JUDGING UNDER CONSTRAINT

As international courts have risen in prominence, policymakers, practitioners, and scholars observe variation in judicial deference. Sometimes international courts defer, whereby they accept a state's exercise of authority, and other times not. Differences can be seen in case outcomes, legal interpretation and reasoning, and remedial orders. How can we explain variation in deference? This book examines deference by international courts, offering a novel theoretical account. It argues that deference is explained by a court's strategic space, which is structured by formal independence, seen as a dimension of institutional design, and state preferences. An empirical analysis built on original data of the East African Court of Justice, Caribbean Court of Justice, and African Court on Human and Peoples' Rights demonstrates that robust safeguards to independence and politically fragmented memberships lend legitimacy to courts and make collective state resistance infeasible, combining to minimize deference. Persuasive argumentation and public legitimation also enable nondeference.

THERESA SQUATRITO is an associate professor in international relations at the London School of Economics and Political Science. She is a coauthor of *The Opening Up of International Organizations* (Cambridge University Press) and a coeditor of *The Performance of International Courts and Tribunals* (Cambridge University Press).

STUDIES ON INTERNATIONAL COURTS AND TRIBUNALS

Studies on International Courts and Tribunals contains theoretical and interdisciplinary scholarship on legal aspects as well as the legitimacy and effectiveness of international courts and tribunals.

Other books in the series:

Mads Andenas and Eirik Bjorge (eds.) *A Farewell to Fragmentation: Reassertion and Convergence in International Law*

Cecilia M. Bailliet and Nobuo Hayashi (eds.) *The Legitimacy of International Criminal Tribunals*

Amrei Müller with Hege Elisabeth Kjos (eds.) *Judicial Dialogue and Human Rights*

Nienke Grossman, Harlan Grant Cohen, Andreas Follesdal and Geir Ulfstein (eds.) *Legitimacy and International Courts*

Theresa Squatrito, Oran R. Young, Andreas Føllesdal and Geir Ulfstein (eds.) *The Performance of International Courts and Tribunals*

Robert Howse, Hélène Ruiz-Fabri, Geir Ulfstein and Michelle Q. Zang (eds.) *The Legitimacy of International Trade Courts and Tribunals*

Marlene Wind (ed.) *International Courts and Domestic Politics*

Christina Voigt (ed.) *International Judicial Practice on the Environment: Questions of Legitimacy*

Martin Scheinin (ed.) *Human Rights Norms in 'Other' International Courts*

Freya Baetens (ed.) *Legitimacy of Unseen Actors in International Adjudication*

Shai Dothan *International Judicial Review: When Should International Courts Intervene?*

Silje Langvatn, Mattias Kumm and Wojciech Sadurski (eds.) *Public Reason and Courts*

Daniel Behn, Szilárd Gáspár-Szilágyi and Malcolm Langford (eds.) *Adjudicating Trade and Investment Disputes: Convergence or Divergence?*

Sondre Torp Helmersen *The Application of Teachings by the International Court of Justice*

Daniel Behn, Ole Kristian Fauchald and Malcolm Langford (eds.) *The Legitimacy of Investment Arbitration: Empirical Perspectives*

Eric De Brabandere *International Procedure in Interstate Litigation and Arbitration: A Comparative Approach*

Chiara Giorgetti and Mark Pollack (eds.) *Beyond Fragmentation: Cross-Fertilization, Cooperation and Competition among International Courts and Tribunals*

Stavros Brekoulakis and Georgios Dimitropoulos (eds.) *International Commercial Courts: The Future of Transnational Adjudication*

Matthew Gillett *Prosecuting Environmental Harm before the International Criminal Court*

Sassan Gholiagha *The Humanisation of Global Politics: International Criminal Law, the Responsibility to Protect, and Drones*

Ezgi Yildiz *The European Court of Human Rights and the Norm Against Torture: Between Forbearance and Audacity*

Christina Voigt and Caroline Foster (eds.) *International Courts versus Non-Compliance Mechanisms: Comparative Advantages in Strengthening Treaty Implementation*

Luise Müller *The Right to Punish: Political Authority and International Criminal Justice*

Theresa Squatrito *Judging under Constraint: The Politics of Deference by International Courts*

JUDGING UNDER CONSTRAINT

The Politics of Deference by International Courts

THERESA SQUATRITO

London School of Economics and Political Science

CAMBRIDGE UNIVERSITY PRESS

CAMBRIDGE
UNIVERSITY PRESS

Shaftesbury Road, Cambridge CB2 8EA, United Kingdom

One Liberty Plaza, 20th Floor, New York, NY 10006, USA

477 Williamstown Road, Port Melbourne, VIC 3207, Australia

314–321, 3rd Floor, Plot 3, Splendor Forum, Jasola District Centre, New Delhi – 110025, India

103 Penang Road, #05–06/07, Visioncrest Commercial, Singapore 238467

Cambridge University Press is part of Cambridge University Press & Assessment, a department of the University of Cambridge.

We share the University's mission to contribute to society through the pursuit of education, learning and research at the highest international levels of excellence.

www.cambridge.org
Information on this title: www.cambridge.org/9781009607612

DOI: 10.1017/9781009607636

When citing this work, please include a reference to the DOI 10.1017/9781009607636

First published 2025

Cover image: Robert Delaunay, "Circular Forms. Sun and Moon", oil on canvas, 1912–31 / IanDagnall Computing / Alamy

A catalogue record for this publication is available from the British Library

A Cataloging-in-Publication data record for this book is available from the Library of Congress

ISBN 978-1-009-60761-2 Hardback

To my parents

CONTENTS

FIGURES

TABLES

ACKNOWLEDGMENTS

This book began during my postdoctoral fellowship at PluriCourts – the Centre for the Study of the Legitimate Roles of the Judiciary in the Global Order at the University of Oslo. I was fortunate to be a part of the wonderful intellectual community of friends that was PluriCourts, and I am indebted to all who were a part of that community. First and foremost, without the support of Andreas Føllesdal and Geir Ulfstein, this book would never have come to fruition. Andreas and Geir believed in me from day one, provided me with the resources to make this book happen, and offered countless words of encouragement and feedback. I am also grateful for advice, support, and feedback from Daniel Naurin, Øyvind Stiansen, Taylor St John, Tarald Berge, Ole Kristian Fauchald, Laura Létourneau-Tremblay, Cecilia Bailliet, Siri Gloppen, Matthew Saul, Christina Voigt, Alain Zysset, Antoinette Scherz, Malcolm Langford, Runar Lie, Nicola Strain, and Tom Pavone. I also thank the advisory board at PluriCourts, including Beth Simmons, Tom Ginsburg, and Andreas Paulus, all of whom provided feedback and words of encouragement. Silje Langvatn has not only been a wonderful friend to me, but she taught me so much about legitimacy and challenged my thinking in so many ways – thank you! To Daniel Behn, I wish I could thank you in person, share the final product with you and then we could argue about it.

I have also had the fortune of receiving feedback and support from friends and colleagues in London. Carmen Pavel generously organized a book workshop for me at King's College London, in addition to offering constructive feedback and encouragement. At this workshop, I benefited from critical yet generous comments from Ian Higham, Peter Brett, Chris Hanretty, Octavio Ferraz, Derek O'Brien, and James Scott. I owe huge thanks to each of these individuals for their time, comments, and careful reading of the manuscript. I also thank participants at the 2022 LSE workshop on International Public Policy for their constructive comments, including Mathias Koenig-Archibugi, Mette Eilstrup

Sangiovanni, Michael Lerner, Dan Berliner, Thomas Bernauer, Christel Koop, Robert Basedow, and Jason Sharman. Thanks are also due to participants at a workshop of the Empirical Network on Law and Judicial Politics at UCL, especially Michal Ovadek, Veronika Fifak, and Ezequiel Gonzalez-Ocantos.

I am grateful to iCourts at the University of Copenhagen for supporting my visit during the winter of 2023. I was warmly welcomed and enjoyed my stay enormously. This project was at a critical point during my visit. I received excellent and very useful comments from many at iCourts, but I owe special thanks to Michael Rask Madsen, Salome Addo Ravn, Zusanna Godzimirska, and Shai Dothan.

I have had the opportunity to present various parts of the book at several conferences, workshops, and seminars, including at the Kolleg-Forschungsgruppe in Berlin/Potsdam on The International Rule of Law – Rise or Decline?, the University of Geneva, Technical University of Munich, the ECPR law and courts section, ISA, and IPSA. I am especially grateful for comments from Andrea Liese, Nina Reiners, Dana Burchardt, Philipp Schroeder, Arthur Dyevre, Sean Richmond, Jonas Tallberg, Mackenzie Eason, Mark Pollack, Simone Dietrich, Tim Büthe, Frans Viljoen, and Wayne Sandholtz. Along the way, I have received invaluable comments from so many people, some of whom I unfortunately fail to mention here. To all, I thank you! I also thank anonymous reviewers for their constructive feedback. Also, several people deserve thanks for their research assistance, including Eirik Torsvoll, Annette Hovdal, Max Usynin, and AJ Davies.

I owe gratitude to several colleagues and friends who have shown me patience, taught me much, and given me encouragement. For this, I especially thank Jonas Tallberg, Thomas Sommerer, Birte Gippert, Ana Maria Daza Vargas, Katerina Dalacoura, and Sinja Graf. To Marie-Therese Gustafsson, thank you for your endless support and laughter. Last, but not least, I thank my family for keeping me grounded and giving me strength to persevere.

CITED LEGAL TEXTS

African Charter on Democracy, Elections and Governance (adopted January 30, 2007, entered into force February 15, 2012), https://au.int/en/treaties/african-charter-democracy-elections-and-governance.

African Charter of Human and Peoples' Rights (adopted June 27, 1981, entered into force October 21, 1986), U.N.T.S. 1520, at 217–92.

Agreement establishing the Caribbean Court of Justice (adopted February 14, 2001, entered into force July 23, 2002), U.N.T.S. 2255, at 319–41.

American Convention on Human Rights (adopted November 22, 1969, entered into force July 18, 1978), U.N.T.S. 1144, at 143–212, Art. 46(1)(d).

Charter of the Organization of African Unity (adopted May 25, 1963, entered into force September 13, 1963), U.N.T.S. 479, at 70–88.

Constitutive Act of the African Union (adopted July 11, 2000, entered into force May 26, 2001), U.N.T.S. 2158, at 3–58.

Convention on the Statute of the Central American Court of Justice (adopted December 10, 1992, entered into force February 2, 1994), U.N.T.S. 1821, at 292–303.

European Convention for the Protection of Human Rights and Fundamental Freedoms (adopted November 4, 1950, entered into force September 3, 1953), U.N.T.S. 213, at 221–70.

Olivos Protocol for the Settlement of Disputes in Mercosur (adopted February 18, 2002, entered into force January 1, 2004), U.N.T.S. 2251, at 288–303.

Protocol A/SP1/12/01 on Democracy and Good Governance Supplementary to the Protocol Relating to the Mechanism for Conflict Prevention, Management, Resolution, Peacekeeping and Security (adopted December 21, 2001), www2.ohchr.org/english/law/compilation_democracy/ecowasprot.htm.

Protocol No. 11 to the Convention for the Protection of Human Rights and Fundamental Freedoms of November 4, 1950, restructuring the control machinery established thereby (adopted May 11, 1994, entered into force November 1, 1998), U.N.T.S. 2061, at 7–24.

Protocol No. 14 to the Convention for the Protection of Human Rights and Fundamental Freedoms, amending the control system of the Convention (adopted May 13, 2004, entered into force June 1, 2010), U.N.T.S. 2677, at 3–21.

Protocol to the African Charter on Human and Peoples' Rights on the Establishment of an African Court on Human and People's Rights (adopted June 10, 1998, entered into force January 25, 2004), accessed August 27, 2024, http://au.int/en/treaties/protocol-african-charter-human-and-peoples-rights-establishment-african-court-human-and.

Revised Treaty for the establishment of the East African Community (as amended December 14, 2006 and August 20, 2007). Arusha: EAC, www.eacj.org//wp-content/uploads/2012/08/EACJ-Treaty.pdf.

Revised Treaty of Chaguaramas establishing the Caribbean Community including the CARICOM Single Market and Economy (adopted July 5, 2001, entered into force February 4, 2002), U.N.T.S. 2259, at 293–443.

Statute of the International Court of Justice (adopted June 26, 1945, entered into force October 24, 1945), UNCIO XV, at 355–64.

Treaty establishing the Caribbean Community (adopted July 4, 1973, entered into force August 1, 1973), U.N.T.S. 946, at 17–542.

Treaty establishing the Common Market for Eastern and Southern Africa (adopted November 5, 1993, entered into force December 8, 1994), U.N.T.S. 2314, at 265–385.

Treaty for the establishment of the East African Community (adopted November 30, 1999, entered into force July 7, 2000), U.N.T.S. 2144, at 255–327.

Treaty related to the Revisions to the Treaty on the Harmonisation of Business Law in Africa (adopted October 17, 2008), www.ohada.com/traite.html.

ABBREVIATIONS

AB	Appellate Body
ACmHPR	African Commission on Human and Peoples' Rights
ACtHPR	African Court on Human and Peoples' Rights
APDF	Association pour le Progrès et la Défense des Droits des Femmes Maliennes
ATJ	Andean Tribunal of Justice
AU	African Union
CACJ	Central American Court of Justice
CARICOM	Caribbean Community
CARIFTA	Caribbean Free Trade Association
CCJ	Caribbean Court of Justice
CHOG	Conference of Heads of Government
CJEU	Court of Justice of the European Union
COMESA CJ	Common Market for Eastern and Southern Africa Court of Justice
COTED	Council for Trade and Economic Development
COV	coefficient of variation
DRC	Democratic Republic of the Congo
DSM	Dispute Settlement Mechanism
EAC	East African Community
EACA	East African Court of Appeal
EACJ	East African Court of Justice
EACSO	East African Common Service Organization
EALA	East African Legislative Assembly
EALS	East African Law Society
ECJ	European Court of Justice
ECOWAS	Economic Community of West African States
ECtHR	European Court of Human Rights
EU	European Union
GATT	General Agreement on Tariffs and Trade
IACtHR	Inter-American Court of Human Rights
IHRDA	Institute for Human Rights and Development in Africa

IC	international court
ICC	International Criminal Court
ICJ	International Court of Justice
IO	international organization
IR	international relations
ITLOS	International Tribunal for the Law of the Sea
NARC	National Rainbow Coalition
NGO	nongovernmental organization
OAU	Organization of African Unity
OECS	Organisation of Eastern Caribbean States
OHADA CCJA	Common Court of Justice and Arbitration for the Organization for the Harmonization of Business Law in Africa
PALU	Pan African Lawyers Union
PRT	Permanent Review Tribunal
RJLSC	Regional Judicial and Legal Services Commission
RTC	Revised Treaty of Chaguaramas
SADC	Southern African Development Community
TCL	Trinidad Cement Limited
TOC	Treaty of Chaguaramas
UN	United Nations
WIC	West Indian Commission
WIF	West Indies Federation
WTO	World Trade Organization

1

Introduction

After years of demands and pressure from domestic civil society groups and the international community, on August 3, 2009, the Malian National Assembly unanimously adopted legislation that would transform the country's family law. Drafted in concert with experts, nongovernmental organizations (NGOs), and international donors, the new family law would mark a significant development for women's rights in Mali. Among other things, it would raise the minimum age for marriage to eighteen for girls, remove legal provisions requiring a wife's obedience to her husband, and provide equal inheritance for men and women. Yet, much of the public was outraged because the legislation would not guarantee the recognition of religious marriage, and on August 22, 2009, a public demonstration drew an estimated 50,000 protesters.[1] Rather than sign the legislation into force, President Amadou Toumani Touré returned it to the National Assembly, which then consulted with Islamic organizations to revise it.

A new Family Code was finally promulgated on December 30, 2011. It set the minimum age for marriage at eighteen for men and sixteen for women, but it permitted marriage from the age of fifteen with parental consent: Either parent could give consent for a boy to marry, but only the father could do so for a girl. Moreover, clergymen were not required to verify consent. The law also provided that a wife must obey her husband, defined the husband as the head of the household, and protected discriminatory inheritance practices, inter alia. In 2016, the Association pour le Progrès et la Défense des Droits des Femmes Maliennes (APDF) – a Malian women's rights organization – and the Institute for Human Rights and Development in Africa (IHRDA) – a pan-African organization – filed an application at the African Court on Human and

[1] Brenda K. Kombo, "Napoleonic Legacies, Postcolonial State Legitimation, and the Perpetual Myth of Non-Intervention: Family Code Reform and Gender Equality in Mali," *Social & Legal Studies* 30, no. 5 (2021): 713.

Peoples' Rights (ACtHPR or African Court) that challenged the new Family Code. The APDF and IHRDA asked the African Court to determine whether the Family Code violated Mali's international human rights obligations, and, if so, whether they were entitled to legal remedies such as an order to reform the law.[2]

In another – yet entirely different – instance, the East African Court of Justice (EACJ or the East African Court) was presented with a case in which it was asked to determine whether Uganda had violated its treaty obligations, including the protection of human rights, due to the government's handling of protests. On April 11, 2011, activists comprising opposition politicians and civil society actors began staging "walk to work" protests in response to high fuel and living costs against the backdrop of widespread discontent with President Museveni's election to a fourth term of office.[3] The police were informed of the planned peaceful protests, which drew thousands of protesters from a broad cross section of Ugandans.[4] Over the ensuing days, the police – under the direction of the government – declared the protests illegal and responded with excessive force, using tear gas, beatings, and live bullets, and detained, arrested, and charged protesters. The violence attracted international media coverage and widespread criticism. By the end of April, the protests and violence had ended, but at least nine people had been killed. The East African Law Society (EALS) filed a petition with the EACJ on May 31, 2011, asking the East African Court to determine whether the Ugandan government had violated its obligations to protect human rights according to the Treaty for the Establishment of the East African Community and the African Charter on Human and Peoples Rights.[5]

In both these instances, international courts (ICs) were presented with a dilemma: Should it defer to the responding state, thereby accepting actions or decisions of the state, or should it not defer, thus rejecting how the state decided to exercise its authority? In the case of the Malian

[2] *Association pour le Progrès et la Défense des Droits des Femmes Maliennes & The Institute for Human Rights and Development v Republic of Mali*, Application No. 46/2016, ACtHPR (May 11, 2018) [herein *ADPF & IHRDA v Mali*, App. 46/2016].

[3] Michael Mutyaba, "From Voting to Walking: The 2011 Walk-to-Work Protest Movement in Uganda," in *Popular Protest, Political Opportunities, and Change in Africa*, ed. Edalina Rodrigues Sanches (Abingdon: Routledge, 2022).

[4] Ibid., 170.

[5] *East African Law Society v The Attorney General of the Republic of Uganda & The Secretary General of the East African Community*, Reference No. 2/2011, EACJ (March 28, 2018).

Family Code, the ACtHPR rejected Mali's decision, finding that the government had misconstrued the relevant human rights law and failed in its international obligations, and ordered the government to amend its law. In contrast, the EACJ dismissed the lawsuit against Uganda for its response to the "walk to work" protests, finding the applicant had submitted inadequate or unauthenticated evidence that protesters were beaten, tear-gassed, or killed, despite the notoriety of the events, and therefore, it could not conclude that the government had contravened its legal obligations. This dismissal amounted to the Court's acceptance of Uganda's actions. In short, the EACJ deferred to the state, while the ACtHPR did not. How can we account for the differences in these international judicial decisions? What factors contributed to the EACJ's decision to defer and the ACtHPR's decision to not defer?

This book aims to understand why international courts can come to such disparate conclusions, as depicted in these two illustrative examples, about whether to defer to states. The book develops a novel theoretical account of judicial decision-making. It approaches decision-making in terms of deference: whether courts, through their decisions, accept a state's (or other governing entities') exercise of authority. I argue that deference is determined by an international court's strategic space – the scope of possible decisions that could satisfy a court's legal and political constraints. When a court's strategic space is broader, the potential for nondeference expands. A combination of structural factors and judicial practices shapes this strategic space by contributing to the credibility of state resistance and the legitimacy of ICs. Overall, five factors are integral to explaining judicial deference due to their impact on a court's strategic space: formal independence, political fragmentation, past resistance, persuasive argumentation, and public legitimation. Formal independence expands the strategic space because it improves the perceived legitimacy of a court and imposes institutional hurdles, both of which make state resistance less credible to courts. Political fragmentation also imposes institutional hurdles, making state resistance less credible, and thereby expands the strategic space. Conversely, past episodes of successful resistance, enabled by weaker independence and political unity among member states, narrows the strategic space by leading a court to view state resistance as practicable in the future. Overall, these political constraints impact an IC's strategic space, but ICs can exercise agency over this strategic space through practices of persuasive argumentation and public legitimation. These practices dampen legitimacy deficits and the potential of state resistance, and thus enable more nondeference.

An original empirical analysis of three international courts – the EACJ, ACtHPR, and the Caribbean Court of Justice (CCJ) – supports this argument. The analysis reveals that the EACJ has been consistently more deferential than the ACtHPR and CCJ. Among the three courts, it has the weakest safeguards to independence and its membership is moderately fragmented (as preference heterogeneity among members is low-to-moderate), both of which facilitated an important episode of collective resistance. The combined effect of low formal independence, moderate political fragmentation, and successful past resistance has been a relatively high degree of deference by the EACJ. The EACJ, however, does not always defer to states. Rather, to the extent that the EACJ does not defer, nondeference has been enabled by the Court's practices of persuasive argumentation and public legitimation. In contrast, the ACtHPR enjoys a broad strategic space because of its high formal independence and significant political fragmentation, and thus, it has been less inclined to defer to states. Unilateral resistance by states, however, in the form of exit contributes to this court's efforts to couple nondeference with persuasive argumentation and public legitimation and its move toward more deference in recent years. The CCJ enjoys the highest levels of formal independence, while its membership has mostly homogeneous preferences, which together provide it with a midrange strategic space. This closely corresponds with its tendency to not defer, except when states' preferences strongly align. The CCJ also relies on persuasive argumentation and public legitimation to bolster its strategic space and minimize resistance when it does not defer to states.

The Puzzle: Deference by International Courts

The end of the Cold War was a pivotal moment for international cooperation as it ushered in the consolidation of the liberal international order. As part of this transition, we have witnessed a proliferation of international courts that were to be part and parcel with a rule-based order.[6] No longer are international courts concentrated in the liberal, democratic core of the international community. Today, ICs operate in nearly all

[6] Karen J. Alter, *The New Terrain of International Law: Courts, Politics, Rights* (Princeton: Princeton University Press, 2014); Robert O. Keohane, Andrew Moravcsik, and Anne-Marie Slaughter, "Legalized Dispute Resolution: Interstate and Transnational," *International Organization* 54, no. 3 (2000).

world regions and have jurisdiction over states with varying histories of judicial power, democracy, and respect for the rule of law.

States, international organizations (IOs), civil society groups (e.g., NGOs), and private actors regularly petition these courts, asking them to interpret and apply the law, to facilitate the peaceful settlement of disputes, to determine whether states and IOs have complied with their legal obligations, and to provide remedies for wrongs. ICs respond to these pleas in varying ways. For instance, the EACJ found no violations in roughly 54 percent of its merits judgments, while the ACtHPR did in only 18 percent. By several accounts, the Court of Justice of the European Union (CJEU) – previously known as the European Court of Justice (ECJ) – frequently expands legal obligations such that is appears to make law, even though it avoids ordering intrusive remedies.[7] On the other hand, the Andean Tribunal of Justice (ATJ) is typically restrained in its legal interpretations.[8] The International Court of Justice's (ICJ) often relies on restrictive interpretation[9] and nonintrusive remedies.[10] The European Court of Human Rights (ECtHR) operated for nearly a decade before declaring a state had violated its obligations, but gradually its interpretations significantly expanded human rights protections,[11] even though its remedies remained nonintrusive.[12] The Inter-American Court of Human Rights (IACtHR) is known for the way it leaves little discretion to states by adopting extensive remedies.[13] This quick review of several international courts suggests that decision-making by ICs varies

[7] Christine Gray, "Remedies," in *The Oxford Handbook of International Adjudication*, ed. Cesare Romano, Karen Alter, and Yuval Shany (Oxford: Oxford University Press, 2014).

[8] Karen J. Alter and Laurence Helfer, "Nature or Nurture? Judicial Lawmaking in the European Court of Justice and the Andean Tribunal of Justice." *International Organization* 64, no. 4 (2010).

[9] Robert Kolb, *The Elgar Companion to the International Court of Justice* (Cheltenham: Edward Elgar, 2014); Deepak Mawar, "The Perils of Judicial Restraint: How Judicial Activism Can Help Evolve the International Court of Justice," *Goettingen Journal of International Law* 9, no. 3 (2018).

[10] Gray, "Remedies"; Chester Brown, *A Common Law of International Adjudication* (Oxford: Oxford University Press, 2007).

[11] Mikael Rask Madsen, "The European Court of Human Rights: From the Cold War to the Brighton Declaration and Backlash," in *International Court Authority*, ed. Karen J. Alter, Laurence R. Helfer, and Mikael Rask Madsen (Oxford: Oxford University Press, 2018).

[12] Gray, "Remedies"; Dinah Shelton, *Remedies in International Human Rights Law* (Oxford: Oxford University Press, 2006).

[13] Gray, "Remedies"; Jo M. Pasqualucci, *The Practice and Procedure of the Inter-American Court of Human Rights*, 2nd ed. (Cambridge: Cambridge University Press, 2013); Shelton, *Remedies in International Human Rights Law*.

and raises several questions. How can we conceptualize this variation? Do judicial decisions vary both across courts and over time? What factors account for variation in international judicial decisions?

These are the questions that motivate this book. I approach them by focusing on a core feature of judicial decisions, namely, *deference.* Sometimes, international courts defer, whereby they accept a state's exercise of authority. This acceptance is revealed by rulings that declare a member state has not violated its legal obligations, use restrictive treaty interpretation or limited scrutiny, or deliver remedies that do not intrude on sovereignty. Other times, they do not defer and, thereby, reject a state's exercise of authority. Such rejection can be seen in court decisions that declare a member state has violated its legal obligations, eschew restrictive interpretations and intensely scrutinize states' decisions or actions, or deliver remedies that intrude on state sovereignty. In short, I define judicial deference as a court's acceptance of a state or other governing entities' (e.g., an organ of an international organization) exercise of authority. This definition builds on a definition proposed by the international relations (IR) scholars Asif Efrat and Abraham Newman and adapts it for international courts.[14] Moreover, based on this definition, I operationalize deference along three dimensions of judicial decisions: case outcomes, legal interpretation and reasoning, and remedies.[15]

The focus on deference distinguishes this book from work that characterizes judicial decisions on an activism/restraint continuum. Shifting the conversation to deference is advantageous for a few reasons. First, activism/restraint is largely in reference to legal interpretation and lawmaking (or lack thereof) by courts. Yet, judicial decisions have other important dimensions of potential interest and through which deference may be visible or practiced, such as remedies.[16] In other words, deference, as I conceive of it, is a broader concept and encompasses more aspects of judicial decision-making. Second, judicial activism – and conversely restraint – is a loaded concept. Activism can refer to decisions

[14] Asif Efrat and Abraham L. Newman, "Deciding to Defer: The Importance of Fairness in Resolving Transnational Jurisdictional Conflicts," *International Organization* 70, no. 2 (2016). Their definition refers to deference by one state to another state.

[15] This definition and operationalization differ from legal approaches. I elaborate on this in Chapter 2.

[16] Some authors describe remedies in terms of activism; see, for example, Cecilia Bailliet, "Measuring Compliance with the Inter-American Court of Human Rights: The Ongoing Challenge of Judicial Independence in Latin America," *Nordic Journal of Human Rights* 31, no. 4 (2013): 490.

where a court invalidates another authority's decision, ignores precedent, engages in lawmaking, or departs from accepted interpretive methods or standards of judging, among others.[17] In addition to having multiple meanings, activism is laden with political connotation, and identifying which decisions are activist or not is often subjective. Thus, deference is conceptually cleaner and less subjective or politically charged.

De facto independence is another concept often used to characterize judicial decision-making. While this concept and deference are related, and both refer to judicial behavior, they accord to different units of analysis. Deference is a characteristic of discrete judicial decisions, while de facto independence is a characteristic of a court. I am primarily interested in studying the decisions of courts, for which deference is more suitable. Deference, however, can also be used to describe a court's case law in the aggregate and is useful for comparative purposes.

The Argument: Strategic Space, Structural Constraints, and Adaptive Practices

The core argument that I advance in this book is that judicial deference is the result of a court's strategic space. This space is constructed by two structural political constraints – formal independence and political fragmentation – which jointly condition how a court is perceived (i.e., its legitimacy) and the feasibility with which states can collectively resist or curtail it. Courts that lack formal robust institutional safeguards to their independence and have unfragmented memberships (i.e., homogeneous state preferences) are more politically constrained than their peers that have greater formal independence and fragmented memberships; hence, their strategic space is relatively narrow, and they will therefore demonstrate more widespread deference. Without robust institutional safeguards to protect a court, it will appear to be vulnerable to the whims and influence of states or those that wield power over it. State defiance of such a court comes with fewer political costs to politicians, and formal independence also means that institutional opportunities for resistance are greater or more practicable. In this setting, courts perceive state resistance to be more credible or plausible, leading them to exercise more caution. Nondeference is thus inhibited by this political setting, especially if resistance has been success in the past. But, when courts enjoy robust

[17] Keenan D. Kmiec, "The Origin and Current Meanings of 'Judicial Activism'," *California Law Review* 92, no. 5 (2004).

safeguards to independence and its member states are politically fragmented (meaning their preferences are heterogeneous), legitimacy is greater and state resistance more limited. This essentially expands the opportunity to exercise nondeference. In slightly different terms, formal judicial independence and political fragmentation enable less deferential decision-making.

These structural political constraints, however, do not straitjacket a court. Rather, my argument suggests that judicial power is also constructed through agency. ICs exercise some degree of agency over their strategic space by adopting practices that also affect their perceived legitimacy and the credibility of state resistance. In particular, ICs often employ persuasive argumentation, in the form of unanimous decisions or referencing authoritative sources, and engage in public legitimation to boost their legitimacy and disincentivize state resistance. These judicial practices help to build and maintain a court's strategic space to have an impact on decision-making.

My argument contrasts, yet complements, the view that judicial decision-making is explained by the strength of a court's support network. Previous literature suggests that courts with strong support networks will demonstrate nondeference, irrespective of states and institutional rules.[18] My argument complements this perspective in two ways. First, it sheds light on decision-making when support networks are forming. Second, it assumes that courts themselves play a role in the construction of their power. Aside from the explanations focused on support networks, I also consider perspectives that highlight ideational factors relating to political norms and legal culture.

An empirical analysis of the EACJ, CCJ, and ACtHPR supports the theoretical argument. An examination of these three courts is valuable for a few reasons. First, it offers insights into newer, less studied international courts. As these are regional courts, it also complements a wealth of research on European regional courts, namely, the CJEU and the ECtHR. The empirical analysis therefore sheds light on the extent to which the European experiences travel to other regions operating within different legal, political, and socioeconomic contexts.

[18] For example, Alter and Helfer, "Nature or Nurture?"; Rachel A. Cichowski, *The European Court and Civil Society: Litigation, Mobilization and Governance* (Cambridge: Cambridge University Press, 2007). This perspective recognizes the importance of institutional rules that guarantee access to international courts for private, substate, and supranational actors.

The EACJ, CCJ, and ACtHPR are embedded within settings of rich legal pluralism, fragile faith and trust in state (or formal) legal order, colonial legacies, and mostly low- and middle-income economies. In addition, these are relatively new courts. Thus, this study expands knowledge on how ICs develop their initial jurisprudence, struggle for recognition, grapple with political constraints, and more during their nascent stages. The cases illustrate how differences in the formal safeguards that are in place to isolate courts from the political control of states engender opportunities for courts to reject the state's exercise of authority in accord with legal constraints. Divisions among states also differ, which can be leveraged to determine how political fragmentation enables nondeference.

Three main findings come from the empirical analysis. First, there is substantial variation in the formal independence of international courts. While previous literature has focused on other design features of international courts, such as formal powers and access,[19] this book introduces formal independence as a design feature and presents original data on the formal independence of twenty-six international courts. A mapping of this data reveals that ICs are not all created alike in terms of their formal safeguards to independence. These safeguards relate to rules on the selection and tenure of judges, the managerial autonomy of courts, and the terms of office for judges. Most variation in formal independence is driven by the former two types of rules.

Second, an analysis of the decisions taken by the EACJ, ACtHPR, and CCJ reveals that the three courts defer in different ways and to different degrees. We can see unique patterns of deference in terms of their case outcomes, legal interpretation and reasoning, and remedies. This threefold approach to assessing judicial deference not only illustrates how courts can rely on different aspects of their decisions to balance legal and political imperatives, but it also offers a more nuanced account of judicial decision-making. Broadly speaking, the EACJ demonstrates substantial deference, while the CCJ shows moderate deference and the ACtHPR minimal deference.

Third, the analysis shows that the observed variation in deference aligns with each court's respective strategic space and political constraints in support of my argument. The EACJ's substantial deference corresponds to its pervasive constraints, which arise from low formal

[19] See, for example, Alter, *The New Terrain of International Law.*

independence and moderate political fragmentation. The CCJ has high formal independence that offsets low political fragmentation, providing for intermediate constraints and thus enabling moderate deference. In contrast, the ACtHPR's subtle constraints, due to formal independence and political fragmentation that are both relatively high, enable its minimal deference. On the other hand, while each court has an emerging support network that is responsible for the lion's share of litigation, these networks' access opportunities, strengths, and activities do not systematically vary with the patterns of deference. That is, stronger and more active networks do not consistently correspond with less deference.

The empirical evidence lends strong support to my argument. Yet, the argument is developed in the context of specific conditions. First and foremost, the argument is a story of *new* international courts and their early years of development. In this context, institutional design has special importance because relationships with states and societal actors are nascent, and thus the reservoir of support that an IC enjoys at its origin depends more on the appearance of constraints, as presented by institutional design. Appearances matter in the absence of past performance. Moreover, support networks may themselves be works in progress early on. New international courts, their rules and legal framework are less knowable to substate and nonstate actors. Courts and their judges grow into their relationship with states. They begin with not knowing exactly how states will react or how well states can collectively coordinate. While early years can be formative, they are not necessarily determinative. First impressions fade and are replaced with stories of success (or failures), and courts' unique cultures develop. In the end, evolving political, social, and political realities contribute to the development of law and courts, even when considering self-reinforcing processes of path dependency or organizational culture.

Second, the courts that I look at are embedded within similar socioeconomic and ideational contexts that distinguish them from those studied elsewhere (e.g., CJEU, ECtHR). The EACJ, CCJ, and ACtHPR are regional courts whose members are in the Global South and mostly low- and middle-income countries. Socioeconomic considerations may have a range of possible effects related to law and courts, including state legal capacity, opportunities and resources for individuals to litigate, and legal knowledge and consciousness. Previous research, for example, shows that the rule of law and economic development or wealth are closely connected.[20] Similarly, international development assistance often emphasizes the rule of law. Additionally, the EACJ, CCJ, and ACtHPR share similar legal cultures characterized by complex legal pluralism, often poor societal confidence in state legal order or insecure judiciaries, and enduring legacies of colonialism. If and how my argument extends beyond these contexts requires further investigation.

Third, my argument does not directly address ICs in their interstate jurisdiction. The empirical analysis does not include an examination of judicial decision-making on interstate disputes, and the theoretical argument is developed primarily with thinking about how courts deal with petitions from private (nonstate) litigants. For this reason, I am cautious to not draw conclusions about judicial decision-making on interstate disputes or claims. While I measure the formal independence of ICs with exclusively or primarily interstate jurisdiction – the Appellate Body (AB) of the World Trade Organization (WTO), the ICJ, or the International Tribunal of the Law of the Sea (ITLOS) – I do not make any claims about how their decision-making is affected by this aspect of their institutional design. I leave this to future empirical analysis to determine whether their deference is best conceptualized in the threefold manner that I rely on and whether deference corresponds to their level of formal independence or political fragmentation. I recognize that a court's relations with states differ somewhat in this context because parties are always states, and therefore dynamics like the relative power of state parties might be an alternative or additional political constraint that affects decision-making in ways not theorized in this book.

Last, I want to be clear that my argument does not ignore how the law itself constrains, or conversely enables, ICs to generate patterns of deference. I assume that it does. This is most obvious in the attention I give to institutional design, which are in fact legal rules that limit state and court behavior. Beyond this, I am attentive to how the law interacts with the political. That said, my primary aim is to identify and understand political constraints.

Research Design

The argument of this book combines a complex set of factors to explain deference and how it varies across ICs and over time. To empirically

[20] Jerg Gutmann and Stefan Voigt, "The Rule of Law: Measurement and Deep Roots," *European Journal of Political Economy* 54 (2018); Stephan Haggard and Lydia Tiede, "The Rule of Law and Economic Growth: Where Are We?" *World Development* 39, no. 5 (2011).

assess these complexities, I use a nested and mixed methods research design. This approach is beneficial because it exploits the comparative advantages of different kinds of data and types of analysis to enhance the validity of causal inferences.[21] While nesting and mixed methods are widely advocated, they are utilized less often. The research approach used here therefore forges new methodological ground for the study of international courts. In the following, I describe the research design, beginning with how it is nested and then its use of mixed methods.

The research design is nested, meaning that the same case studies are analyzed in both cross-case and within-case comparison.[22] On the one hand, I draw inferences about the causal factors contributing to deference by comparing the EACJ, CCJ, and ACtHPR. The courts were selected to ensure variation on the key explanatory variables while controlling for confounding factors – making this a most similar systems research design. The EACJ, CCJ, and ACtHPR are "typical" or "pathway" case studies. Methodologists suggest that selecting case studies according to these principles is appropriate for theory-building,[23] which is the aim here. The three courts differ in terms of formal independence and political fragmentation, both of which are key explanatory variables considered by the theoretical argument. The EACJ, CCJ, and ACtHPR enjoy different institutional safeguards to independence. An analysis of formal independence among twenty-six international courts supports this position, and it forms the basis of the case selection. As Chapter 3 illustrates, the EACJ has low formal independence, the CCJ's is high, and the ACtHPR lies between. The memberships of these three ICs also vary in terms of their political fragmentation, especially when considering developments across time. Generally speaking, political fragmentation

[21] Sidney Tarrow, "Bridging the Quantitative–Qualitative Divide," in *Rethinking Social Inquiry: Diverse Tools, Shared Standards*, 2nd ed., ed. Henry E. Brady and David Collier (Lanham: Rowman & Littlefield Publishers, 2010); Dimiter Toshkov, *Research Design in Political Science* (London: Bloomsbury Publishing, 2016), 312–13.

[22] Toshkov, *Research Design in Political Science*, 312–13. This type of a nested design is distinct from nested designs that apply different methods in separate stages: for example, quantitative methods followed by qualitative methods as described by Evan S. Lieberman, "Nested Analysis as a Mixed-Method Strategy for Comparative Research," *American Political Science Review* 99, no. 3 (2005).

[23] John Gerring, *Case Study Research: Principles and Practices*, 2nd ed. (Cambridge: Cambridge University Press, 2016); Derek Beach and Rasmus Brun Pedersen, *Causal Case Study Methods: Foundations and Guidelines for Comparing, Matching, and Tracing* (Ann Arbor: University of Michigan Press, 2016).

among the members of the EACJ is moderate but low in the case of the CCJ and high for the ACtHPR.

The case selection controls for confounding factors. In particular, the EACJ, CCJ, and ACtHPR have important similarities in their institutional design, especially as they all feature modes of private access. They also have similarities in the types of legal issues that they tend to decide on: human rights, domestic governance, and rule of law. This is seemingly at odds with their formal mandates and general impressions of these courts. While the EACJ and CCJ are regional integration courts, like the CJEU, and do not formally have human rights jurisdiction, a notable portion of their jurisprudence pertains to human rights, domestic governance, and rule of law issues, like the ACtHPR. Additionally, there are parallels between the socioeconomic and ideational contexts of these courts. Their member states are mostly low- and middle-income countries in the Global South, their legal cultures are pluralistic, and there is a lack of faith in and access to the state's legal order (to be distinguished from legal order that is rooted in customary or traditional law and dispute resolution). Moreover, the courts were established and operate in postcolonial settings where legacies of the past are enduring. Among other things, colonial legacies contribute to a unique dualism of political norms, whereby ideas of sovereignty, noninterference, and independence are frequently in tension with extant beliefs in regionalism, unity, and cooperation. Last, their newness means that each court's sui generis legal culture is developing and not yet deeply entrenched. In other words, these similarities present a unique opportunity to control – albeit imperfectly – for alternative explanations.

On the other hand, the book draws causal inferences from within-case comparisons. Within-case analysis entails an in-depth study of each court over time and across legal issues. This part of the research design is essential to showing how political fragmentation, past resistance, and judicial practices contribute to deference. In other words, looking at variations within each court's jurisprudence allows me to determine whether shifts in political fragmentation, resistance, and changes in judicial practices track with the temporal patterns of deference in each of the three courts.

The within-case analyses provide an additional advantage, namely, that each intensive case study makes an important empirical contribution. The analysis of the EACJ, CCJ, and ACtHPR provides detailed data on their decisions. While more and more research has been produced on these courts, the entire corpus of their jurisprudence has yet to be examined. Rather, researchers have so far focused on more limited aspects of their decisions. For instance, James Gathii has analyzed the EACJ's decisions in response to opposition politicians, Andrew Heinrich has studied the EACJ's decisions on governance in Burundi, or Adamantia Rachovitsa has examined the ACtHPR's jurisprudence on its material jurisdiction.[24] In contrast, the contribution here is a coverage of all judgments from their first decision up to and through 2020.

The research design also relies on mixed methods, drawing from a mix of data types and methods. Overarching both the within- and cross-case comparisons is a congruence analysis. Congruence analysis differs from both correlation analysis and process-tracing. It relies on deductively positing a relationship between variation on the independent and dependent variables, then examining whether there is evidence of a correlation between these variables.[25] It also provides (minimalist) theoretical specification and empirical evidence of a causal process in addition to demonstrating a correlation.[26] In contrast, correlation analysis focuses on correlation, not causation. Put different, correlation analysis treats the causal process as a black box – not to be examined – while congruence analysis treats it as a "grey box" that is partially examined. On the other hand, process-tracing is less focused on correlation and instead focus on completely demystifying the causal process such that it is a transparent box.[27] As Beach and Pedersen argue, many researchers claim to be doing process-tracing when they in fact are doing congruence analysis.[28] Thus, congruence analysis maps associations between independent and dependent variables while also revealing aspects of causality.

[24] James Thuo Gathii, "International Courts as Coordination Devices for Opposition Parties: The Case of the East African Court of Justice," in *The Performance of Africa's International Courts: Using Litigation for Political, Legal, and Social Change*, ed. James Thuo Gathii (Oxford: Oxford University Press, 2020); Andrew Heinrich, "Sub-Regional Courts as Transitional Justice Mechanisms: The Case of the East African Court of Justice in Burundi," in *The Performance of Africa's International Courts: Using Litigation for Political, Legal, and Social Change*, ed. James Thuo Gathii (Oxford: Oxford University Press, 2020); Adamantia Rachovitsa, "On New 'Judicial Animals': The Curious Case of an African Court with Material Jurisdiction of a Global Scope," *Human Rights Law Review* 19, no. 2 (2019).

[25] Alexander L. George and Andrew Bennett, *Case Studies and Theory Development in the Social Sciences* (Cambridge, MA: MIT Press, 2005), chapter 9.

[26] Beach and Pedersen, *Causal Case Study Methods*, chapter 8.

[27] Ibid.

[28] Ibid.

Congruence analysis is beneficial to research where there is limited previous documentation of a causal relationship and when process-tracing is impracticable.[29] These considerations apply to this research project. Deference has been minimally studied in terms of a causal relationship, and even less research has speculated on the link between deference and formal independence and political fragmentation. Moreover, there are significant barriers to process-tracing because the researcher cannot sit in the room when judges deliberate and make decisions, deliberations are not documented, and judges legally and ethically cannot divulge details of deliberations or their exchanges with one another. Put differently, this may be an instance where "grey-boxing" is as good as it gets. As Beach and Pedersen argue, congruence analysis is appropriate in such cases.

Causal inferences can be strengthened in congruence analysis when combined with cross-case comparison.[30] Even better is when congruence tests are clustered, meaning that a battery of evidence is provided to support a proposition. In other words, it is a cumulation of evidence, as opposed to any smoking gun, that enables a "relatively strong overall confirmation of the theory."[31] For this reason, I rely on a series of tests and data types. First, I produce original data on the decisions of each court. I hand-coded the judgments of the three courts, from their first judgments to those finalized by the end of 2020, along several dimensions (case outcomes, remedies, citations, vote distribution, etc.).[32] This data is triangulated with information drawn from each of the courts' judgments, official reports, websites, and public communication. Interview data and secondary research also complement the quantitative data for the within-case and cross-case analyses. Interviews were conducted between 2015 and 2016 in Arusha, Tanzania; and Port of Spain, Trinidad; and

[29] Beach and Pedersen suggest that congruence analysis applies to typical cases for within-case comparison; see Beach and Pedersen, *Causal Case Study Methods*, chapter 8. Others argue that it can also be used in small-n cross-case comparison; see George and Bennett, *Case Studies and Theory Development*; Joachim Blatter and Markus Haverland, *Designing Case Studies Explanatory Approaches in Small-N Research* (Basingstoke, UK: Palgrave Macmillan, 2012), chapter 4.

[30] Beach and Pedersen, *Causal Case Study Methods*, 280.

[31] Ibid., 287.

[32] The data includes decisions by the EACJ in ninety-four cases, the CCJ in eighteen cases, and the ACtHPR in ninety-one cases. Some cases include more than one ruling. All cases are listed in the Appendix.

additional interviews were conducted virtually in 2023 and 2024.[33] Finally, I also rely on secondary cross-national data related to human rights, democracy, rule of law, and so on. In all, the concurrent use of qualitative and quantitative data improves not only measurement validity but also the robustness of the causal inferences.

While details on data and measurement are specified in each of the empirical chapters, I take this opportunity to briefly describe the measurement strategy for the key explanatory factors. To measure deference, I use my data on each court's decisions to calculate descriptive statistics on case outcomes (e.g., rates at which violations are found) and remedial orders (e.g., the portion of judgments that include intrusive remedial orders). Deference through legal interpretation and reasoning is assessed qualitatively. Formal independence is measured with an original index on formal independence, described in Chapter 3. I measure political fragmentation as the degree of variation in state preferences, where state practices on issues such as human rights, democracy, and the rule of law serve as a proxy for preferences. For this purpose, I use Varieties of Democracy (V-Dem) and Freedom House data.[34] I use my original data on the courts' decisions to assess persuasive argumentation by calculating the rates at which each court issues unanimous judgments and descriptive statistics on citation practices. I assess public legitimation qualitatively from the courts' official reports, press releases, websites, and social media. I make special use of Facebook profiles, extracting all posts from each court's Facebook page with a web-scraping tool. Text analysis of the posts is used to measure the relative prominence of narratives in the public communication of the courts. Finally, support networks are assessed qualitatively, but also using my data on the courts' jurisprudence to determine the proportion of legal cases supported by repeat lawyers, NGOs, and similar.

[33] See Table A1.1 in the Appendix for interview details. All interviews are anonymous and no identifying information is provided, as required by the relevant ethics approval and guaranteed to interviewees. Interviews are referenced as an assigned number throughout the book. In total, ten judges; ten lawyers with direct experience with the ACtHPR, EACJ, or CCJ; six registry staff members; and two staff from external funders were formally interviewed. Some interviewees were able to comment on both the EACJ and the ACtHPR.

[34] Michael Coppedge et al., "V-Dem [Country-Year] Dataset V12," (Varieties of Democracy (V-Dem) Project, 2022), https://www.v-dem.net/data/dataset-archive/; Freedom House, "Freedom in the World: Aggregate Category and Subcategory Scores, 2003–2022," (2023), https://freedomhouse.org/report/freedom-world. Freedom House data is used for the CCJ because it includes most of the CCJ's member states, unlike V-Dem.

Theoretical Implications of the Argument

This book sits squarely at the crossroads of legal scholarship and political science and speaks directly to a growing body of interdisciplinary research on international courts. It has implications for debates on the performance of international courts,[35] showing that political constraints structure performance – that is, ICs judge under *political* constraints.[36] While I am not the first to come to this conclusion, this book uniquely contributes by demonstrating how formal independence and political fragmentation combine to structure these political constraints. It suggests that future research should revisit how institutional design and state preferences interact to affect IC performance. Similarly, it points to a need to improve our understanding of why substate and supranational actors do (not) engage with international courts and how these actors themselves face political constraints that may limit their capacity to utilize the international judiciary.[37] In addition, the book has implications for debates about how hierarchy shapes international judicial politics. While previous work suggests that hierarchy – akin to domestic separation of powers – affects international judicial politics,[38] the case studies reveal impacts of global hierarchies and inequalities (that have

35 Clifford J. Carrubba and Matthew J. Gabel, *International Courts and the Performance of International Agreements: A General Theory with Evidence from the European Union* (Cambridge: Cambridge University Press, 2014); James Thuo Gathii, *The Performance of Africa's International Courts: Using International Litigation for Political, Legal, and Social Change* (Oxford: Oxford University Press, 2020); Tamar Gutner and Alexander Thompson, "The Politics of IO Performance: A Framework," *Review of International Organizations* 5, no. 3 (2010); Theresa Squatrito et al., eds., *The Performance of International Courts and Tribunals* (Cambridge: Cambridge University Press, 2018); Jonas Tallberg et al., "The Performance of International Organizations: A Policy Output Approach," *Journal of European Public Policy* 23, no. 7 (2016).

36 Tom Ginsburg, "Bounded Discretion in International Judicial Lawmaking," *Virginia Journal of International Law* 45, no. 3 (2005); Tom Ginsburg, "Political Constraints on International Courts," in *The Oxford Handbook of International Adjudication*, ed. Cesare Romano, Karen Alter, and Yuval Shany (Oxford: Oxford University Press, 2014); Richard H. Steinberg, "Judicial Lawmaking at the WTO: Discursive, Constitutional, and Political Constraints," *American Journal of International Law* 98, no. 2 (2004).

37 These questions have been studied in reference to the EU; see, for example, Karen J. Alter, *Establishing the Supremacy of European Law: The Making of an International Rule of Law in Europe* (Oxford: Oxford University Press, 2001); R. Daniel Kelemen and Tommaso Pavone, "Where Have the Guardians Gone? Law Enforcement and the Politics of Supranational Forbearance in the European Union," *World Politics* 75, no. 4 (2023). To my knowledge, however, they have received minimal attention outside of the EU.

38 Jeffrey K. Staton and Will H. Moore, "Judicial Power in Domestic and International Politics," *International Organization* 65, no. 3 (2011).

little to do with formal authority).[39] This suggests that future research on international courts, ranging from questions about their origins, accessibility, and practices, might benefit from a closer consideration of the role of global hierarchies and inequalities.[40]

The book also contributes to the literature on international organizations in contemporary world politics.[41] Two dynamics appear to have new effects on IOs today – a heightened public awareness and salience of IOs and the politics of noncooperation and contestation (e.g., backlash, pushback, delegitimation, competitive regime creation). This book integrates these dynamics into its theoretical framework. Drawing from scholarship on the legitimacy of IOs as well as IOs and public opinion,[42]

[39] Janice Bially Mattern and Ayşe Zarakol, "Hierarchies in World Politics," *International Organization* 70, no. 3 (2016).

[40] Some recent work goes in this direction; see, for example, Tobias Lenz and Mariel Reiss, "Globalising the Study of Diffusion: Multiple Sources and the East African Community," *Journal of European Public Policy* (2023); Lora Anne Viola, *The Closure of the International System: How Institutions Create Political Equalities and Hierarchies* (Cambridge: Cambridge University Press, 2020); Christoph Valentin Steinert, "Elitist Remedies? Complaint Resources and Representation in International Human Rights Bodies," *International Studies Quarterly* 68, no. 2 (2024). TWAIL ("Third World Approaches to International Law") scholarship can be added to this list; see, for example, Antony Anghie, *Imperialism, Sovereignty and the Making of International Law* (Cambridge: Cambridge University Press, 2007); Antony Anghie, "Rethinking International Law: A TWAIL Retrospective," *European Journal of International Law* 34, no. 1 (2023); James Thuo Gathii, "Promise of International Law: A Third World View (Including a TWAIL Bibliography 1996–2019 as an Appendix)," *American Society of International Law, Proceedings of the Annual Meeting* 114 (2020).

[41] International courts are a type of IO, and they are typically embedded as subunits within larger IOs.

[42] Jonas Tallberg and Michael Zürn, "The Legitimacy and Legitimation of International Organizations: Introduction and Framework," *Review of International Organizations* 14, no. 4 (2019); Allen Buchanan and Robert Keohane, "The Legitimacy of Global Governance Institutions," *Ethics and International Affairs* 20, no. 4 (2006); Ian Hurd, *After Anarchy: Legitimacy and Power in the United Nations Security Council* (Princeton: Princeton University Press, 2007); Andreas Follesdal, "Survey Article: The Legitimacy of International Courts," *Journal of Political Philosophy* 28, no. 4 (2020); Dominik Zaum, ed., *Legitimating International Organizations* (Oxford: Oxford University Press, 2013); Terrence L. Chapman, "Audience Beliefs and International Organization Legitimacy," *International Organization* 63, no. 4 (2009); Lisa Dellmuth and Jonas Tallberg, *Legitimacy Politics: Elite Communication and Public Opinion in Global Governance* (Cambridge: Cambridge University Press, 2023); Brian Greenhill, "How Can International Organizations Shape Public Opinion? Analysis of a Pair of Survey-Based Experiments," *Review of International Organizations* 15, no. 1 (2020); Tana Johnson, "Guilt by Association: The Link between States' Influence and the Legitimacy of Intergovernmental Organizations," *Review of International Organizations* 6, no. 1 (2011); Erik Voeten, "Public Opinion and the Legitimacy of International Courts,"

the book offers an account of IO decision-making that considers how IO legitimacy and public perceptions affect the relationship between IOs and states and thus IO decisions. Additionally, the book contributes to research on IO responses to noncooperation and institutional resilience.[43] While recent research provides insights into the causes and consequences of noncooperation and contestation,[44] we know less about IO responses. This book suggests that institutional resilience amid backlash and resistance derives – at least partially – from their modifications to decision-making and adaptive practices.

Structure of the Book

The remainder of this book develops the theoretical framework and empirical analysis. The theoretical framework is the focus of Chapter 2. Chapters 3–6 empirically evaluate this framework.

The theoretical framework is presented in Chapter 2, which proceeds in three steps. It first specifies the key concept of interest (or dependent variable) – judicial deference. After describing how I conceptualize and operationalize judicial deference, the chapter outlines two main

Theoretical Inquiries in Law 14, no. 2 (2013); Joseph M. Grieco et al., "Let's Get a Second Opinion: International Institutions and American Public Support for War," *International Studies Quarterly* 55, no. 2 (2011); Klaus Dingwerth et al., eds., *International Organizations Under Pressure: Legitimating Global Governance in Challenging Times* (Oxford: Oxford University Press, 2019).

43 Ezequiel Gonzalez-Ocantos and Wayne Sandholtz, "The Sources of Resilience of International Human Rights Courts: The Case of the Inter-American System," *Law & Social Inquiry* 47, no. 1 (2022).

44 Karen J. Alter, James T. Gathii, and Laurence R. Helfer, "Backlash Against International Courts in West, East and Southern Africa: Causes and Consequences," *European Journal of International Law* 27, no. 2 (2016); Courtney Hillebrecht, *Saving the International Justice Regime: Beyond Backlash Against International Courts* (Cambridge: Cambridge University Press, 2021); Mikael Rask Madsen, Pola Cebulak, and Micha Wiebusch, "Backlash Against International Courts: Explaining the Forms and Patterns of Resistance to International Courts," *International Journal of Law in Context* 14, no. 2 (2018); Inken von Borzyskowski and Felicity Vabulas, "Hello, Goodbye: When Do States Withdraw from International Organizations?" *Review of International Organizations* 14, no. 2 (2019); Julia C. Morse and Robert O. Keohane, "Contested Multilateralism," *Review of International Organizations* 9, no. 4 (2014); Andreas Kruck and Bernhard Zangl, "The Adjustment of International Institutions to Global Power Shifts: A Framework for Analysis," *Global Policy* 11, no. S3 (2020); Catherine E. De Vries, Sara B. Hobolt, and Stefanie Walter, "Politicizing International Cooperation: The Mass Public, Political Entrepreneurs, and Political Opportunity Structures," *International Organization* 75, no. 2 (2021).

theoretical explanations for judicial deference. The first explanation, which forms the basis of my argument, focuses on the strategic setting in which ICs operate. It maintains that a court's strategic setting is shaped by formal judicial independence and political fragmentation. Together, these two factors share a negative relationship with deference as they reduce the likelihood of state resistance and improve IC legitimacy. Put differently, deference declines as independence and fragmentation increase. However, ICs can also exercise agency over their strategic space by adopting practices in the form of persuasive argumentation and public legitimation. These practices also affect an IC's strategic space by way of the credibility of state resistance and the court's legitimacy. The second explanation focuses on the role of judicial support networks and suggests that ICs are less deferential when they have strong support networks. The chapter describes each of these theoretical logics and concludes by identifying observable implications for each explanation.

Chapter 3 asks whether international courts are designed with institutional safeguards to preserve independence. It first conceptualizes formal independence as the formal rules that aim to safeguard autonomous judicial decision-making. Based on this definition, the chapter then develops an original measure of formal independence, which is used to estimate the formal independence of twenty-six ICs from 1945 to 2015. Next, the chapter compares formal independence across these ICs and reveals significant variation in formal independence. It shows that rules pertaining to the selection and tenure of international judges as well as the managerial autonomy of ICs are the sources of most of the observed variation.

Chapters 4–6 examine the judicial decision-making of the East African Court of Justice, the Caribbean Court of Justice, and the African Court, respectively. Each of these chapters begins by situating the courts within the context of their historical origins and surrounding political norms and legal culture. The chapters then describe deference as it is revealed by case outcomes, interpretation and reasoning, and remedies of each court. Following the description of deference, the chapters consider the extent to which deference aligns with the strength and activity of the courts' support networks. Each chapter then analyzes the court's formal independence and political fragmentation, followed by the practices that help to build or maintain its strategic space. These analyses focus on drawing out the relationship between each of these factors and each court's distinct patterns of deference.

These chapters reveal three varieties of deference and related constraints. The EACJ is best described as having *substantial deference* due to its *pervasive constraints*, which result from low formal independence and medium political fragmentation. On the other hand, the CCJ has been *moderately deferential* as a result of its *intermediate constraints.* While the CCJ enjoys high formal independence, political fragmentation among its member states is low, and thus, the CCJ's strategic space is especially affected by the degree of homogeneity of state preferences on the matters before the Court. Finally, the ACtHPR is characterized by *minimal deference* because of its more *subtle constraints*, which derive from having generally high formal independence and high political fragmentation.

Chapter 7 summarizes the empirical findings on the EACJ, CCJ, and ACtHPR by comparing the three international courts and reviews the core results of the within-case comparisons. It also outlines the book's implications for interdisciplinary research on international courts and IR literature on IOs in contemporary world politics.

2

Judicial Deference and the Strategic Space of International Courts

The main instrument through which international courts serve their functions, whether settling disputes, interpreting and applying the law, or enforcing compliance, is their decisions. This contrasts with other types of international organizations that typically have a range of instruments to draw upon in fulfilling their governing roles, such as data collection, technical assistance, resource distribution, sanctions, or even interstate negotiations. In other words, international courts uniquely govern by decision. For this reason, understanding what underlies international judicial decision-making is crucial to debates about the legitimacy and performance of ICs.

This book studies international courts, defined as international judicial bodies that (1) take decisions on the basis of international law – as opposed to domestic law; (2) follow predetermined rules of procedure; (3) issue legally binding outcomes; (4) are composed of permanent independent members;[1] and (5) require at least one party to a dispute is a state or an international organization.[2] Moreover, it conceives of ICs as a unique type of international organization, which is any association of more than two states that has membership criteria, is a formal entity, and possesses a permanent secretariat or other indication of institutionalization such as headquarters and/or staff.[3]

[1] Permanence is defined as having a fixed term of appointment (e.g., predetermined number of years), in contrast to an ad hoc appointment to preside over a single dispute or decision.

[2] Cesare Romano, Karen Alter, and Yuval Shany, "Mapping International Adjudicative Bodies, the Issues, and Players," in *The Oxford Handbook of International Adjudication*, ed. Cesare Romano, Karen Alter, and Yuval Shany (Oxford: Oxford University Press, 2014), 6.

[3] Jon C. W. Pevehouse et al., "Tracking Organizations in the World: The Correlates of War IGO Version 3.0 Datasets," *Journal of Peace Research* 57, no. 3 (2020): 464; see also Lisa L. Martin and Beth A. Simmons, "International Organizations and Institutions," in *Handbook of International Relations*, ed. Walter Carlsnaes, Thomas Risse, and Beth A. Simmons (London: Sage, 2012).

The aim of this book is to shed light on the decisions of international courts. It does so by focusing on a core feature of judicial decision-making – deference. Judicial deference varies extensively in international adjudication. Yet, why some courts defer more than others or why deference ebbs and flows is not fully understood. This chapter advances an account of deference by international courts, which focuses on their strategic space. It presents a theoretical argument about the factors that structure a court's strategic space and distinguishes itself from other prominent accounts of judicial decision-making in existing research.

I lay out this approach in three steps. First, I conceptualize judicial deference in terms of if and how a court, through its decisions, either accepts or rejects the exercise of authority by states or other governing entities (e.g., international organization). Based on this definition, I operationalize deference in terms of three features of judicial decisions: case outcomes, legal interpretation and reasoning, and remedies. This threefold view of judicial decisions facilitates a comprehensive assessment of deference. It also helps to elucidate distinctions between deference and other related concepts, namely, judicial activism/restraint and de facto independence.

Second, I develop a theoretical framework that explains judicial deference. Informed by rational institutionalism, this framework centers on the strategic setting in which ICs operate. The key political factors shaping this strategic setting are states' preferences and the institutional rules governing an IC. I suggest that formal rules that safeguard judicial independence and political fragmentation, as in the heterogeneity of states' preferences, enable less deferential decision-making. These factors construct a court's strategic setting by way of their impact on the perceived legitimacy of the court and the credibility of state resistance against the court. Additionally, ICs exercise agency over their strategic setting by adopting practices that also affect perceived legitimacy and the credibility of resistance. I outline the logic behind this argument and identify theoretical expectations, or observable implications, to be evaluated empirically.

Third, I discuss alternative approaches, which offer different expectations about whether and when ICs would be inclined to defer to states. The most prominent of these alternatives looks to an IC's support network. This approach expects that courts with a strong and active network of proponents will demonstrate less deference, irrespective of states' preferences and institutional rules. I also consider approaches that emphasize ideational factors, like political norms and legal culture.

Conceptualizing Judicial Deference

Deference is a critical characteristic of international judicial decisions because it relates to the allocation of authority. Accordingly, it has consequences for how ICs fulfill their governing roles, namely, the settlement of international disputes, the clarification of international law, and the enforcement of international legal obligations.[4] This section conceptualizes deference for the purpose of this book. In doing so, it discusses the advantages of approaching judicial decision-making in terms of deference as conceived here and describes how three features of a judicial decision – case outcome, legal interpretation and reasoning, and remedial orders – are used to operationalize deference.

Judicial deference is defined as a court's acceptance of the state's exercise of authority (or that of any other governing entity within the court's jurisdiction). This definition builds on the concept of deference developed by Efrat and Newman to understand transnational jurisdictional conflicts and whether one state accepts the authority of another state.[5] Others have adapted Efrat and Newman's definition to apply to other governing actors. For instance, Pratt used it to describe the allocation of authority among different international organizations, or whether one IO accepts the exercise of authority by another IO.[6] Like Pratt, I adapt Efrat and Newman's definition to address other authority actors, specifically, international courts.

While international courts typically review acts or actions of states or their constitutive organs (e.g., legislature, judiciary or executive agency), many international courts review and decide on the acts or actions of

[4] Theresa Squatrito et al., "A Framework for Evaluating the Performance of International Courts and Tribunals," in *The Performance of International Courts and Tribunals*, ed. Theresa Squatrito et al. (Cambridge: Cambridge University Press, 2018); Yuval Shany, "No Longer a Weak Department of Power? Reflections on the Emergence of a New International Judiciary," *European Journal of International Law* 20, no. 1 (2009); José Alvarez, "What Are International Judges For? The Main Functions of International Adjudication," in *The Oxford Handbook of International Adjudication*, ed. Cesare Romano, Karen Alter, and Yuval Shany (Oxford: Oxford University Press, 2014); Karen J. Alter, "The Multiple Roles of International Courts and Tribunals: Enforcement, Dispute Settlement, Constitutional and Administrative Review," in *Interdisciplinary Perspectives on International Law and International Relations*, ed. Jeffrey Dunoff and Mark Pollack (Cambridge: Cambridge University Press, 2013).

[5] Efrat and Newman, "Deciding to Defer," 410; they define deference as "one state's acceptance of the exercise of jurisdiction by another state."

[6] Tyler Pratt, "Deference and Hierarchy in International Regime Complexes," *International Organization* 72, no. 3 (2018).

supranational or intergovernmental organs.[7] For example, some judgments of the CJEU concern an act or action of a member state (i.e., infringement) while others address an act or action of a European Union (EU) institution, such as the EU Commission or EU Council (i.e., annulment). For simplicity, the remainder of this chapter discusses deference in terms of the relationship between an IC and states, even though my conceptualization also applies to ICs' acceptance or not of the exercise of authority by any intergovernmental and supranational organs within their jurisdiction.

I am not the first to study deference by international courts; in fact, international judicial deference has received the attention of legal scholars.[8] My conceptualization of deference shares similarities with legal approaches but is also unique. Shirlow's contribution to legal scholarship on deference provides a prominent definition. She defines it as "techniques used by international adjudicators to recognise a domestic actor's superior 'authority' to decide issues relevant to the settlement of the dispute" and thus "deference equates to a recognition of another actor's decision-making authority."[9] Similarly, Cheyne conceives of deference as a court's "acknowledgement of the primacy of the State to make decisions and the need to avoid substituting the State's judgment with its own."[10] These definitions, like mine, relates to the allocation of authority. However, I do not conceive of deference in terms of the substitution or replacement of authority per se. Rather, I conceptualize deference as acceptance, which according to Efrat and Newman can take two forms: abstention and validation.[11] A court accepts a state's exercise of authority either by *abstaining* from exercising its own authority or by *validating* a decision or action of the state.

Abstention and validation can be seen in various features of a judicial decision. For instance, dismissal of a legal complaint because it falls outside a court's jurisdiction is one way a court might abstain. A court can also abstain by not dictating what actions a state must take to remedy

[7] Many, but not all, courts have authority over intergovernmental and supranational organs; see Alter, *The New Terrain of International Law.*

[8] Esmé Shirlow, *Judging at the Interface: Deference to State Decision-Making Authority in International Adjudication* (Cambridge: Cambridge University Press, 2021); Lukasz Gruszczynski and Wouter Werner, *Deference in International Courts and Tribunals: Standard of Review and Margin of Appreciation* (Oxford: Oxford University Press, 2014); Ilona Cheyne, "Deference and the Use of the Public Policy Exception in International Courts and Tribunals," in *Deference in International Courts and Tribunals*, ed. Lukasz Gruszczynski and Wouter Werner (Oxford: Oxford University Press, 2014).

[9] Shirlow, *Judging at the Interface*, 16.

[10] Cheyne, "Deference and the Use of the Public Policy Exception," 38.

[11] Efrat and Newman, "Deciding to Defer," 413–14.

a violation. In the first instance, deference affects the outcome of the dispute (who wins or loses), while remedial orders are implicated in the second instance. A decision whereby a court finds a state's interpretation and application of the law to be valid, and therefore dismisses the state of any wrongdoing, also constitutes deference.

Nondeference occurs when a court rejects the state's exercise of authority, either by *not abstaining* or by *not validating* an act or action taken by the state. It can also be seen in different features of a judicial decision. When a court finds a violation, for example, it has withheld validation of the state's exercise of authority. If a court agrees that it has jurisdiction, it has not abstained. Likewise, when a court expands an interpretation of the law or specifies how a state must remedy a wrong, it has foregone abstention. In these instances, the court's decision withholds acceptance while also substituting the state's judgment with its own.

Conceived as acceptance (validation or abstention), deference can be observed in the outcome of a legal case, in the way in which law is interpreted and reasoned, as well as the remedial orders. This contrasts with prominent legal approaches, which examine deference based on the intensity of judicial scrutiny or standards of review (e.g., margin of appreciation). These approaches focus on questions such as what doctrines lend themselves to deference or nondeference, what is the legal reasoning behind different levels of judicial scrutiny, and what ought to be the standard of review.

The contrasts between legal approaches and my own are primarily analytical. On a practical level, they will typically agree on what decisions are deferential or not because a deferential standard of review will often result in acceptance. As Fahner explains, "the intensity of review affects the likelihood that the adjudicators will find that the decision under review is lawful: if they exercise a low intensity of review, it is likely that the original decision will be approved; conversely, a high intensity of review increases the chances that the original decision will be overturned."[12] However, differences can exist on a practical level. For example, according to Shirlow, deference is low in de novo review because the domestic court's decision is highly scrutinized,[13] irrespective of whether the IC comes to a similar conclusion as the domestic court. The sheer fact that the court exercises intense review removes authority from the state and constitutes nondeference. My approach, in contrast,

[12] Johannes Hendrik Fahner, *Judicial Deference in International Adjudication: A Comparative Analysis* (Oxford: Hart Publishing, 2020), 7.

[13] Shirlow, *Judging at the Interface.*

focuses on whether the de novo review results in acceptance or rejection of a domestic court's decision.

Characterizing judicial decision-making in terms of deference has advantages over alternatives. Scholars and policymakers alike typically characterize judicial decisions as "activism" or – conversely – "restraint." Yet, this way of describing judicial decisions poses problems. Importantly, judicial activism is a term fraught with multiple meanings. The first noted use of "judicial activism" and "restraint" was by Arthur Schlesinger in 1947, who described the justices of the US Supreme Court as either "activists" or "champions of restraint."[14] According to him, activist judges used judicial power for "their own conception of the social good" while those who exercised restraint expanded "the range of allowable judgment for legislatures."[15] Kmiec identifies five widespread definitions and argues that activism is used to refer to instances where a court: (1) invalidates the decision of another authority (e.g., a legislature); (2) ignores precedent; (3) legislates; (4) departs from accepted interpretive methods; or (5) engages in result-oriented judging.[16] Others include additional components to determine activism, such as "institutional aggrandizement."[17] Attempts to refine the concept have led others to define judicial activism as a departure from "cultural standards of judicial role"[18] or "prevailing standards of adjudicatory conduct."[19] This definition, however, is difficult to apply when considering courts comparatively, as the cultural standards will differ from court to court and with time.[20] Moreover, judicial activism is laden with political connotations and subjective assessments – it is often in the eye of the beholder.[21]

Criticisms wielded against the WTO's Appellate Body exemplify the challenges with exploring judicial decision-making through the lens of

[14] Cited in Stefanie A. Lindquist and Frank B. Cross, *Measuring Judicial Activism* (Oxford: Oxford University Press, 2009), 1; Fahner, *Judicial Deference in International Adjudication*, 7.

[15] Ibid.

[16] Kmiec, "The Origin and Current Meanings of 'Judicial Activism'."

[17] Lindquist and Cross, *Measuring Judicial Activism*.

[18] Craig Green, "An Intellectual History of Judicial Activism," *Emory Law Journal* 58, no. 5 (2009): 1226.

[19] Fuad Zarbiyev, "Judicial Activism in International Law: A Conceptual Framework for Analysis," *Journal of International Dispute Settlement* 3, no. 2 (2012); Fuad Zarbiyev, "Judicial Activism," in *Max Planck Encyclopedia of International Procedural Law*, ed. Hélène Ruiz Fabri (Oxford: Oxford University Press, 2018).

[20] Zarbiyev, "Judicial Activism in International Law."

[21] Lindquist and Cross, *Measuring Judicial Activism*, 1.

activism versus restraint. The United States has accused the WTO AB of "judicial activism" and "overreach" because it has created new rights and obligations for members.[22] A significant part of the charges of overreach by the United States relates to how the AB treats previous decisions as binding precedent.[23] The application of the term "activism" to the WTO AB is somewhat confusing because adherence to established interpretations is a typical marker of restraint, not activism. Whether we view the WTO AB as activist is further complicated by additional considerations. For instance, decisions of most international courts are formally binding only on the direct parties to a dispute, so departure from this principle is arguably overreach. On the other hand, the AB's gap-filling might be more indicative of states' failures to develop the law through intergovernmental negotiations than it is of the AB's activism.[24] Overall, this example shows that assessments of activism can be varied and its key markers context dependent or subjective.

Deference is thus useful because it does not suffer from the same politically charged connotations as activism or restraint or from being subjective. It is also beneficial for comparative analysis of the decision-making of international courts and tribunals because it operates with a common benchmark – the acceptance (or not) of the state's exercise of authority.

Last, I distinguish deference from de facto independence. While both terms refer to judicial behavior, they speak to different units of analysis. As I conceive of it, deference is a characteristic of discrete judicial decisions – although it can be used to describe a body of decisions. On the other hand, de facto independence is a characteristic of a court. While de facto independent courts are less likely to be deferential in any given decision and vice versa, it may in practice make some deferential decisions.

[22] US Trade Representative, *Report on the Appellate Body of the World Trade Organization* (2020) accessed August 27, 2024, https://ustr.gov/sites/default/files/enforcement/DS/USTR.Appellate.Body.Rpt.Feb2020.pdf; Congressional Research Service, *The World Trade Organization's Appellate Body: Key Disputes and Controversies*, R46852 (2021) accessed August 24, 2024, https://crsreports.congress.gov/.

[23] Ibid.

[24] Henry Gao and Weihuan Zhou, "'Overreaching' or 'Overreacting'? Reflections on the Judicial Function and Approaches of WTO Appellate Body," *Journal of World Trade* 53, no. 6 (2019); Amrita Bahri, "Appellate Body Held Hostage: Is Judicial Activism at Fair Trial?" *Journal of World Trade* 53, no. 2 (2019).

Deference: Three Indicators

Having elaborated on how I define deference, I now turn to how it is operationalized or observed empirically. As alluded to above, an international court makes several determinations that reveal acceptance or rejection of the state's (or other entity's) exercise of authority, including the determinations on (1) *case outcome*, (2) *legal interpretation and reasoning*, and (3) *remedial orders*. The first two are determinations about whether there has been a breach of law, while the third concerns the consequences or sanctions against the state for its breach. Each of these determinations roughly speaks to one of the main functions of ICs. Case outcome relates most clearly to a court's dispute resolution function, legal interpretation and reasoning to clarification and development of law, and remedies to issues of compliance. This leads me to adopt a threefold operationalization of judicial deference, which I describe below.

First, we can observe deference through a case outcome, or in whose favor the court rules (e.g., admissible or not, win or loss). I assume that deference occurs when an IC decides that the respondent state has complied with its legal obligations (validation), or it dismisses a case as being inadmissible or outside its jurisdiction (abstention). Conversely, decisions that declare the respondent state has violated a legal obligation are indicative of nondeference. While case outcomes can provide insights into judicial deference, measuring deference by case outcomes alone "risks missing potentially more interesting and important aspects of international adjudication."[25] Also, case outcomes overestimate deference because they capture considerations other than a court's intention to accept the state's exercise of authority. For instance, a decision in which a court declares a petition is outside its jurisdiction may indicate that the law clearly denies the court authority rather than being an act of abstention on the part of said court. Similarly, a ruling that finds the state has not violated the law might not be indicative of the court's acceptance of the state's exercise of authority but instead that there was poor evidence to support the allegation. Put differently, a case outcome may be a poor indicator of deference in any given legal case, and case outcomes will overestimate judicial deference in the aggregate. Nonetheless, case outcomes, especially in the aggregate, can approximate a court's tendency to accept or reject states' exercise of authority, which is necessary for comparative analysis.

[25] Shirlow, *Judging at the Interface*, 72.

To balance the advantages and disadvantages, I combine case outcomes with additional features of judicial decisions to operationalize deference. Namely, deference is also observed through the method of interpretation and legal reasoning applied by a court in any given decision. Treaty interpretation is defined as "the activity through which international tribunals give meaning to a treaty in the context of a particular case or fact pattern."[26] There are several methods used to interpret treaties, each of which relies on a specific reference point. For example, judges will often use the text, party intent, or underlying treaty objective as the baseline for understanding treaty obligations. For several methods of interpretation, there is no clear pattern with deference. For instance, interpretative methods based on the text, party intent, or underlying objective of a treaty are not rock-solid ways of identifying deference.[27] One method that provides the most insight into deference relies on a reference point concerned with the envisaged role of a court, or what Pauwelyn and Elsig label as either a "work-to-rule" approach or alternatively a "gap-filling" approach.[28] A work-to-rule approach takes the view that a court's role is typically secondary to the state and applies only what the treaty provides for according to the strictest, most conservative reading. A work-to-rule approach resembles "restrictive interpretation," in which a court limits the scope of vague provisions or "assumes that state intends to be bound by the least of any obligation which could be read from a provision of doubtful content or ambiguous expression."[29] A "work to rule" approach most closely resembles a court abstaining from anything that resembles law-making by way of interpretation or validating any reasonable interpretation given by a state. Conversely, gap-filling assumes a court's job is to fill in gaps left by a treaty to complete a contract.[30] Gap-filling is what scholars often associate with judicial lawmaking,[31] and it is sometimes called

[26] Joost Pauwelyn and Manfred Elsig, "The Politics of Treaty Interpretation: Variations and Explanations across International Tribunals," in *Interdisciplinary Perspectives on International Law and International Relations*, ed. Jeffrey Dunoff and Mark Pollack (Cambridge: Cambridge University Press, 2014), 446.

[27] Ibid.

[28] Ibid., 454–55.

[29] Richard K. Gardiner, *Treaty Interpretation*, 2nd ed. (Oxford: Oxford University Press, 2015), 59; see also Johannes Hendrik Fahner, "In Dubio Mitius: Advancing Clarity and Modesty in Treaty Interpretation," *European Journal of International Law* 32, no. 3 (2021).

[30] Pauwelyn and Elsig, "The Politics of Treaty Interpretation," 454–55.

[31] Steinberg, "Judicial Lawmaking at the WTO."

purposive or expansive interpretation.[32] It will typically require a court to not abstain.

A work-to-rule approach is deferential.[33] Gap-filling is often nondeferential, but not always. Thus, to determine deference in interpretation I look first and foremost at whether there is a work-to-rule approach. On the other hand, if there is what appears to be a nondeferential form of gap-filling, I also consider three other pieces of information: (1) Does the court's interpretation diverge from the respondent state's argued position or preferred interpretation in the dispute; (2) does the court rely on legal reasoning or doctrines that are known to reflect deference;[34] and (3) does legal scholarship or legal opinion view the interpretation or reasoning as deferential. In all instances, I am attentive to whether an interpretation generally broadens or narrows obligations in ways that reflect abstention or validation. Ultimately, determining deference in legal interpretation and reasoning requires qualitative assessment on a case-by-case basis. However, as I use a threefold indicator of deference, I see these challenges as less problematic than if my measure was based solely on this aspect of a judicial decision. Also, as a separate note, this aspect of my measure closely overlaps with what legal scholarship tends to associate with deference.

Third, deference can also manifest in a court's decision on remedies, or the legal consequences to a state once it has been found to have failed in its obligations. Remedies are also seen as the way in which relief or justice is afforded to a wronged applicant. IR scholars tend to pay little attention to judicial remedies.[35] Yet, legal remedies are an integral part of an international court's judgment.[36] While there is some debate about what remedial powers international courts have, three types are more or less recognized: (1) declaratory judgments, (2) reparations, and (3) consequential orders.[37] While not all ICs have the power to use all of these

[32] Pauwelyn and Elsig, "The Politics of Treaty Interpretation," 455.

[33] Ibid.

[34] This includes doctrines or standards of review like a margin of appreciation, good faith, evidentiary burdens, and state discretion; see, for example, Shirlow, *Judging at the Interface*.

[35] For exceptions, see William Phelan, "Enforcement and Escape in the Andean Community: Why the Andean Community of Nations Is Not a Replica of the European Union," *Journal of Common Market Studies* 53, no. 4 (2014); Øyvind Stiansen, "Directing Compliance? Remedial Approach and Compliance with European Court of Human Rights Judgments," *British Journal of Political Science* 51, no. 2 (2021).

[36] Gray, "Remedies"; Shelton, *Remedies in International Human Rights Law*.

[37] Gray, "Remedies."

remedies – some remedial powers may be proscribed by the constitutive instruments (i.e., founding treaties, statutes, etc.) of an IC – they are generally recognized as the main remedies of international legal practice.[38] Declaratory judgments are the declaration of wrongdoing by the respondent state. This type of remedy "leaves it to the discretion of the wrongdoing state to take appropriate measures to comply with international law."[39] Declaratory judgments are the least intrusive to states because they simply declare wrong-doing[40] but allow the respondent state to determine how it will remedy the legal violation. In other words, these remedies are acts of abstention by courts and do not impose any particular act or action on the state about providing a wronged party with relief. Reparations include restitution, compensation, and satisfaction.[41] Restitution is an obligation to restore the status quo before the wrong was committed. Sometimes restitution is materially impossible or would incur a disproportionate burden on the state when compared to the benefit. Compensation is an order obligating a state to monetarily compensate a wronged party for the damage caused. Satisfaction is an obligation that the violating state acknowledge its wrongdoing, express regret, issue an apology, or similar.[42] Reparations overall are focused on giving relief to the wronged party by committing the state to take some form of action. While reparations limit state discretion on how to offer relief, it does not encroach largely on state sovereignty because there is no mandated change to law or policies. Consequential (or mandatory) orders "direct the respondent state to take or abstain from some form of specific action."[43] Consequential orders include orders for specific performance, which aim to ensure the state complies with the underlying obligation, and negative injunctions, which prevent the state from taking certain action. Both reparations and consequential orders reflect a court choosing not to abstain from determining an appropriate remedy. However, as consequential orders are the most intrusive on state sovereignty, removing state policy discretion and replacing state authority

[38] Brown, *A Common Law of International Adjudication.*

[39] Gray, "Remedies."

[40] Shelton, *Remedies in International Human Rights Law*, 255.

[41] Brown, *A Common Law of International Adjudication*, 190. See also, UN International Law Commission, *Articles on the Responsibility of States for Internationally Wrongful Acts*, Report of the ILC on the Work of its Fifty-third Session, UNGA Official Record, 56th session, Supplement No. 10, A/56/10 (2001).

[42] Ibid., 191.

[43] Ibid., 209.

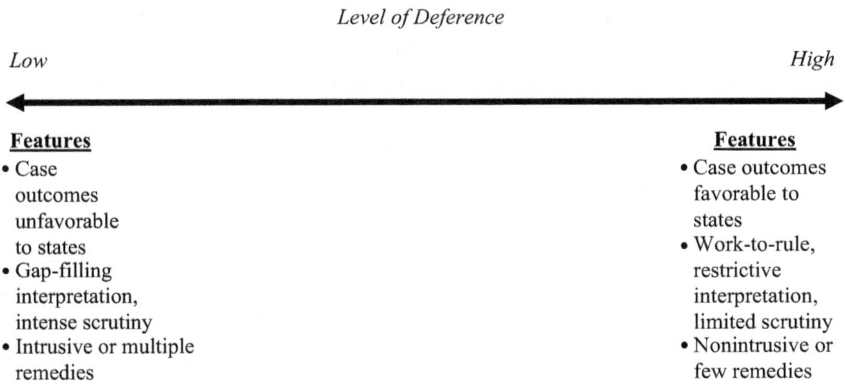

Figure 2.1 Operationalization of deference.

with that of the court, I consider consequential orders to be the least deferential type of remedy. Finally, nondeference can become greater in any given decision when a court combines remedies. If a court orders both restitution and compensation, for example, it is less deferential than if it were to only order compensation.

Figure 2.1 depicts this threefold operationalization of deference. A few considerations inform this approach to measuring judicial deference. First is the observation that courts can employ different levels of deference across the three dimensions of a single judgment. For example, they can take expansive interpretations while adopting minimally intrusive remedies. This operationalization helps to capture these nuances. Additionally, this threefold approach facilitates measurement at the level of individual court decisions but can be aggregated to say something about the tendencies of a court for both temporal and cross-sectional comparisons. It provides a comparative metric that is especially workable and appropriate for courts in which individuals or private actors can have standing.[44] It also bears in mind the newness of the courts being studied. Alternatives such as text analysis based on a dictionary approach might be useful for courts like the ECtHR or CJEU because they have hundreds of judgments and have developed a uniform internal language. Newer courts do not have these advantages. Last, this measure roughly captures the various functions or roles of courts: dispute resolution (case outcome), legal clarification and application (legal interpretation and reasoning), and

[44] A different operationalization may be necessary for interstate disputes.

compliance (remedies). Thus, while other approaches to observing and studying deference can be instructive, this operationalization is adopted to accommodate the comparative research design and aims of this book.

International Courts and Their Strategic Space: Political Constraints and Judicial Practices

International courts differ in terms of the degree to which they defer to states in their decision-making. For example, the CJEU has been described as being less deferential because it is viewed as making law,[45] despite its preference for nonintrusive remedies.[46] In contrast, the ICJ shows more deference because of its restrictive interpretation[47] and minimally intrusive remedies.[48] The ECtHR has been less deferential to states in its legal interpretation[49] while employing less intrusive remedies.[50] This, however, has varied throughout the Court's lifetime, across states and individual judgments.[51] The IACtHR is also known for non-deference due to its intrusive remedies.[52] How can we explain this variation? What factors influence whether an IC defers to states or not?

45 Bruno Witte, Elise Muir, and Mark Dawson, *Judicial Activism at the European Court of Justice* (Cheltenham: Edward Elgar, 2013); Alter and Helfer, "Nature or Nurture?"; R. Daniel Kelemen, "The Court of Justice of the European Union: Changing Authority in the Twenty-First Century," in *International Court Authority*, ed. Karen J. Alter, Laurence Helfer and Mikael Rask Madsen (Oxford: Oxford University Press, 2018); Weiler, "The Transformation of Europe," *Yale Law Journal* 100 (1991); Wasserfallen, "The Judiciary as Legislator?" *Journal of European Public Policy* 17, no. 8 (2010); Dorte Sindbjerg Martinsen, "Conflict and Conflict Management in the Cross-Border Provision of Healthcare Services," *West European Politics* 32, no. 4 (2009). Some scholars contest this characterization of the CJEU; see, for example, Andreas Grimmel, "Judicial Interpretation or Judicial Activism? The Legacy of Rationalism in the Studies of the European Court of Justice," *European Law Journal 18*, no. 4 (2012); Davies, "Activism Relocated: The Self-Restraint of the European Court of Justice in Its National Context," *Journal of European Public Policy* 19, no. 1 (2012).

46 Gray, "Remedies."

47 Kolb, *The Elgar Companion to the International Court of Justice*; Mawar, "The Perils of Judicial Restraint."

48 Gray, "Remedies"; Brown, *A Common Law of International Adjudication.*

49 Madsen, "The European Court of Human Rights."

50 Gray, "Remedies"; Shelton, *Remedies in International Human Rights Law.*

51 Madsen, "The European Court of Human Rights"; Shai Dothan, "Judicial Tactics in the European Court of Human Rights," *Chicago Journal of International Law* 12, no. 1 (2011).

52 Gray, "Remedies"; Shelton, *Remedies in International Human Rights Law*; Pasqualucci, *The Practice and Procedure of the Inter-American Court of Human Rights.*

To address these questions, I begin with the widely accepted observation that international courts, like their domestic counterparts, operate by their very nature within a strategic space.[53] Some have labeled this "strategic space"[54] as "bounded discretion"[55] or "constrained independence."[56] A court's strategic space derives from its competing incentives, which it has by virtue of being a court. On the one hand, a court has legal incentives – to build and maintain a reputation as a legitimate legal authority. This requires a court to demonstrate legal competence and its respect for the law and legal procedures. The ability to speak as an authority on the law also necessitates the appearance of being neutral. Courts must appear to be unaffected by political pressure and as dealing only in law, not in politics. Without a reputation for neutrality, international courts risk becoming irrelevant and unable to serve their core functions. Thus, ICs have incentives to maintain a reputation as a neutral and expert interpreter of the law.

On the other hand, ICs also have political interests – to maintain the support of those who wield power. Courts are traditionally described as the "weakest" or the "least dangerous" types of governing institutions because they lack the ability to enforce their rulings. Courts must rely upon other political actors or power holders to implement their decisions and to continually support their functioning. This is also the case for international courts. Without compliance and support from power

[53] Olof Larsson and Daniel Naurin, "Judicial Independence and Political Uncertainty: How the Risk of Override Affects the Court of Justice of the EU," *International Organization* 70, no. 2 (2016); Steinberg, "Judicial Lawmaking at the WTO"; Lee Epstein and Jack Knight, *The Choices Justices Make* (Washington, DC: Congressional Quarterly Press, 1998); R. Daniel Kelemen, "The Limits of Judicial Power: Trade-Environment Disputes in the GATT/WTO and the EU," *Comparative Political Studies* 34, no. 6 (2001); Geoffrey Garrett, R. Daniel Kelemen, and Heiner Schulz, "The European Court of Justice, National Governments, and Legal Integration in the European Union," *International Organization* 52, no. 1 (1998); Anne-Marie Burley and Walter Mattli, "Europe Before the Court: A Political Theory of Legal Integration," *International Organization* 47, no. 1 (1993); Laurence Helfer and Anne-Marie Slaughter, "Why States Create International Tribunals: A Response to Professors Posner and Yoo," *California Law Review* 93, no. 3 (2005); Georg Vanberg, *The Politics of Constitutional Review in Germany* (Cambridge: Cambridge University Press, 2005). Even though scholars debate what factors influence this strategic space and the extent to which ICs are themselves able to restructure the strategic space (e.g., by changing states' preferences or mobilizing compliance constituencies), it is generally accepted that ICs operate within this space.

[54] Steinberg, "Judicial Lawmaking at the WTO."

[55] Ginsburg, "Bounded Discretion in International Judicial Lawmaking."

[56] Helfer and Slaughter, "Why States Create International Tribunals."

wielders, a court's ability to serve its core roles in governance can be threatened. Because of their need for compliance and support from power holders, ICs seek to avoid state resistance and defiance. Resistance can come in many forms and can include what others refer to as backlash and pushback.[57] States can unilaterally resist a court through threats or execution of "exit" and "voice."[58] Exit transpires when a state withdraws from the jurisdiction of a court. Voice occurs when a state publicly "attacks" a court, implicitly or explicitly communicating displeasure with a court, or by ignoring it through nonparticipation[59] or willful noncompliance. States can also resist an IC through collective measures, aiming to rein in or curb a court's authority by restricting the resources, mandate or authority of a court.[60] States might also override a court. These possible means of resistance constrain a court politically and give courts reason to accommodate states' preferences.

To summarize, a court's competing incentives relate to its perceived legitimacy and the feasibility and credibility of state resistance. International courts formulate and issue their decisions against this backdrop. While it is accepted that this is the context in which judges make decisions, the boundaries of their strategic space and what factors determine the breadth of this strategic space are debated. In the following, I develop a theoretical account to explain variation in courts' strategic space and its impact on judicial decision-making. This account highlights how two structural factors – formal independence and political fragmentation – combine to affect the strategic space in which courts operate and make decisions. The two political factors are causally linked to an IC's strategic space, and hence deference, due to their impact on the perceived legitimacy of a court and the feasibility and credibility of state resistance.

57 Madsen, Cebulak, and Wiebusch, "Backlash Against International Courts."

58 Albert O. Hirschman, *Exit, Voice, and Loyalty Responses to Decline in Firms, Organizations, and States* (Cambridge, MA: Harvard University Press, 1970); Ginsburg, "Bounded Discretion in International Judicial Lawmaking"; Joost Pauwelyn and Rebecca J. Hamilton, "Exit from International Tribunals," *Journal of International Dispute Settlement* 9, no. 4 (2018).

59 For example, the Russian Federation did not participate in the judicial proceedings in the Arctic Sunrise case before the ITLOS; see A. G. Oude Elferink, "The Russian Federation and the Arctic Sunrise Case: Hot Pursuit and Other Issues Under the LOSC," *International Law Studies* 92 (2016).

60 This form of resistance most closely resembles backlash, as defined by Hillebrecht, when it is a sustained effort to restrict a court; see Hillebrecht, *Saving the International Justice Regime*.

The framework also points to a set of intervening factors. These include practices that ICs adopt to purposively broaden their strategic space, namely, persuasive argumentation and public legitimation. Previous state resistance can also intervene to affect the strategic space; when states have previously been successful at implementing resistance, a court's strategic space narrows. If and how international courts practice persuasive argumentation and public legitimation as well as their past experiences with resistance will be affected by structural conditions. Their impact on a court's strategic space occurs because they affect the credibility and feasibility of efforts to curb a court. They also have an impact on a court's strategic space by affecting the legitimacy of ICs and their judgments. In turn, their impact on a court's strategic space shapes judicial deference.

Structural Factors: Formal Independence and Political Fragmentation

The **formal independence** of a court facilitates its ability to balance its competing incentives. Judicial independence relates to the ability of courts to deliberate and reach judgments in light of the law and without undue pressure or influence from external sources, governmental or otherwise.[61] Independence can be conceived as either de facto independence or de jure independence.[62] De facto independence is a matter of whether a court demonstrates independent behavior in practice. On the other hand, de jure independence, or what I label *formal independence*, is a feature of institutional design that relates to the availability of ex ante and ex post mechanisms of state control over a court and thereby if and how independence is formally safeguarded. Chapter 3 develops the concept and measurement of formal independence, but in short it is rooted in the codified rules governing a court that determine the extent to which a court enjoys safeguards to independence.

Previous literature suggests that independence has bearing on the performance of international courts.[63] Although not expressed in the

[61] Keohane, Moravcsik, and Slaughter, "Legalized Dispute Resolution."

[62] James Melton and Tom Ginsburg, "Does De Jure Judicial Independence Really Matter? A Reevaluation of Explanations for Judicial Independence," *Journal of Law and Courts* 2, no. 2 (2014).

[63] Laurence Helfer and Anne-Marie Slaughter, "Towards a Theory of Effective Supranational Adjudication," *Yale Law Journal* 107, no. 2 (1997); Helfer and Slaughter, "Why States Create International Tribunals"; Keohane, Moravcsik, and Slaughter,

language of independence, research has shown that the formal rules defining state control of a court affect judicial decision-making.[64] Some scholars have argued that the independence of ICs is associated with judicial activism.[65] More recent research highlights the relationship between specific elements of formal independence, like reappointment rules, and judicial decision-making.[66] In addition, formal independence has been shown to facilitate judicial activism[67] and autonomy of domestic constitutional courts.[68]

Formal independence affects a court's strategic space, or how ICs experience and perceive the balance of legal and political imperatives, via two mechanisms: (1) the credibility and political feasibility of coordinated resistance against a court, and (2) its legitimacy. First, formal independence shapes the credibility and feasibility of coordinated state resistance (e.g., court reform, removal of judges, budgetary consequences). When formal independence is low, there is a greater availability of possible means for curtailing a court through coordinated action. All else equal, the feasibility and credibility of state resistance will be greater.

"Legalized Dispute Resolution"; Yuval Shany, *Assessing the Effectiveness of International Courts* (Oxford: Oxford University Press, 2014); Andrew T. Guzman, "International Tribunals: A Rational Choice Analysis," *University of Pennsylvania Law Review* 157, no. 1 (2008). Some scholars contest this claim and argue that the dependence of a court ensures effectiveness; see, for example, Eric Posner and John Yoo, "Judicial Independence in International Tribunals," *California Law Review* 93, no. 1 (2005).

64 Mark A. Pollack, *The Engines of European Integration: Delegation, Agency, and Agenda Setting in the EU* (Oxford: Oxford University Press, 2003); Steinberg, "Judicial Lawmaking at the WTO."

65 Keohane, Moravcsik, and Slaughter, "Legalized Dispute Resolution," 459.

66 Øyvind Stiansen, "(Non)Renewable Terms and Judicial Independence in the European Court of Human Rights," *Journal of Politics* 84, no. 2 (2022).

67 Kenneth Holland, ed., *Judicial Activism in Comparative Perspective* (New York: St. Martin's Press, 1991); Shannon Ishiyama Smithey and John Ishiyama, "Judicial Activism in Post-Communist Politics," *Law & Society Review* 36, no. 4 (2002).

68 Bernd Hayo and Stefan Voigt, "The Long-Term Relationship between De Jure and De Facto Judicial Independence," *Economics Letters* 183 (2019); Melton and Ginsburg, "Does De Jure Judicial Independence Really Matter?"; Bernd Hayo and Stefan Voigt, "Explaining De Facto Judicial Independence," *International Review of Law & Economics* 27, no. 3 (2007); Daniel Brinks, "Judicial Reform and Independence in Brazil and Argentina: The Beginning of a New Millennium?" *Texas International Law Journal* 40, no. 3 (2005); Siri Gloppen, "The Accountability Function of the Courts in Tanzania and Zambia," *Democratization* 10, no. 4 (2003). Other researchers find the relationship between domestic de jure and de facto independence to be weak or more limited; see, for example, Melton and Ginsburg, "Does De Jure Judicial Independence Really Matter?"; Julio Ríos-Figueroa and Jeffrey K. Staton, "An Evaluation of Cross-National Measures of Judicial Independence," *Journal of Law, Economics, and Organization* 30, no. 1 (2014).

Conversely, independence-enhancing safeguards reduce the likelihood that states can credibly threaten to or successfully curtail a court because the means of doing so are more limited.

The credibility and feasibility of state resistance can impact decision-making. Credible threats have a chilling effect on judicial decision-making and increase their inclination to exercise caution.[69] For instance, Stiansen and Voeten show that when democratic states resist a court, the court responds with restraint.[70] Thus, formal independence shapes decision-making, by way of its impact on the credibility and plausibility of state resistance, such that deference decreases.

Formal independence also has an impact on a court's strategic space and, therefore, decision-making, because it strengthens a court's legitimacy – or "beliefs within a given constituency or other relevant audience that a political institution's exercise of authority is appropriate."[71] Formal independence, especially in the absence of a history of practice, can lead stakeholders to believe a court is unbiased and isolated from political pressure and thereby strengthen public trust, confidence, or support for said court. It gives the appearance of independence. This is because independence is typically seen as a crucial property of a legitimate court.[72] Conversely, rules that limit formal independence can tarnish a court's legitimacy, giving it the appearance of being politically vulnerable. Legitimacy can also impede state (coordinated and unilateral) resistance. Defiance or resistance against a rightful and appropriate institution creates audience costs for states and can require large amounts of social capital to defy or resist. Endowed with more legitimacy, because of its formal independence, a court will face reduced political constraints and

69 Gretchen Helmke, *Courts Under Constraints: Judges, Generals, and Presidents in Argentina* (Cambridge: Cambridge University Press, 2005); Vanberg, *The Politics of Constitutional Review*.

70 Øyvind Stiansen and Erik Voeten, "Backlash and Judicial Restraint: Evidence from the European Court of Human Rights," *International Studies Quarterly* 64, no. 4 (2020).

71 Tallberg and Zürn, "The Legitimacy and Legitimation of International Organizations," 74–75; see also Dane Imerman, "Contested Legitimacy and Institutional Change: Unpacking the Dynamics of Institutional Legitimacy," *International Studies Review* 20, no. 1 (2018). Legitimacy is understood as a subjective and intersubjective quality of an institution, not an objective quality about its moral justifiability or its "right to rule" – even though beliefs about an institution may be informed by its objective quality. In other words, it is understood in this book as a sociological, empirical, or descriptive concept.

72 Follesdal, "Survey Article"; Theresa Squatrito, "A Comparative Analysis of Formal Independence," in *The Legitimacy of International Trade Courts and Tribunals*, ed. Robert Howse, Helene Ruiz-Fabri, and Michelle G. Zang (Cambridge: Cambridge University Press, 2018).

demonstrate less willingness to defer. The impact of formal independence via an IC's legitimacy is likely to be especially important in its earlier years of operation because, with time, an IC's performance and practice will also factor into legitimacy assessments.[73]

Another factor affecting the breadth of a court's strategic space, primarily because of its impact on the credibility of state resistance, is the degree of **political fragmentation** between those actors who wield control over a court. Comparative judicial politics research illustrates that greater political fragmentation makes it more challenging for those who wield control over a domestic court to curtail or punish it.[74] On the international stage, political fragmentation – understood as the degree of preference heterogeneity among member states – similarly affects the credibility or feasibility of coordinated resistance against an IC.

The membership of an IC is not a monolith, but a set of multiple principals who have individual preferences. IR scholarship provides ample evidence to suggest that preference heterogeneity affects the coordinated action of states. Generally speaking, states are less likely to cooperate when their preferences diverge.[75] Intergovernmental decision-making is more cumbersome when there is minimal overlap in states' preferences because the scope for agreement is narrow.[76] The degree of heterogeneity of states' preferences similarly affects how states interact with international bodies to which they have delegated authority.[77] When states' preferences diverge, not only is the original act of delegation affected but so is any process of "de-delegation," "recontracting" or

[73] Dellmuth and Tallberg, for instance, show that institutional performance affect legitimacy beliefs; see Lisa Dellmuth and Jonas Tallberg, "The Social Legitimacy of International Organisations: Interest Representation, Institutional Performance, and Confidence Extrapolation in the United Nations," *Review of International Studies* 41, no. 3 (2015).

[74] John A. Ferejohn and Larry D. Kramer, "Independent Judges, Dependent Judiciary: Institutionalizing Judicial Restraint," *New York University Law Review* 77, no. 4 (2002); Julio Ríos Figueroa, "Fragmentation of Power and the Emergence of an Effective Judiciary in Mexico, 1994-2002," *Latin American Politics & Society* 49, no. 1 (2007); Diana Kapiszewski, Gordon Silverstein, and Robert A. Kagan, eds., *Consequential Courts: Judicial Roles in Global Perspective* (Cambridge: Cambridge University Press, 2013); Rebecca Bill Chavez, *The Rule of Law in Nascent Democracies: Judicial Politics in Argentina* (Stanford: Stanford University Press, 2004).

[75] Robert Axelrod and Robert O. Keohane, "Achieving Cooperation Under Anarchy: Strategies and Institutions," *World Politics* 38, no. 1 (1985).

[76] Fritz W. Scharpf, *Games Real Actors Play: Actor-Centered Institutionalism in Policy Research* (Boulder, CO: Westview Press, 1997).

[77] Darren G. Hawkins et al., *Delegation and Agency in International Organizations* (Cambridge: Cambridge University Press, 2006).

similar.[78] Political fragmentation is one reason why EU member states have only rarely collectively resisted the CJEU.[79] Resistance against the Court is complicated by the "joint decision trap,"[80] meaning that efforts to collectively resist the Court would most likely require the support of some states whose preferences align with the judgment(s) of the Court. While fragmentation is likely to affect an IC's strategic space primarily because it sends signals about the probability of collective state resistance, fragmentation might also have an impact on how an IC is viewed or its legitimacy. Some research suggests that preference heterogeneity has an impact on how the public views IO decisions, such that fragmentation boosts the legitimacy of an IO's decision.[81]

Therefore, courts will typically view fragmentation, or heterogeneous preferences among states, as an opportunity to reject the state's exercise of authority – when deemed appropriate on the basis of law – because state resistance is unlikely to unfold.[82] These dynamics are, however, slightly complicated by two other considerations: (1) the voting rule by which intergovernmental decisions are taken, and (2) the distance between the court's preferred position and that of states. For instance, the notion of "majoritarian activism" suggests that a court's nondeference is enabled by having a majority of states with preferences that overlap with that of the court – as no coordinated resistance can occur when a majority agrees with a court.[83] Various scholars have modeled one or both of these considerations in relation to the CJEU.[84] While I do not dispute the relevance of these two considerations, I do not

78 Daniel L. Nielson and Michael J. Tierney, "Delegation to International Organizations: Agency Theory and World Bank Environmental Reform," *International Organization* 57, no. 2 (2003); Eugénia Heldt, "Regaining Control of Errant Agents? Agency Slack at the European Commission and the World Health Organization," *Cooperation and Conflict* 52, no. 4 (2017).

79 Kelemen, "The Court of Justice of the European Union."

80 Fritz W. Scharpf, "The Joint-Decision Trap: Lessons from German Federalism and European Integration," *Public Administration* 66, no. 3 (1988).

81 See Chapman, "Audience Beliefs and International Organization Legitimacy."

82 Some research on the ECJ corroborates this expectation. Clifford J. Carrubba, Matthew Gabel, and Charles Hankla, "Judicial Behavior Under Political Constraints: Evidence from the European Court of Justice," *American Political Science Review* 102, no. 4 (2008).

83 Alec Stone Sweet and Thomas L. Brunell, "Trustee Courts and the Judicialization of International Regimes: The Politics of Majoritarian Activism in the European Convention on Human Rights, the European Union, and the World Trade Organization," *Journal of Law and Courts* 1, no. 1 (2013).

84 Larsson and Naurin, "Judicial Independence and Political Uncertainty"; Garrett, Kelemen, and Schulz, "The European Court of Justice"; George Tsebelis and Geoffrey

incorporate them into the theoretical model (even though the empirical analysis keeps them in mind). My reasoning is twofold. First, the expectations would only change at the margins. For instance, we would only expect high fragmentation to correspond with deference when the court's position diverges significantly from a sizeable portion of states and when decisions can be taken by a majority as opposed to consensus. Meanwhile if a court's preference overlaps with unfragmented preferences of states, deference remains the likely result, even though it will be an act of validation and not abstention. Second, such a model is difficult to apply across international courts given different voting rules and changing state preferences. Parsimony is more amenable to comparative analysis at this stage. All else equal, I expect that a lack of political fragmentation among states will lead an IC to view coordinated responses from states as politically practicable, and therefore to defer.

Formal independence and political fragmentation, I argue, combine to shape a court's strategic space by way of their impact on the political feasibility and credibility of state resistance and a court's legitimacy. The combined effect of these two structural factors on strategic space and deference is visualized as a two-dimensional space in Figure 2.2. As formal independence and political fragmentation increase so does a court's strategic space. Where the strategic space is larger, nondeference is more likely. Conversely, deference is more likely when formal independence and political fragmentation are low. Additionally, if formal independence is high, yet fragmentation is low – or vice versa – the gains from independence are partially offset by the absence of fragmentation. In these scenarios, there will be a midrange strategic space.

This account explains variation in aggregate levels of deference across courts, while also offering insights into temporal variation for individual courts. Deference over time for an international court can arise from changes in formal independence and political fragmentation. While formal independence changes infrequently, it is not unheard-of. Occasionally states change rules governing courts that expand their formal independence.[85] I have not observed in my data any instances

Garrett, "The Institutional Foundations of Intergovernmentalism and Supranationalism in the European Union," *International Organization* 55, no. 2 (2001).

85 An example is the ECtHR following the entry into force of Protocol No. 14 to the European Convention for Human Rights. See Protocol No. 14 to the Convention for the Protection of Human Rights and Fundamental Freedoms, amending the control system of the Convention (adopted May 13, 2004, entered into force June 1, 2010),

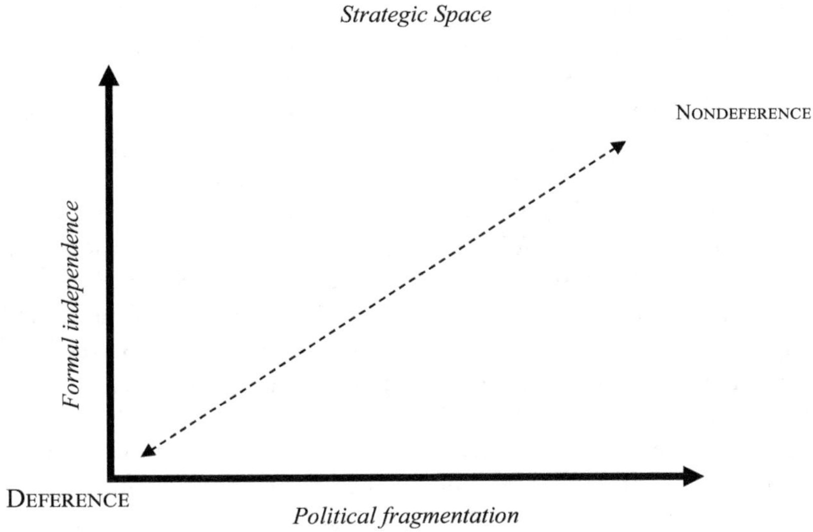

Figure 2.2 Visualization of strategic space.

where formal independence has decreased. Political fragmentation can also drive changes in deference, and it is more susceptible to fluctuations for two reasons. First, state preferences are not static. A variety of dynamics contributes to changes in state preferences, including developments in: (1) domestic interests, ideas and institutions,[86] and (2) international institutions, power structures, and social interactions.[87] Some

U.N.T.S. 2677, at 3-21 [herein "ECHR Protocol No. 14"]. This protocol removed the possibility for reappointments while increasing the length of terms from six to nine years.

86 Andrew Moravcsik, "Taking Preferences Seriously: A Liberal Theory of International Politics," *International Organization* 51, no. 4 (1997); Kathleen McNamara, *The Currency of Ideas: Monetary Politics in the European Union* (Ithaca: Cornell University Press, 1998); Judith Goldstein and Robert O. Keohane, *Ideas and Foreign Policy: Beliefs, Institutions and Political Change* (Ithaca: Cornell University Press, 1993); Ronald Rogowski, *Commerce and Coalitions: How Trade Affects Domestic Political Alignments* (Princeton: Princeton University Press, 1989); David A. Lake and Robert Powell, *Strategic Choice and International Relations* (Princeton: Princeton University Press, 1999); Jeffrey W. Legro, "Culture and Preferences in the International Cooperation Two-Step," *American Political Science Review* 90, no. 1 (1996).

87 Peter Gourevitch, "The Second Image Reversed: The International Sources of Domestic Politics," *International Organization* 32 (1978); Lloyd Gruber, *Ruling the World Power Politics and the Rise of Supranational Institutions* (Princeton: Princeton University Press, 2000); Alastair Iain Johnston, "Treating International Institutions as Social Environments," *International Studies Quarterly* 45, no. 4 (2001); Martha Finnemore

argue that ICs can also contribute to changes in states' preferences.[88] Second, the membership of international courts expands and contacts at times. The latter is a relatively rare phenomenon but not unprecedented.[89] Several withdrawals from international courts exemplify membership contraction. Zimbabwe withdrew from the jurisdiction of the SADC Tribunal following an initial decision of the Tribunal.[90] In 2012, Venezuela denounced the American Convention and exited the jurisdiction of the IACtHR, following a series of decisions that placed Venezuela at odds with the Court.[91] In 1998, Trinidad and Tobago also withdrew from the IACtHR in anticipation of the Court's decision on the death penalty.[92] France and the United States withdrew their acceptance of the compulsory jurisdiction of the ICJ. France withdrew from the ICJ's jurisdiction in 1974 following the Court's decision in the *Nuclear Test* cases in 1974, and the United States did the same following the ICJ's decision in the *Nicaragua* case in 1995.[93] In 2012, Colombia also exited the ICJ's compulsory jurisdiction.[94] More recent are the withdrawals of Burundi and the Philippines from the International Criminal Court (ICC).[95] Membership suspension or expulsion can also occur, such as the extraordinary expulsion of Russia from the Council of Europe, and consequently the ECtHR, in 2022. Expansions in membership are more common and apply to many courts, including the European Court of Human Rights and the WTO AB. For example, the membership of the European Court of Justice expanded from its original six members to its highest at twenty-eight members from 2013 to

and Kathryn Sikkink, "International Norm Dynamics and Political Change," *International Organization* 52, no. 4 (1998); Robert O. Keohane, *After Hegemony Cooperation and Discord in the World Political Economy* (Princeton: Princeton University Press, 1984).

88 Alter, *The New Terrain of International Law.*

89 von Borzyskowski and Vabulas, "Hello, Goodbye"

90 Laurie Nathan, "The Disbanding of the SADC Tribunal: A Cautionary Tale," *Human Rights Quarterly* 35, no. 4 (2013): 876.

91 Alexandra Huneeus and René Urueña, "Treaty Exit and Latin America's Constitutional Courts," *AJIL Unbound* 111 (2017).

92 Gisella Gori, "Compliance," in *The Oxford Handbook of International Human Rights Law*, ed. Dinah Shelton (Oxford: Oxford University Press, 2013), 918.

93 Pauwelyn and Hamilton, "Exit from International Tribunals."

94 Ibid., 682.

95 Ibid., 681–82.

2019. Changes in membership have occurred in all three ICs that are studied in-depth in this book.

Intervening Factors: Persuasive Argumentation, Public Legitimation, and Past Resistance

Robust formal judicial independence and political fragmentation do not mean unfettered judicial decision-making. At the same time, courts with minimal independence and political homogeneity should not be seen as politically captured or automatically deferential. This is because legal constraints still exist and matter. In addition, courts exercise agency over their strategic space to some degree; they have some capacity to influence their legitimacy and therefore their political constraints. ICs can develop practices that help to (re)constitute their strategic space. I consider two specific practices: persuasive argumentation and public legitimation. I refer to these practices collectively as *adaptive practices*, as they are simultaneously a court's adaptation to its political environments while also reflecting efforts to adapt or change that setting. I consider these two practices because they are implicated by the same underlying causal mechanisms of the political feasibility or credibility of state resistance and legitimacy. Persuasive argumentation and public legitimation can be seen as intervening variables in the explanatory model because if and how ICs employ these behaviors is determined, at least in part, by the nature of formal independence and political fragmentation.

Persuasive argumentation[96] is a tool for ICs to manage political and legal constraints, aiming to persuade states and other power holders to internalize the court's interpretation of the law and view its judgments as legitimate and authoritative. Elsewhere, it has been argued that international courts change the interests of states.[97] An IC's ability to do so is rooted in legal argumentation and what Risse calls "communicative behavior."[98] As the well-known adage goes, courts lack the power of the purse and sword, and so their power of influence resides largely in their capacity to persuade

[96] I use the term "persuasive argumentation" to reflect that communicative behavior can fall within the logic of consequentialism and appropriateness (for the purposes of bargaining and persuasion) or communicative rationality (for arguing and truth-seeking); see Thomas Risse, "'Let's Argue!': Communicative Action in World Politics," *International Organization* 54, no. 1 (2000). I do not assume that the communicative behavior of ICs is purely persuasion or arguing.

[97] Alter, *The New Terrain of International Law.*

[98] Risse, "Let's Argue!."

and argue. "Rhetoric is certainly a weapon of the weak."[99] Persuasive argumentation relates to the use of rhetoric and arguments to persuade or convince others to change their beliefs, preferences, and identities as well as to communicate validity claims (i.e., assertions of moral justification, truthfulness, and trustfulness).[100] Communicative behaviors – arguing and persuasion – can be instrumental in explaining states behaviors and international decision-making.[101]

Persuasive argumentation is a powerful tool for international courts. First, it can serve as a means by which ICs are able to shape state's preferences, beliefs, and identities – either because they are authentically persuaded[102] or because they are rhetorically coerced and rationally persuaded.[103] In changing states' preferences, beliefs, or identities, ICs thereby reduce the likelihood of state resistance by bringing states along to view the law as it does. Second, persuasive argumentation can facilitate compliance. As Franck argues, the legitimacy of a norm contributes to the "compliance pull" that it has over actors.[104] International actors, such as courts, can use argumentation to boost the compliance pull of a norm.[105] For example, states comply more with the IACtHR when its judgments are linguistically clear and precise.[106] Similarly, court

[99] Ronald R. Krebs and Patrick Thaddeus Jackson, "Twisting Tongues and Twisting Arms: The Power of Political Rhetoric," *European Journal of International Relations* 13, no. 1 (2007): 38.

[100] Risse, "'Let's Argue!'."

[101] Frank Schimmelfennig, "The Community Trap: Liberal Norms, Rhetorical Action, and the Eastern Enlargement of the European Union," *International Organization* 55, no. 1 (2001); Krebs and Jackson, "Twisting Tongues and Twisting Arms"; Risse, "'Let's Argue!'."; Jeffrey T. Checkel, "Why Comply? Social Learning and European Identity Change," *International Organization* 55, no. 3 (2001); Christian Grobe, "The Power of Words: Argumentative Persuasion in International Negotiations," *European Journal of International Relations* 16, no. 1 (2010).

[102] Nicole Deitelhoff, "The Discursive Process of Legalization: Charting Islands of Persuasion in the ICC Case," *International Organization* 63, no. 1 (2009).

[103] Krebs and Jackson, "Twisting Tongues and Twisting Arms"; Grobe, "The Power of Words."

[104] Thomas M. Franck, *The Power of Legitimacy Among Nations* (Oxford: Oxford University Press, 1990).

[105] Steven R. Ratner, "Persuading to Comply: On the Deployment and Avoidance of Legal Argumentation," in *Interdisciplinary Perspectives on International Law and International Relations: The State of the Art*, ed. Jeffrey Dunoff and Mark Pollack (Cambridge: Cambridge University Press, 2010).

[106] Jeffrey K. Staton and Alexia Romero, "Rational Remedies: The Role of Opinion Clarity in the Inter-American Human Rights System," *International Studies Quarterly* 63, no. 3 (2019).

judgments that are more authoritative and reflect certainty, as conveyed through rhetoric, are more likely to be followed.[107] Thus, an IC's persuasive argumentation, or how it employs rhetorical devices and constructs legal arguments, can facilitate compliance or minimize the risk of state resistance.

In addition to the language used, whether affect-laden, precise, or certain, citations are an important means by which judges can communicate to external audiences, including states and legal communities.[108] Moreover, a court's citation practices are not only a matter of legal considerations but also nonlegal, political factors.[109] Citations are used strategically to construct a persuasive and compelling argument.[110] ICs cite their own jurisprudence, but they also cite other authorities, such as external jurisdictions. While it is normal for international courts to cite external jurisdictions, especially other international courts, they do so to different extents.[111] External citations can shield a court from the appearance of "making law." In other words, referencing external jurisprudence signals that a court judgment does not "make law," but rather brings it into harmony or alignment with already established and esteemed views on the law. In all, we would expect that external citations will be more prevalent when the strategic space of a court is relatively narrow.

The type of external jurisdiction cited, however, may also differ depending on the strategic space. Reference to national jurisprudence might be an especially useful way for an international court to signal its respect for national law and that its decision accords with state authority.

[107] Pamela C. Corley and Justin Wedeking, "The (Dis)Advantage of Certainty: The Importance of Certainty in Language," *Law & Society Review* 48, no. 1 (2014).

[108] Yonatan Lupu and Erik Voeten, "Precedent in International Courts: A Network Analysis of Case Citations by the European Court of Human Rights," *British Journal of Political Science* 42, no. 2 (2012); Erik Voeten, "Borrowing and Nonborrowing Among International Courts," *Journal of Legal Studies* 39, no. 2 (2010); Olof Larsson et al., "Speaking Law to Power: The Strategic Use of Precedent of the Court of Justice of the European Union," *Comparative Political Studies* 50, no. 7 (2017).

[109] Jens Frankenreiter, "The Politics of Citations at the ECJ – Policy Preferences of E.U. Member State Governments and the Citation Behavior of Judges at the European Court of Justice," *Journal of Empirical Legal Studies* 14, no. 4 (2017); Yonatan Lupu and James H. Fowler, "Strategic Citations to Precedent on the U.S. Supreme Court," *Journal of Legal Studies* 42, no. 1 (2013); Larsson et al., "Speaking Law to Power."

[110] Mattias Derlén and Johan Lindholm, "Characteristics of Precedent: The Case Law of the European Court of Justice in Three Dimensions," *German Law Journal* 16, no. 5 (2015); Robert J. Hume, "The Use of Rhetorical Sources by the U.S. Supreme Court," *Law & Society Review* 40, no. 4 (2006).

[111] Voeten, "Borrowing and Nonborrowing Among International Courts."

The CJEU, for example, "strengthens its own legal legitimacy by making it appear that its own authority flows from the national courts."[112] Nods to domestic law, especially when a court has a narrow strategic space, will help to minimize state resistance or preserve and potentially enhance a court's legitimacy.

ICs with broad strategic space, due to higher formal independence and political fragmentation, are less likely to rely on external citations overall. They should still use external citations to make key decisions of non-deference compelling. However, they can probably rely on their own jurisprudence to construct persuasive arguments more because their political constraints are less pervasive.

Another method for making arguments more compelling, while helping an IC to cope with its political constraints, is to speak with a single voice. Unanimous judgments suggest to a court's various audiences that there is no dissention among the judges, and that the position of the court holds across the various national, political, and legal identities of the judges. If the court or individual judges are especially concerned about their individual or collective position vis-à-vis states or political power holders, unanimous decisions are preferable. Recent scholarship suggests that unanimous decisions can lead to less resistance of states in the form of better compliance.[113] Other research suggests unanimous decisions are more likely to be accepted.[114] For this reason, I expect ICs with narrow strategic space, arising from less formal independence or low political fragmentation, to speak with a single voice (when not formally required to do so) in order to avoid political retribution, especially when not deferring. I should note that not all ICs are allowed to have dissenting or separate written opinions.[115] Among the courts I look at in-depth, two (the ACtHPR and EACJ) are permitted by their relevant statutes to have dissenting or separate opinions.

112 Burley and Mattli, "Europe Before the Court," 64.

113 Daniel Naurin and Øyvind Stiansen, "The Dilemma of Dissent: Split Judicial Decisions and Compliance with Judgments from the International Human Rights Judiciary," *Comparative Political Studies* 53, no. 6 (2020).

114 James R. Zink, James F. Spriggs, and John T. Scott, "Courting the Public: The Influence of Decision Attributes on Individuals' Views of Court Opinions," *Journal of Politics* 71, no. 3 (2009).

115 Jonathan W. Kuyper and Theresa Squatrito, "International Courts and Global Democratic Values: Participation, Accountability, and Justification," *Review of International Studies* 43, no. 1 (2017).

Courts can respond to political constraints and thereby seek to alter their strategic space through **public legitimation**, defined as strategies whereby an institution deliberately seeks to generate and promote public beliefs in the rightfulness of a political institution.[116] Recent scholarship on international organizations finds evidence of broad efforts by IOs to legitimize themselves in the eyes of stakeholders and to shape how the public views them.[117] International courts are no exception, as they demonstrate practices of legitimation.[118] As a case in point, Ecker-Erhardt finds that the ICC, the Council of Europe, and the Organization of American States have the highest degrees of public communication (which he associates with legitimation),[119] and they each have highly salient ICs attached to them (the ICC's judicial chambers, ECtHR and IACtHR, respectively).

International courts depend on public support and care about how they are viewed publicly, despite not having a direct electoral connection with the public. Based on the general view that international processes interact with domestic politics,[120] public support is likely to matter to ICs for a few reasons. First, public support has bearing on state compliance with international judicial decisions. If an international court is viewed favorably by domestic constituencies, state policymakers may incur audience costs if they resist or defy that court.[121] Conversely, when an IC enjoys minimal public support, states have few domestic incentives to comply. Second, favorable public opinion insulates ICs from political attack.[122] As Kelemen argues, "the higher the levels of diffuse public support for a court, the greater the costs politicians will face for attempting to undermine that court's independence or to other wise

116 Tallberg and Zürn, "The Legitimacy and Legitimation of International Organizations," 5.

117 Ibid.; Matthias Ecker-Ehrhardt, "Self-Legitimation in the Face of Politicization: Why International Organizations Centralized Public Communication," *The Review of International Organizations* 13, no. 4 (2018).

118 Theresa Squatrito, "Judicial Diplomacy: International Courts and Legitimation," *Review of International Studies* 47, no. 1 (2021).

119 Ecker-Ehrhardt, "Self-Legitimation in the Face of Politicization," 535.

120 Robert D. Putnam, "Diplomacy and Domestic Politics: The Logic of Two-Level Games," *International Organization* 42, no. 3 (1988).

121 Xinyuan Dai, "Why Comply? The Domestic Constituency Mechanisms," *International Organization* 59, no. 2 (2005); Beth A. Simmons, *Mobilizing for Human Rights: International Law in Domestic Politics* (Cambridge: Cambridge University Press, 2009).

122 R. Daniel Kelemen, "The Political Foundations of Judicial Independence in the European Union," *Journal of European Public Policy* 19, no. 1 (2012); Ginsburg, "Political Constraints on International Courts."

challenge its rulings."[123] When an international court enjoys public esteem, states' attempts to curb said court or to disobey it come at the risk of politicians losing face for defying what the public views as rightful law. Third, public support can affect judicial decision-making. For example, policy-specific public opinion appears to influence the decisions of the CJEU.[124] Fourth, public interest in ICs is growing, as can be seen by Google searches,[125] and outreach by courts can affect the public's opinion of an IC.[126] Fifth, international judges often believe public esteem of their court is instrumental to their work. As one international judge said, courts "need to establish their relevance, their integrity, and their effectiveness. To do so, they need to be seen and heard, not just by the legal and diplomatic communities, but also by a broad cross-section of the citizenry."[127]

Given the significance of the public to ICs, we should expect to see ICs practice public legitimation. This will manifest in broad efforts to "speak" with the public, and not only its core, direct constituency (e.g., lawyers, national judges, advocacy groups). In other words, we should see outreach that targets a public audience or for their communications to be *public-oriented.* While this may occur through judicial decisions, ICs can rely on a wide array of "off-the-bench" or outreach activities, ranging from its public communication (e.g., social media profiles, press releases) and public events, to communicate with the public.

Public legitimation will target the public while portraying the "rightfulness" of the court through value-laden messages about its processes and outcomes.[128] It will focus less on conveying the appropriateness of the law and its interpretations, and instead highlight "norm-referential"

[123] Kelemen, "The Political Foundations of Judicial Independence," 45.

[124] Michael F. Harsch and Vladislav Maksimov, "International Courts and Public Opinion: Explaining the CJEU's Role in Protecting Terror Suspects' Rights," *Journal of Common Market Studies* 57, no. 5 (2019); Michael Blauberger et al., "ECJ Judges Read the Morning Papers. Explaining the Turnaround of European Citizenship Jurisprudence," *Journal of European Public Policy* 25, no. 10 (2018).

[125] Voeten, "Public Opinion and the Legitimacy of International Courts"; Krzysztof J. Pelc, "Googling the WTO: What Search-Engine Data Tell Us About the Political Economy of Institutions," *International Organization* 67, no. 3 (2013).

[126] Geoff Dancy et al., "What Determines Perceptions of Bias toward the International Criminal Court? Evidence from Kenya," *Journal of Conflict Resolution* 64, no. 7–8 (2019).

[127] Daniel Terris, Cesare P. R. Romano, and Leigh Swigart, *The International Judge: An Introduction to the Men and Women Who Decide the World's Cases* (Oxford: Oxford University Press, 2007), 170.

[128] Squatrito, "Judicial Diplomacy."

narratives about the IC.[129] In particular, their legitimation narratives are likely to reflect on how the IC represents or reflects the people or communities governed by the court, and thus be *people-centered.*[130] An IC might also emphasize its commitment to and fulfillment of its *political purpose*, such as its founding principles or mandate.[131]

Given the significance of the public to ICs, we would expect ICs to develop practices of public legitimation with a goal of broadening its strategic space, or to cope with its political imperatives and impact its legitimacy. As public support is necessary for all courts, public legitimation may be observed to some degree for all courts. However, ICs are more likely to rely on public legitimation when they have low formal independence or homogeneous state preferences. Additionally, if states can exit or withdraw from the court's jurisdiction (or conversely voluntarily accept its jurisdiction), public legitimation is also likely to be critical. Exit is a unilateral form of resistance, meaning formal independence and political fragmentation are irrelevant, leading a court to rely more on the public to insulate it from exit – or conversely gain accessions. This may mean that people-centered narratives could be especially powerful tools for ICs where unilateral exit from a court's jurisdiction (or a portion thereof) is an option for states.

Finally, **past resistance** is likely to affect a court's strategic space and hence deference. Past resistance gives a court information about the credibility and plausibility of future resistance. Past episodes of resistance, either collective or unilateral, suggest that resistance is possible, especially when successfully implemented. This means that courts will see themselves as more politically vulnerable if they have previously experienced curtailments from states than if they have not. Previous resistance can also have legitimacy costs for courts, adding to their sense of vulnerability and political constraint. The likelihood that a court has experienced past resistance is greater for courts that have lower independence and memberships with homogeneous preferences. This means that past resistance is best understood as an intervening variable, as with persuasive argumentation and public legitimation.

[129] Klaus Dingwerth and Antonia Witt, "Legitimation Contests: A Theoretical Framework," in *International Organizations Under Pressure* (Oxford: Oxford University Press, 2019); Michael N. Barnett and Martha Finnemore, *Rules for the World: International Organizations in Global Politics* (Ithaca: Cornell University Press, 2004), 166–67.

[130] Dingwerth et al., *International Organizations Under Pressure.*

[131] Ibid.

Figure 2.3 depicts in broad strokes the theoretical argument. It shows that formal independence and political fragmentation are the key explanatory variables at t_0, all else equal (e.g., the law or legal dispute). These two factors combine to influence a court's strategic space, and hence its deference. When formal independence and political fragmentation are low, the conditions are ripe for more deference at t_0. (Non) deference at t_0 can potentially inform state preferences, and subsequently fragmentation, at t_1. On rare occasions, (non)deference at t_0 might also lead to changes in formal independence at t_1.

Also informed by (non)deference at t_0 and against the backdrop of formal independence and political fragmentation, a court develops practices of persuasive argumentation and public legitimation at t_1. For those courts with previously narrow strategic space, persuasive argumentation will entail references to external jurisprudence and unanimous decisions, and public legitimation that conveys messages about the court's people-centeredness or commitment to its political purpose. For those with broad space, internal jurisprudence may be more central to their construction of persuasive arguments. Regardless, nondeference will be associated with external citations. Public legitimation is likely to be more people-centered, and less focused on its political purpose, when individual states have exit or entry options. Also, (past) resistance can narrow a court's strategic space and make deference more likely.[132]

A few additional points should be noted. First, while I study deference as a manifestation of a court's strategic space, other aspects of a court's performance also exist within a court's strategic space. This is why Figure 2.3 situates persuasive argumentation and public legitimation within strategic space. Put differently, these practices are both constituted by and constitutive of a court's strategic space. The same might be said of efforts to mobilize and socialize pro-compliance constituencies. Second, the intervening variables might be affected by other conditions. For example, a court's resources influence the extent to which it can employ higher degrees of public legitimation. Third, this model, as depicted by Figure 2.3, does not show all potential feedback loops, such as how

[132] Resistance is difficult to illustrate in a diagram with only two points in time because it can happen in the interim. For this reason, the diagram calls it "resistance" and not past resistance, although the framework assumes resistance will affect future deference – not deference at the exact same point in time. Some readers might find it easier to think of resistance as happening at $t_{0.5}$, which has an impact on deference at t_1. Chapter 4 on the EACJ provides an example.

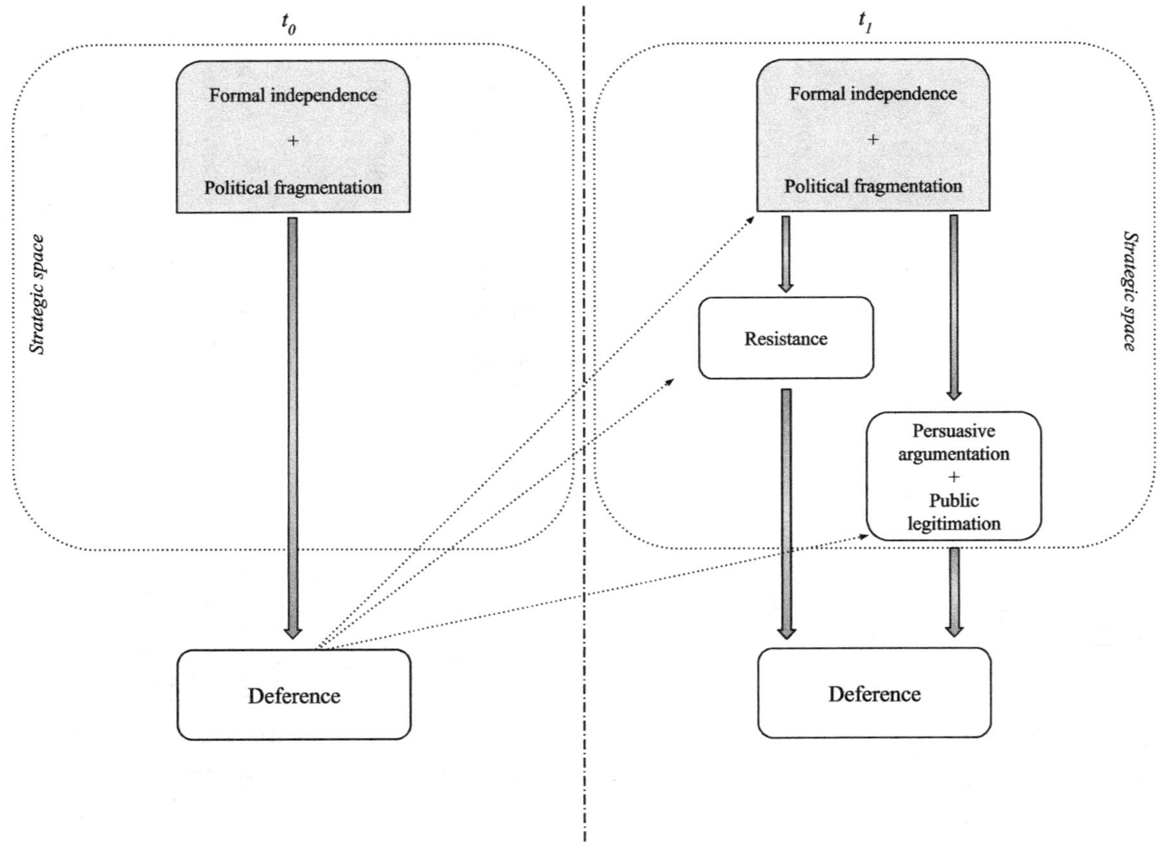

Figure 2.3 Diagram of theoretical framework.

(non)deference, persuasive argumentation, or public legitimation could feed into member state preferences and consequently homogeneity or heterogeneity of preferences over time. I recognize that these feedback loops could exist and indirectly contribute to the reconstitution of a court's strategic space. Fourth, the main causal mechanisms that link these pieces together are the plausibility and feasibility of resistance and perceived legitimacy.

Overall, this framework leads to five core theoretical expectations, summarized by the following hypotheses:

H_1: The higher an IC's formal independence is, the less it will defer.

H_2: The more politically fragmented the membership of an IC is, the less it will defer.

H_3: The narrower an IC's strategic space is (as a result of either formal independence or political fragmentation), the more it will rely on persuasive argumentation to facilitate nondeference.

H_4: The narrower an IC's strategic space is (as a result of either formal independence or political fragmentation), the more it will rely on public legitimation to facilitate nondeference.

H_5: All else equal, an international court will defer more when it has experienced past resistance.

Aside from these five hypotheses, I have also speculated that persuasive argumentation will rely more on domestic versus international citations when the IC's strategic space is narrow. Additionally, I have posited that public legitimation and the relevant narratives might also vary depending on whether states can unilaterally exit a court's jurisdiction. I do not label these expectations as hypotheses as they are more speculative and less theoretically grounded.

This theoretical framework aims to cast a wide net and I claim to offer an account that extends beyond the three ICs that I examine. Nonetheless, the scope of the argument (or limits to its generalizability) is worth recalling at this point. First, the argument is developed with newer international courts in mind. In the long term, these posited dynamics may change, especially as a court develops its own norms, support networks, and jurisprudence.[133] Second, I recognize these dynamics may be different for courts that have interstate jurisdiction

[133] Clifford Carrubba, "A Model of the Endogenous Development of Judicial Institutions in Federal and International Systems," *Journal of Politics* 71, no. 1 (2009).

only or that predominantly decide interstate disputes (e.g., ITLOS). This is because these courts weigh state against state. Here other factors may be important additional confounding factors (e.g., relative power and legal capacity of disputing states). Third, the law is an important constraint that also conditions a court's strategic space. I nonetheless assume that typically there is more than one reasonable way to interpret and apply the law – that is, the law is not determinant – and courts are among the actors engaged in an ongoing process of determining what the law is.

Alternative Accounts

The above puts forward a theory of judicial deference by international courts that is based on the structural political constraints and judicial practices that (re)constitute a court's strategic space. However, there are other possible theoretical accounts of deference. In the following, I outline these accounts. The first privileges the support networks of courts, while the second emphasizes ideational factors. In contrast to my argument, both accounts are generally skeptical about the centrality of states and institutional design (or at least the aspects of design that define the relationship between states and a court, or the separation of powers). While I articulate them as alternative explanatory accounts, I do not view them as competing. In fact, they are mostly complementary. I, however, leave this issue for now and return to it in the Conclusion.

Support Networks

One prominent account suggests that whether a court tends toward deference is determined by the strength and activity of its support network. When a court has a strong, broad, and active support network, it is less likely to defer. This builds on the perspective that judicial power is socially constructed.[134] From this perspective, courts draw power from other actors who do have the capacity to induce state compliance and impose costs on states for resistance against a court. If courts have the

[134] Charles Epp, *The Rights Revolution: Lawyers, Activists, and Supreme Courts in Comparative Perspective* (Chicago: University Press of Chicago, 1998); Cichowski, *The European Court and Civil Society*; Alter, *The New Terrain of International Law*; Terence C. Halliday, Lucien Karpik, and Malcolm M. Feeley, *Fighting for Political Freedom: Comparative Studies of the Legal Complex and Political Liberalism* (Oxford: Hart Publishing, 2007); Jennifer Widner, *Building the Rule of Law: Francis Nyalali and the Road to Judicial Independence in Africa* (New York: WW Norton, 2001).

backing of a robust and vital support network, they have less reason to exercise politically cautious decision-making. In other words, a strong and active support network shields a court and creates the conditions for it to be less deferential, if legally merited.

ICs cultivate the support of these actors and form partnerships (often informally) with them through their jurisprudence. For example, ICs can reveal to wider audiences how the relevant law can serve the interests of constituencies.[135] Their decisions can implicitly invite litigation in certain areas through assertive statements on jurisdiction or by expanding channels of access, such as for amicus curiae. Courts can also foster relationships with substate and private actors through "off-the-bench" activities.[136] These can range from the participation of judges in professional associations and legal training opportunities to courtesy calls with national officials.[137] For example, Burley and Mattli claim that the CJEU courted national judges "through seminars, dinners, regular invitations to Luxembourg, and visits around the community."[138] Put differently, support networks are a product of a court's agency.

Not all aspects of a support network are necessarily the result of a court's efforts to cultivate partners. Sometimes, formal rules may help a court to cultivate these interlocutors. Rules on access for private litigants in particular provide societal actors with opportunity to mobilize the law.[139] Also, some partnerships are the result of societal mobilization, where advocacy groups and lawyers identify opportunities provided by the law. That is, they can mobilize law on their own initiative in hopes that a court will provide recourse.[140] Moreover, some partners were proponents of courts before they were established, such as the Coalition for the International Criminal Court.[141]

135 Helfer and Slaughter, "Towards a Theory of Effective Supranational Adjudication."

136 Alexei Trochev and Rachel Ellett, "Judges and Their Allies: Rethinking Judicial Autonomy through the Prism of Off-Bench Resistance," *Journal of Law and Courts* 2, no. 1 (2014).

137 Burley and Mattli, "Europe Before the Court"; Walter Mattli and Anne-Marie Slaughter, "Revisiting the European Court of Justice," *International Organization* 52, no. 1 (1998).

138 Burley and Mattli, "Europe Before the Court" 62.

139 Helfer and Slaughter, "Towards a Theory of Effective Supranational Adjudication"; Keohane, Moravcsik, and Slaughter, "Legalized Dispute Resolution"; Darren Hawkins and Wade Jacoby, "Agent Permeability, Principal Delegation and the European Court of Human Rights," *Review of International Organizations* 3, no. 1 (2008); Alter, *The New Terrain of International Law*.

140 Cichowski, *The European Court and Civil Society*.

141 Deitelhoff, "The Discursive Process of Legalization."

Judicial support networks are comprised of various types of actors, but crucial to a network are private, substate, and supranational actors. Private actors include individuals, advocacy groups, NGOs, interest groups, legal professionals, and for-profit actors.[142] These types of actors have been shown to affect the decision-making of domestic courts and the extent to which they advance rights.[143] Substate actors include government officials, administrative agencies, and national judiciaries.[144] Supranational actors, or entities of international organizations, in their capacity as compliance monitors (prosecutors) or administrators can also act as supporters.[145]

These accounts have significant evidence to give them credence. ICs' abilities to mobilize or benefit from support networks, and the decisions of these actors to engage in international litigation, are crucial to understanding judicial decision-making. However, it remains unclear what explains nondeference in the presence of weak or inactive support networks. Thus, my account seeks to address these instances.

Ideology, Political Norms, and Legal Culture

Existing research suggests that ideational factors contribute to domestic judicial behavior. A well-known explanation for judicial decision-making, called the attitudinal model, comes out of studies on the Supreme Court of the United States, which suggests that judges' attitudes and policy preferences determine the Supreme Court's decision-making.[146] Hönnige finds evidence of the attitudinal model in the

[142] Cichowski, *The European Court and Civil Society*; Heidi Nichols Haddad, *The Hidden Hands of Justice: NGOs, Human Rights, and International Courts* (Cambridge: Cambridge University Press, 2018); Dai, "Why Comply?"; Tommaso Pavone, "From Marx to Market: Lawyers, European Law, and the Contentious Transformation of the Port of Genoa," Article, *Law & Society Review* 53, no. 3 (2019).

[143] Epp, *The Rights Revolution*; Halliday, Karpik, and Feeley, *Fighting for Political Freedom.*

[144] Alter, *Establishing the Supremacy of European Law*; Alter and Helfer, "Nature or Nurture?"

[145] Alec Stone Sweet and Thomas L. Brunell, "Constructing a Supranational Constitution: Dispute Resolution and Governance in the European Community," *American Political Science Review* 92, no. 1 (1998); Alter, *The New Terrain of International Law*; Jonas Tallberg and James McCall Smith, "Dispute Settlement in World Politics: States, Supranational Prosecutors, and Compliance," *European Journal of International Relations* 20, no. 1 (2014).

[146] Jeffrey A. Segal and Harold J. Spaeth, *The Supreme Court and the Attitudinal Model Revisited* (Cambridge: Cambridge University Press, 2002).

French and German constitutional courts.[147] Voeten finds that political ideology of the appointing states significantly influences the judicial ideology of ECtHR judges and, ultimately, their decision-making.[148]

Other insights consider how political norms and shared conceptions of the role of law and the judiciary's political functions, rather than the political values and ideology of individual judges, affect judicial decision-making. This approach has been more prominent in scholarship on judicial politics in Latin America.[149] For example, Hilbink argues that the Chilean judiciary's institutional ideology, or the shared ideas of the social function and role of the judiciary, significantly affected the way in which the courts responded to the illiberal policies of the Pinochet regime.[150] She argues, "the Chilean judiciary, historically constructed around the concept of apoliticism, provided professional understandings and incentives that rendered even democratic-minded judges unequipped and disinclined to take stands in defense of liberal democratic principles."[151]

The role of ideational factors has been less prominent in the study of international law and courts. Nevertheless, there are some important insights. Domestic legal culture has been shown to have bearing on state willingness to accept compulsory jurisdiction of ICs and their design.[152] Domestic legal culture, however, does not significantly determine judicial decisions in the case of the ECtHR.[153] Some scholarship following in the

147 Christoph Hönnige, "The Electoral Connection: How the Pivotal Judge Affects Oppositional Success at European Constitutional Courts," *West European Politics* 32, no. 5 (2009).

148 Erik Voeten, "The Politics of International Judicial Appointments: Evidence from the European Court of Human Rights," *International Organization* 61, no. 4 (2007).

149 Lisa Hilbink, *Judges Beyond Politics in Democracy and Dictatorship: Lessons from Chile* (Cambridge: Cambridge University Press, 2007); Diana Kapiszewski, "How Courts Work: Institutions, Culture, and the Brazilian *Supremo Tribunal Federal*," in *Cultures of Legality: Judicialization and Political Activism in Latin America*, ed. Alexandra Huneeus, Javier Couso, and Rachel Sieder (Cambridge: Cambridge University Press, 2010); Javier Couso, Alexandra Huneeus, and Rachel Sieder, eds., *Cultures of Legality: Judicialization and Political Activism in Latin America* (Cambridge: Cambridge University Press, 2010); Matthew C. Ingram, "Crafting Courts in New Democracies: Ideology and Judicial Council Reforms in Three Mexican States," *Comparative Politics* 44, no. 4 (2012).

150 Hilbink, *Judges Beyond Politics in Democracy and Dictatorship*.

151 Ibid., 5.

152 Sara McLaughlin Mitchell and Emilia Justyna Powell, *Domestic Law Goes Global: Legal Traditions and International Courts* (Cambridge: Cambridge University Press, 2011).

153 Voeten, "The Politics of International Judicial Appointments" (2007).

tradition of Bourdieu[154] suggests that courts develop their own set of values, norms, and practices – or a sui generis legal culture – which helps to explain international judicial decision-making.[155]

Ideational factors, including ideology, political norms, and legal culture, may affect the courts I examine to some extent, but a few reasons cast doubt on their sufficiency as an explanation for deference. Across the three courts there are important similarities related to ideational factors. First, the judges on all three courts have mixed backgrounds; they come from different domestic contexts and professional backgrounds. This means that the ideological views present on the courts are likely to be similarly mixed. Second, the colonial pasts have had similar lasting impacts on political norms within the regions under analysis. One important legacy of colonialism is the duality of political norms. Namely, beliefs in regionalism, unity, or international cooperation are prominent, yet are also in tension with strong norms of sovereignty, noninterference, and state independence. The courts I study were constituted within this dualism of political norms and function in its shadows. Third, the legal culture(s) relevant to each court have important similarities. Legal culture includes not only the legal order(s) governing a society but also includes beliefs and attitudes about the law and courts, or legal consciousness.[156] The member states of all three courts encounter dilemmas with regard to the constitutional order and access to courts.[157] Despite some variation, there is a tendency for African domestic judiciaries to have experience with political interference and vulnerability to executives.[158] Also, scholars have noted that the public lack confidence or

[154] Pierre Bourdieu, "The Force of Law: Toward a Sociology of the Juridical Field," *Hastings Law Journal* 38, no. 5 (1987).

[155] Mikael Rask Madsen, "From Cold War Instrument to Supreme European Court: The European Court of Human Rights at the Crossroads of International and National Law and Politics," *Law & Social Inquiry* 32, no. 1 (2007); John Hagan, Ron Levi, and Gabrielle Ferrales, "Swaying the Hand of Justice: The Internal and External Dynamics of Regime Change at the International Criminal Tribunal for the Former Yugoslavia," *Law & Social Inquiry* 31, no. 3 (2006); Yves Dezalay, *Dealing in Virtue: International Commercial Arbitration and the Construction of a Transnational Legal Order* (Chicago: University of Chicago Press, 1996).

[156] Sally Engle Merry, "What Is Legal Culture - an Anthropological Perspective Using Legal Culture," *Journal of Comparative Law* 5, no. 2 (2010).

[157] For example, see "Rule of Law Index," World Justice Project, accessed June 27, 2024, https://worldjusticeproject.org/rule-of-law-index/global. The rankings reveal that states in the Caribbean and Africa fall within the midrange of adherence to the rule of law.

[158] Tabeth Masengu, "The Vulnerability of Judges in Contemporary Africa: Alarming Trends," *Africa Today* 63, no. 4 (2017); Peter VonDoepp and Rachel Ellett,

trust in domestic courts.[159] The Caribbean nations have a better record of democracy and the rule of law than many African states, but scholars have remarked on a lack of faith in the capacity of the constitutional order to guarantee justice and equality in Caribbean states.[160] Moreover, a shared colonial legacy of African and Caribbean states is legal pluralism.[161] Also, as new courts, the EACJ, ACtHPR, and CCJ have not yet developed their own set of values, norms, and practices, even though this is an ongoing process. Put simply, there are many parallels in their respective legal cultures.

I do not exclude the possibility that ideational factors contribute to judicial decision-making. Instead, I aim to hold ideational factors more or less constant through the selection of cases.

Conclusion

This chapter has specified the central phenomenon under examination in this book. In contrast to previous work that focuses on judicial activism or restraint to describe judicial decisions, I focus on deference. Judicial deference describes if and how a court either accepts or rejects the exercise of authority by states or other governing entities (e.g., an organ of an international organization). Deference can be indicative of a court either abstaining from exercising its own authority or validating state

"Reworking Strategic Models of Executive-Judicial Relations: Insights from New African Democracies," *Comparative Politics* 43, no. 2 (2011).

159 H. Kwasi Prempeh, "Marbury in Africa: Judicial Review and the Challenge of Constitutionalism in Contemporary Africa," *Tulane Law Review* 80, no. 4 (2006).

160 Se-shauna Wheatle and Yonique Campbell, "Constitutional Faith and Identity in the Caribbean: Tradition, Politics and the Creolisation of Caribbean Constitutional Law," *Commonwealth & Comparative Politics* 58, no. 3 (2020).

161 Diego López-Medina, "The Latin American and Caribbean Legal Traditions: Repositioning Latin America and the Caribbean on the Contemporary Maps of Comparative Law," in *The Cambridge Companion to Comparative Law*, ed. Mauro Bussani and Ugo Mattei (Cambridge: Cambridge University Press, 2012); Rose-Marie B. Antoine, "Waiting to Exhale: Commonwealth Caribbean Law and Legal Systems," *Nova Law Review* 29, no. 2 (2005); Bonny Ibhawoh, *Imperial Justice: Africans in Empire's Court* (Oxford: Oxford University Press, 2013); Berihun A. Gebeye, "Decoding Legal Pluralism in Africa," *Journal of Legal Pluralism and Unofficial Law* 49, no. 2 (2017); H. Kwasi Prempeh, "Africa's 'Constitutionalism Revival': False Start or New Dawn?" *International Journal of Constitutional Law* 5, no. 3 (2007); Lindsay Stirton and Martin Lodge, "Constitutionalism and Colonial Legacies in the Caribbean," in *The Oxford Handbook of Caribbean Constitutions*, ed. Richard Albert, Derek O'Brien, and Se-shauna Wheatle (Oxford: Oxford University Press, 2020).

authority. I put forward an operationalization of deference based on three features of judicial decisions, namely, the case outcome, legal interpretation and reasoning, and remedies.

The chapter presented a theoretical account to explain variation in judicial deference. This account focuses on situating judicial decision-making within the strategic space of international courts. Deference, therefore, will correspond with the breadth of this space. I have argued that the key factors shaping a court's strategic space are the rules safeguarding judicial independence and the degree of political fragmentation. I have posited that deference is more likely to occur when an IC has weaker safeguards to independence and a politically unfragmented membership, and thus a narrower strategic space. Additionally, I have argued that persuasive argumentation, public legitimation, and prior experiences with state resistance against an IC can all contribute to if and how it defers to states. These factors construct a court's strategic setting by way of their impact on the perceived legitimacy of the court and the feasibility and credibility of state resistance against the court.

Last, I discussed alternative accounts, which focus primarily on the network of proponents that support an international court and ideational factors, such as political norms and legal culture. As this chapter has suggested, these alternative perspectives are likely to be applicable, yet insufficient, explanations of deference. Consequently, the research design does not treat these approaches as competing explanations, but rather controls for their potential impact to the best extent possible.

As this chapter has argued, formal independence is crucial to understanding judicial decision-making. Chapter 3 shifts attention to formal independence and begins the empirical analysis. It develops the concept of formal independence before introducing how it is measured for the purposes of this book and examines the extent to which formal independence varies across international courts.

3

Formal Independence of International Courts

The theoretical framework presented in Chapter 2 highlights formal independence as a key factor shaping deference. It argues that formal independence, alongside political fragmentation, structures an international court's strategic space and consequently deference. In particular, formal independence shapes the perceived legitimacy of a court. The more a court has robust safeguards to independence, the more its subjects and constituents will see it as independent and by extension legitimate. A court's perceived legitimacy affects the costs to states for resisting that court. Defiance and resistance of a legitimate court are politically costly and risky because constituents are likely to view such actions as disregard for rightful law and authority. Second, formal independence also affects the extent to which states can credibly resist or curb a court through collective formal means. Greater formal independence translates into fewer opportunities or higher barriers for collective resistance. Thus, greater formal independence is likely to reduce political constraints faced by courts and thereby expand their strategic space to enable less deference.

This begets the question: Are international courts formally independent? This chapter addresses this question. To do so, it conceptualizes and measures the formal independence of international courts. I conceptualize *formal independence* as the formal rules that aim to safeguard autonomous judicial decision-making. This understanding of formal independence contrasts with informal independence. Based on this definition, the chapter develops an original measure of formal independence, which is used to estimate the formal independence of twenty-six ICs from 1945 to 2015. The chapter then maps and compares formal independence across these ICs. The mapping reveals significant variation in the formal independence of ICs. Rules pertaining to the appointment and terms of office for international judges as well as the managerial autonomy of ICs are the sources of most of the observed variation.

International Courts and Judicial Independence

Judicial independence is the ability of courts to deliberate and reach legal judgments based on legal considerations and without undue pressure or influence from external sources, governmental or otherwise. It relates to a court's ability to act autonomously, how it is held accountable, and whether nonlegal pressures unduly impact judicial deliberation and decision-making.[1] Even though the independence of a court is linked to the independence and impartiality of its judges, the focus here is on independence as an institutional attribute of a court.

Policymakers and scholars alike view independence as a desirable feature for courts. For example, the United Nations (UN) calls upon all states to secure, promote, and respect judicial independence.[2] While independence is valued for normative or moral reasons, it is also desirable for judicial effectiveness. The link between independence and effectiveness is increasingly recognized for international courts, and not only domestic courts. Guillaume argues, "[t]he international judiciary, like national judiciaries, cannot effectively perform its functions unless it enjoys the requisite independence."[3] Scholars have argued that independence shapes compliance with ICs,[4] and it has an impact on the role of ICs in dispute settlement and legal clarification.[5] Moreover, the

[1] Judicial accountability is a trade-off with judicial independence; see Georg Vanberg, "Establishing and Maintaining Judicial Independence," in *The Oxford Handbook of Law and Politics*, ed. Gregory A. Caldeira, R. Daniel Kelemen, and Keith E. Whittington (Oxford: Oxford University Press, 2008); Jeffrey L. Dunoff and Mark A. Pollack, "The Judicial Trilemma," *American Journal of International Law* 111, no. 2 (2017). Yet, it is also features in some definitions of judicial independence; see Stefan Voigt, "The Independence of International Courts – Making Reputation Work?" *Maastricht Journal of European and Comparative Law* 24, no. 4 (2017): 516.

[2] UN General Assembly, *Basic Principles on the Independence of the Judiciary*, Resolution A/RES/40/32 (November 29,1985) and A/RES/40/146 (December 13, 1985), adopted by the Seventh United Nations Congress on the Prevention of Crime and the Treatment of Offenders (1985).

[3] Gilbert Guillaume, "Some Thoughts on Independence of International Judges," *The Law & Practice of International Courts and Tribunals* 2, no. 1 (2003): 163.

[4] Helfer and Slaughter, "Why States Create International Tribunals."

[5] Helfer and Slaughter, "Towards a Theory of Effective Supranational Adjudication"; Helfer and Slaughter, "Why States Create International Tribunals"; Keohane, Moravcsik, and Slaughter, "Legalized Dispute Resolution"; Shany, *Assessing the Effectiveness of International Courts*. Others argue that the effectiveness of international adjudication is associated with dependence; see Posner and Yoo, "Judicial Independence in International Tribunals."

independence of an international court improves its ability to ensure the rule of law.[6]

Independence is also a desirable attribute for international courts because it improves their legitimacy, or how they are perceived by other actors.[7] As Benvenisti and Downs argue,

> the perceived independence of a given international tribunal from the handful of powerful states that have tended to dominate the institutional design process continues to be the most significant factor in shaping the extent to which judge made law is regarded as legitimate in the eyes of less powerful states. Such political independence on the part of the international tribunals continues to be a necessary, if not sufficient, condition for the perceived legitimacy of their lawmaking.[8]

Independence confers legitimacy on international courts because it implies ICs are fair and unbiased.[9] Interview research substantiates the link between independence and perceptions. In one study, for instance, the ECtHR's independence shaped interviewee's views of the Court.[10] Another study found that independence improves the perceived legitimacy of the ECtHR by way of advancing procedural justice.[11]

While there is wide-scale agreement that independence is a desirable attribute, whether international courts are in fact independent is debated. On the one hand, there are those who contend that international courts are politically constrained and lack independence.[12] In this camp is literature that builds on principal-agent theory. It treats international courts as agents of states who are the principals responsible for delegating authority to courts. Courts are understood to have their own interests that may diverge from those of states. Consequently, states will seek to

[6] Theodor Meron, "Judicial Independence and Impartiality in International Criminal Tribunals," *American Journal of International Law* 99, no. 2 (2005).

[7] It may also be a necessary requirement for normative legitimacy.

[8] Eyal Benvenisti and George W. Downs, "Prospects for the Increased Independence of International Tribunals," *German Law Journal* 12, no. 5 (2011): 1058.

[9] Nienke Grossman, "Legitimacy and International Adjudicative Bodies," *George Washington International Law Review* 41, no. 1 (2009).

[10] Başak Cali, Anne Koch, and Nicola Bruch, "The Legitimacy of Human Rights Courts: A Grounded Interpretivist Analysis of the European Court of Human Rights," *Human Rights Quarterly* 35, no. 4 (2013).

[11] Eva Brems and Laurens Lavrysen, "Procedural Justice in Human Rights Adjudication: The European Court of Human Rights," *Human Rights Quarterly* 35, no. 1 (2013).

[12] Garrett, Kelemen, and Schulz, "The European Court of Justice"; Carrubba, Gabel, and Hankla, "Judicial Behavior under Political Constraints"; Manfred Elsig and Mark Pollack, "Agents, Trustees, and International Courts: The Politics of Judicial Appointment at the World Trade Organization," *European Journal of International Relations* 20, no. 2 (2014).

curtail or curb "agency slack." Court-curbing mechanisms include ex ante controls, which aim to prevent "adverse selection." States, for example, rely on appointment procedures to identify judges whose ideological preferences closely align with their own. Other court-curbing mechanisms are ex post means of sanctioning a court, such as declining to reappoint a judge or altering the jurisdiction or powers of the court following a controversial decision.[13] This perspective suggests that court-curbing mechanisms, typically governed by formal rules, constrain judicial independence. Another strand of literature draws less from principal-agent theory, but nonetheless arrives at the conclusion that international courts have "bounded discretion,"[14] "constrained independence,"[15] and operate within a "strategic space."[16] Both strands recognize that international judicial independence is limited because they operate with states in the background and political constraints that limit judicial autonomy.

On the other hand, several scholars argue that international courts are independent and exercise their authority without concern for the preferences of states.[17] A prominent argument from this perspective approaches international courts as "trustees" of states. Unlike delegation to an agent, trusteeship has the foremost objective of making states' commitments credible, for which independence is essential.[18] Judges and courts can act as trustees because they have moral authority, serving higher values or "the law," and expert authority based on respect for their competence and relevant knowledge.[19] Put differently, the independence of an IC is the result of its expert and moral authority. A slightly different take suggests that states have limited means of controlling ICs because disunity among principals reduces the political feasibility of curbing and therefore ICs operate "in an unusually permissive zone of discretion."[20]

13 Elsig and Pollack, "Agents, Trustees, and International Courts"; Ginsburg, "Political Constraints on International Courts"; Kelemen, "The Political Foundations of Judicial Independence in the EU."

14 Ginsburg, "Bounded Discretion in International Judicial Lawmaking."

15 Helfer and Slaughter, "Why States Create International Tribunals."

16 Steinberg, "Judicial Lawmaking at the WTO."

17 Cichowski, *The European Court and Civil Society*; Karen J. Alter, "Agents or Trustees? International Courts in Their Political Context," *European Journal of International Relations* 14, no. 1 (2008); Alec Stone Sweet and Thomas L. Brunell, "The European Court of Justice, State Noncompliance, and the Politics of Override," *American Political Science Review* 106, no. 1 (2012).

18 Giandomenico Majone, "Two Logics of Delegation: Agency and Fiduciary Relations in EU Governance," *European Union Politics* 2, no. 1 (2001).

19 Alter, "Agents or Trustees?"

20 Stone Sweet and Brunell, "Trustee Courts and the Judicialization of International Regimes," 65.

Moreover, the risks of court-curbing are narrow because states' preferences are often changed by courts.[21]

Empirical studies have informed this debate. Most of these studies examine the CJEU and/or the WTO dispute settlement mechanism. The wider population of international courts has received limited attention. Additionally, these empirical studies do not measure the independence of these courts. This chapter addresses these limitations by conceptualizing and measuring formal judicial independence of twenty-six ICs. The section "Conceptualizing and Measuring Formal Independence" describes how I conceive of and measure formal independence.

Conceptualizing and Measuring Formal Independence

Judicial independence is a complex concept, consisting of two dimensions. First, independence has a behavioral dimension, which describes whether in practice behavior is independent. This can be called informal independence (also referred to as de facto independence).[22] Second, formal independence (sometimes called de jure independence) concerns the institutional design of a court and whether judicial independence is formally safeguarded through codified rules. Drawing the distinction between these two dimensions of independence is essential as one connotes rules and the other behavior or practice. It also has significant implications for measurement. Yet, those who study judicial independence at the international level rarely make a point of drawing the conceptual difference between formal and informal independence.

Literature on domestic courts illustrates the benefits of the conceptual distinction. It facilitates examination of whether rules that safeguard independence enable courts to behave independently.[23] Similarly, distinguishing between formal and informal independence sheds light on independence as a key design feature of international institutions more broadly.[24] Finally, it can be useful for identifying how independence affects the outcomes, such as compliance, or impacts of international courts.

21 Alter, "Agents or Trustees?"; Alter, *The New Terrain of International Law.*

22 Hayo and Voigt, "Explaining De Facto Judicial Independence"; Melton and Ginsburg, "Does De Jure Judicial Independence Really Matter?"

23 Melton and Ginsburg, "Does De Jure Judicial Independence Really Matter?"; Hayo and Voigt, "Explaining De Facto Judicial Independence"; Hayo and Voigt, "The Long-Term Relationship between De Jure and De Facto Judicial Independence."

24 Yoram Haftel and Alexander Thompson, "The Independence of International Organizations: Concept and Applications," *Journal of Conflict Resolution* 50, no. 2 (2006).

While there are various measures of formal independence of domestic courts, no such measure exists for ICs.[25] I develop an original dataset that measures the formal independence of international courts. The ICs included in the dataset comprise the full universe of permanent ICs that were operational at any point between 1945 until 2015.[26] Excluded are quasi-judicial bodies (such as the UN human rights committees), tribunals with ad hoc appointments (such as investor–state arbitration tribunals), hybrid criminal courts (such as the Special Court for Sierra Leone), or ICs that were "nipped in the bud."[27] This selection of ICs closely matches other prominent comparative research on ICs.[28] Table 3.1 lists the included ICs, along with their abbreviations and the year they became operational.

Formal independence is operationalized as the codified rules governing each court, as regulated by their founding treaties, regulations, and rules of procedure (or similar). I construct a composite measure based on eleven codified rules that provide institutional safeguards of judicial independence. The rules of interest are those that define the ex ante and ex post mechanisms of control that states might have over a court. These rules address: (a) the appointment of judges and their terms of office, (b) the managerial autonomy of courts, and (c) additional safeguards that insulate and protect judges from inappropriate external pressures. This selection of rules is guided by theoretical literature, which I refer to when discussing each rule below. Also, this selection closely parallels those that are included in measures of domestic de jure independence or proposed measures for international courts.[29] I exclude other rules that might be associated with independence, such as the permanence of a court, admissibility, or access because they have no

[25] Voigt discusses a possible measure; several components of my measure overlap with his proposed measure. See Voigt, "The Independence of International Courts"

[26] Permanence is defined as having judges who hold fixed positions, in contrast to ad hoc appointments. See Cesare Romano, "A Taxonomy of International Rule of Law Institutions," *Journal of International Dispute Settlement* 2, no. 1 (2011): 262.

[27] Cesare Romano, "Trial and Error in International Judicialization," in *The Oxford Handbook of International Adjudication*, ed. Cesare Romano, Karen Alter, and Yuval Shany (Oxford: Oxford University Press, 2014).

[28] Alter, *The New Terrain of International Law.*

[29] For domestic measures, see Melton and Ginsburg, "Does De Jure Judicial Independence Really Matter?"; Hayo and Voigt, "Explaining De Facto Judicial Independence"; Lars P. Feld and Stefan Voigt, "Economic Growth and Judicial Independence: Cross-Country Evidence Using a New Set of Indicators," *European Journal of Political Economy* 19, no. 3 (2003). For one on international courts, see Voigt, "The Independence of International Courts."

Table 3.1 *Population of international courts, 1945–2015*

International court	Year in operation
African Court on Human and Peoples' Rights (ACtHPR)	2006
Andean Tribunal of Justice (ATJ)	1984
Arab Investment Court (AIC)	2003
Benelux Court of Justice (BCJ)	1974
Central American Court of Justice (CACJ)	1992
Caribbean Court of Justice (CCJ)	2005
Central African Economic and Monetary Community Court of Justice (CEMAC CJ)	2000
Common Market for Eastern and Southern Africa Court of Justice (COMESA CJ)	1998
Court of Justice of the European Union (CJEU)	1952
East African Court of Justice (EACJ)	2001
Economic Court of the Commonwealth of Independent States (ECCIS)	1993
Economic Community of West African States Court of Justice (ECOWAS CJ)	2002
Eurasian Economic Union Court (EAEU CT)	2015
European Court of Human Rights (ECtHR)	1959
European Free Trade Agreement Court of Justice (EFTA CJ)	1994
Inter-American Court of Human Rights (IACtHR)	1979
International Criminal Court (ICC)	2002
International Court of Justice (ICJ)	1947
International Criminal Tribunal of Rwanda (ICTR)	1994
International Criminal Tribunal of the former Yugoslavia (ICTY)	1993
International Tribunal for the Law of the Sea (ITLOS)	1996
Mercosur Permanent Review Tribunal (Mercosur PRT)	2002
Organization for the Harmonization of Business Law in Africa Common Court of Justice and Arbitration (OHADA CCJA)	1996
Tribunal of the Southern African Development Community (SADCT)	2005–2010
Western African Economic and Monetary Union Court of Justice (WAEMU CJ)	1995
World Trade Organization Appellate Body (WTO AB)	1994

direct ability to safeguard independence on their own, even though they may, in conjunction with other factors, have an impact on informal independence. For similar reasons, I exclude rules more clearly related to impartiality. The following discussion elaborates on how each rule can safeguard independence and relates to the idea of ex ante or ex post mechanisms of state control.

Selection and Terms of Judicial Office

While appointment of judges is likely to be politically charged for all ICs, appointment procedures and the terms of judicial office vary.[30] Some appointment procedures provide better safeguards to independence than others. Five rules concerning appointment and the terms of judicial office relate to independence:

Selection: The procedure for appointing judges varies across ICs, including: the direct appointment by a single state; by a unanimous vote or consensus of all member states; by a supermajority vote of states; by a majority vote; or by selection of an independent body.[31] Direct appointments by a single state occur in some "full representation" courts, meaning that the number of seats on the court equals the number of member states so that each state is "represented" by one judge. The ECtHR is an example of a full representation court. "Selective representation" courts, where there are fewer seats than states (e.g., WTO AB), or courts which have more seats than there are member states (e.g., EACJ), do not have direct appointments for obvious reasons. Generally speaking, the independence of international institutions increases as the size of the veto group (or the blocking coalition) becomes larger.[32] Thus, as Keohane, Moravcsik, and Slaughter explain, judges appointed either directly by an individual state or by unanimity (or consensus) – thereby providing any one

[30] Ruth Mackenzie and Philippe Sands, "International Courts and Tribunals and the Independence of the International Judge," *Harvard International Law Journal* 44, no. 1 (2003); Voeten, "The Politics of International Judicial Appointments"; Elsig and Pollack, "Agents, Trustees, and International Courts"; Ruth Mackenzie et al., *Selecting International Judges: Principle, Process, and Politics* (Oxford: Oxford University Press, 2010).

[31] The CCJ is the only IC with judges appointed by an independent commission; see Chapter 5 for details.

[32] Haftel and Thompson, "The Independence of International Organizations," 258.

state with a veto – have low independence because one state on its own can influence the composition of a court.[33] For example, when a state can directly appoint a judge, it can select judges who have ideological leanings that align with its preferences. Similarly, if appointment is by unanimity (or consensus), any one state can prevent the selection of a judge whose preferences diverge from its own. Supermajority rules make it more difficult for a state to block the selection of a judge because it would need the support of a portion of other states to join in blocking the appointment. Majority voting rules enable even more independence because it requires at least half of all member states to block a selection of judges.

Reappointment: Rules on reappointment are also believed to influence independence.[34] If judges can be reappointed, they have more incentives to maintain the good will of states. In other words, states might rely on reappointment as a carrot to nudge judges toward favorable decisions. Thus, the possibility of reappointment reduces independence.

Tenure: Tenure can also affect judicial independence, such that longer terms bolster independence.[35] When judges are appointed for short terms, they might have more insecurities about their career prospects once their term expires. Moreover, states can influence a judge's career options once she completes her term of office. For example, the state may later nominate her for a judgeship to another court. Judges, especially if they are younger, may therefore seek to protect their long-term career by remaining in the high esteem of states. Voeten finds that there is some indication that career insecurities make judges more likely to favor their national governments in disputes.[36] All else equal, longer terms help to insulate judges from political retribution for unpopular decisions and reduce concerns for their career.

Removal from office: Rules governing the dismissal of judges also affect judicial independence.[37] When states control the removal of judges

33 Keohane, Moravcsik, and Slaughter, "Legalized Dispute Resolution."

34 Erik Voeten, "The Politics of International Judicial Appointments," *Chicago Journal of International Law* 9, no. 2 (2009), 400–401; Stiansen, "(Non)Renewable Terms and Judicial Independence."

35 Voeten, "The Politics of International Judicial Appointments," 400.

36 Erik Voeten, "The Impartiality of International Judges: Evidence from the European Court of Human Rights," *American Political Science Review* 102, no. 4 (2008).

37 Dominik Zimmermann, *The Independence of International Courts: The Adherence of the International Judiciary to a Fundamental Value of the Administration of Justice* (Baden-Baden: Nomos, 2014).

from office, judges have greater incentive to maintain the good esteem of states, negatively affecting independence. Independence is better safeguarded by rules that ensure removal from office is determined by a judge's peers or the court itself.

Oath of office: Another means of safeguarding independence is a sworn oath of office.[38] An oath of office, or disclosure statement, safeguards independence because it binds a judge to remain independent. Moreover, an oath is a public commitment to remain independent, which is likely to be important for perceived legitimacy.

Managerial Autonomy

The extent to which a court has control over its material and human resources is likely to affect judicial independence. Resources and leadership affect the ability of ICs to process their caseloads and how they do so. For example, autonomy over resources "may permit a court or tribunal to develop a factual record independent of that of state litigants before them."[39] Moreover, research suggests that those working within the registries and secretariats of international courts, while often unseen and unheard, are instrumental to the administrative and legal operations of ICs.[40] I consider four rules that relate to managerial autonomy.

Budget: A court's ability to determine its budget provides it with discretion to determine how its resources are allocated. If states control the budget, they determine the amount of funding a court has as well as how resources are allocated, such as whether funding can go to fact-finding, expert testimony, support staff, or public relations. Thus, the more influence a court has over its budget, the greater its independence.[41]

38 Guillaume, "Some Thoughts on Independence of International Judges," 164; Grossman, "Legitimacy and International Adjudicative Bodies," 135.

39 Keohane, Moravcsik, and Slaughter, "Legalized Dispute Resolution," 462.

40 Freya Baetens, ed. *Legitimacy of Unseen Actors in International Adjudication* (Cambridge: Cambridge University Press, 2019); Joost Pauwelyn and Krzysztof Pelc, "Who Guards the 'Guardians of the System'? The Role of the Secretariat in WTO Dispute Settlement," *American Journal of International Law* 116, no. 3 (2022); Stéphanie Cartier and Cristina Hoss, "The Role of Registries and Legal Secretariats in International Judicial Institutions," in *The Oxford Handbook of International Adjudication*, ed. Cesare Romano, Karen J. Alter, and Yuval Shany (Oxford: Oxford University Press, 2014).

41 While the size of a court's budget is important, I assume the most relevant aspect of budgeting for a court's independence concerns who controls how resources are allocated.

Registrar: Also critical for a court's independence is its ability to decide who works in its registry or secretariat. As staffing and managerial decisions are made by a registrar or secretary, whoever appoints the registrar or secretary indirectly shapes many aspects of a court's operation, including staffing choices and case processing. The more influence a court has over the appointment of its registrar, the higher its independence.

President: A court's leader influences how it operates and processes cases. The president (or chairperson) of the court, for example, can determine how cases are allocated or who writes decisions.[42] Courts that appoint their own president therefore have more independence than when they are selected by states.

Rules of Procedure: The control over a court's rules of procedure can also affect its independence. When courts can determine these rules of procedure on their own, they have some autonomy over the internal administration of the court, the functioning of its registrar, as well as some aspects of judicial proceedings. Thus, courts that can determine their rules of procedure are likely to have more discretion over their management and internal operation, and thus functionally have greater independence.

Insulation of Judges from Undue External Pressure

Other rules can help to safeguard the judges on the bench from being subject to inappropriate pressure from external actors. Two rules provide such safeguards.

Secret deliberations: Rules governing the secrecy or confidentiality of judicial deliberation may foster independence. When courts have confidential deliberations, we can assume that secrecy enables judges to freely deliberate without concern for how their statements may be perceived, interpreted, or used against them by external actors. Thus, secret deliberation may go a long way toward enhancing judicial independence.[43]

Immunities and Privileges: Provisions that grant diplomatic privileges and immunities to judges also safeguard independence. Protections for judges from politically motivated prosecutions may be essential to their ability to act free from the pressure of states. "If the individual

[42] Silje Synnøve Lyder Hermansen, "Building Legitimacy: Strategic Case Allocations in the Court of Justice of the European Union," *Journal of European Public Policy* 27, no. 8 (2020).

[43] Guillaume, "Some Thoughts on Independence of International Judges," 165.

judges cannot feel safe from sanctions for the decisions he makes on the bench, if he has to fear negative consequences that affect other aspects of his life, then the most competent individual will either decline to serve as a judge or be disposed to surrender to the pressure."[44] Privileges and immunities that benefit judicial independence include protections for judges from prosecution for actions taken in fulfilling the obligations of office.

Before a discussion of how these rules are coded for the purpose of constructing a composite measure, it is worth noting that some might question the inclusion of any given rule that I incorporate. For example, a rule concerning an oath of office may have minimal impact on the overall protection of a court. I, however, contend that the hypothesized impact of formal independence is not purely about whether any one given rule guarantees noninterference, but whether the rules in combination safeguard independence by making interference difficult for states. The degree of difficulty states face in resisting a court is affected by whether a court appears to be independent. Thus, my purpose of including such rules is to not discount the symbolic significance of something like a sworn oath, as it shapes the appearance of independence and thereby makes state resistance more costly and difficult than if there were no oath.

An Index of IC Formal Independence

To construct a composite measure of formal independence, each international court is coded along these eleven rules. Each rule is coded on a scale of 0 to 1, where 0 represents low independence and 1 is high independence. The coding for each rule is summarized in Table 3.2.

Based on this coding scheme, I develop an additive measure, which equally weights all eleven rules on independence and then normalizes the sum on a 0 (low independence) to 1 (high independence) scale.[45] The *Formal Independence Index* is based on this composite measure for all

[44] Zimmermann, *The Independence of International Courts*, 191.

[45] The combination of tenure and reappointment is carefully considered. Tenure and reappointment could be either additive or interactive. I use the additive approach. Interacting tenure and reappointment (adjusting the scale from 1 to 2 to avoid multiplying zero scores) results in the same order ranking as the additive approach. The order ranking from least to highest independence for the additive approach is: short tenure with reappointment, average tenure with reappointment, short tenure with no reappointment = long tenure with reappointment, average tenure with no reappointment, and long tenure with no reappointment.

Table 3.2 *Measuring the formal independence of international courts*

	Rule	Low independence = 0	Moderate independence = 0.5	High independence = 1
Appointment and Term of Office	• Appointment	Direct appointment or vote by consensus	Vote by supermajority†	Vote by majority, or selection by independent body
	• Reappointment*	Possible	n/a	Not possible
	• Tenure	Less than average tenure (<6 years)	Average tenure (6 years)	Greater than average (>6 years)*
	• Removal	Decided by states	Decided by states, court consulted	Decided by court
	• Oath	No oath	n/a	Yes
Managerial Autonomy	• Budget	Decided by states	Decided by states, court consulted	Decided by court
	• Registrar/Secretary	States appoint	States and court jointly appoint	Court appoints
	• President	States appoint	States and court jointly appoint	Court appoints, or rotating position
	• Rules of Procedure	States adopt	Court adopts its rules of procedure with approval by states	Court adopts
Insulation of Judges	• Secret deliberations	Not guaranteed	n/a	Yes
	• Diplomatic privileges and immunities	Not guaranteed	n/a	Yes

* CCJ judges hold their tenure until the age of seventy-two and therefore can have terms that exceed six years. See Chapter 5 for further details.

† The CJEU's new procedure for appointment under the Lisbon Treaty, requiring an independent panel to consult on appoints, is unique. It is coded as 0.5 as it increases independence.

twenty-six ICs from 1945 to 2015. I also consider alternative methods for constructing a composite measure. One alternative is to weigh rules differently. I elect to use equal weighting for three reasons. First, weighting requires additional theoretical insights into what rules are most crucial to independence. Second, the rules that are arguably less critical for independence, such as oath or secret deliberations, are similar across most, if not all, courts. In other words, most of the variation is explained by a fewer set of variables. Third, several measures of de jure independence of domestic judiciaries use a similar additive approach.[46]

Another possibility for measuring formal independence is to exclude those rules that are arguably less important to ensuring independence. I calculate another index (*Index2*), which includes only the rules concerning appointment and terms of office and managerial autonomy. *Index2* and the *Formal Independence Index* are highly correlated ($r = .99$).[47] Another view is that there is a clear distinction between judicial independence and judicial accountability.[48] Excluding the rules most associated with accountability, or the ability to sanction the court or its judges (reappointment, removal of judges, and budget), I calculate a third version of the index (*Index3*). It is also highly correlated with the *Formal Independence Index* ($r = .89$). Finally, I considered using factor analysis to create an index. This reveals four factors with Eigen values above 1.[49] The factor with the highest Eigen value explains only 28 percent of the variation. In all, the benefit of using these alternatives indices is limited, and without further theoretical justification for excluding certain rules, I proceed with the full *Formal Independence Index*.

Mapping Formal Judicial Independence of ICs

Do international courts differ in their formal independence? A comparison of formal independence of all twenty-six ICs sheds light

[46] For example, see Feld and Voigt, "Economic Growth and Judicial Independence"; Linda Camp Keith, "Judicial Independence and Human Rights Protection around the World," *Judicature* 85, no. 4 (2002).

[47] I calculate this index with and without the oath of office. Both have the same correlation with the full index.

[48] Dunoff and Pollack, "The Judicial Trilemma"; Vanberg, "Establishing and Maintaining Judicial Independence."

[49] These four factors together account for 70 percent of the variation in the data. The rules that contribute most strongly to the first factor are the selection of the president and the secrecy of deliberations.

Table 3.3 *Prevalence of rules that hamper independence over time*

	1995 (N = 12)	2015 (N = 25)
Judges selected by consensus	50 percent	44 percent
Reappointment	91.67	68
Term less than 6 years	25	28
States decide on removal	33.3	24
States decide on budget	33.3	28
States select registrar	0	8
States select president	0	8
States decide on rules of procedure	0	8
Deliberation not in secret	0	4

Note: Immunities and oath are not included because they are present in both years for all courts.

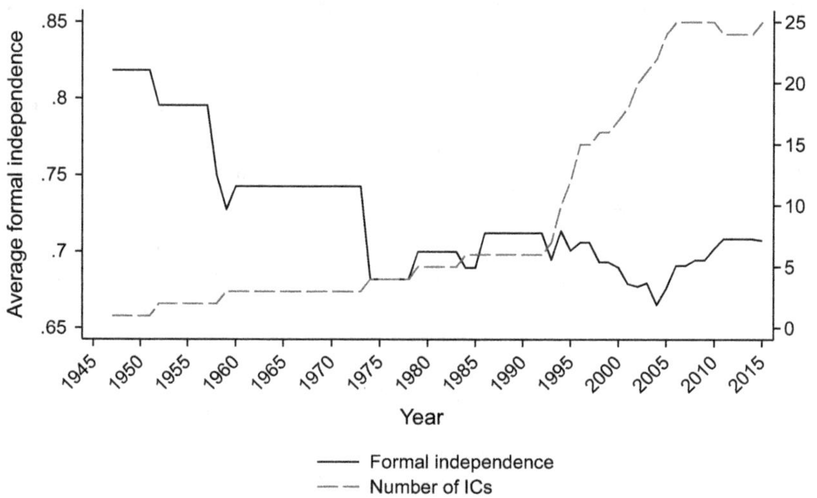

Figure 3.1 Formal independence from 1945 to 2015.

on this question. Figure 3.1 illustrates that on average judicial independence has declined over time. This development coincides with the increase in the number of ICs.

What rules are used typically to limit judicial independence, and has this changed over time? Table 3.3 shows what percentage of ICs in 1995 and 2015 featured rules that hamper judicial independence. By comparing 1995 to 2015, we can see that some provisions have

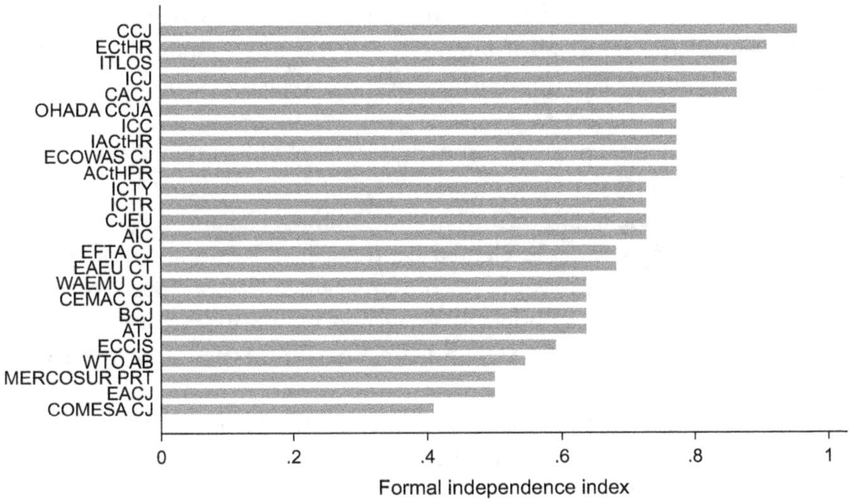

Figure 3.2 Variation in formal independence by court (2015).

become less common over time, including rules that allow for reappointment and appointment by consensus. However, state control over the selection of court presidents, registrars, and rules of procedure has increased. While most of these differences do not on their own affect a large percentage of ICs, they contribute to a decline in the average level of judicial independence. Additionally, it suggests that the decline in formal independence of the international judiciary is driven by the proliferation of new courts. That is, new courts are created with less robust measures to safeguard judicial independence when compared to older courts.

Figure 3.2 compares the formal independence of twenty-five ICs in 2015.[50] It shows that the Court of Justice of the Common Market for Eastern and Southern Africa (COMESA CJ), Mercosur Permanent Review Tribunal (PRT), and the East African Court of Justice have the lowest levels of formal independence. All three of these courts' judges are appointed by consensus. COMESA's court also scores low because, among other things, its judges hold renewable five-year terms, and states control the removal of judges and the selection of the Court's president.[51]

[50] The SADC Tribunal was disbanded in 2010, and therefore, it was not in operation in 2015.

[51] Treaty establishing the Common Market for Eastern and Southern Africa (adopted November 5, 1993, entered into force December 8, 1994) U.N.T.S. 2314, at 265–385: Art. 8 and 20–22.

The Mercosur PRT's arbitrators hold renewable two-year terms and states control the removal of judges.[52] For the EACJ, states control the removal of judges, the appointment of the registrar, and the Court's budget.[53]

The international court with the highest level of formal independence is the Caribbean Court of Justice. The CCJ's independence is provided by its rules on judicial appointments and managerial autonomy. Judges, as well as the registrar, are elected by the CCJ's Regional Judicial and Legal Services Commission (RJLSC), which is an independent commission.[54] Also, its budget is governed by a tripartite relationship between the Court, the RJLSC, and the Board of Trustees of the CCJ's Trust Fund.[55]

The ECtHR, ITLOS, ICJ, and Central American Court of Justice (CACJ) also score comparatively high in terms of judicial independence. For example, the CACJ's institutional safeguards to independence include judicial appointments that are for a ten-year, nonrenewable term. Judicial appointments to the ECtHR are also nonrenewable and last for nine years.[56] The ICJ also scores high because of its rules pertaining to judicial appointments. Judges are elected by a majority vote of the UN Security Council and the General Assembly to serve a nine-year, renewable term.[57] Also, all four of these courts decide on their rules of procedure and select their registrars and presidents.[58]

[52] Olivos Protocol for the Settlement of Disputes in Mercosur (adopted on February 18, 2002; entry into force January 1, 2004) U.N.T.S. 2251, at 288–303: Art. 18. The fifth arbitrator is appointed for a nonrenewable three-year term.

[53] Treaty for the establishment of the East African Community (adopted November 30, 1999, entered into force July 7, 2000) U.N.T.S. 2144, at 255–327: Art. 26, 45 and 132, respectively [herein "EAC Treaty"].

[54] Agreement establishing the Caribbean Court of Justice (adopted February 14, 2001, entered into force July 23, 2002) U.N.T.S. 2255, at 319–341: Art. 4 and 5 [herein "CCJ Agreement"].

[55] The CCJ is funded by a Trust Fund, which is directed by an independent Board of Trustees.

[56] This was a change instituted by the adoption of Protocol No. 14 of the European Convention; see ECHR Protocol No. 14.

[57] Statute of the International Court of Justice (adopted June 26, 1945, entered into force October 24, 1945), UNCIO XV, at 355–364: Art. 10 and 13. The coding on the ICJ (and other ICs for which it is relevant) does not include the appointment of ad hoc judges.

[58] The presidency of the CACJ rotates among the members; see Convention on the Statute of the Central American Court of Justice (adopted December 10, 1992, entered into force February 2, 1994) U.N.T.S. 1821, at 292–303: Art. 16.

Appointment and Terms of Office

The rules concerning judicial appointment and the terms of office are often designed to limit independence. In 2015, 68 percent of ICs featured the possibility of re-appointment (Table 3.3), which can hinder judicial independence.[59] We also know that judges are appointed by a consensus of member states or by direct appointments in nearly half of all ICs. Do ICs systematically differ in the extent to which their rules on appointment and terms of office are weak or strong safeguards to independence? To address this question, I create a subindex on the *appointment and terms of office* that includes the following rules: appointment, reappointment, length of tenure, removal from office, and oath of independence. The subindex is a cumulative score of these five rules, equally weighted and normalized on a scale of 0 (low independence) to 1 (high independence). Figure 3.3 compares ICs on the basis of the *appointment and terms of office* subindex in 2015.

Figure 3.3 shows that appointment and terms of office rules of the CCJ and the Common Court of Justice and Arbitration for the Organization for the Harmonization of Business Law in Africa (OHADA CCJA) are among the most robust in furnishing formal judicial independence. As mentioned before, the CCJ stands out because the RJLSC, not the member states, appoint its judges.[60] Apart from the President of the Court, the removal of judges on the CCJ is also determined by RJLSC.[61] In addition, judges hold office until the age of seventy-two, and thus reappointment does not apply.[62] The judges of the OHADA CCJA are elected by an absolute majority by the Council of Ministers, which is an intergovernmental decision-making body, for a seven year, nonrenewable term.[63] On the other end of the spectrum, there are a number of ICs that lack strong protections to independence through appointment procedures and the terms of judicial office. The Court of Justice of COMESA (COMESA CJ) and Mercosur's PRT score the lowest, followed by Andean's Tribunal and Court of Justice for the Economic

[59] Elsig and Pollack, "Agents, Trustees, and International Courts"; Stiansen, "(Non) Renewable Terms and Judicial Independence."

[60] CCJ Agreement, Art. 4(6–7).

[61] Ibid.

[62] Ibid., Art. 9(3).

[63] Treaty related to the Revisions to the Treaty on the Harmonisation of Business Law in Africa (adopted October 17, 2008): Art. 31, accessed August 27, 2024, www.ohada.com/traite.html.

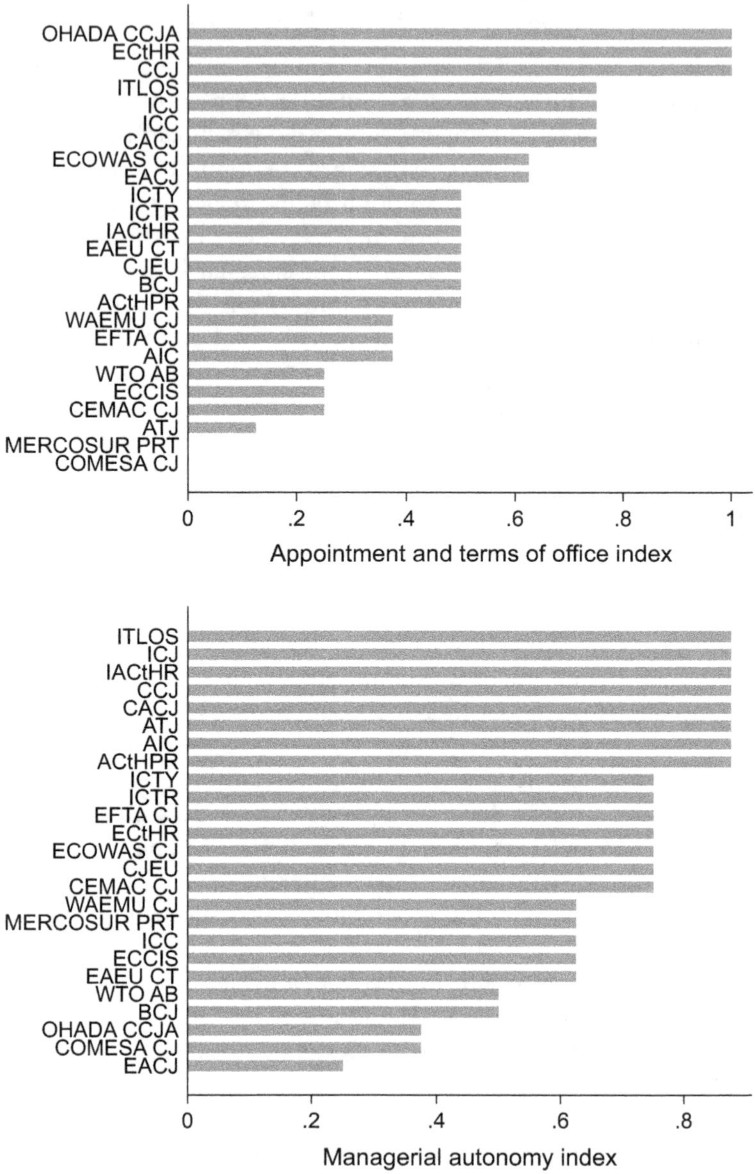

Figure 3.3 Variation in appointment and terms of office safeguards and managerial autonomy (2015).

Community of West African States (ECOWAS). Except for the WTO AB, only regional courts have below average (0.58) formal independence in terms of appointment and terms of office.

Managerial Autonomy

Rules concerning the management of ICs also appear to have varying impact on the degree of formal independence of international courts. How do ICs compare in their autonomy over their management? To address this question, I use a subindex on *managerial autonomy* to summarize the rules determining control over a court's budget and rules of procedure, as well as the selection of the registrar and president. The subindex is a cumulative score of these four rules, equally weighted and normalized on a scale of 0 (low independence) to 1 (high independence). A comparison of IC in 2015 in terms of managerial autonomy is depicted in Figure 3.3.

From this figure we can see that several ICs that have relatively little managerial autonomy also scored low in terms of appointment and terms of office (e.g., EACJ, COMESA CJ, WTO AB, and Mercosur PRT). The OHADA CCJA is quite interesting in that while it has high independence in terms of the appointment of judges and their terms of office, it has limited managerial autonomy. Several courts (both regional and global) have relatively high levels of managerial autonomy, including the ITLOS, ICJ, IACtHR, CCJ, CACJ, ATJ, and the ACtHPR. Also, as Table 3.3 reveals, states rarely retain control over courts' rules of procedure or the selection of registrars and presidents. The lack of managerial autonomy that exists for many ICs is driven largely by their limited control over their budgets. In other words, states seem to be especially wary about turning the purse strings over to courts which could affect the administration of justice in significant ways.

Case Selection

Mapping formal independence across a wide selection of ICs reveals that they are designed with different arrangements of formal rules to safeguard judicial independence. Whether these arrangements have an impact on judicial decision-making, and deference in particular, requires a more focused examination of ICs and their decisions. To trace the impact of formal independence, alongside the other explanatory factors specified in Chapter 2, I rely on comparison. Namely, I examine variation within each court's decisions (i.e., within-case comparison) and compare across courts (i.e., cross-case comparison). For this purpose, I draw heavily on this mapping of formal independence when selecting the EACJ, CCJ, and ACtHPR to study in-depth. Here I briefly detail the logic behind the selection of these courts.

First, an overarching aim of the research is to examine the deference of newer international courts in the Global South for which we have less knowledge, to see how deference is structured in the infancy of a court's life. Early years for institutions can be formative, and path dependency and organizational culture can take root from the beginning. Observing courts in their nascent stage is therefore important. My goal was also to contribute empirically, which led me to focus on courts that have received less scholarly attention. Also, previous research suggests that states' economic development or wealth can have bearing on the rule of law, even though this is minimally documented with regard to the international rule of law.

The second motivation for the case selection was to ensure variation on the key explanatory variables, especially formal independence, knowing that this was a factor for which variation would be primarily cross-sectional: Temporal changes to institutional design are much rarer than changes in political fragmentation. In addition, I aimed to identify a selection of cases that would feature some control over alternative explanatory factors. Specifically, I considered rules on access and relative strength of civil society, legal culture and political norms, and legal issues within the courts' jurisprudence.[64]

Reflecting on the cross-sectional differences in formal independence, as depicted in Figures 3.2 and 3.3, I noted that the CCJ is consistently high in formal independence, while the ACtHPR features a mid-to-high level of independence. The EACJ, on the other hand, stands out for its low level of formal independence. All three courts were established and became operational roughly around the same time. When I began this project in 2014, it was clear that they had a growing body of case law that related to similar issues of human rights, rule of law, and domestic governance. The member states of these courts also have shared histories of colonialism that have had significant impacts on their legal cultures and political norms and most are considered by the World Bank to be low- and middle-income countries.

[64] The accessibility and language of judgments were also considered.

Conclusion

This chapter has introduced and explored original data estimating the formal independence of twenty-six international courts. In doing so, it makes three main points which are revealed by the data. First, ICs are designed with varying degrees of formal independence. Differences in the rules concerning the appointment and terms of judicial office, as well as those addressing the managerial autonomy of ICs, are responsible for most of the overall variation. ICs do, however, have a few safeguards to independence in common. Nearly all ICs require judges to take an oath of office, guarantee judges diplomatic privileges and immunities, and require secret deliberations. Second, the data reveals that the average level of formal independence has declined as new courts have been created over time.

With the variation in formal independence having been identified, the next question becomes: does it matter? I have posited that formal independence is consequential for judicial decision-making. The remaining chapters examine the link between formal independence and deference, alongside other factors, in the cases of the East African Court of Justice, the Caribbean Court of Justice, and the African Court on Human and Peoples' Rights.

4

The East African Court of Justice

Pervasive Constraints and Substantial Deference

In the late 1990s, Kenya, Tanzania, and Uganda renewed their efforts toward regional integration, which culminated in the creation of the East African Community (EAC) in 2000. The East African Court of Justice was established as the EAC's core judicial organ and was tasked with interpreting and applying the founding treaty and ensuring compliance with Community law. Since the EACJ issued its first decision in 2006, the Court has delivered important decisions on a range of issues, including domestic governance, human rights, and the rule of law as well as key aspects of regional integration. By studying the EACJ's decision-making, this chapter examines the theoretical argument in the case of an international court with narrow strategic space. Specifically, the EACJ faces pervasive political constraints due to low formal independence, as shown in the Chapter 3, and a lack of political fragmentation. Additionally, the EACJ has experienced political resistance by states. According to the theoretical framework presented in Chapter 2, the EACJ should demonstrate a substantial degree of deference.

This chapter assesses the extent to which the EACJ defers to states and whether its deference is best explained by the nature of Court's structural political constraints and adaptive practices, or alternatively its support networks. The analysis reveals that the EACJ's deference is substantial, meaning that the Court is highly prone to accept, either through abstaining or through not validating, the states' exercise of authority. This is observed through the rates at which case outcomes are decided in favor of states and how the Court relies on restrictive interpretations and minimal scrutiny in its legal reasoning. However, the EACJ has shown less deference in its remedies when it finds a violation. The analysis further illustrates how these patterns of deference are associated with the Court's political vulnerability due to its weaker safeguards to independence and the lack of fragmentation among the EAC's member states. Past resistance has also played a role in confining the Court. On the other hand, to the extent that the Court does not defer, it has been bolstered by increasing political fragmentation among member states and by the Court's own agency. In particular, the Court adapts to its political environment by practicing persuasive argumentation and public legitimation that facilitates less deference. Last, the patterns of deference are loosely associated with the Court's support network.

The chapter begins by describing the process leading to the creation of the EAC to place the EACJ within its historic and ideational context. It then describes the Court's workload before examining the extent to which and how the Court defers. Next, the chapter shows how the Court's support network is stronger than its deference would imply. This is followed by an analysis of how the Court's deference corresponds with its pervasive political constraints and adaptive practices. The chapter concludes with a review of the core findings.

The EACJ's Ideational Setting: Colonial Legacies, Political Norms, and Legal Culture

The EACJ has been affected by its ideational context. For this reason, I set the stage for the analysis by briefly describing this context. Notably, this discussion reveals that the political norms behind regionalism and the legal culture in East Africa are tied to the region's colonial experience. The legacies of colonialism include political tensions between integration and independence, and legal pluralism. In addition to legal pluralism, legal culture is defined by a prominence of "judicial insecurity" and limited societal confidence in the state legal order.

Regionalism in East Africa has a long history and integration occurred in three iterations prior to the formation of the current EAC. The first iteration was an effort to generate economies of scales by the British Empire. During the nineteenth century, Kenya, Zanzibar (now part of Tanzania), and Uganda were British protectorates or colonies, while Tanganyika (the present-day mainland Tanzania), Burundi, and Rwanda were controlled by Germany.[1] British interests propelled cooperation between Kenya and Uganda. For example, colonial rulers constructed a Kenya-Uganda Railway in the final years of the nineteenth century, established a single currency in 1905, a postal union in 1911, and a customs union in 1917.[2] Following the end of World War I and the

[1] Richard E. Mshomba, *Economic Integration in Africa: The East African Community in Comparative Perspective* (Cambridge: Cambridge University Press, 2017), 35.

[2] Ibid., 37–38.

creation of the League of Nations, Burundi and Rwanda were transferred to Belgian control, and Tanganyika became a mandated territory under British control.[3] With the transfer of Tanganyika to British rule, it was integrated into the prior cooperation between the territories of Uganda and Kenya. Tanganyika, for instance, joined the common currency in 1921, the customs union in 1923, and the postal union in 1933.[4] Keen on further integration, the territorial governors began holding conferences (which included Kenya, Tanganyika, Uganda, Zanzibar, and present-day Malawi and Zambia) that led to deeper and wider cooperation.[5] In 1940, the Conference of Governors established a secretariat,[6] and later transformed the Conference into the East African High Commission in 1948, which included cooperation on administration, finance, post and communications, railways and harbors, civil aviation, social services, research and scientific services, economic services, and defense.[7]

An important feature of the colonial attempts to integrate East Africa was a certain degree of legal integration. As with other regions under British imperial rule, the East African territories shared a regional court of appeal, called the East African Court of Appeal (EACA).[8] Established in 1902, this court was part of the British imperial legal order, and it was the penultimate court of appeal for citizens of the British colonies and protectorates in East Africa. Its decisions were binding, but litigants could seek an appeal to the Judicial Committee of the Privy Council in London.[9] It addressed both criminal and civil matters, and it was staffed by British judges.[10] Even though it considered local customary law and often was called upon to remedy conflicts between colonial statutes and treaties, the common law and customary law, it was nonetheless an imperial court.[11] The EACA's administration was transferred to the East African High Commission in 1948.

This remained the situation until the dawn of independence in the early 1960s. At that time, and marking the second iteration of

[3] Ibid., 38.
[4] Ibid., 39.
[5] Ibid., 40.
[6] Ibid.
[7] Ibid., 41–42.
[8] The name was modified at various points and included the Eastern African Court of Appeal and the Court of Appeal for East Africa.
[9] Ibhawoh, *Imperial Justice*, 35.
[10] Ibid., 36.
[11] Ibid., 42–44.

integration, British and East African leaders transformed the East African High Commission into the East African Common Service Organization (EACSO).[12] Tanganyika became independent in 1961, Uganda in 1962 and Kenya in 1963. Zanzibar and Tanganyika united to form the United Republic of Tanzania in 1964. The newly independent states recognized the EACA as their court of last resort according to the EACSO agreements and state constitutions.[13] While the EACSO persisted, nationalist sentiments and discontent with the unequal distribution of common resources created disruptions, leading to the abandonment of the single currency in 1965.[14] Efforts to redress some of the discontent led to the Kampala Agreement in 1965, which aimed to address trade imbalances.[15]

In a third iteration, the Treaty for East African Cooperation was adopted in 1967 and the now former East African Community was created to help sustain a common market.[16] This cooperation continued the status of the EACA as the court of last resort for the member states.[17] The former East African Community survived for ten years, but collapsed after states were unable to agree on a budget in 1977.[18] This also marked the end of the EACA. A combination of unrealistic expectations, clashing political ideologies, the rise of Ugandan dictator Idi Amin, economic hardships from the 1970s oil crisis, and severe draught contributed to the collapse and pressures to disintegrate.[19] Tensions between the states were high, and the situation deteriorated when Uganda invaded Tanzania in 1978, and an eight-month-long war broke out. It took nine years and interventions by the World Bank and the UN for Kenya,

[12] Mshomba, *Economic Integration in Africa*, 47.

[13] Neil Orloff, "Economic Integration in East Africa: The Treaty for East-African Co-Operation," *Columbia Journal of Transnational Law* 7, no. 2 (1968): 318; L. L. Kato, "The Court of Appeal for East Africa: From a Colonial Court to an International Court," *East African Law Journal* 7, no. 1 (1971).

[14] Mshomba, *Economic Integration in Africa*, 52.

[15] Ibid., 50.

[16] Ibid., 53.

[17] Kato, "The Court of Appeal for East Africa"; J. W. Katende and George W. Kanyeihamba, "Legalism and Politics in East Africa: The Dilemma of the Court of Appeal for East Africa," *Transition*, no. 43 (1973).

[18] Mshomba, *Economic Integration in Africa*, 67.

[19] Ibid., 56–66; John Ravenhill, "Regional Integration and Development in Africa: Lessons from the East African Community," *Journal of Commonwealth & Comparative Politics* 17, no. 3 (1979); Arthur Hazlewood, "The End of the East African Community: What Are the Lessons for Regional Integration Schemes?" *Journal of Common Market Studies* 18, no. 1 (1979).

Tanzania, and Uganda to agree on a distribution of common assets from their former cooperation.[20]

As this account suggests, regional integration can be traced back to the initiatives of colonial oppressors. In the postcolonial era, political elites recognized the value of regional integration, yet some opposing pressures encouraged disintegration. Revival of integration began when government leaders met in 1991 and later created a Permanent Tripartite Commission for East African Cooperation in 1993.[21] Eventually, the new and current EAC was created in 2000 by the Treaty Establishing the East African Community (EAC Treaty).[22] The founding members are Kenya, Tanzania, and Uganda. Rwanda and Burundi joined in 2007, South Sudan in 2016, and the Democratic Republic of the Congo (DRC) in April 2022. The EAC's primary objective is a customs union, a common market, a monetary union, and, ultimately, a political federation.

The establishment of the new EAC was likely the product of several factors. The idea of integration had never been fully outrooted. Even the 1984 mediation agreement on the distribution of former community assets left open the possibility for future cooperation.[23] Shared resources, such as Lake Victoria, and intraregional trade provided additional motivations.[24] The conflicting economic and political ideologies which drove states apart were somewhat alleviated by the 1990s. For example, the World Bank and IMF structural adjustment programs in the 1980s meant that Kenya, Tanzania, and Uganda had compatible economic policies by the 1990s.[25] External economic and political factors also put pressure on leaders to recommit to regional integration. For example, globalization generally incentivized regionalism,[26] and

20 Mshomba, *Economic Integration in Africa*, 67.

21 Ibid., 74–75.

22 The EAC Treaty was amended in 2006 and 2007; see Revised Treaty for the establishment of the East African Community (as amended December 14, 2006 and August 20, 2007) (Arusha: EAC), www.eacj.org//wp-content/uploads/2012/08/EACJ-Treaty.pdf [herein "Amended EAC Treaty"].

23 Mshomba, *Economic Integration in Africa*, 74.

24 Mariel Reiss, *Constructing the East African Community: Diffusion from African and European Regional Organizations* (Abingdon: Routledge, 2022), 53.

25 Mshomba, *Economic Integration in Africa*, 74–75.

26 Wanyama Masinde and Christopher Otieno Omolo, "The Road to East African Integration," in *East African Community Law: Institutional, Substantive and Comparative EU Aspects*, ed. Emmanuel Ugirashebuja et al. (Leiden: Brill Nijhoff, 2017); Edward D. Mansfield and Eric Reinhardt, "Multilateral Determinants of Regionalism: The Effects of GATT/WTO on the Formation of Preferential Trading Arrangements," *International Organization* 57, no. 4 (2003).

interorganizational learning and emulation, as well as some active influence of actors like the EU, also contributed to the development of the new EAC.[27]

Political norms supportive of regional unity and cooperation ultimately contributed to the creation of the EAC, but they also coexisted with norms supportive of national sovereignty and disunity. This duality can be seen in aspects of the EAC's decisions. For example, when designing the EACJ some actors, mostly from civil society, called for the Court to have jurisdiction over human rights. States resoundingly rejected these proposals in favor of a regional court that better preserved sovereignty.[28] We can also see these tensions in the EAC's relatively high delegation (whereby a third party is granted authority by the states, such as the EACJ), alongside lower levels of pooling (or the transfer of authority from individual member states to a collective IO member state body).[29]

Beyond political norms, colonialism left its mark on legal culture across the region. Importantly, colonialism significantly contributed to legal pluralism within East Africa, which is an important aspect of the legal identity and culture across East Africa. Pluralism is reflected in the mix of state legal orders across and within EAC's member states. The EAC's founding members (Kenya, Uganda, Tanzania) have common law systems, reflecting their former status as British colonies. South Sudan also uses common law. Burundi and Rwanda are civil law states, indicating their former colonial ties. Moreover, Islamic law operates – albeit to varying extents – in Kenya,[30] Tanzania, and South Sudan. In addition to state and religious law, customary law is an integral part of the legal order in all member states.[31]

27 Reiss, *Constructing the East African Community*; Tobias Lenz, *Interorganizational Diffusion in International Relations: Regional Institutions and the Role of the European Union* (Oxford: Oxford University Press, 2021).

28 Mihreteab Tsighe Taye, "The Role of the East African Court of Justice in the Advancement of Human Rights: Reflections on the Creation and Practice of the Court," *African Journal of International and Comparative Law* 27, no. 3 (2019).

29 Liesbet Hooghe and Gary Marks, "Delegation and Pooling in International Organizations," *Review of International Organizations* 10, no. 3 (2015): 310.

30 In Kenya, for example, Islamic law applies only on issues of marriage, divorce, and inheritance when all parties are Muslim and agree to the jurisdiction of Kahdi's courts. See Jamil Ddamulira Mujuzi, "The Islamic Law of Marriage and Inheritance in Kenya," *Journal of African Law* 65, no. 3 (2021); Hooghe and Marks, "Delegation and Pooling in International Organizations."

31 Jeanmarie Fenrich, Paolo Galizzi, and Tracy E. Higgins, eds., *The Future of African Customary Law* (Cambridge: Cambridge University Press, 2011); Uwe Kischel, *Comparative Law* (Oxford: Oxford University Press, 2019). Customary law has changed

Aside from plurality of legal orders governing a society, legal culture is also constituted by beliefs and attitudes about the law and courts.[32] In East Africa, and elsewhere in Africa, state courts are not the sole mode of dispute settlement pursued by local and regional actors. Customary modes of dispute settlement are frequently utilized.[33] Their judiciaries and state legal order face many challenges. For instance, judges can face retaliation for their decision.[34] Access to justice is often illusive. The United Nations Development Programme (UNDP) finds significant gaps in the rule of law and access to justice in several of the EAC's member states; the reality "is that of unfairly enforced laws that are not accessible to all, weak institutions unable to increase access to justice, or citizens who are not empowered to make effective use of the law."[35] Moreover, constitutionalism has a history of lacking empirical legitimacy.[36] For instance, trust in courts is often low according to Afrobarometer surveys.[37] Overall, we might describe this as a culture of judicial insecurity and fragile trust.

To summarize, the EACJ's ideational environment is significantly shaped by the colonial history of its member states. Colonial legacies, alongside a range of other political and economic factors, have simultaneously promoted political norms that are supportive of integration and regional cooperation alongside competing values like independence and sovereignty. Additionally, the EACJ's ideational context includes legal

since the (pre-)colonial eras and might best described as the living law of indigenous people; see, for example, Abdulmumini A. Oba, "The Future of Customary Law in Africa," in *The Future of African Customary Law*, ed. Jeanmarie Fenrich, Paolo Galizzi, and Tracy E. Higgins (Cambridge: Cambridge University Press, 2011).

32 Merry, "What Is Legal Culture?."

33 James Thuo Gathii, "Variation in the Use of Subregional Integration Courts between Business and Human Rights Actors: The Case of the East African Court of Justice," *Law and Contemporary Problems* 79, no. 1 (2016): 50.

34 See for example, Martha Gayoye, "'Constitutions Without Constitutionalism' and Judicial Leadership in Kenya," *Journal of Eastern African Studies* 18, no. 3 (2024); VonDoepp and Ellett, "Reworking Strategic Models of Executive-Judicial Relations."

35 UNDP, *Rule of Law and Access to Justice in Eastern and Southern Africa: Showcasing Innovations and Good Practices* (Addis Ababa: UNDP, 2013), iii, accessed April 1, 2024, www.undp.org/sites/g/files/zskgke326/files/migration/africa/Rule-of-Law-and-Access-to-Justice-in-Eastern-and-Southern-Africa-2013_EN.PDF.

36 Prempeh, "Marbury in Africa."

37 See "Online Data Analysis," Afrobarometer, accessed August 27, 2024, www.afrobarometer.org/online-data-analysis/. In the sixth survey round from 2014 to 2015, on average less than 30 percent of respondents from Burundi, Kenya, Tanzania, and Uganda had a lot of trust in courts. Other EAC states were not included in the round.

cultures defined by pluralism, judicial insecurity, and fragile faith in the state legal order.

The East African Court at Work

Against this backdrop, the EACJ was established by chapter 8 of the EAC Treaty, which entered into force in 2000. The Court resides in Arusha, Tanzania, at the EAC's headquarters. The EACJ is responsible for "ensur[ing] the adherence to law in the interpretation and application of and compliance with [the EAC] Treaty."[38] Since 2007, it has had a First Instance and Appellate Division.[39] Member states may refer to the EACJ another member or Community "organ"[40] or "institution"[41] for an infringement or failure to fulfill Treaty obligations.[42] Upon the direction of the Council of the EAC, the Secretary General can also refer a member state to the EACJ for an infringement or failure to fulfill its Treaty obligations.[43] Private actors (i.e., legal and natural persons) can refer any Act, regulation, directive, decisions, or action of a member state or an EAC institution to the EACJ for a determination of its lawfulness according to the Treaty.[44] Member states' domestic courts can refer questions on the interpretation or application of the Treaty to the EACJ for a preliminary ruling.[45] Also, the Summit of Heads of State (herein the Summit), the Council, or member states may request advisory opinions from the Court.[46] Decisions of the Court are binding on member states, subject to appeal to the Appellate Division, and jurisdiction is compulsory with membership in the EAC.

The EACJ became operational in 2001, received its first "reference" (i.e., application) in 2005, and delivered its first judgment in 2006. Since then,

38 Amended EAC Treaty, Art. 23(1).

39 The Appellate Division was created by amendment to the EAC Treaty in 2006.

40 Ibid., Art. 9(1). EAC organs include the Summit, Council, Coordination Committee, Sectoral Committees, the EACJ, EALA, Secretariat, or any that are later established by the Summit.

41 Ibid., Art. 9(2). Institutions are bodies established by the Summit, and the East African Development Bank, and the Lake Victoria Fisheries Organization, which existed prior the adoption of the EAC Treaty.

42 Ibid., Art. 28(1).

43 Ibid., Art. 29.

44 Ibid., Art. 30(1). This provision does not expressly include community organs among the entities that private litigants can make claims against, but the Court has interpreted it to include organs; see *East African Law Society & Others v Attorney General of Kenya & Others*, Reference No. 3/2007, EACJ (August 31, 2008) [herein *EALS & Ors. v Kenya & Ors.*, Ref. 3/2007].

45 Amended EAC Treaty, Art. 34.

46 Ibid., Art. 36.

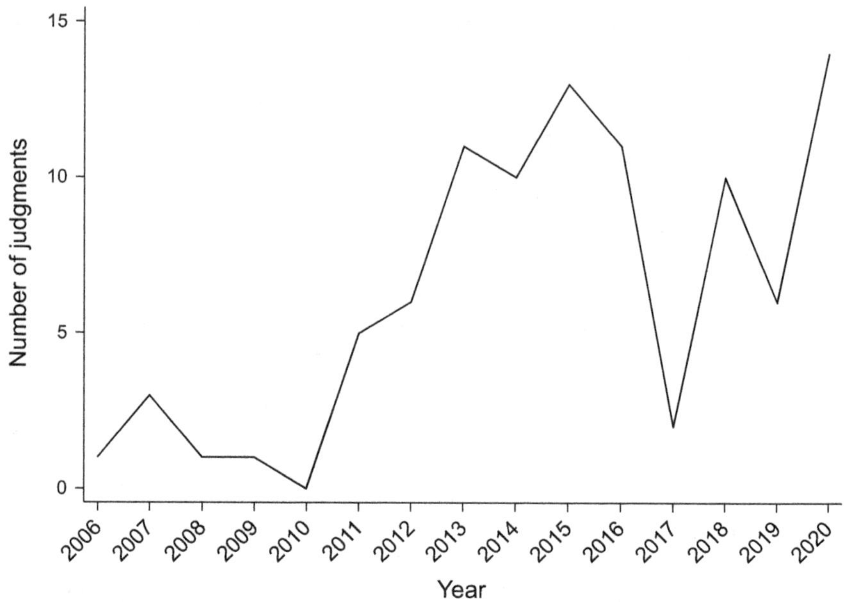

Figure 4.1 Number of EACJ finalized cases by year (2006–2020).

the Court's caseload has grown, despite some lulls. The proceeding analysis is based on original data of all EACJ's finalized cases from 2006 until the end of 2020. This data includes a total of ninety-four cases, of which seventy-one were delivered by the First Instance Division and twenty-three by the Appellate Division.[47] Figure 4.1 shows how many cases the EACJ finalized each year. In 2020, it issued fourteen judgments, the highest number in any year up to 2020. It averaged 6.3 final judgments per year. While the EACJ's caseload is smaller than, for example, the ECJ in its first fifteen to twenty years (see Figure A4.1 in Appendix), these figures are on par with other international courts, such as the ACtHPR (see Chapter 6).

Nearly all references to the EACJ (excluding appeals) have been initiated by private actors, except for one filed by a member state against an EAC institution[48] and one reference for a preliminary ruling.[49] The

[47] See Appendix for a complete list of all cases included in the dataset. I distinguish between finalized First Instance cases and appeals.

[48] *The Attorney General of the Republic of Burundi v The Secretary General of the East African Community*, Reference No. 2/2018, EACJ (July 2, 2019).

[49] *Preliminary Ruling in the case of the Attorney General of the Republic of Uganda v Tom Kyahurwenda*, Case Stated 1/2014, EACJ (July 31, 2015).

Table 4.1 *Number of EACJ's cases by respondent, First Instance Only (2006–2020)*

Respondent	Total	Decided on merits	No treaty violation	Treaty violation
East African Community	29	25	17	8
Burundi	19	13	8	5
Kenya	12	9	5	4
Rwanda	8	8	6	2
South Sudan	1	1	0	1
Tanzania	12	9	4	5
Uganda	24	19	13	6

Note: These figures do not include references where a respondent is struck off for being wrongly enjoined in the dispute. Preliminary references and appeals are also excluded.

respondents to references are not evenly distributed. Table 4.1 shows the number of references by each respondent, bearing in mind that references can have more than one respondent. The EAC was a respondent in twenty-nine instances. Among member states, Uganda was the respondent in the most disputes, or twenty-four in total. Burundi has also been a respondent in a comparatively large number of disputes.[50] South Sudan was a respondent in only one finalized dispute, but it had only been a member for four years within the timeframe under analysis.

The EACJ has addressed a variety of issues. Two-thirds of claims concerned the EAC's fundamental and operational principles – espoused in Article 6(d)[51] and 7(2)[52] of the EAC Treaty – and relate to democracy, human rights, and the rule of law. Article 6(d) or Article 7(2) violations

[50] For an excellent account of cases against Burundi, see Heinrich, "Sub-Regional Courts as Transitional Justice Mechanisms."

[51] Article 6(d) says: "The fundamental principles that shall govern the achievement of the objectives of the Community by the Partner States shall include: (d) good governance including adherence to the principles of democracy, the rule of law, accountability, transparency, social justice, equal opportunities, gender equality, as well as the recognition, promotion and protection of human and peoples rights in accordance with the provisions of the African Charter on Human and Peoples' Rights."

[52] Article 7(2) says: "The Partner States undertake to abide by the principles of good governance, including adherence to the principles of democracy, the rule of law, social justice and the maintenance of universally accepted standards of human rights."

were each alleged in forty-one of the EACJ first instance cases, while both were cited in thirty-eight cases. Matters relating to the East African Legislative Assembly (EALA), such as the election of EALA members or the election of the Speaker, were brought to the Court in nine first instance cases.[53] Eight first instance cases concerned the common market or customs union, and the powers and responsibilities of the EAC Secretariat (EAC Treaty Articles 66–73) were raised in nine first instance cases.[54]

Judicial Deference by the East African Court of Justice

This section examines the EACJ's decisions to determine the extent to which it accepts the states' and EAC's exercise of authority. It illustrates that the Court defers to a substantial degree, as seen in the tendency of case outcomes to be favorable to states and the EAC as well as the Court's reliance on restrictive interpretation. However, the Court is less likely to defer when it comes to remedies.

Case Outcomes

Case outcomes, or the rates at which states or the EAC win a case, provide information on the extent to which the EACJ defers, or accepts the state's or EAC's exercise of authority. Table 4.2 provides descriptive statistics on the EACJ's case outcomes and its deference rates. I examine case outcomes and deference rates by type of respondents (states, EAC, or both) and types of decisions (decided on the merits or all decisions). The *merits deference rate* is calculated as the number of judgments in which the EACJ found the respondent(s) had not violated the law divided by the total number of merits judgments – this gives an indication of how often the EACJ validates the respondent's exercise of authority. The *total deference rate* equals the number of decisions in which the Court found no violation (validation), the case was inadmissible (abstention), or it did not have jurisdiction (abstention) divided by the total number of all case outcomes.

[53] For an excellent account of these cases, see Gathii, "International Courts as Coordination Devices for Opposition Parties."

[54] This count includes references in which the initial claim invokes the relevant treaty provisions related to the Secretary General, irrespective of whether the claims relating to the Secretary General were dropped or struck out by the Court.

Table 4.2 *Summary of EACJ's case outcomes (2006–2020)*

	Number of judgments	Percent of category
All		
• *Inadmissible or no jurisdiction*	25	28.09
• *No violation found*	34	38.20
• *At least one violation*	30	33.71
	Deference rate (percent)	
Total (N = 89)	66.29	
Merits (N = 64)	53.13	
State respondent		
• *Inadmissible or no jurisdiction*	25	32.47
• *No violation*	28	36.36
• *At least one violation*	24	31.17
	Deference rate (percent)	
Total (N = 77)	68.83	
Merits (N = 52)	53.85	
EAC respondent (N = 30)		
• *No violation or dismissed*	21	70.00
• *At least one violation*	9	30.00

Note: These data exclude the one preliminary ruling and four instances where the Court affirmed its jurisdiction and remanded the reference back to the First Instance Division. Total deference rate = (*no violation* + *inadmissible or no jurisdiction*) ÷ Total N. Merits deference rate = *no violation* ÷ Merits N.

A few observations can be made from Table 4.2. First, the EACJ rules in favor of states and the EAC more than it does applicants, so it has a general propensity to accept the respondents' exercise of authority either through abstention or validation. When states are respondents, the EACJ has deferred in approximately 69 percent of all cases. The rate of deference in cases against states is lower if the dispute gets past the hurdles of jurisdiction and admissibility and is considered on the merits. In these instances, the EACJ ruled in favor of states in slightly more than half of its decisions. The Court defers more to EAC organs than it does to individual states. Overall, applicants typically do not get favorable outcomes when they bring complaints to the EACJ.

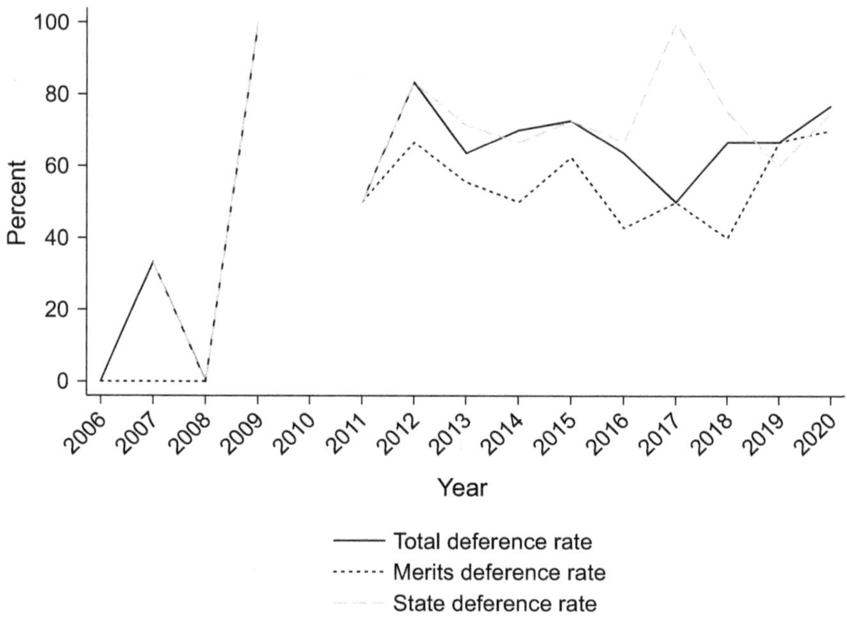

Figure 4.2 EACJ's deference rate by year (2006–2020).
Note: This figure does not include preliminary references or Appellate decisions that remand a case back to the First Instance Division.

Has the Court's deference changed over time? Figure 4.2 speaks to this question, depicting temporal patterns in case outcomes. This figure should be interpreted with caution because year-on-year changes can be large as the number of judgments in any given year is relatively small. This is especially the case in the first five years. For example, the deference rate was zero in 2008 and 100 percent in 2009, but this apparent surge in deference occurred because there was only one judgment in each of these years. There is also a gap in the figure because there were no final judgments in 2010.

Changes in deference, nonetheless, are easier to discern from 2011 onward. Three main observations can be made. First, the EACJ's tendency to defer to states is relatively consistent over time. This is depicted in Figure 4.2, which shows deference to states is equal to or higher than the total deference rate in most years since 2011 and does not drop below 50 percent. In fact, the average yearly *state deference rate* (including cases against states only) for the 2010s is 72 percent, suggesting that states receive a favorable outcome in close to three out of every four judgments.

Second, applicants fare slightly better, and states less so, if the Court considers the merits of a case. Figure 4.2 shows that the merits deference rate is lower than total deference in all years. On average, the yearly merits deference rate is 55 percent and does not surpass 70 percent from 2010 onward, although it never drops below 40 percent. Last, we can see a slight downward trend in deference from 2012 to 2018.

While the EACJ defers more than it does not, it does not overtly succumb to political pressures or blindly rule in favor of states: The Court has refused to abstain in numerous instances, and it has declined to validate a state's or the EAC's exercise of authority at times. As the section "Legal Interpretation and Deferential Reasoning" shows, the Court's legal interpretations and reasoning is sometimes nondeferential.

Legal Interpretations and Deferential Reasoning

The EACJ has adopted nondeferential interpretations in some notable instances. For example, the Court has twice declined to validate the Treaty amendments adopted by the EAC Summit in 2006, in one case for a failure to conduct a public consultation prior to adoption[55] and the other because the amendments undermine the supremacy of the EACJ.[56] In the first of these cases, the Court addressed the question of whether Article 30 of the Amended EAC Treaty permitted private litigants to refer cases against Community organs to the EACJ. Article 30(1) does not expressly include EAC "organs" among the entities against which private litigants can allege infringement. The respondents to the case urged the Court:

> to interpret the provisions of Article 30 of the Treaty strictly, and not to construe them as impugned on the sovereignty of the Partner States; emphasizing that under that article, only an Act, regulation, directive, decision or action of a single Partner State or an institution of the Community may be challenged; but not that of an organ of the Community. He argued that to the extent that in this reference the applicants challenge the legality of the decision of the Summit to amend the Treaty, the reference does not fall within the ambit of Article 30 and is therefore not properly before this Court.[57]

[55] *EALS & Ors. v Kenya & Ors.*, Ref. 3/2007.

[56] *East African Centre for Trade Policy and Law v The Secretary General of the East African Community*, Reference No. 9/2012, EACJ (May 9, 2013).

[57] *EALS & Ors. v Kenya & Ors.*, Ref. 3/2007, 10–11.

States made clear to the Court in their arguments that anything other than a narrow interpretation of Article 30 would impose on their sovereignty. The Court nonetheless rejected the respondents' preferred interpretation. It stated: "we are not persuaded by the respondents' urging that we give to Article 30, a narrow interpretation that excludes from the application of the Article, infringement of the Treaty by an organ of the Community. With due respect to learned counsel, it seems to us that such a restrictive interpretation is not based on a sound ground."[58] In this instance, the Court eschewed restrictive interpretation and instead embraced a purposive interpretation that permits private litigants to sue Community organs.

Previous scholarship identifies other notable instances where the Court adopted nondeferential interpretations of its jurisdiction.[59] For example, Gathii calls the Court's judgment in *Katabazi* "mission creep" because it declared it indirectly had jurisdiction over human rights, the rule of law, and good governance.[60] *Katabazi* concerned fourteen Ugandans who were granted bail by the High Court of Uganda and then promptly rearrested by security personnel in defiance of the High Court.[61] The arrestees were then taken before a military court martial, charged with possession of firearms and terrorism. The Ugandan Constitutional Court declared their detention unconstitutional and ordered their release. After the Government failed to comply, the applicants filed a complaint with the EACJ, claiming that the re-arrests, charges, and detention violated Articles 6 and 7 of the EAC Treaty, which commit member states to objectives and principles of human rights and the rule of law.[62] The EACJ ruled that it had jurisdiction to hear the case, even though the Treaty did not expressly grant it human rights jurisdiction and reserved the authority to expand the jurisdiction of the Court, including for human rights issues, to states.[63] The Court

58 Ibid., 15.

59 James Gathii, "Mission Creep or a Search for Relevance: The East African Court of Justice's Human Rights Strategy," *Duke Journal of Comparative & International Law* 24, no. 2 (2013); James Thuo Gathii, "Saving the Serengeti: Africa's New International Judicial Environmentalism," *Chicago Journal of International Law* 16, no. 2 (2016).

60 Gathii, "Mission Creep or a Search for Relevance."

61 *James Katabazi & 21 Others v The Secretary General of the East African Community & The Attorney General of the Republic of Uganda*, Reference No. 1/2007, EACJ (October 31, 2007) [herein *Katabazi v EAC & Uganda*, Ref. 1/2007].

62 The claim cited Article 6, 7(2), and 8(1)(c) of the EAC Treaty.

63 Amended EAC Treaty, Art. 27(2).

found the case nevertheless concerned the interpretation of the EAC Treaty because the Community and states committed to objectives and principles of human rights and the rule of law according to Article 6(d) and 7(2). For this reason, the EACJ would not "abdicate from exercising its jurisdiction of interpretation [of the Treaty] ... merely because the reference includes allegation of human rights violation."[64] By rejecting a restrictive interpretation of its jurisdiction, the Court refused to abstain from reviewing how states exercise their authority relating to human rights. This essentially rebuffed states' earlier decision to exclude human rights from the EACJ's jurisdiction.[65]

While *Katabazi* and a few other judgments are exemplars of nondeferential interpretation and reasoning, they are exceptional. In fact, the EACJ employed restrictive interpretation in the aftermath of *Katabazi* to mitigate its impact, notably in the *Independent Medical Legal Unit* case.[66] In this case, the complainant alleged that Kenya and the EAC failed to prevent, investigate, and punish the execution, torture, cruelty, and inhuman and degrading treatment of over 3,000 residents in the Mount Elgon region between 2006 and 2008. The Kenyan government challenged the EACJ's jurisdiction to hear the case, among other things, based on the time limitation imposed by Article 30(2) of the Amended EAC Treaty. This provision asserts that individual complaints "shall be instituted within two months" of the alleged violation.[67] The EACJ's First Instance Division on July 29, 2011, ruled against Kenya, reasoning that "the matters complained of are failures in a whole continuous chain of events from when the alleged violations started until the Claimant decided that the Republic of Kenya had failed to provide any remedy for the alleged violations."[68] This decision drew on the concept of a "continuous violation" which is a widely recognized principle in international human rights law.

Kenya appealed this ruling, and the Appellate Division reversed the First Instance Division's decision, dismissing the complaint as time-barred according to Article 30(2). The Appellate Division argued:

64 *Katabazi v EAC & Uganda*, Ref. 1/2007, 16.

65 Taye, "The Role of the East African Court of Justice in the Advancement of Human Rights," 360.

66 *Independent Medical Legal Unit v The Attorney General of the Republic of Kenya & 4 Others*, Reference No. 3/2010, EACJ (July 20, 2011) [herein *IMLU v Kenya*, Ref. 3/2010].

67 Amended EAC Treaty, Art. 30(2).

68 *IMLU v Kenya*, Ref. 3/2010, 10.

> In our view, there is no enabling provision in the Treaty to disregard the time limit set by Article 30(2). Moreover, that Article does not recognize any continuing breach or violation of the Treaty outside the two months after a relevant action comes to the knowledge of the Claimant; nor is there any power to extend that time limit . . . Again, no such intention can be ascertained from the ordinary and plain meaning of the said Article or any other provision of the Treaty.[69]

The Appellate Division deferred to states; it relied on restrictive interpretation to abstain as much as possible from imposing on states' sovereignty. The EACJ's interpretation, in essence, accepted the states' decision to limit the Court jurisdiction – as reflected in Article 30(2) – when they amended the Treaty in 2006.

The restrictive interpretation of Article 30(2) has been significant. While the *Katabazi* case potentially "opened the flood gates" and extended the authority of the EACJ, the outcome of the *Independent Medical Legal Unit* case minimized the effects of *Katabazi*. Since then, the Court has consistently applied the same narrow interpretation of the two-month time limit, making successful application to the EACJ exceedingly difficult.[70] This was especially the case in the years immediately following the Appellate Division's judgment. My data reveal that twelve applications have been time-barred from review by the Court. In several other instances, the Court found that some, but not all, of an applicant's claims were time-barred.[71]

Other important decisions of the Court reflect deference through interpretation. For instance, the Appellate Division relied on restrictive interpretation to determine the EACJ's ratione personae jurisdiction, or rules on standing, for a nonresident citizen.[72] The Appellate Division interpreted Article 30(1) of the EAC Treaty, which provides that "any person who is resident in a Partner State may refer for determination by the Court" a complaint of an alleged Treaty violation by a state or EAC institution. The Court determined that this provision guarantees jurisdiction of the Court only if the complainant resides in a member state,

[69] *Attorney General of the Republic of Kenya v Independent Medical Legal Unit,* Appeal No. 1/2011, EACJ (March 15, 2012) [herein *Kenya v IMLU,* Appeal 1/2011], 17.

[70] Interview 13.

[71] See for example, *Ronald Ssembuusi v The Attorney General of the Republic of Uganda,* Reference No. 16/2014, EACJ (November 23, 2020).

[72] *Manariyo Desire v The Attorney General of the Republic of Burundi,* Appeal No. 1/2017, EACJ (November 28, 2018) [herein *Desire v Burundi,* Appeal 1/2017]. In this matter, the EACJ speaks of ratione personae jurisdiction and standing interchangeably.

and therefore excludes from the jurisdiction of the Court any reference from nonresident citizens.[73] Based on the ordinary meaning, the Court concluded that "the word 'resident' as used in Art. 30(1) cannot be construed to mean that it was intended by the drafters of the Treaty to engraft 'non-resident citizens' of EAC Partner States as part of the phrase '. . . any person who is resident in a Partner State'."[74] The Court further argued that this interpretation would not be absurd or unreasonable results or effects that are counter to the object and purpose of the Treaty. The exclusion of nonresident citizens from the right to petition the EACJ is significant, as the Court has been increasingly used by opposition politicians or regime opponents to seek redress,[75] and it is not uncommon for members of the opposition to be in exile.[76]

Some members of the Court, in fact, called this interpretation restrictive, when they issued the first dissenting opinion the EACJ had ever seen (two of five judges dissented). The dissenting judges contended that the majority's interpretation was "narrow and restrictive . . . and amounts to a retrogressive and backward move in Treaty interpretation for this Court."[77] They argued that Treaty was created to benefit the East African people and therefore empowered them to challenge infringements before the Court. As such, "it could not have been the intention of the framers of the Treaty that access to justice under the Treaty would be unequal or disproportionate."[78] A good faith interpretation would require the Court to consider the object and purpose of the Treaty. As the dissent argues, "it follows therefore that a Good Faith interpretation does not import a simple literal interpretation of words and terms as would be had from a dictionary, but rather a consideration of those terms and words in light of the object and purpose of the Treaty."[79] Ultimately, the Court's interpretation restricted access to the EACJ, requiring the Court to abstain from exercising its authority more often than it would have otherwise.

A closer look at legal reasoning reveals EACJ's scrutiny is usually light, as the Court often concludes the EAC Treaty reserves discretion for states

[73] Ibid.
[74] Ibid., para. 44.
[75] Gathii, "International Courts as Coordination Devices for Opposition Parties."
[76] Ntagahoraho Z. Burihabwa and Devon E. A. Curtis, "Postwar Statebuilding in Burundi: Ruling Party Elites and Illiberal Peace," *International Affairs* 97, no. 4 (2021).
[77] *Desire v Burundi* (Dissenting opinion), Appeal 1/2017, para. 2.
[78] Ibid., para. 27.
[79] Ibid., para. 29.

or complainants have not met evidentiary standards. I identify sixteen instances of deference arising from an interpretation that the EAC Treaty reserves discretion for states, typically because the Treaty is silent on the matter. The Court also applies high evidentiary standards, which Shirlow argues "can be used to restrict the circumstances in which an international court or tribunal will review domestic acts, thereby expanding the decision-making autonomy of particular domestic actors."[80] Thus, the EACJ's high evidentiary standards can be viewed as a mode of deference; I find fifteen cases where deference arose from high standards of evidence. In one of these cases, the Court was asked to determine whether Uganda's repression of the peaceful "walk to work" protests in 2011 violated the state's obligation to respect human rights. The Court's approach to the issue was to address the evidence. Even though the brutality of the protests were noted by both local and international media, and shamed by organizations such as Human Rights Watch, the Court concluded newspaper cuttings were not properly tended as evidence, that the Court could not rely on the notoriety of events as evidence, and the Court rejected video evidence because its authenticity was not proven by the applicants. Witness testimony was also insufficient as no evidence was provided to confirm the veracity of their testimonies. For example, the applicants did not provide medical records documenting personal injuries.[81]

While deference is often based on reasons of state discretion or inadequate evidence, I find several cases where the Court decided state action was reasonable or that the Court has limits to its power based on a "work-to-rule" or restrictive interpretation. The Court rarely applies intense scrutiny based on practices of, for instance, balancing, proportionality assessments, or a margin of appreciation. All in all, the evidence suggests that the Court's methods of interpretation and reasoning are more deferential than not, irrespective of case outcome.

Remedies

The EACJ rules in favor of states in most judgments and tends to rely on restrictive or "work-to-rule" interpretations or relaxed scrutiny. Do the Court's remedies similarly reflect deference? The EAC Treaty and the

80 Shirlow, *Judging at the Interface*, 167.

81 *East Africa Law Society vs The Attorney General of Uganda & the Secretary General of the EAC*, Reference No. 2/ 2011, EACJ (March 28, 2018).

Table 4.3 *Summary of EACJ's remedies (2006–2020)*

Type of remedy	Number of instances
Declaratory judgments	30
. With one additional remedy = 16 (53%)	
. With two additional remedies = 2 (7%)	
Reparations	7
. Against EAC = 2	
Consequential orders	14
. Against EAC = 2	
. Against state* = 10	
. Against state and EAC = 2	
Remit to FI in favor of applicant	3

* In one instance, a consequential order was delivered without a declaratory judgment.

Note: Judgments can have more than one remedy type. The coding included up to four per case. This does not include cost awards. Some declaratory judgments are against both the state respondent(s) and the EAC.

EACJ Rules of Procedure permit a wide range of remedies and do not explicitly limit the Court's remedial powers. An analysis of the remedial orders reveals that the EACJ has used the full range of its powers, and it frequently shows nondeference to states through its remedies for successful litigants.

Table 4.3 summarizes the remedial orders delivered by the EACJ. As shown, the most common remedy is declaratory orders, which the Court delivered in all thirty cases where it found a violation (as we would expect). In sixteen of these, or 53 percent, the Court issued one additional remedy. In two cases, representing 7 percent of instances where a breach was declared, the Court ordered two additional remedies. The additional remedies included reparations, like compensation or restitution, which the EACJ ordered in seven cases. They also included consequential orders, which is the type of remedy that intrudes most on state sovereignty. Consequential orders are the EACJ's second most common remedy, after declaratory judgments. The EACJ has given consequential orders in thirteen instances, or 43 percent of cases where a violation is found. It has also issued a consequential order in one case where it did not declare a violation.[82] Also noteworthy, the EACJ issued consequential orders against the EAC and states at similar rates. Among the cases in which the EAC was found to have failed in its obligation, the EACJ delivered a consequential order in 44 percent. Similarly, the Court delivered a consequential order in 46 percent of cases where a state was found to be in violation. Additionally, the Appellate Division gave remedies in the form of remanding references to the First Instance Division in three cases. There were also three cases in which the EACJ granted interim orders (temporary injunction),[83] although applicants requested them in twelve other cases included in the data (not shown in Table 4.3).

Table 4.4 describes the Court's consequential orders. It shows that most of the EACJ's consequential orders against states mandate changes to domestic law or policy, while two of the four orders against the EAC require the Secretary General to investigate or carry out fact-finding inquiries related to alleged failures of states. Table 4.4 also shows that the EACJ tempers the intrusiveness of its remedies at times, as seen by its use of prospective annulment. These consequential orders apply prospectively only. In other words, these orders signal some deference because they do not reverse or invalidate past decisions, but rather set expectations for future action. For instance, in *East African Law Society & Others v Kenya & Others*,[84] the Court declared that the states had not followed correct procedures when amending the EAC Treaty by failing to hold public consultations. The Court nonetheless did not void the relevant amendments. Rather, it said that public consultations were necessary for any future amendments. The *Serengeti*[85] case is another instance

[82] *Democratic Party & Mukasa Mbidde v The Secretary General of the East African Community & The Attorney General of the Republic of Uganda*, Reference No. 6/2011, EACJ (May 9, 2012) [herein *Democratic Party & Mbidde v EAC & Uganda*, Ref. 6/2011]. The EACJ did not declare a violation because a domestic court had already declared the impugned rules null and void, and amendments were ongoing. The EACJ, however, proscribed Uganda from using the impugned rules for future EALA elections.

[83] *Bonaventure Gasutwa & 2 Others v The Attorney General of the Republic of Burundi*, Reference No. 13/2014, EACJ (November 26, 2015); *Democratic Party & Mbidde v EAC & Uganda*, Ref. 6/2011; *Prof. Peter Anyang' Nyong'o & 10 Others v The Attorney General of Kenya & 5 Others*, Reference No. 1/2006, EACJ (March 29, 2007) [herein *Anyang' Nyong'o v Kenya & Ors.*, Ref. 1/2006].

[84] *EALS & Ors. v Kenya & Ors.*, Ref. 3/2007.

[85] *African Network for Animal Welfare v The Attorney General of the United Republic of Tanzania*, Reference No. 9/2010, EACJ (June 20, 2014) [herein *ANAW v Tanzania*, Ref. 9/2010].

Table 4.4 *Summary of EACJ's consequential orders*

Orders against state only	
Mandates change to domestic law or policy	• *Mohochi v Uganda*, Ref. 5/2011: orders relevant provision of Citizenship and Immigration Control Act inoperative, when pertaining to EAC citizens. • *Anita v Uganda & EAC*, Ref. 6/2012: orders state to amend rules of procedure for election of EALA members. • *Burundi Journalist Union v Burundi*, Ref. 7/2013: orders state to take measures to implement judgment, indirectly specifying what provisions must be repealed. • *Raphael & Anor v Burundi*, Ref. 15/2014: ordering state "to cause the amendment of Article 5 of Act No. 1/26 within its internal legal mechanisms." • *Media Council of Tanzania v Ors. v Tanzania*, Ref. 2/2017: orders state "to take such measures as are necessary, to bring the Media Services Act, into compliance" with EAC Treaty. • *Mseto & Anor. v Tanzania*, Ref. 7/2016: orders the government minister "to annul the order forthwith and allow the Applicant to resume publication." • *BAT Ltd. v Uganda*, Ref. 7/2017: orders state to interpret and apply law in accord with EAC law and to align tax laws with Community law applicable to goods from EAC states. • *Democratic Party & Mbidde v EAC & Uganda*, Ref. 6/2011: bars state from electing members of EALA until law amended, even though no violation was declared; dismissed EAC of wrongdoing.
Prospective application	• *ANAW v Tanzania*, Ref. 9/2010: orders state to refrain "from operationalising its initial proposal or proposed action of constructing or maintaining a road of bitumen standard across the Serengeti National Park subject to its right to undertake such other programmes or initiate policies in the future which would not have a negative impact on the environment and ecosystem." • *Tanzania v ANAW*, Appeal 3/2014: upholds permanent injunction.

Orders against state(s) and EAC	
Prospective application	• *EALS & Ors. v Kenya & Ors.*, Ref. 3/2007: orders public consultations for future amendments to EAC Treaty.
Administrative action; discretion for state	• *EALS v Burundi & EAC*, Ref. 1/2014: orders Secretary General of EAC "to immediately operationalize the Task Force . . . to investigate alleged violations of Treaty" and state "to take, without delay, the measures required to implement th[e] judgment, including allowing the Secretary General's Task Force to carry out its investigative mission."
Orders against EAC only	
Prospective application	• *Mwatela & Ors. v EAC*, App. 1/2005: annuls contested decisions of Council, without retrospective effect, and any future decisions where Council not properly constituted.
Administrative action	• *EALS v EAC*, Ref. 7/2014: orders Secretary General "to submit to. . .the Council of Ministers for consideration, the findings and recommendations of the factfinding mission."

Note: Case names are listed in short form. See Appendix for full citation.

where an order had only prospective application. In this case, the EACJ issued a permanent injunction against Tanzania, preventing the state from constructing a paved road through the Serengeti National Park. Ostensibly, this order significantly intruded on Tanzania's sovereignty; however, the Tanzanian government had already abandoned its plan to pave a road when the injunction was issued.[86] While the Court did limit action going forward, it was also cautious to recognize that the state could pursue future initiatives, so long as there was no negative environmental impact. Put differently, it left some discretion to the government. In the appeal that followed, the Appellate Division upheld

[86] Ibid.; see also Gathii, "Saving the Serengeti," 407.

the permanent injunction (the data counts this as another consequential order).[87]

The Court has occasionally left some degree of discretion to states on how to remedy a wrong. Most notably, in *East Africa Law Society v Attorney General of Burundi*,[88] the Court responded to allegations that Burundi had violated rule of law principles by disbarring without due process an attorney who had criticized the government. The Court ruled in favor of the applicant and ordered the government to take measures to implement the judgment. The Court, however, did not specify what these measures should be, and importantly did not say the government must reinstate the lawyer to the bar. In other instances, when the Court mandated changes to domestic law or policy, it has done so with varying degrees of intervention.

To summarize, the EACJ's remedial orders paint a somewhat different picture about deference. On remedies, the EACJ is less acceptant of the state or EAC's exercise of authority. Nonetheless, there is a perception that its remedies are limited and that the Court exercises restraint in orders.[89] This perception may reflect how the consequential orders give some discretion to states.

Explaining the East African Court's Substantial Deference

Despite notable instances of nondeference, the EACJ's decisions show substantial levels of deference in terms of case outcomes and legal interpretation, and to a lesser degree remedies. How can we explain the Court's tendency to defer?

The Role of Support Networks

Previous scholarship suggests that support networks play a key role in determining whether ICs defer to states or not. An account based on the logic of support networks expects higher degrees of deference, such as that shown by the EACJ, when a court provides insufficient opportunities for supporters to access the Court, it fails to adequately mobilize

87 *The Attorney General of the United Republic of Tanzania v African Network for Animal Welfare*, Appeal No. 3/2014, EACJ (July 29, 2015) [herein *Tanzania v ANAW*, Appeal 3/2014].

88 *East African Law Society v The Attorney General of the Republic of Burundi & The Secretary General of the East African Community*, Reference No. 1/2014, EACJ (May 15, 2015).

89 Interview 27.

supporters or if its support network is weak or inactive. The following section assesses this logic by looking at the channels of access for supporters, the Court's efforts to mobilize potential supporters, and the strength and activity of its support network. It considers three types of supporters: private actors (e.g., nongovernmental actors, civil society, for-profit actors), substate actors (e.g., national courts), and supranational actors. It shows that the EACJ's support network is better situated than its deference would suggest based on the logic of support networks. Moreover, the greatest source of support for the EACJ comes from private actors, not substate or supranational actors.

The Court features several channels of access for its would-be supporters to utilize. First, private actors have direct access to petition the Court. The EAC Treaty entitles individuals or other private actors (NGOs, businesses, etc.) to directly petition the Court for determination of the legality of a state or EAC act or action.[90] The Court also has provisions for third-party access. Specifically, private actors can act as either amicus curiae or interveners before the EACJ,[91] although the Court must first grant them leave to intervene or submit an amicus curiae brief.[92] Last, private actors can indirectly access the Court through referrals for preliminary rulings from national courts. When questions of Community law arise in the context of domestic litigation, national courts are entitled to refer these issues for a preliminary ruling to the EACJ.[93]

Moreover, the Court has sought to mobilize its supporters and encourage their use of these channels of access. Important aspects of the Court's jurisprudence are pro-litigant and expand opportunities for private actors to access the Court. The EACJ has asserted its willingness to review complaints that involve alleged violations of the principles of good governance, rule of law, and human rights.[94] It has also determined

[90] Amended EAC Treaty, Art. 30. There is no requirement that domestic remedies are first exhausted.

[91] Ibid., Art. 40.

[92] The Court has not always granted access for amici. For example, the Court rejected amicus curiae applications from the UHAI EASHRI, due to a lack of neutrality, and the Health Development Initiative-Rwanda, for its lack of interest; see Applications No. 20 & 21/2014, arising from *Human Rights Awareness and Promotion Forum v The Attorney General of the Republic of Uganda*, Reference No. 6/2014, EACJ (September 27, 2016).

[93] Amended EAC Treaty, Art. 34.

[94] *Katabazi v EAC & Uganda*, Ref. 1/2007.

that it can review environmental disputes.[95] The Court's awards on costs (i.e., recoverable expenses of litigation, such as lawyers' fees and payments to expert witnesses) have also been pro-litigant at times. For instance, the Court has adopted the practice of not awarding costs in public interest litigation. It has also determined that it will consider an applicant's hardship, such of loss of employment, when deciding whether to award costs to litigants.[96]

The EACJ has also made structural reforms, with the support of member states, to facilitate access and cultivate its support network. In 2013, the EACJ's rules were amended to remove filing fees.[97] Sub-registries were also created in 2010, at the request of the EACJ.[98] The first sub-registry opened in 2012, and currently there is a sub-registry in the capital of five partner states. (There is not yet one in South Sudan or the DRC.) Prior to having the sub-registries, the only way to file a complaint was to travel to the EACJ registry in Arusha and file there. For most private actors, namely, individuals, this was prohibitive to filing a complaint. The sub-registries thus are important contact points for stakeholders, which enhance the accessibility and visibility of the Court.[99]

The EACJ has worked to mobilize actors through its outreach, or "off-the-bench," activities. For example, it has hosted numerous workshops with lawyers, national judges, and civil society organizations.[100] Likewise, these organizations invite representatives of the Court to participate in their activities.[101] The Court also produces material to improve information about how to access and use the Court. For instance, it has published a user guide and manual.[102]

[95] *ANAW v Tanzania*, Ref. 9/2010; *Tanzania v ANAW*, Appeal 3/2014.

[96] *Eric Kabalisa Makala v The Attorney General of the Republic of Rwanda*, Reference No. 1/2017, EACJ (June 18, 2020).

[97] EAC, *EACJ Rules of Procedure 2013*, Legal Notices Supplement No. 1 to the East African Community Gazette No. 7 (Arusha: EAC, 2013); EAC, *EACJ Rules of Procedure 2004*, Rule 82 (Arusha: EAC, 2004). See also EACJ, *Court Manual: A Practical Guide to the Law and Practice of the East African Court of Justice* (Arusha: EACJ, 2020): 21, accessed August 18, 2024, www.eacj.org/wp-content/uploads/2023/02/EACJ-Manual.pdf.

[98] John Eudes Ruhangisa, "The East African Court of Justice: Ten Years of Operation (Achievements and Challenges)," Sensitisation Workshop on the Role of the EACJ in the EAC Integration (Kampala, November 2, 2011), accessed August 25, 2024, www.eacj.org/wp-content/uploads/2013/09/EACJ-Ten-Years-of-Operation.pdf.

[99] Interview 15; Interview 14.

[100] Interview 14.

[101] Interview 15.

[102] EACJ, *Court Manual.*

Table 4.5 *Legal counsel representing applicants at the EACJ*

	Number of cases	Percent
Repeat counsel	38	53.52
Not repeat	23	32.39
Unknown	6	8.45
Self-represented	4	5.63

Note: N = 71. Appeals and preliminary references are excluded.

Not only does the EACJ feature access opportunities and work to mobilize its support network, but its network is relatively active. In fact, the EACJ's support network has been responsible for a large portion of the cases brought to the Court, and in particular the Pan African Lawyers Union (PALU) and the EALS "have been very active in bringing cases . . . and they have actually kept [the Court] very busy."[103] Additionally, political elites, especially members of the political opposition within the member states, have also been active in utilizing the Court.[104] My data record the legal counsel in each case, when stated in the judgment. The data reveal that a significant portion of cases were litigated by a repeat lawyer, or a lawyer who served as counsel in at least one prior case before the EACJ. Table 4.5 illustrates what portion of cases are represented by a repeat lawyer at the First Instance Division. It excludes appeals because counsel does not typically change as cases progress to the appellate stage. Preliminary references are also excluded because private actors behind the domestic dispute do not have representation before the EACJ in these types of cases. As Table 4.5 shows, approximately 54 percent of cases were litigated by a repeat lawyer. In fact, eight lawyers alone acted as legal counsel across thirty-three disputes. Repeat lawyers thus are critical to litigation before the EACJ. NGOs have been applicants in nine cases excluding appeals and preliminary references. Also, a third party has been granted leave as either an amicus or an intervener in fourteen cases (15 percent of cases).[105] All in all, a support network is at the core of much of the Court's workload.

[103] Interview 15.

[104] Gathii, "International Courts as Coordination Devices for Opposition Parties."

[105] This excludes the one preliminary reference in my data. Observations were submitted in that case.

Table 4.6 *Cross-tabulations of EACJ's deference by support network*

	Repeat counsel		NGO participation	
Applicant wins	No	Yes	No	Yes
No (deferred)	14 (51.85)	26 (68.42)	44 (64.71)	17 (65.38)
Yes	13 (48.15)	12 (31.58)	24 (35.29)	9 (34.62)
	Fisher's Test p-value: 0.204 χ^2 p-value: 0.177 N = 65		Fisher's Test p-value: 1.000 χ^2 p-value: 0.951 N = 94	
Consequential order, if violation declared				
No (deferred)	8 (61.54)	5 (41.67)	16 (72.73)	1 (12.50)
Yes	5 (38.46)	7 (58.33)	6 (27.27)	7 (87.50)
	Fisher's Test p-value: 0.434 χ^2 p-value: 0.319 N = 25		Fisher's Test p-value: 0.009** χ^2 p-value: 0.002** N = 30	
Additional remedy, if violation declared				
No (deferred)	7 (53.85)	2 (16.67)	11 (50.00)	1 (12.50)
Yes	6 (46.15)	10 (83.33)	11 (50.00)	7 (87.50)
	Fisher's Test p-value: 0.097* χ^2 p-value: 0.048** N = 25		Fisher's Test p-value: 0.099* χ^2 p-value: 0.050** N = 30	

Note: *p < 0.10, **p < 0.05, ***p < 0.001. These data exclude cases in which the legal counsel is unknown and appeals judgments. In each cross-tabulation, the first number is the frequency and the second number (in parentheses) is the column percentage.

Can this support network account for the EACJ's deference? I test whether applicants win more often when cases involve a repeat lawyer or an NGO, as would be expected if a support network were a strong explanatory determinant of nondeference (see Table 4.6). The results are mixed. On the one hand, when cases are represented by repeat lawyers or NGOs participate (either as an applicant or a third party), the applicants are less successful than if no repeat lawyer or NGO participates. This finding runs counter to the expectations of a support network. On the other hand, the overall pattern on remedial orders lends evidence to the role of a judicial support network. Consequential orders were delivered in 58 percent of instances when a repeat lawyer was involved in contrast to

38 percent when there was no repeat lawyer. Similarly, when NGOs participate, 88 percent of decisions included a consequential order whereas only 27 percent of cases without NGO participation conclude with a consequential order. The same pattern is present when comparing the involvement of judicial supporters with whether the Court orders any remedy in addition to a declaratory judgment.

While it is quite telling that the EACJ is less deferential in terms of its remedial orders depending on the participation of its judicial support network, it is difficult to understand how the Court's decisions on outcomes and interpretation, which are more deferential, were driven by the role of support networks. Many of the case outcomes are the result of deferential standards of review. For instance, the Court has interpreted the law in ways that undermine access for would-be supporters. As described earlier, the restrictive interpretation of the two-month time limit for filing a case has led to several complaints being dismissed by the Court. Moreover, the decision in which this restrictive interpretation was adopted was a reference filed by an NGO and another NGO acted as an amicus.[106] As one interviewee expressed, "You can't take a case there anymore," suggesting how limiting the two-month rule is and how would-be supporters see opportunities with the Court.[107] A more recent decision relied on restrictive interpretation to exclude nonresident citizens from direct access to the Court; the applicant in this case was represented by a repeat lawyer.[108] The EACJ also penalizes unsuccessful applicants by rewarding legal costs to successful state respondents or the EAC if the case does not reflect a public interest in the eyes of the Court. I have recorded fourteen instances where the EACJ awarded costs to a state or the EAC at the expense of the private actor. Ultimately, the EACJ applies more deference in cases prior to arriving at the question of possible remedies, despite the participation of an active support network. If and when the Court does, however, conclude that it cannot defer to states on jurisdiction or the merits of the case, the support network provides some cover for its more intrusive remedies.

Finally, it is worth noting that the Court appears to have minimal support from substate actors, such as national judiciaries, and supranational actors. Domestic courts are disinclined to refer cases to the EACJ. By the end of 2020, there had only been one preliminary reference. While the reasons why domestic courts have not made more referrals are

[106] *Kenya v IMLU*, Appeal 1/2011.
[107] Interview 11.
[108] *Desire v Burundi*, Appeal 1/2017.

beyond the scope of this analysis, insufficient knowledge of the preliminary referral or the relevant EAC law by lower court judges or concurrent appointments may offer partial explanations.[109] Additionally, national court judges may believe that the EACJ poses a threat to themselves, or the courts they preside over. For instance, a referral may be viewed as ceding their otherwise limited power to a supranational court, or judges may fear political retribution from their executives for making a referral. Domestic courts within the EAC are often politically constrained by the executives,[110] and a referral would limit their ability to make regime friendly judgments when the political stakes are high. These explanations are speculative. Yet, it remains clear that domestic courts have so far been unable or unwilling to provide the EACJ with substate partnerships like that which have been documented for other international courts, such as the CJEU. Support from supranational actors, namely, the EAC Secretary General, is also unlikely. While the Secretary General can initiate proceedings if it finds a state has infringed its duties, it cannot refer the case to the Court on its own discretion but needs the support of the EAC Council (an intergovernmental organ). Thus, the EACJ is unlikely to find a supranational actor among its advocates. This is a marked difference to the CJEU.

In sum, to the extent that the Court demonstrates a willingness to not defer to states in terms of its remedies, the EACJ's support network, especially from private actors, may embolden it. However, other aspects of the EACJ's decision-making do not align with the expectation of a support network. In particular, the generally high levels of activity of the private actor contingent of a support network are not congruent with the EACJ's substantial deference on outcomes and legal interpretation. More aligned with the high levels of deference are, however, the inactivity or weakness of the EACJ's substate and supranational actors.

The Structural Determinants of the East African Court's Strategic Space

The previous discussion alluded to explanatory gaps that arise from the logic of support networks. Does the Court's strategic space fill these gaps? In what follows, I consider the structural determinants of the Court's

[109] Some judges have concurrent appointments on national high courts and the EACJ.

[110] VonDoepp and Ellett, "Reworking Strategic Models of Executive-Judicial Relations"; Masengu, "The Vulnerability of Judges in Contemporary Africa."

Table 4.7 *Rules constituting the formal independence of the EACJ*

	Independence enhancing	Independence hampering
Appointment and Terms of Office	• Seven-year term • Nonrenewable terms • Oath of office	• Judges elected by consensus • Removal of judges decided by states
Managerial autonomy	• Court adopts its rules of procedure	• States selects registrar and president • States decide on budget
Insulation of Judges	• Diplomatic privileges and immunities of office • Secret deliberations	

strategic space and their role in shaping the EACJ's substantial deference. I begin by examining the EACJ's formal independence.

Formal Independence

The comparative mapping of ICs' formal independence in Chapter 3 revealed that the EACJ is among the ICs with lowest levels of formal independence. Table 4.7 summarizes the rules that constitute the formal independence of the EACJ and whether they enhance or hamper independence. First among the rules that limit the Court's independence are those governing the selection of judges and their tenure. The Court can have a maximum of fifteen judges (ten for the First Instance Division and five for the Appellate Division),[111] who are selected by consensus of the Summit.[112] Selection by consensus allows any state to veto potential appointees. States also have the capacity to remove judges from office for misconduct, an inability to perform the duties of office, or criminal behavior. Removal can occur through two means: (1) the Summit can remove a judge upon the recommendation of an ad hoc tribunal appointed by the Summit for the purposes of adjudging fitness; or (2) the Summit can remove a judge if they have been removed from office domestically or resigns from office domestically following allegations of misconduct.[113] The provision about the removal of EACJ judges differs

[111] Amended EAC Treaty, Art. 24.
[112] Ibid., Art. 12 and 24.
[113] Ibid., Art. 26.

from other ICs, which tend to have the sitting judges of the court decide on the merits of a fellow judge's removal.

Second, rules pertaining to the Court's managerial autonomy weaken formal independence. The EACJ does not have formal input over the selection of its registrar, president (for Appellate Division) and principal judge (for the First Instance Division), or its budget. States through the Council of Ministers appoint the registrar,[114] and the Summit selects the president of the Court and the principal judge.[115] The Court's budget is proposed by the Secretariat of the EAC, which is then considered by the Council of Ministers and approved by the EALA.[116] There is no formal requirement that the Court be consulted on its budget.

In contrast to the rules that hamper independence, some governing rules enhance the EACJ's formal independence. Importantly, judges are elected to a seven-year (or until the age of seventy, whichever comes first), nonrenewable term.[117] Also, a degree of managerial autonomy is provided by the Court's ability to determine its own rules of procedure.[118] Last, the EACJ's independence is enhanced by rules that help to insulate judges from political pressure, namely, judges enjoy diplomatic privileges[119] and are "immune from legal action for any act or omission committed in the discharge of their judicial functions,"[120] and the Court's decisions are "reached in private."[121]

While distinct from independence, I also mention two rules that relate to impartiality. First, judges must recuse themselves from hearing cases in which they were previously involved or in which they have a conflict of interest.[122] Second, the Summit on the recommendation of the Council determines the salary and conditions of service for EACJ judges, which are otherwise not mentioned in the Treaty.[123]

On the whole, key elements of the EACJ's safeguards to independence are weak, making the Court potentially vulnerable to political pressure from states. The formal rules provide states with an arsenal of formal

[114] Ibid., Art. 45.
[115] Ibid., Art. 24(4) and (5).
[116] Ibid., Art. 132; see also Art. 14, 71, and 71.
[117] Ibid., Art. 25(1) and (2).
[118] Ibid., Art. 42(1).
[119] Ibid., Art. 138.
[120] Ibid., Art. 43(1).
[121] Ibid., Art. 35(2).
[122] Ibid., Art. 26(6).
[123] Ibid., Art. 25(5).

mechanisms, both ex ante and ex post, to employ against the Court if they wished to do so. Moreover, these rules have a bearing on how the Court is perceived. Two rules in particular have been the subject of controversy and criticism. First, politicians, the media, regional lawyers, and even the Court itself have criticized the rules governing the removal of EACJ judges. The EAC Treaty was amended in 2006, in an episode of "backlash" against the Court. Among the rules modified were those related to the removal of judges. Article 26 of the original EAC Treaty from 1999, provided:

(1) *The President of the Court or other Judge shall not be removed from office except by the Summit for misconduct or for inability to perform the functions of his or her office due to infirmity of mind or body.*
(2) *Notwithstanding the provisions of paragraph 1 of this Article, a Judge of the Court shall only be removed from office if the question of his or her removal from office has been referred to an ad hoc independent tribunal appointed for this purpose by the Summit and the tribunal has recommended that the Judge be removed from office for misconduct or inability to perform the functions of his or her office.*
(3) *The tribunal appointed under paragraph 2 of this Article shall consist of three eminent Judges drawn from within the Commonwealth of Nations.*

According to the original Treaty, states controlled the removal of judges, upon the recommendation of a tribunal for misconduct or infirmity. In 2006, the Treaty was amended to increase states' control over the removal of judges. The revisions were widely seen as a maneuver by Kenya to punish the Court, and two of its appointees, for the EACJ's decision in the *Anyang Nyong'o* case,[124] which halted Kenya's selection of members for the EALA. Article 26 of the Revised Treaty states that:

1. *A Judge shall not be removed from office except by the Summit –*

   (a) *for misconduct or for inability to perform the functions of his or her office due to infirmity of mind or body;*

   Provided that a Judge shall only be removed from office under this subparagraph if the question of his or her removal from office

[124] Bernard Namunane, "Leaders Petitioned Over Regional Court," *The Nation*, December 19, 2006; Ernest Mpinganjira, "Lawyers Protest Move to Weaken Regional Court," *The East African Standard*, December 19, 2006. See also *Anyang' Nyong'o v Kenya & Ors.*, Ref. 1/2006.

has been referred to an ad hoc independent tribunal appointed for this purpose by the Summit and the tribunal has recommended that the Judge be removed from office for misconduct or inability to perform the functions of his or her office; or

(b) in the case of a Judge who also holds judicial office or other public office in a Partner State–

(i) is removed from that office for misconduct or due to inability to perform the functions of the office for any reason; or

(ii) resigns from that office following allegation of misconduct or of inability to perform the functions of the office for any reason;

(c) if the Judge is adjudged bankrupt under any law in force in a Partner State; or

(d) if the Judge is convicted of an offence involving dishonesty or fraud or moral turpitude under any law in force in a Partner State.

The most notable part of the revised provision is paragraph (b) to (d), which allows any state to remove a judge from office by using domestic channels. Local elites openly criticized the amended article, viewing it as a way for states to unilaterally remove judges simply by indicting a sitting judge within their national jurisdiction. For instance, the President of the EALS, Tom Ojienda, said, "'the amendments, among other things, provide that EACJ judges automatically surrender their positions upon being indicted in their countries'... He added the reforms pursued by Kenya 'constituted a travesty of judicial independence and a threat to regional integration within the EAC'."[125] Similarly, the then Deputy Secretary General of the EALS, Otiende Amollo, told the media that the changes were "unwarranted and could lead to emasculation of the Judiciary by the Executive."[126] In an opinion piece, one regional lawyer claimed, "The decision means that the judges will be in office only at the mercy of their respective presidents, which will amount to absence of security of tenure. Once this is done, the EACJ will have graduated into a toothless watchdog, incapable of deciding against their governments."[127] A Kenyan opposition politician at the time, Joseph Kamotho, wrote in an opinion piece in a local newspaper that "From the look of things, there is an

[125] Ibid.

[126] Mpinganjira, "Lawyers Protest Move to Weaken Regional Court."

[127] Abudu Sallam Waiswa, "EACJ—Kenya's Move Shows Political Immaturity," *The East African*, January 2, 2007.

attempt to subjugate the jurisdiction of the court to that of member states. That could prove problematic in the long run."[128]

The Court itself has criticized the new provisions on the removal of judges. When the EACJ was presented with a case contesting the validity of the Treaty amendments, it argued, "The introduction of automatic removal and suspension on grounds raised or established in the home State, and applicable to only those in judicial or public office, makes possibilities of applying un-uniform standards to judges of the same court endanger the integrity of the Court as a regional court."[129] The EACJ's strategic plan identified some of the rules related to formal independence as source of its weakness. In particular, the 2010–15 strategic plan listed the "lack of security of tenure of judges" as a weakness.[130] To my knowledge, there has been one incident where a judge has been removed from the Court. Justice Moijo ole Keiwua from Kenya was suspended from the EACJ in 2007 following his removal from the bench in Kenya after facing allegations of corruption, which was enabled by the amendments to the Treaty.[131] All in all, the rules on the removal of judges have undermined the Court's safeguards from political interference, which tarnishes societal perceptions about the Court.

Another important aspect of the Court's formal independence that has had a notable impact on how the Court is viewed are the rules related to its managerial autonomy. Political elites have expressed dissatisfaction with the current rules and advocated for greater financial and administrative autonomy for the Court. For instance, the EAC Development Strategy for 2006–10 called for financial autonomy for the EACJ.[132] Similarly, the EALA recommended the EAC Summit pass the "Administration of the EACJ Bill of 2016,"[133] which aimed to strengthen the independence of the EACJ by, among other things, giving the Court greater say in the allocation of its financial resources. The Court also identified its lack of managerial autonomy as problematic for its

[128] Joseph Kamotho, "Changes to the EAC Treaty Unwise," *The Nation*, January 25, 2007.

[129] *EALS & Ors. v Kenya & Ors.*, Ref. 3/2007, 45.

[130] EACJ, *Strategic Plan: 2010–2015* (Arusha: EACJ, 2010), 21.

[131] David Mugonyi, "Kenya Removes Judge from Arusha Court," *The Nation*, March 20, 2007.

[132] EAC, *EAC Development Strategy: 2006–2010* (Arusha: EAC, 2006): 90, accessed June 18, 2024, http://repository.eac.int/bitstream/handle/11671/214/3rd-EAC-Development-Strategy.pdf?sequence=1&isAllowed=y.

[133] EAC, *Bills Supplement*, No. 9 of November 18, 2016 (Arusha: EAC, 2016), accessed June 18, 2024, www.eala.org/uploads/EACJ_bill2.pdf.

independence and performance, and it has lobbied states to increase the EACJ's managerial autonomy. For example, its Strategic Plan of 2018–23 recognized that its capacity was limited by not having financial or administrative autonomy.[134] In 2021, the President of the Court, Justice Nestor Kayobera, told the media that "financial autonomy would also boost the independence of the Court."[135] The previous President of the Court, Emmanuel Ugirashebuja, similarly went to the press in 2020, arguing that financial autonomy would "give the Court financial muscle to carry its activities independently."[136]

The situation remains unchanged into 2024, and the current President of the Court continues to press for increased financial and administrative autonomy. President Kayobera, when speaking at an event in Kampala, said: "The other arms of the EAC have independence. We need the EACJ to have financial and administrative autonomy to discharge our mandate properly."[137] While these pleas have been ongoing, the Court's limited budget and need to go to states to ask for budgetary autonomy have an impact on how the Court is perceived by its stakeholders. As one interviewee explained, sometimes the Court has to go begging the heads of state, and "that ruins the credibility of the Court."[138]

The EACJ's rules related to managerial autonomy and the selection and removal of judges curtail its independence. While these rules negatively affect the perceived legitimacy of the Court, they are unlikely to chill judicial decision-making on their own. Rather, the coupling of these rules with a politically aligned, or unfragmented, membership gives the Court greater reason to anticipate and view coordinated state resistance as credible.

Political Fragmentation

I have shown that the EACJ delivers judgments under constraints imposed by its formal rules. These rules both provide channels for political interference and weaken the Court's legitimacy in the eyes of

134 EACJ, *Strategic Plan: 2018–2023* (Arusha: EACJ, 2018), accessed June 18, 2024, www.eacj.org/?page_id=1359.

135 Quoted in Zephania Ubwani, "Why Financial Autonomy 'Is Good' for EACJ," *The Citizen*, July 5, 2021.

136 President Justice Emmanuel Ugirashebuja quoted in Zephania Ubwani, "Why East African Court Wants More Financial Freedom," *The Citizen*, December 7, 2020.

137 Quoted in Jackson Mutinda, "EACJ President Nestor Kayobera Says Court Needs More Autonomy," *The East African*, October 26, 2022.

138 Interview 27.

its stakeholders. While the formal rules constrain the Court, my core argument also expects political fragmentation to affect decision-making. Specifically, I have posited that deference and fragmentation have a negative relationship (H_2). Fragmentation, understood as heterogeneous preferences among member states, reduces the feasibility and credibility of collective state resistance. This begs the question: Do we observe a negative relationship between deference and fragmentation in the case of the EACJ?

To address this question, I identify three issues that have been repeatedly addressed by the EACJ. The issues are: (1) press freedom, (2) freedom of association, and (3) due process guarantees. I select these issues because the Court has addressed them in more than one of its merits decisions and corresponding data are available for measuring fragmentation. The issues that meet these criteria are limited. Table 4.8 catalogs the EACJ's decisions on these issues. It shows that the EACJ did not defer on issues of press freedom (2015–19), but that it did on the freedom of association (2018–19). On due process, the Court did not defer between 2012 and mid-2018, but thereafter it began to defer. The table also specifies the theoretically expected level of fragmentation, based on H_2, in each case: Where deference is absent, we expect to observe high fragmentation, and when the Court deferred, fragmentation should be low. The final column shows the actual degree of fragmentation.

To measure fragmentation, or preference heterogeneity, I use V-Dem data, inferring preferences from state practice.[139] I rely on three V-Dem indicators to capture preferences on each of the selected issues: *government censorship effort* as an indicator of state preferences on press freedom, *civil society repression* for freedom of association, and *transparent laws with predictable enforcement* for due process guarantees.[140] For each of the indicators, I calculate the yearly coefficient of variation (COV) for all EAC member states, adjusted for changes in the EAC membership. The COV is a statistical measure of variability, which indicates the size of a sample's standard deviation in relation to its mean.

[139] Michael Coppedge et al., "V-Dem Codebook V12," Varieties of Democracy (V-Dem) Project, 2022, www.v-dem.net/static/website/img/refs/codebookv12.pdf; Michael Coppedge et al., "V-Dem [Country-Year] Dataset V12."

[140] The V-dem codebook provides descriptions of these data; see Michael Coppedge et al., "V-Dem Codebook V12." I select indicators based on their relevance to the cases analyzed.

Table 4.8 *EACJ deference and EAC fragmentation on select issues*

Issue	Case name	Year of judgment	Deference	Theoretically expected fragmentation	Observed fragmentation
Press freedom	*Burundi Journalist Union v Burundi*, Ref. 7/2013	2015	No	High	High; increase from previous year
	Mseto & Anor. v Tanzania, Ref. 7/2016	2018	No	High	High; increase from previous year
	Media Council of Tanzania & Ors. v Tanzania, Ref. 2/2017	2019	No	High	High; no change from previous year
Freedom of association	*EALS v Uganda & EAC*, Ref. 2/2011	2018	Yes	Low	Low; decrease from previous year
	FORSC & Ors. v Burundi & EAC, Ref. 12/2016	2019	Yes	Low	Low; decrease from previous year
Due process	*Rwanda v Rugumba*, Appeal 1/2012	2012	No	High	Low; no change from previous year
	Mohochi v Uganda, Ref. 5/2011	2013	No	High	Low; increase from previous year
	EALS v Burundi & EAC, Ref. 1/2014	2015	No	High	Low; increase from previous year
	Grands Lacs Suppliers & Ors. v Burundi, Ref. 6/2016	2018	No	High	High; increase from previous year

Issue	Case name	Year of judgment	Deference	Theoretically expected fragmentation	Observed fragmentation
	Christophe v Rwanda, Ref. 10/2014	2018	Yes	Low	High; increase from previous year
	M/S Quick Telecommunications v Tanzania, Ref. 10/2016	2019	Yes	Low	Low; decrease from previous year
	Makala v Rwanda, Ref. 1/2017	2020	Yes	Low	Low; decrease from previous year
	Ssembuusi v Uganda, Ref. 16/2014	2020	Yes	Low	Low; decrease from previous year

Note: Low is defined as a COV of 50 percent or below, and high is defined as above 50 percent. Cells are shaded in gray when the observed fragmentation is congruent with the expected fragmentation. Case names are listed in short form; see Appendix for full citation.

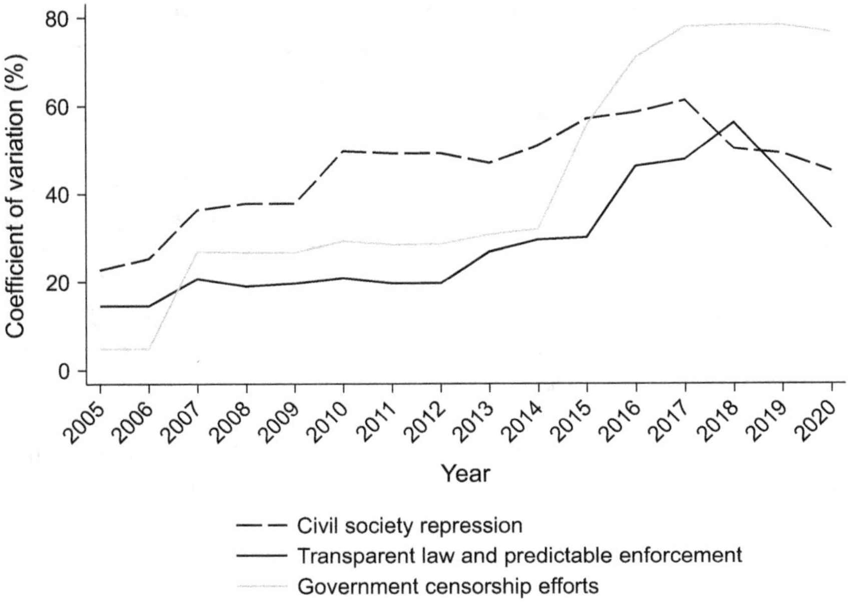

Figure 4.3 EAC political fragmentation on select issues.
Note: Calculations and illustration by author.
Data: Michael Coppedge et al., "V-Dem [Country-Year] Dataset V12."

It is useful because it is a standardized measure of variability, allowing for comparison across indicators.[141] Higher values indicate greater variability in the data, or, in other words, more heterogeneous preferences. Figure 4.3 illustrates the preference heterogeneity of EAC members from 2005 to 2020 on each of the three indicators.

Table 4.8 compares the observed heterogeneity, based on the data shown in Figure 4.3, with the theoretically expected level of heterogeneity. All instances where the observed and expected heterogeneity are congruent are shaded in gray. As Table 4.8 shows, the EACJ delivered three merits judgments related to press freedom between 2015 and 2019. All three of these judgments represent nondeference, as the Court declared that the respondent state violated its treaty obligations through its treatment of the media. We therefore expect to observe high

[141] The COV is calculated as the standard deviation of a sample divided by the sample mean.

fragmentation on *government censorship* between 2015 and 2019. Figure 4.3 shows that the COV for *government censorship* grew steeply in 2014 and remained high in the following years, as expected according to H_2. There is also a negative relationship between fragmentation and deference on the issue of freedom of association. Between 2018 and 2019, the Court ruled twice in favor of states on the freedom of association, reflecting deference. Using data on the *repression of civil society*, Figure 4.3 shows that preference heterogeneity peaked in 2017 and then declined, suggesting growing alignment between states in 2017. While preferences heterogeneity in 2018 was higher than in the EAC's first five years, the years these judgments came out were marked by a declining fragmentation on civil society repression.

The Court has addressed due process rights in several cases. The circumstances in each case differ. Some relate to criminal detention and trials, others to civil matters. At their core, however, they concern whether applicants were treated fairly during domestic judicial processes and according to established rules and principles. Deference on due process claims has changed over time, along with fragmentation. The EACJ was nondeferential between 2012 and June 2018. Since that time, the Court deferred to states in all related cases. According to data on *transparent law and predictable enforcement* (Figure 4.3), there was a steep increase in the heterogeneity of states' preferences from 2012 to 2018. This roughly corresponds with expectations, as deference was low during a period of rising fragmentation, even if heterogeneity was relatively low. In 2019 and 2020, the EACJ was more deferential, which coincides with low and declining heterogeneity. If we were to include how fragmentation shifts from year to year (as opposed to the absolute level in any given year) for all three issues, the evidence is even stronger. In that case, all but one row would be shaded.

Overall, the evidence largely aligns with the theoretical expectation that deference and fragmentation have a negative relationship (H_2). While these data cover only roughly a quarter of all merits judgments against states and a subset of issues, another observation speaks to the patterns in deference overall. Figure 4.3 suggests that political fragmentation increased from approximately 2012 to 2017, but then began to decline. This roughly corresponds with temporal changes in deferral rates. As seen in Figure 4.2, both total and merit deferral rates decreased between 2012 and 2017, before there was an uptick around 2018 and 2019. Broadly speaking, there is strong evidence to suggest that the EACJ has been more deferential at times and on issues where states' preferences are homogeneous. Conversely, as states' preferences diverge, the Court is less inclined to defer. This suggests that political fragmentation alleviates some of the political constraints faced by the Court. Finally, examining fragmentation in this way sheds light on what explains both temporal patterns in deference and cross-sectoral ones.

Past Resistance

The EACJ experienced coordinated state resistance early in its operations. This important episode of resistance has been documented by other scholars,[142] but I briefly recount the main contours of the story here before discussing its impact on the EACJ.

Shortly after the Court began operating, opposition politicians from Kenya sought the EACJ's intervention over Kenya's selection of members to the EALA.[143] The EAC Treaty requires the national assemblies of each member state to "elect, not from among its members, nine members of the Assembly, who shall represent as much as it is feasible, the various political parties represented in the National Assembly, shades of opinion, gender and other special interests groups in that Partner state."[144] Kenya's National Assembly conducted an "election" of its EALA members in October 2006. For this "election," the major political parties – the Kenya African National Union, the Forum for the Restoration of Democracy-People, and the National Rainbow Coalition (NARC) – put forward a list of nominees to the EALA. However, a schism within the NARC, which was a coalition party that came to power in 2002, led it to have two lists: one proposed by the Government from among politicians loyal to President Kibaki and another proposed by a new opposition group but former coalition partner (the Liberal Democratic Party). It was the Government's list for NARC nominees that was presented to the National Assembly for approval. Those nominees listed by Liberal Democratic Party, including Professor Peter Anyang' Nyong'o, filed a reference with the EACJ contesting Kenya's selection of members. Anyang' Nyong'o and others also sought an interim injunction that would prevent the selected members from taking office until the Court had decided the reference. The EACJ granted this temporary order on

[142] Henry Onoria, "Botched-Up Elections, Treaty Amendments and Judicial Independence in the East African Community," *Journal of African Law* 54, no. 1 (2010); Alter, Gathii, and Helfer, "Backlash Against International Courts in West, East and Southern Africa."

[143] See *Anyang' Nyong'o v Kenya & Ors.*, Ref. 1/2006.

[144] Amended EAC Treaty, Art. 50(1).

November 27, 2006. Immediately after this order was handed down, Kenya took steps to punish the EACJ for what it viewed as interference in domestic political affairs. For instance, Kenya tried to have the Court disbanded and intimidated the Kenyan judges in hopes they would recuse themselves from the case.[145] Kenya collaborated with the other member states to curb the EACJ. This began on November 30, when the EAC Summit condemned the decision of the Court.[146] In December 2006, the Summit amended the EAC Treaty to restrain the Court, which came into force in March 2007.

The amendments restructured the Court into the First Instance and Appellate Division and added provisions aiming to restrict the jurisdiction of the Court. In addition, the amendments revised the provisions related to the removal of judges, which are described in detail above. Changes to the rules governing the removal of judges were seen as Kenya's strategy to intimidate and remove its judges from the Court. The member states also added paragraph 2 to Article 30, barring references from private actors that are filed more than two months following an alleged violation.

This entire episode had implications for how the Court was viewed. The Summit's condemnation of the Court in its Communique of November 30, 2006, damaged the legitimacy of the Court, as did some media coverage which claimed the Court's order had "thrown [the EALA] into disarray"[147] and that by not hearing from all parties, namely, the nominees who were prevented from taking office, the Court "violated the rule of natural justice," caused them "irreparable damage," and "paralysed the regional assembly."[148] Proponents of the Court also suggested the episode was damaging to the Court. For instance, Donald Deya, chief of the EALS, wrote in an opinion piece that states were "denigrating the Court" as well as the Treaty and that the EALS "condemns any attacks on the independence and integrity of the EACJ."[149]

[145] Alter, Gathii, and Helfer, "Backlash Against International Courts in West, East and Southern Africa"; see also *Anyang' Nyong'o v Kenya*, Ref. 1/2006, Ruling on Application 5/2007 (February 6, 2007).

[146] EAC, *Joint Communiqué of the Eighth Summit of EAC Heads of State*, November 30, 2006 (Arusha: EAC 2006).

[147] Zephania Ubwani, "Swearing-in of Kenyan MPs Blocked," *The Nation*, November 28, 2006.

[148] Jibril Adan, "EALA Nominees Contest Ruling," *The East African Standard*, December 12, 2006.

[149] Donald Deya, "Why Undermining EA Court Is Sheer Folly," *The East African*, December 12, 2006.

In a press interview, the EALS called out states for their "disparaging and ridiculing tone" of the Court, which amounted to "contempt of court."[150] Thus, the states' collective resistance affected perceptions of the Court.

This experience also provided important information to judges sitting on the Court: States are capable of curtailing and undermining the Court if it steps too much out of line. For instance, when the Court was asked to interpret the amendment that imposed a two-month time limit on references, the Appellate Division narrowly interpreted this time limit.[151] In fact, one interviewee suggested that the Court's fear of another "backlash" led it to be "very narrow and restrictive in the interpretation" of the two-month rule.[152] The Court's restrictive interpretation of this provision should be read in light of the fact that the provision resulted from an episode of collective state resistance.

Also telling is how the Court has tended to respond to requests for interim orders. Applicants have requested interim orders on fourteen occasions in the aftermath of *Anyang' Nyong'o*.[153] Orders were granted in only two of these instances. For stakeholders, the EACJ's rulings on interim orders have been "very hesitant," and even though there is sympathy for the Court, it "has refrained on some occasions to exercise its mandates when they are highly needed and they abscond from their duty ... because people, they expect them to do more than what they are doing."[154] Another interviewee speculated that the EACJ's decision to deny interim orders in relation to President Nkurunziza of Burundi's bid to run for a third presidential term was due to the "potential for another backlash."[155] The reluctance to grant interim orders occurs in the background of prior resistance that arose from the Court's delivery of interim orders.

The temporal patterns in deference resonate with interviewees' impressions that past resistance has affected the Court's decision-making. The Court's deferral rate increased in the aftermath of *Anyang' Nyong'o* (see Figure 4.2). Thus, the evidence suggests that the Court's experience with state resistance narrowed its strategic space, leading the Court to prefer deference in order to avoid similar episodes, as expected by H_5.

150 Quoted in "Wagging Tongues over EALA Ruling 'Is Contempt of Court'," *Arusha Times*, December 11, 2006.

151 *Kenya v IMLU*, Appeal 1/2011, 17.

152 Interview 2.

153 *Anyang' Nyong'o v Kenya & Ors.*, Ref. 1/2006.

154 Interview 27.

155 Interview 2.

The EACJ's Adaptive Practices

The formal independence and political fragmentation, along with past resistance, have structured the EACJ's strategic space in important ways. They combine to shape the credibility and feasibility of resistance as well as how the Court is perceived by its stakeholders, setting the conditions for the EACJ's substantial deference. As I have shown, however, the EACJ sometimes decides not to defer. The nature of fragmentation in any given dispute, as well as the participation of a support network, shed light on the nondeference by the EACJ. I have posited that the Court might also adapt to its political constraints by developing practices that help to restore or broaden its strategic space, thus enabling the Court to not defer when in accord with underlying legal constraints. The following discussion explores the EACJ's practices of persuasive argumentation and public legitimation to discern their significance.

Persuasive Argumentation

The EACJ relies on two forms of *persuasive argumentation* – unanimous decisions and citation of national jurisprudence – to buttress nondeference. First, the EACJ relies on unanimous judgments. Speaking with one voice, according to my argument, enables some protection for judges but also helps to boost the persuasiveness of the Court's judgments. One member of the Court explained that judges have informally agreed to issue unanimous decisions for the purpose of speaking with one voice and to improve the independence of the judges and prevent political retribution.[156] Protecting the individual judges from political retaliation is a salient concern for the judges. Several of the judges come from countries where judicial interference is relatively commonplace. For example, scholars have described Kenya, Burundi, and Uganda as states where judicial interference occurs.[157] Additionally, the experience of the EACJ has been that individual judges can indeed become targets of states, as was the case following the interim order in *Anyang' Nyong'o*, which led one Kenyan judge to be removed from office.

The Court has issued unanimous decisions in all but two judgments. In the first instance, the Appellate Division ruled in favor of the

[156] Interview 15.

[157] VonDoepp and Ellett, "Reworking Strategic Models of Executive-Judicial Relations"; Masengu, "The Vulnerability of Judges in Contemporary Africa"; Makau Mutua, "Justice under Siege: The Rule of Law and Judicial Subservience in Kenya," *Human Rights Quarterly* 23, no. 1 (2001).

Table 4.9 *Descriptive statistics on EACJ's citation practices*

Type of citation	Mean	Standard deviation	Min	Max
EACJ jurisprudence	4.71	4.01	0	23
External jurisprudence	3.84	4.42	0	22
. *International*	1.36	1.92	0	7
. *Domestic*	2.48	3.51	0	16

Note: All ninety-four cases are included. The coding records citations made by the Court in the reasoned part of its rulings or judgments. It does not include references that are cited in the summary of parties' arguments or the discussion of case facts. Citations raised by parties in their arguments which are later referenced by the Court in its own reasoning are included in the citation counts. Citations are only counted once, even when the Court cites them more than once in a single decision. Interim rulings are included in coding of case, if applicable and available. Final judgments at the First Instance Division and Appellate Division are coded separately.

respondent state, which had argued that the Court was not entitled to hear applications from nonresident citizens.[158] Two judges dissented, neither of whom were nationals of the respondent state.[159] In the second instance, the Court was responding to a claim raised by Burundi contesting the process leading to the election of the Speaker of the EALA. The Court dismissed Burundi's claim, but one judge dissented in support of Burundi.[160] The dissenting judge in this instance was the appointee from Burundi.[161] It is only in this latter instance where an act of nondeference resulted in a dissenting opinion, yet only by the national judge who would most likely benefit politically from the dissent. Otherwise, unanimous judgments provide means by which the Court prevents its strategic space from narrowing when it decides not to defer.

The second practice of persuasive argumentation that the EACJ has developed relates to how it cites jurisprudence. Table 4.9 summarizes the descriptive statistics of the EACJ's citation practices. It shows that the average EACJ judgment cites 4.71 of its own judgments. On the other hand, the

158 *Desire v Burundi*, Appeal 1/2017.

159 *Desire v Burundi* (Dissenting opinion), Appeal 1/2017.

160 *The Attorney General of the Republic of Burundi v The Secretary General of the East African Community*, Appeal No. 2/2019, EACJ (June 4, 2020) [herein *Burundi v EAC*, Appeal 2/2019].

161 *Burundi v EAC* (Dissenting opinion), Appeal 2/2019.

Table 4.10 *Cross-tabulation of EACJ's citation practices by deference (merits only)*

	Domestic references		International references	
Declared violation	No	Yes	No	Yes
No (defer)	16 (47.06)	18 (52.94)	16 (47.06)	18 (52.94)
Yes	7 (23.33)	23 (76.67)	10 (33.33)	20 (66.67)
	Fisher's Test p-value: 0.068* χ^2 p-value: 0.046**		Fisher's Test p-value: 0.314 χ^2 p-value: 0.263	
Consequential order				
No (defer)	21 (42.00)	29 (58.00)	23 (46.00)	27 (54.00)
Yes	2 (14.29)	12 (85.71)	3 (21.43)	11 (78.57)
	Fisher's Test p-value: 0.067* χ^2 p-value: 0.043**		Fisher's Test p-value: 0.129 χ^2 p-value: 0.088*	
Additional remedy				
No (defer)	20 (44.44)	25 (55.56)	21 (46.67)	24 (53.33)
Yes	3 (15.79)	16 (84.21)	5 (26.32)	14 (73.68)
	Fisher's Test p-value: 0.045** χ^2 p-value: 0.023**		Fisher's Test p-value: 0.169 χ^2 p-value: 0.123	

Note: N = 64. *p<0.10, ** p<0.05, *** p<0.001. This excludes cases where the merits are not considered, or the case is remanded to the FI. In each cross-tabulation, the first number is the frequency and the second number (in parentheses) is the row percentage.

average number of citations to external jurisprudence is 3.84. Among external jurisprudence, the average EACJ judgment cites international courts less than domestic courts, and the maximum number of citations to domestic jurisprudence is more than twice that of international citations.[162]

The Court cites a range of authorities. Domestic jurisdictions that are cited include those of the member states as well as the former EACA and other common law jurisdictions including British, Canadian, Indian, and American courts. As for international jurisprudence, the Court cites several international courts and tribunals, but often the ICJ and the CJEU.

[162] Decisions by UN international human rights committees and regional human rights commissions are coded as international jurisprudence.

The EACJ's citation practices systematically vary by whether it defers or not. Table 4.10 analyzes the relationship between deference and citation practices. This table compares references to both domestic and international jurisdictions against deference in merits decisions based on: (1) case outcomes and (2) remedies. It shows that nondeference – whether measured by a declared violation, consequential order, or any remedy in addition to a declaratory judgment – is reasoned with reference(s) to domestic jurisprudence more often than deference is. For instance, roughly 77 percent of decisions in which violations are declared cite domestic case law, but domestic jurisprudence is cited in only 53 percent of decisions where no violation is found. The contrast is even greater when looking at consequential orders: 86 percent of judgments with consequential orders cite domestic courts, while 58 percent without a consequential order cite domestic jurisprudence. The differences in domestic citations based on deference are statistically significant. That said, the Court does also refer to domestic case law when it defers. References to international jurisprudence are also more typical when there is nondeference than not, even though this difference is not always statistically significant or as large. These patterns hold when looking at all judgments, in contrast to merits-only judgments (see Table A4.1).

The data support H_3 and suggest that external citations (especially from domestic jurisprudence) are integral to how it manages its political constraints and nondeference. To maintain a positive relationship with states, especially when dealing with an issue for the first time, the Court aims to have "a deeply reasoned judgment. Sometimes we even go further and cite the case law of other international tribunals, especially the ECJ. You will also find that given the fact obviously the founding members of [the EAC] have the common law system, we even go further to cite some national cases so that people can start relating to what is happening, especially in member states. Because if we say that even in your own country there's a ruling that supports what we talk about," the Court can begin to receive support from states.[163] For instance, the Court drew upon domestic and international jurisprudence in the *Serengeti*[164] and *Anyang' Nyong'o*[165] cases, and both are among the judgments with the highest number of references to both international and domestic cases. Both decisions cite judgments from courts within the member states,

[163] Interview 15.

[164] *Tanzania v ANAW*, Appeal 3/2014.

[165] *Anyang' Nyong'o v Kenya & Ors.*, Reference No. 1/2006.

other common law jurisdictions, and the former East African Court of Appeal.[166] At the same time, they reflect instances of nondeference. The *Serengeti* decision reflects nondeference in terms of outcomes, legal interpretation, and remedies. Other instances where domestic references are high are cases where interim orders are requested and/or other interim applications are ruled on by the Court. For example, in *Zziwa v EAC*[167] the First Instance Division found that there had been a violation of the EAC Treaty behind the ousting of the Speaker of the EALA, Margaret Zziwa.

The EACJ's strategic space is constrained by lower safeguards to independence and political fragmentation. To cope with these constraints, the Court relies on persuasive arguments to bolster its judgments, especially when it does not defer. Unanimous judgments and references to domestic jurisprudence are key to understanding deference by the EACJ. However, the Court also relies on nonjudicial practices to shape its strategic space. I turn to this next and consider how the EACJ employs public legitimation.

Public Legitimation

The EACJ has also developed practices of public legitimation to expand its strategic space. The Court uses a range of activities that targets public audiences while portraying the Court's commitment to its political purpose and stakeholders.

In its first several years of operations, the Court gave little attention to how it was viewed by its stakeholders.[168] However, by 2010 the Court recognized that policymakers and stakeholders did not "consciously or unconsciously, appreciate its role," which could risk "marginalizing the status of the Court" and "denying East African citizens the right to access the services of an effective regional court."[169] The Court also acknowledged that it was "not visible enough" as "the users and other stakeholders still do not know sufficiently this regional mechanism of dispute resolution."[170] In recognition of these issues, the Court set related objectives: "to proactively influence a positive shift in mindset of EAC Policy Organs and other Stakeholders concerning the role and place of the

166 References to decisions of the EACA are coded as domestic jurisprudence.

167 *Hon. Dr. Margaret Zziwa v The Secretary General of the East African Community*, Reference No. 17/2014, EACJ (February 3, 2017).

168 Interview 7.

169 EACJ, *Strategic Plan: 2010–2015*, 17.

170 Ibid., 18.

Court" and "to make the Court visible and indispensable in matters related to the discharge of its mandate."[171] More concretely, the EACJ aimed to raise the profile of the Court by organizing seminars, meetings, and "sensitization workshops" with stakeholders and holding sessions in the member states.[172]

The EACJ's public image remained a key concern when the Court formulated its second strategic plan in 2018. Specifically, the EACJ identified the appreciation and visibility of the Court as two of its six main strategic issues.[173] The plan stressed the need to engage stakeholders through seminars, workshops, and other outreach activities. It also envisioned plans to disseminate promotional material and revamp the EACJ's webpage and social media presence.[174]

In line with these plans, the Court carries out outreach activities. The Court occasionally holds sessions and meetings in member states.[175] It also hosts and participates in workshops with lawyers, national judges, and civil society organizations.[176] The judges and Registrar speak at external events, typically by invitation, such as delivering a public lecture at universities.[177] While the main objective of these activities is to raise "awareness of this Court to the citizens of the East African Community,"[178] they typically target civil society organizations, like NGOs, the private sector, academic institutions, and bar associations, as opposed to the broader public.[179] The ability to reach a broad audience through its outreach activities has also been hindered by a lack of available funding,[180] which has been remarked upon in the EAC Annual Reports.[181]

The Court targets a wider audience through public communication, namely, press releases, its webpage, and social media. An evaluation of this public communication reveals whether it aims to legitimize the

171 Ibid., 19.
172 Ibid., 23–24.
173 Ibid., 17.
174 EACJ, *Strategic Plan: 2018–2023*, 25–26.
175 Interview 27; Interview 15.
176 Interview 14.
177 Interview 15.
178 Interview 14; Interview 15.
179 Ibid.
180 Ibid.
181 For example, EAC, *Annual Report: Financial Year 2017/2018* (Arusha: EAC Secretariat, 2019), 76; EAC, *Annual Report: Financial Year 2016/2017* (Arusha: EAC Secretariat, 2018), 70.

Court in the eyes of the public. For this purpose, I extracted all press releases from the EACJ's website up through the year 2020. Beginning with the earliest available press release in 2010, a total of 191 press releases were manually coded for their content. The vast majority (79 percent) of the press releases discuss case proceedings and outcomes. The remaining 21 percent discuss the Court's ceremonial events or "off-the-bench" activities, hosted by the Court or attended by judges or the Registrar.

The Court utilizes press releases to convey messages to the public about the Court. The coding reveals that 15 percent of the press releases feature portrayals of the Court's political purpose or its people-centeredness. The press releases convey the Court as an essential instrument for justice and integration. For example, when describing the workshop leading to the first strategic plan in 2010, a press release stated the judges and staff "will work towards the transformation of the EACJ into a well-designed tool of justice to address the legal challenges emanating from the wider and deeper integration of the Community."[182] Similar messaging can be identified at later dates. For instance, a 2018 press release described a sensitization workshop. It reported that Justice Ugirashebuja, the President of the EACJ at the time, stressed that

> "regional integration requires good cooperation between all the partners in the rule of law chain: judges, lawyers, civil servants, academics, businesses and individuals. 'We all must contribute to make the EAC a living legal reality.' His Lordship emphasized on the role of the court, which is crucial in resolving disputes which would otherwise threaten the survival of a Community... Justice Ugirashebuja further added that without an effective dispute resolution mechanism, the survival of the Community is at stake and that without its case law, and many principles that the Court has developed and will continue to develop, the Community will certainly not be where it is today and will not arrive at where it aims to be."[183]

The political purpose of the EACJ is also conveyed through narratives about the value of law, courts, and judiciaries, in general, rather than the Court per se. These narratives signal the EACJ's commitment to principles of the rule of law and its other core purposes. One press release, for instance, reported that Justice Dr. Emmanuel Ugirashebuja "advised the

[182] EACJ, "EACJ to Develop Five-Year Strategic Plan to Guide Its Operations," press release, February 23, 2010.

[183] EACJ, "EACJ President Calls Upon the Stakeholders to Strengthen Their Cooperation & Relationship with the Court," press release, June 21, 2018.

judiciary of any Country in today's World is a critical part of its economic and social infrastructure and therefore, that the judiciary is a vital factor in the rule of law and more broadly in economic development."[184]

Press releases also at times convey the Court's attention to its stakeholders, with references to East Africans, the Community or region and its citizens. For instance, the press release describing a 2014 Workshop for the Judges of National Courts and Civil Society Organizations cited Justice Ugirashebuja as saying: "Together we can give hope to all those who clamor for resurgent East Africa and a region of greater equality, peace and harmonious development."[185] Several press releases praise the Court for "bringing justice closer to East Africans."

Nearly all of the narratives about the Court's political purpose or people-centeredness arise when the EACJ communicates information about its off-the-bench activities. Such messages are rarely found in the press releases about cases proceedings, which instead relate details about cases before the Court, including the factual background of the reference, the parties' arguments, and the invoked Treaty provisions. While the released details about cases can include mentions of democracy, rule of law, good governance, or human rights, the press releases make clear that such values are claimed by the parties to a dispute or are expressed in law. Thus, they do not convey these values as attributes of the Court.

The narratives of the EACJ's political purpose and people-centeredness are also expressed on the Court's website. The homepage presents the Court's visions to be "A world-class Court dispensing quality justice for a prosperous Community" and its mission "To contribute to regional Integration by ensuring adherence to justice, rule of law and fundamental rights and freedoms through the interpretation and application of and compliance with the East African Community Law." Together, the press releases and webpage illustrate that the Court uses legitimation narratives of political purposes and people-centeredness. The press releases especially show that these narratives have been present across time, as I find at least one press release in every year (except 2020, when the Court's ceremonial and outreach activities were significantly affected by the COVID-19 pandemic). Even though we can observe

[184] EACJ, "President of the Court Attends the Conference on Requirements for an Independent and Effective Judiciary in Nairobi," press release, February 17, 2016.

[185] EACJ, "EACJ Workshop for Judges of the National Courts & Civil Society Workshop Officially Open in Kigali, Rwanda," press release, September 24, 2014.

Table 4.11 *Public legitimation narratives in EACJ's Facebook posts*

Legitimation words and phrases	Number of posts	Percent of total
People-centeredness	25	4.73
community	9	1.7
East Africans	4	0.76
East African citizens	0	0
East African people	1	0.19
citizens	8	1.52
people	7	1.33
Political purpose	65	12.31
integration	12	2.27
justice	26	4.92
rule of law	13	2.46
democracy	7	1.33
good governance	12	2.27
human rights	8	1.52
development	9	1.70
community	9	1.7
People-centeredness or political purpose	68	12.88

Note: All terms and phrases are case sensitive.

legitimation narratives, they are missing from a large share of the EACJ's public communication as seen through its press releases.

In addition to press releases and its webpage, the Court uses social media – including Facebook, Twitter, and YouTube – as part of its public communication strategy.[186] I further assess the Court's legitimation narratives by examining its Facebook posts.[187] Using a web-scraping tool, I extracted all of the EACJ's Facebook posts from June 2013 until the end of 2020.[188] In total there were 528 posts extracted. I analyzed the posts for words or phrases that reflect the Court's political purpose and people-centeredness.[189] Table 4.11 displays the prominence of the

[186] Ibid.; Interview 15.

[187] I use Facebook because this is the social media outlet that offers the maximum amount of content to assess with a text analysis.

[188] The EACJ's Facebook profile was created in June 2013. See "Page transparency," Facebook, accessed November 14, 2023, www.facebook.com/eacjcourt/about_profile_transparency.

[189] These words and phrases were identified to match those that were most commonly featured in the messaging found in the press releases.

EACJ's legitimation narratives as revealed by the Facebook posts. Like the Court's press releases, Table 4.11 shows that a relatively small portion (13 percent) of the EACJ's Facebook posts feature an element of public legitimation. It also shows that of the two types of narratives, the EACJ places greater emphasis on its political purpose rather than on its people-centeredness. The Court might stress its political purpose to signal to states that it respects its purpose.

A year-by-year examination reveals an upward trend in the use of terms reflecting people-centeredness or commitment to political purpose (see Table A4.2). From 2013 to 2017, each year featured less than ten percent of posts with public legitimation terms, while more than fifteen percent did so in each of the following years. While the temporal data are limited, there appears to be a positive relationship between public legitimation and nondeference in accord with H_4. Notably, merit deference was at its lowest in 2018 (see Figure 4.2), while public legitimation was at its highest.

Conclusion

This chapter has examined the decision-making of the East African Court of Justice, and its principal findings are best summarized as four main points. First, the ideational setting of the EACJ, much like the other courts studied in this book, reveals legacies of the colonial past for the region. These legacies are most profoundly seen in often opposing political norms; regionalism and integration have been valued and embraced from the colonial era up to today but have also run up against strong commitments to national sovereignty at times. Additionally, legal pluralism and judicial insecurity also shape prominent beliefs in the state legal order.

Second, as will be shown in the following chapters, the EACJ stands out for its high degree of deference. Its case outcomes typically show acceptance of the exercise of authority by the EAC or its member states. Legal interpretations on key questions have followed a work-to-rule approach, and the Court's reasoning prioritizes state discretion and uses high evidentiary standards. The EACJ, however, abstains less in its remedial orders and has been willing to issue intrusive consequential orders. On the whole, the EACJ can be described as exercising substantial deference.

Third, the pattern of deference demonstrated by the Court is puzzling based on the extensiveness of its support network. While the support network still has significant room for strengthening, the Court has benefited from an active private contingent of its support network. Most cases are supported by a repeat lawyer or involve the participation of an NGO. Their involvement in litigation before the EACJ, however, does not systematically determine the outcome of cases or legal interpretation. The Court's high deference, nonetheless, aligns with a lack of support from subnational or supranational actors. All things considered, the patterns in deference are difficult to reconcile based on the Court's support network and suggest there are other aspects of its political environment that matter.

Fourth, to explain the EACJ's deference we need to consider the pervasive constraints faced by the Court. More than the other ICs examined in this book, the EACJ has low formal independence. This constrains the Court in important ways, by affecting the credibility of state resistance and the Court's legitimacy. Past resistance further solidifies a sense that resistance is feasible and harms how stakeholders view the Court. Political fragmentation, or the lack of it, therefore also adds to the Court's constraints. As I have shown, the temporal and cross-sectoral variation in deference closely follows patterns in political fragmentation. The variation in deference is also linked to the Court's practices of persuasive argumentation and public legitimation. Generally speaking, the EACJ's deference and constraints align with the expectations outlined in Chapter 2. As an IC with low formal independence and moderate levels of political fragmentation, the EACJ shows a tendency to defer to states. Chapter 5 examines the Caribbean Court of Justice and demonstrates how an IC with high formal independence, in contrast to the EACJ, tends to not defer.

5

The Caribbean Court of Justice

Intermediate Constraints and Moderate Deference

The Caribbean Court of Justice is the international court at the heart of the Caribbean Community (CARICOM). CARICOM is a regional integration organization comprising fifteen member states: Antigua and Barbuda, the Bahamas, Barbados, Belize, Dominica, Grenada, Guyana, Haiti, Jamaica, Montserrat, Saint Lucia, Saint Kitts and Nevis, Saint Vincent and the Grenadines, Suriname, and Trinidad and Tobago. The CCJ began operating in 2005, and since then it has made a mark on the Caribbean Community by fulfilling its role as the guardian of Community law and as the court of last resort for some member states. Through a close investigation of the CCJ's decision-making, this chapter examines the book's core argument in the case of an international court with a midrange strategic space. In contrast to the EACJ's pervasive political constraints, the CCJ's strategic space is characterized by intermediate political constraints that develop from high formal independence that is partially offset by a lack of political fragmentation. Based on the theoretical framework presented in Chapter 2, we expect the CCJ's deference to be moderate.

This chapter assesses this expectation and whether the CCJ's structural political constraints and adaptive practices account for the observed patterns of deference. It shows that the CCJ's deference is moderate. Its decisions frequently reject states' exercise of authority through outcomes that are in favor of applicants and broad legal interpretations. Yet, the Court frequently stops short of placing high demands on states, preferring to offer recommendations rather than impose intrusive remedies. It also tends to defer to CARICOM institutions or when states reveal uniform preferences. The chapter links these patterns of deference to the CCJ's robust formal safeguards to judicial independence alongside the minimal political fragmentation across CARICOM's membership. While formal independence depresses deference by boosting the legitimacy of the CCJ and reducing the possibilities of collective state resistance, homogeneous state preferences have the opposite effect. The latter effect is especially prominent when the Court reviews decisions and actions taken by CARICOM organs. Moreover, the analysis reveals that the CCJ copes with its political environment by practicing persuasive argumentation and public legitimation. Last, the chapter shows that the CCJ's deference is difficult to reconcile with the strength and activity of its support network.

The chapter unfolds in five steps. First, it introduces the CCJ by way of describing its historical origins and ideational setting. Second, using original data, the chapter provides an overview of the Court's mandate and workload before mapping the extent to which the CCJ defers. Third, the chapter considers the role of the Court's support networks, suggesting that the CCJ's supporters lack sufficient influence to explain the level of observed nondeference. Fourth, the chapter explores how the CCJ's (non)deference corresponds with formal independence and political fragmentation on the one hand and adaptive judicial practices on the other. Last, the chapter reviews the core findings of the case study.

The CCJ's Ideational Setting: Colonial Legacies, Political Norms, and Legal Culture

The CCJ's ideational context, which likely has an impact on the CCJ's performance, resembles that of the EACJ (Chapter 4) and the ACtHPR (Chapter 6) in many ways. To begin with, the CCJ is rooted in the colonial past of the Caribbean nations that it serves. While all but two of CARICOM's members are English-speaking and were most recently British colonies,[1] the Spanish, French, Dutch, and British settled and colonized today's CARICOM nations at various points of time and in various constellation. For instance, during the years of the American War of Independence through the end of the Napoleonic Wars (roughly 1775–1815), "the West Indian territories were tossed between the warring European powers."[2] Despite differences in how the French, British, and Dutch ruled these colonies, colonialism had many homogenizing socioeconomic effects across the region.[3] Colonial rulers established plantation colonies, mostly for sugar exportation, across these territories. Indigenous populations were devastated by disease, slavery, war,

1 Suriname and Haiti were not British territories in the lead-up to independence.

2 Ann Spackman, *Constitutional Development of the West Indies 1922–1968: A Selection from the Major Documents* (Barbados: Caribbean Universities Press, 1975), 2.

3 Stirton and Lodge, "Constitutionalism and Colonial Legacies in the Caribbean."

brutality, and displacement,[4] while millions of enslaved Africans and later indentured servants from India were transported to the colonies to work the plantations.[5] Moreover, plantation landowners were largely absent.[6]

Colonial governors, especially among the former British colonies, experimented with intraregional administration, or some version of integration. As Payne describes, the island nations "suffered from a bewildering and unsettling series of experiments in inter-colonial administration for a period which lasted for more than two and half centuries. Only the relatively remote territories of Jamaica, British Guiana [Guyana] and British Honduras [Belize] were excluded from the merry-go-round."[7] Despite these efforts to integrate the colonies, a sense of regional unity did not develop and was impeded because intraregional administration was pursued solely for purposes of administrative efficiency, intraregional communication and transport were poor, and plantation competition spurred inter-colonial rivalries.[8] It was not until the early twentieth century that regionalism truly began to develop. At this point, intraregional communication and transport improved and several regional institutions and associations were formed, including the West Indian Court of Appeal (1919), the Imperial College of Tropical Agriculture (1924), and the Associated Chambers of Commerce (1917).[9] With time, unity started to have a political purpose – independence and self-governance.[10] Yet, support for integration waxed and

4 Alexander Koch et al., "Earth System Impacts of the European Arrival and Great Dying in the Americas After 1492," *Quaternary Science Reviews* 207 (2019). Many refer to the "extinction" of the indigenous population, while recent work contests this characterization; see, for example, Tony Castanha, *The Myth of Indigenous Caribbean Extinction: Continuity and Reclamation in Borikén (Puerto Rico)* (New York: Palgrave Macmillan, 2011); Maximilian C. Forte, "Extinction: Ideologies Against Indigeneity in the Caribbean," *Southern Quarterly* 43, no. 4 (2006).

5 Lomarsh Roopnarine, "Indo-Caribbean Migration: From Periphery to Core," *Caribbean Quarterly* 49, no. 3 (2003); Philip D. Morgan, "Slavery in the British Caribbean," in *The Cambridge World History of Slavery: Volume 3*, ed. David Eltis and Stanley L. Engerman (Cambridge: Cambridge University Press, 2011).

6 Spackman, *Constitutional Development of the West Indies 1922–1968*, 3–17; Stirton and Lodge, "Constitutionalism and Colonial Legacies in the Caribbean," 27–28.

7 Anthony J. Payne, *The Political History of CARICOM* (Kingston, Jamaica: Ian Randle Publishers, 2008), xv.

8 Ibid., xvi.

9 Ibid., xxi–xxiii.

10 Ibid., xvii; Derek O'Brien, "CARICOM: Regional Integration in a Post-Colonial World," *European Law Journal* 17, no. 5 (2011): 633.

waned in the decades leading up to independence, with some territories being more and others less eager to pursue political cooperation or regional unification. For some, pan-Caribbean unity was the most viable path toward full self-governance, especially because the small size of the former colonies was viewed as an impediment to their capacity to function as sovereign states.[11] For others, it conflicted with nationalist sentiments.[12]

By the end of WWII, many local elites supported, albeit with some nudging from British authorities, a closer political unity of the colonies.[13] Ten of the now fifteen members of CARICOM (which included most of the British West Indies) were consolidated into the West Indies Federation (WIF) in 1958, with the understanding that it would constitute a self-governing sovereign state.[14] Designing a constitutional order for the new federation was politically challenging due to competing interests and visions,[15] and because the different colonies were reluctant to concede elements of self-governance over to a federal government, which they were increasingly enjoying.[16] The WIF was short-lived and ultimately failed before it became a fully autonomous state. By popular referendum in 1961, Jamaica withdrew from the federation, and Trinidad

[11] Payne, *The Political History of CARICOM*, xxv; Patsy Lewis, *Caribbean Regional Integration: A Critical Development Approach* (London: Routledge, 2022); Spencer Mawby, *Ordering Independence: The End of Empire in the Anglophone Caribbean, 1947–69* (London: Palgrave Macmillan, 2012).

[12] Payne, *The Political History of CARICOM*, xix; O'Brien, "CARICOM: Regional Integration in a Post-Colonial World," 633; Jesse Harris Proctor, "The Framing of the West Indian Federal Constitution: An Adventure in National Self-Determination," *Revista de Historia de América*, no. 57/58 (1964); Spackman, *Constitutional Development of the West Indies 1922–1968*, 39–40.

[13] Payne, *The Political History of CARICOM*; Hamid A. Ghany, *Constitutional Development in the Commonwealth Caribbean* (Kingston, Jamaica: Ian Randle Publishers, 2018).

[14] The ten territories that are now CARICOM states which were included in the West Indies Federation are: Antigua and Barbuda, Barbados, Dominica, Grenada, Jamaica, Montserrat, Saint Kitts-Nevis-Anguilla, Saint Lucia, Saint Vincent and the Grenadines, Trinidad and Tobago. The Federation also included the Turks and Caicos Islands and the Cayman Islands. The British West Indies territories which were not included in the Federation were British Honduras (Belize), British Guiana (Guyana), the British Virgin Islands, the Bahamas, and Bermuda. CARICOM members that were not part of the Federation were the Bahamas, Belize, Guyana, Haiti, and Suriname.

[15] Proctor, "The Framing of the West Indian Federal Constitution"; Ghany, *Constitutional Development in the Commonwealth Caribbean*.

[16] O'Brien, "CARICOM: Regional Integration in a Post-Colonial World," 634; Spackman, *Constitutional Development of the West Indies 1922–1968*, 39–40.

and Tobago quickly followed.[17] With the absence of the region's two largest economies, the WIF collapsed in 1962.

Integration, nevertheless, was not completely sidelined. Some of the newly independent states – along with some of the still dependent territories – set aside aims for a closer political union and instead focused on economic cooperation. Driven not only by earlier aspirations for unification but also anxiety that the nations would lose preferential trade status with the impending entry of the United Kingdom (UK) into the European Economic Communities (the precursor to the EU), leaders created the Caribbean Free Trade Association (CARIFTA) which came into effect in 1968.[18] In 1972, the Conference of Heads of Government (CHOG) decided to transform the CARIFTA into a common market and established the Caribbean Community in 1973 with the adoption of the Treaty of Chaguaramas (TOC).[19] States dominated CARICOM through the main intergovernmental decision-making bodies (the CHOG and the Council of Ministers), which took decisions by consensus,[20] and CARICOM had weak enforcement powers. Consequently, CARICOM relied heavily on the willingness of governments to give effect to the Community's decisions. Ultimately, poor economic performance led Community leaders to contemplate reforms. They established the West Indian Commission (WIC), also known as the Ramphal Commission because Sir Shridath Ramphal served as the chair, to make proposals on how to fulfill the ambitions of the TOC.[21] The WIC found faults with CARICOM's inability to ensure implementation, in other words, its limited monitoring and enforcement capacity. The WIC's report in 1992 recommended a variety of changes to ensure better implementation of the common market, including the establishment of a court.[22] The WIC argued: "Integration rests on rights and duties; it requires the support of the rule of law applied regionally and

[17] O'Brien, "CARICOM: Regional Integration in a Post-Colonial World," 634; Payne, *The Political History of CARICOM.*

[18] O'Brien, "CARICOM: Regional Integration in a Post-Colonial World," 636.

[19] Treaty establishing the Caribbean Community (adopted July 4, 1973, entered into force August 1, 1973) U.N.T.S. 946, at 17–542.

[20] O'Brien, "CARICOM: Regional Integration in a Post-Colonial World," 638–39.

[21] CHOG, *Communiqué of the Tenth Meeting of the Conference of Heads of Government of the Caribbean Community*, July 3–7, 1989 (Grande Anse, Grenada: CARICOM Secretariat, 1989), https://caricom.org/communique-issued-at-the-conclusion-of-the-tenth-meeting-of-the-conference-of-heads-of-government-of-the-caribbean-community-3-7-july-1989-grand-anse-grenada/.

[22] WIC, *Time for Action: Report of the West Indian Commission* (Kingston: University of the West Indies Press, 1993).

uniformly. A CARICOM Supreme Court interpreting the Treaty of Chaguaramas, resolving disputes arising under it… declaring and enforcing Community law … is absolutely necessary to the integration process."[23] Thus, the court that would eventually become the CCJ was viewed as integral to economic integration and global competitiveness for the region.

At the same time, a regional court was also believed to be necessary to complete the process of independence for the former British colonies. When the members of CARICOM gained independence from the UK beginning in the 1960s, most states gained self-governance in legislative and executive affairs only, and not judicial matters.[24] In fact, most of the newly independent states kept the UK's Judicial Committee of the Privy Council in London as their court of last resort. Only Guyana severed ties with the Privy Council after gaining independence, as did Grenada for the period of 1979 to 1991.[25] This important vestige of colonialism was not to everyone's liking. For years, various legal and political elites circulated ideas of establishing a supreme court for the Commonwealth Caribbean to replace the Privy Council.[26] For instance, the Organisation of Commonwealth Caribbean Bar Associations in 1972 recommended the establishment of a Caribbean court of appeal.[27]

The tides began to shift in the late 1980s, when Trinidad and Tobago proposed the establishment of a Caribbean court of appeal at a meeting of CHOG in 1987. The CHOG concluded this proposal should be considered and mandated the attorney generals of CARICOM states, in consultation with national judiciaries and representative bodies of the legal profession, to study and make recommendations on this proposal.[28]

[23] Ibid., 500.

[24] David Simmons, "The Caribbean Court of Justice: A Unique Institution of Caribbean Creativity," *Commonwealth Law Bulletin* 31, no. 1 (2005): 73; Salvatore Caserta, *International Courts in Latin America and the Caribbean: Foundations and Authority* (Oxford: Oxford University Press, 2020), 28–33.

[25] Hugh Rawlins, *The Caribbean Court of Justice: The History and Analysis of the Debate* (Georgetown, Guyana: CARICOM, 2000), 5.

[26] Leonard Birdsong, "The Formation of the Caribbean Court of Justice: The Sunset of British Colonial Rule in the English Speaking Caribbean," *University of Miami Inter-American Law Review* 36, no. 2/3 (2005): 200; see also Caserta, *International Courts in Latin America and the Caribbean*.

[27] Duke E. Pollard, *The Caribbean Court of Justice: Closing the Circle of Independence* (Kingston, Jamaica: Caribbean Law Publishing Co., 2004), 2.

[28] CHOG, *Communiqué of the Eighth Meeting of the Conference of Heads of Government of the Caribbean Community*, June 29–July 3, 1987 (Castries, St Lucia: CARICOM, 1987),

The CHOG endorsed the progress made toward creating an appellate court in 1989.[29] The WIC echoed the conclusions of the CHOG, also recommending the replacement of the Privy Council with a Caribbean court that would have appellate jurisdiction.[30] Many establishment elites, however, were opposed to the idea. The holdouts against a court of appeal acquiesced in the 1990s after the Privy Council determined that Caribbean countries' use of the death penalty violated human rights standards.[31]

Finally, with an eye toward improving integration and completing independence, the CHOG decided to establish a Caribbean Court of Justice in 1998.[32] When the CCJ was finally created in 2001 by the Agreement Establishing the Caribbean Court of Justice (CCJ Agreement) and the Revised Treaty of Chaguaramas (RTC),[33] it was vested with appellate and original jurisdiction to meet both demands of replacing the Privy Council and ensuring greater implementation of the Community's objectives.

By looking back, we can see that the CCJ is deeply rooted in the colonial legacies of the region. The dualism of two existent political norms – independence and sovereignty versus regionalism and unity – meant the path to CARICOM and the CCJ was often unsteady and fraught with tensions that are still noticeable today. For example, only five states recognize the appellate jurisdiction of the CCJ,[34] indicating a

https://caricom.org/communique-of-the-eighth-meeting-of-the-conference-of-heads-of-government-of-the-caribbean-community-29-june-3-july-1987-castries-saint-lucia/.

29 Ibid.

30 WIC, *Time for Action.*

31 *Pratt and Morgan v The Attorney General for Jamaica and another* (Jamaica) [1993] UKPC 1 (November 2, 1993).

32 CHOG, *Communiqué of the Nineteenth Meeting of the Conference of Heads of Government of the Caribbean Community*, June 30–July 4, 1998 (Castries, St Lucia: CARICOM Secretariat, 1998), https://caricom.org/communique-issued-at-the-conclusion-of-the-the-nineteenth-meeting-of-the-conference-of-heads-of-government-of-the-caribbean-community-30-june-4-july-1998-castries-saint-lucia/.

33 Agreement establishing the Caribbean Court of Justice (adopted February 14, 2001, entered into force July 23, 2002) U.N.T.S. 2255, at 319–341. For a discussion of the dual nature of the CCJ, see Armand De Mestral, "The Constitutional Functions of the Caribbean Court of Justice," *McGill Journal of Dispute Resolution* 1, no. 2 (2015).

34 As of May 2023, only Barbados, Guyana, Belize, Dominica, and Saint Lucia have accepted the CCJ's appellate jurisdiction. Guyana severed ties with the Privy Council in 1973, Barbados in 2005, Belize in 2010, Dominica in 2015, and Saint Lucia most recently in May 2023. The following states retain the Judicial Committee of the Privy Council as the court of last resort: Antigua and Barbuda, Bahamas, Grenada, Jamaica, Montserrat, Saint

less than wholehearted embrace of the CCJ among the CARICOM members or that some member states "do not have full confidence in the Court."[35] More broadly, CARICOM – as it was adopted by member states – is "a model of regional integration which involved virtually no concession of national sovereignty."[36] These tensions might be reflected in CARICOM's institutional design, which features midrange delegation (meaning the granting of authority to an independent body) alongside low pooling (defined as joint decision-making where the national veto is surrendered).[37]

In addition, the colonial past has contributed to the legal culture within which the Court operates. Most notably, an important legacy is legal pluralism. The CCJ presides over disparate legal systems, despite their commonalities. While most of the member states are rooted in common law legal traditions, and all began with externally imposed law, their legal traditions are not uniform. The common law was not uniformly received in the Caribbean, there was no historical aim toward legal harmonization across the region, and "law-making and most judicial decision-making in the Caribbean is markedly local and national, not regional."[38] Moreover, Guyana and Saint Lucia retain aspects of the civil law system – poignant reminders of their tumultuous colonial past[39] – and Haiti and Suriname are civil law systems.[40] Thus, the legal regimes are best described as "disparate but closely connected."[41]

Moreover, state law exists alongside other "legal orders," to varying degrees across the CARICOM states. Custom is a source of law "of particular importance in the area of land law or property law and family law."[42] Other informal systems of law and justice have emerged, such as that found in garrison communities in Jamaica[43] or within Maroon

Kitts and Nevis, Trinidad and Tobago, and Saint Vincent and Grenadines. Haiti and Suriname maintain their own court of last resort.

35 Interview 22.

36 Derek O'Brien and S. Foadi, "CARICOM and Its Court of Justice," *Common Law World Review* 37, no. 4 (2008): 337.

37 Hooghe and Marks, "Delegation and Pooling in International Organizations."

38 Tracy Robinson, "A Caribbean Common Law," *Race & Class* 49, no. 2 (2007): 119.

39 Antoine, "Waiting to Exhale," 144. Antoine explains that Saint Lucia switched hands between French and British rulers fourteen times.

40 Rose-Marie B. Antoine, *Commonwealth Caribbean Law and Legal Systems*, 2nd ed. (New York: Routledge-Cavendish, 2008), 41.

41 Robinson, "A Caribbean Common Law," 118.

42 Antoine, *Commonwealth Caribbean Law and Legal Systems*, 178.

43 Wheatle and Campbell, "Constitutional Faith and Identity in the Caribbean," 356.

communities.[44] Religious legal traditions also have recognition in some CARICOM states.[45] Thus, pluralism is an important aspect of the legal identity both across and within CARICOM states.

In addition, the legal culture across the Caribbean has been described as lacking a "constitutional faith."[46] Wheatle and Campbell argue the lack of constitutional faith is reflected in and due to the widespread beliefs that the judicial system is slow or unresponsive. Failures to respect constitutional rights also "make it difficult to cultivate reliance, trust and positive stories about the constitution and the state."[47] Several studies similarly reveal that public perceptions of the justice system are often poor, although there is variation across countries and according to the year under study.[48] As some have argued, the lack of faith in the judicial system and the state legal order, like legal pluralism, is part of the legacy of colonialism.

Overall, the CCJ today exists within an ideational context characterized by colonial legacies, political norms that value regionalism alongside commitments to preserving sovereignty and independence, and legal culture rooted in pluralism and a lack of trust or faith in the state legal order. With this in mind, the section "The Caribbean Court at Work" provides an overview of CCJ's workload.

The Caribbean Court at Work

The Agreement Establishing the Caribbean Court of Justice entered into force in 2003, and the CCJ became operational in 2005.[49] Its seat is in Port of Spain, Trinidad and Tobago. The CCJ had dual jurisdiction: (1) it has appellate jurisdiction and serves as a supreme court for states that accede to this jurisdiction; and (2) it has original jurisdiction in respect of

[44] Antoine, *Commonwealth Caribbean Law and Legal Systems*, 293; Werner Zips, "Laws in Competition: Traditional Maroon Authorities Within Legal Pluralism in Jamaica," *Journal of Legal Pluralism & Unofficial Law* 28, no. 37–38 (1996).

[45] Antoine, *Commonwealth Caribbean Law and Legal Systems*, 49–50.

[46] Wheatle and Campbell, "Constitutional Faith and Identity in the Caribbean."

[47] Ibid., 354.

[48] For a summary of these studies, see UNDP, *Caribbean Justice: A Needs Assessment of the Judicial System in Nine Countries* (Panama City: UNDP, 2020), accessed May 10, 2023, www.undp.org/sites/g/files/zskgke326/files/migration/bb/Caribbean-Justice_A-Needs-Assessment-of-the-Judicial-System-in-Nine-Countries.pdf.

[49] There are twelve signatories to the CCJ Agreement: Antigua and Barbuda; Barbados; Belize; Dominica; Grenada; Guyana; Jamaica; Saint Kitts and Nevis; Saint Lucia; Saint Vincent and the Grenadines; Suriname; and Trinidad and Tobago.

the interpretation and application of the RTC. Its original jurisdiction is compulsory and exclusive for member states of CARICOM.[50] Within its original jurisdiction, the Court can hear disputes between member states, between member states and the Community, or referrals from national courts of member states concerning the interpretation and application of the RTC.[51] The Court can also review applications from private individuals or entities concerning the interpretation and application of the RTC, if the Court grants special leave to have their application reviewed.[52] In granting special leave, the Court determines whether the applicant has standing based on criteria spelled out in Article 222 of the RTC. If special leave is granted, the Court then proceeds to the merits of the case. Member states and the Community may also request advisory opinions from the Court.[53]

The Court received its first application to its appellate jurisdiction in 2005, while the first application in the original jurisdiction was submitted in 2008. Figure 5.1 shows the yearly number of judgments the Court has issued by jurisdiction from 2005 to 2020. As illustrated by this figure, the lion's share of its workload has consistently been in appellate review. Also, while the number of judgments fluctuates from year to year, there has been a steady increase over time. In total, there have been 256 judgments, 222 of which have been within the CCJ's appellate jurisdiction. Within the original jurisdiction, there have been thirty-four judgments, spread across eighteen contentious applications and one advisory opinion.

The remainder of the analysis focuses on the Court's decision-making within its original jurisdiction because it is only within this jurisdiction that the CCJ acts as an *international court*. In its appellate jurisdiction, the Court functions as a national court. As my overall aim is to understand international judicial decision-making, the appellate jurisdiction falls outside the scope of analysis. To examine deference by the CCJ, I draw from original data based on all cases (i.e., applications) within the original jurisdiction finalized up to and through the end of 2020.[54]

[50] RTC, Art. 211(1). Although full members of CARICOM, three states (the Bahamas, Haiti, and Montserrat) have not ratified the CCJ Treaty.

[51] Ibid., Art. 211(1)(a–c).

[52] Ibid., Art. 211(1)(d).

[53] Ibid., Art. 212.

[54] In some instances, the CCJ issued more than one judgment or ruling in a single application. I treat applications as the unit of analysis. A similar approach is taken for the EACJ and ACtHPR. See Appendix for a complete list of all applications included in the data.

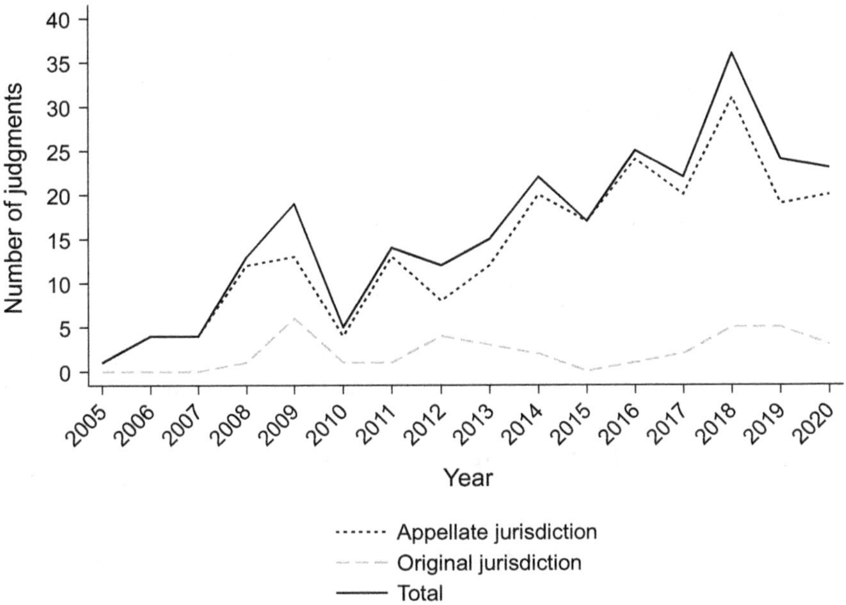

Figure 5.1 Number of CCJ finalized cases by year (2005–2020).

From the first application through the end of 2020, the Court has finalized eighteen applications in its original jurisdiction. These applications address several legal issues, although most relate to one of two issues.[55] Eight applications concern the common external tariff (Article 82 and 83 of the RTC). Four address the freedom of movement (RTC Article 45 and 46). Import duties (RTC Article 87) have been addressed in two applications. Two applications have centered around Community institutions and associate institutions and whether the Court had jurisdiction over disputes arising from the acts and decisions of those institutions. Other applications relate to competition (RTC Article 174 and 175) and freedom of services (RTC Article 36).

A few other applications within the Court's original jurisdiction also stand out. The Court issued its first judgment of friendly settlement in 2020.[56] It received its first interstate dispute in 2022, involving Belize and

[55] The list of cases in the Appendix details the relevant issue for each application.

[56] *Mootilal Ramhit & Sons Contracting Limited v The State of Trinidad & Tobago* [2020] CCJ 3 (OJ), July 23, 2020.

Trinidad and Tobago.[57] The fact that the RTC recognizes alternative dispute resolution mechanisms may partially account for the lack of interstate disputes.[58] Last, the Court received its first request for an advisory opinion in 2019 and delivered the opinion in 2020.[59]

As the above makes clear, in any given year the Court decides only a handful of cases, if that, within its original jurisdiction. The CCJ's workload lags that of other courts. For instance, the CCJ has had far fewer cases than the European Court of Justice in its first fifteen years (see Figure A4.1 in the Appendix); between 1953 and 1967 the ECJ issued 236 rulings. The comparative sluggishness of the CCJ's caseload, as will be discussed further below, is partially attributable to the absence of cases brought by CARICOM and referrals from national courts. The CCJ's caseload also lags that of the EACJ (see Chapter 4). We should also bear in mind that CARICOM comprises smaller nations and markets than both the EU and EAC. Regardless, even though the caseload within the original jurisdiction has grown slowly, the decisions taken by the Court so far have been crucial in laying the foundation for future applications and the development of Community law. Understanding the Court's decision-making, even with the relatively small number of applications, sheds light on what we might expect of it in the coming years while also offering insights into the factors shaping international courts and their jurisprudence throughout their infancy.

Judicial Deference by the Caribbean Court of Justice

How can we characterize the Caribbean Court of Justice's decision-making? To what extent does it defer to states? As explained in Chapter 2, deference can be observed in case outcomes, a court's legal interpretation and reasoning, and its use of remedies. This section examines the CCJ's deference on each of these dimensions. The examination reveals that deference by the CCJ is generally moderate but varies.

[57] *The State of Belize v The State of Trinidad & Tobago* [2022] CCJ 1 (OJ) (February 1, 2022).

[58] Interview 19; see also Adrian D. Saunders, "A Commentary on the Early Decisions of the Caribbean Court of Justice in Its Original Jurisdiction," *International and Comparative Law Quarterly* 59, no. 3 (2010): 766.

[59] Advisory Opinion, requested by the Caribbean Community [2020] CCJ 1 (OJ) (March 18, 2020).

Case Outcomes

Whether the CCJ defers depends on the respondent. The picture of deference also differs for merits-only decisions in contrast to all decisions (this includes admissibility and jurisdiction plus merits decisions). Table 5.1 provides descriptive statistics for case outcomes, based on the respondent and type of decisions. The *total deference rate* is 50 percent, reflecting outcomes for all applications, irrespective of respondent or type of decision. This suggests that the Court deferred half of all applications because it either abstained or validated the state or CARICOM's exercise of authority. Put differently, the applicant won in only half of applications. The deference rate, however, is lower among merits judgments. Specifically, the *merits deference rate* is 36 percent, regardless of respondent. This means that if applicants are granted leave and the Court

Table 5.1 *Summary of CCJ's case outcomes (2009–2020)*

	Number of judgments	Percent of category
All		
• *Inadmissible or no jurisdiction*	4	22.2
• *No violation found*	5	27.8
• *At least one violation*	9	50.0
	Deference rate (percent)	
Total (N =18)	50.0	
Merits (N = 14)	35.7	
State respondent		
• *No jurisdiction*	2	14.9
• *No violation*	4	28.6
• *At least one violation*	8	57.1
	Deference rate (percent)	
Total (N = 14)	42.9	
Merits (N = 12)	33.3	
CARICOM respondent (N = 8)		
• *No violation or dismissed*	6	75.0
• *At least one violation*	2	25.0

Note: In four cases, respondents were both CARICOM and a state(s). Total deference rate = (*no violation* + *inadmissible or no jurisdiction*) ÷ Total N. Merits deference rate = (*no violation*) ÷ Merits N.

considers the application's merits, the Court accepts the state or CARICOM's exercise of authority in slightly more than one-third of applications.

If we differentiate between the type of respondent (state versus CARICOM), the picture is slightly different. The CCJ more frequently finds states in violation of Community law than it does Community institutions, meaning it defers more to CARICOM than it does states. Of all fourteen applications where a member state was the respondent, the Court deferred 43 percent. Among the applications against states that were considered on the merits, the Court deferred to states in only 33 percent. CARICOM was a respondent in eight applications; the Court deferred to CARICOM in six, or 75 percent, of these applications. All else equal, the CCJ tends to defer less often to states than to CARICOM.[60]

Based on these figures alone, we can surmise that the CCJ defers minimally to states – especially if it considers the merits – but it defers more to CARICOM organs. On balance, we might say that CCJ is moderately deferential. Case outcomes, however, reflect much more than deference alone, such as actual (non)compliance, the quality of legal defense, or the strength of a legal case. For this reason, deference rates provide an incomplete picture of deference and suggest we need to combine this information with that of legal interpretation and reasoning by the Court as well as its use of remedies. I turn to these next.

Legal Interpretations and Reasoning

The Court's legal interpretations and reasoning tend to be nondeferential, often rejecting states' preferred interpretations. The Court's inclination toward nondeference is evident in several pivotal interpretations. First, the Court's interpretation of Article 222 of the RTC, which provides private actors' access to the CCJ, was nondeferential. The Court was required to interpret Article 222 in *TCL v Guyana*, a case which related to Guyana's alleged failure to implement CARICOM's common external tariff on cement.[61] Trinidad Cement Limited (TCL), a Guyanese cement company, filed an application against Guyana because the Government taxed cement imported from outside CARICOM at a lower rate than

[60] In Chapters 4 and 6, I map deference rates temporally. The number of applications in the CCJ does not make such a mapping meaningful, so I do not include one here.

[61] *Trinidad Cement Limited & TCL Guyana Incorporated v The Co-operative Republic of Guyana* [2009] CCJ 1 (OJ) (January 15, 2009) [herein *TCL v Guyana* [2009] CCJ 1 (OJ)].

required by the common external tariff. Before considering the merits of TCL's claim, however, the Court had to decide whether to grant special leave to TCL to have its application reviewed. The Court therefore needed to determine if Article 222(c) required the national state to espouse the private entity's claim or for that state to agree to the complaint.[62] Guyana argued that the RTC required this. The Court argued that such a literal, restrictive interpretation of paragraph (c) would require a state to be both complainant and respondent whenever a private actor has a complaint against the state of which it is a national, thereby precluding nationals from filing a complaint against their own state. The Court rejected Guyana's preferred interpretation, arguing it would be contrary to the "object and purpose of the RTC." Instead, the Court found that it must "interpret the Article in a manner that would render it effective. In effect the Court must adopt a teleological approach."[63] It argued that the contracting parties of the RTC did not intend to prohibit a national from filing a claim against their own state.[64] Paragraph (c), rather, intended to protect states from being "twice vexed," or to prevent the same claim from arising from both a state and a private entity.[65]

The interpretation advocated by Guyana was likely a view shared by several states and would have permitted states greater control over litigation before the CCJ. Pollard, who later became a CCJ judge, in his book on the drafting of the RTC and creation of the CCJ, argued:

> The Agreement Establishing the Caribbean Court of Justice, consonant with traditional international law, does not accord private entities *locus standi* as a matter of right in matters before the court. Consequently, a private entity aggrieved by a member state or any of its nationals in the

[62] Article 222 of the RTC states: "Persons, natural or juridical, of a Contracting Party may, with the special leave of the Court, be allowed to appear as parties in proceedings before the Court where: (a) the Court has determined in any particular case that this Treaty intended that a right or benefit conferred by or under this Treaty on a Contracting Party shall ensure to the benefit of such persons directly; and (b) the persons concerned have established that such persons have been prejudiced in respect of the enjoyment of the right or benefit mentioned in paragraph (a) of this Article; and (c) the Contracting Party entitled to espouse the claim in proceedings before the Court has: (i) omitted or declined to espouse the claim, or (ii) expressly agreed that the persons concerned may espouse the claim instead of the Contracting Party so entitled; and (d) the Court has found that the interest of justice requires that the persons be allowed to espouse the claim."

[63] *TCL v Guyana* [2009] CCJ 1 (OJ), para. 38.

[64] Ibid., para. 40.

[65] Ibid., para. 43.

> enjoyment of rights accorded by or under the Revised Treaty must have its claim espoused by the State of nationality. Alternatively, the party aggrieved may institute proceeding in national courts . . . [and seek a referral to the CCJ]. In both instances, therefore access to the Caribbean Court of Justice by private entities would be indirect either by espousal of the claim through the State of nationality or by a reference pursuant to Article 214.[66]

Pollard suggests that a "work-to-rule," restrictive interpretation that would defer to states was plausible. Ultimately, however, the Court's teleological interpretation of Article 222 in *TCL v Guyana* expanded access, leaving "the Court's door . . . wide open to potential applicants,"[67] while suspending states' authority to decide which complaints the Court could review.

A second crucial instance of the Court's nondeferential interpretation concerned its judicial review and remedial powers. The question of the Court's judicial review and remedial powers arose in another application filed by TCL, namely, *TCL v Caribbean Community*.[68] In this case, the CCJ needed to determine: (1) if it could review the lawfulness of a decision taken by the Council for Trade and Economic Development (COTED) and the Secretary-General of CARICOM to suspend the common external tariff for cement, and (2) if so, whether the Court could strike down as null and void COTED's decision to suspend the tariff as unlawful. In short, it had to ascertain the scope of its judicial review and remedial powers.

The RTC is not clear on this matter. It makes no expressed statement about whether the Court can review an act of a CARICOM organ. The Court concluded that it does have such authority. It reasoned that it "has power to scrutinise the acts of the Member States and the Community to determine whether they are in accordance with the rule of law which is a fundamental principle accepted by all the Member States of the Caribbean Community. It would be almost impossible to interpret the RTC and apply it to concrete facts unless the power of judicial review was implicit in that mandate."[69] Having asserted its authority to determine

[66] Pollard, *The Caribbean Court of Justice*, 223.

[67] David S. Berry, "The Original Jurisdiction Jurisprudence of the Caribbean Court of Justice: Promoting Regional Integration," *Social and Economic Studies* 61, no. 2 (2012): 35.

[68] *Trinidad Cement Limited v The Caribbean Community* [2009] CCJ 4 (OJ) (August 10, 2009) [herein *TCL v CARICOM* [2009] CCJ 4 (OJ)].

[69] Ibid., para. 38.

whether specific acts of a state or the Community were in accord with the RTC, the Court then found that this also implied the authority to declare unlawful acts void. Specifically, the Court argued, "[g]iven the Court's duty to enforce the rule of law and to render the RTC effective, competence to review the legality of acts adopted by Community institutions must perforce include competence to award appropriate relief to private entities that have suffered and established loss as a result of an illegal act or omission on the part of the Community."[70] This interpretation was an expressed rejection of alternative, deferential interpretation proffered by a nonrespondent state.[71] Rather than accept this alternative, the Court bestowed itself with "far-reaching powers"[72] that rejected CARICOM's authority to supervise Community institutions and to decide on how to remedy violations.

A third important interpretation illustrating nondeference, whereby the Court rejected the states' exercise of authority, came about in *Myrie v Barbados*.[73] This dispute concerned Shanique Myrie, a Jamaican national who was travelling to Barbados. Upon arrival at the airport in Barbados, she was detained, body-searched, and denied entry. Among other things, she claimed that this was a violation of Article 45 of the RTC, which ensures free movement for CARICOM nationals, and a 2007 decision of the CHOG, which entitles Community nationals to an automatic definite stay of six months in other CARCIOM states.[74] The Court took several important steps in this case, all of which exemplify nondeference. It affirmed "the Court can and must take into account principles of international human rights law when seeking to shape and develop relevant Community law."[75] The Court did not assert jurisdiction to adjudicate over violations of international human rights law, but rather that Article 217 of the RTC authorized the Court to apply rules of

[70] Ibid., para. 43.

[71] Ibid., para. 34. In its observation submitted to the CCJ, Jamaica argued that the CCJ did not have the power of judicial review because, unlike the EU Treaty, the RTC did not explicitly provide for it. Jamaica also argued that it was inappropriate for the CCJ to have coercive measures of remedy over Community institutions.

[72] David S. Berry, *Caribbean Integration Law* (Oxford: Oxford University Press, 2014), 427.

[73] *Shanique Myrie v The State of Barbados* [2013] CCJ 3 (OJ) (October 4, 2013) [herein *Myrie v Barbados* [2013] CCJ 3 (OJ)].

[74] Myrie further claimed that the search and detention were a serious violation of her fundamental human rights, and that she was discriminated against on grounds of her nationality, which is prohibited by RTC, Art. 7 and 8.

[75] *Myrie v Barbados* [2013] CCJ 3 (OJ), para. 10.

international law when relevant. The Court determined that this included international human rights treaties.

In addition, the Court took steps toward asserting the supremacy of Community law and giving it direct effect. The Court affirmed that states were bound by Community law, even if they had not enacted or transposed it into domestic law, saying, "it is inconceivable that such [transposition] would be necessary in order to create binding rights and obligations *at the Community level.*"[76] Later in this judgment, the Court would clarify that the supremacy of CARICOM law applied at the Community level: "Community law and the limits it imposes on the Member States must take precedence over national legislation, *in any event at the Community level.*"[77] This implies that Community law would supersede domestic law when enforced at the Community level. The Court did not go so far as to say that supremacy was enforceable at the domestic level, but it "leave[s] the door open" for a more encompassing notion of supremacy.[78]

The Court also opened the door for the "direct effect"[79] of CARICOM law based on its interpretation of Article 240. Article 240 of the RTC reads: "(1) Decisions of competent Organs taken under this Treaty shall be subject to the relevant constitutional procedures of the Member States before creating legally binding rights and obligations for nationals of such States. (2) The Member States undertake to act expeditiously to give effect to decisions of competent Organs and Bodies in their municipal law." The Court claimed that Article 240

> speaks to giving effect to such rights and obligations *in domestic law*. This is clearly reflected in its second paragraph which requires Member States to give effect to decisions of competent Organs and Bodies in their *municipal law* so as to enable Community nationals to enforce their rights at the national level and in the municipal courts. If binding regional decisions can be invalidated at the Community level by the failure on the part of a particular State to incorporate those decisions locally the efficacy of the entire CARICOM regime is jeopardized… The Court is therefore entitled, if not required, to adjudicate complaints of alleged breaches of Community law even where Community law is inconsistent

[76] Ibid., para. 51.
[77] Ibid., para. 69, emphasis added.
[78] Berry, *Caribbean Integration Law*, 219.
[79] Direct effect is a doctrine originally developed by the ECJ, whereby the rights conferred on individuals through EU law are binding on states and directly enforceable by national judges.

> with domestic law. It is the obligation of each State, having consented to the creation of a Community obligation, to ensure that its domestic law, at least in its application, reflects and supports Community law.[80]

The CCJ's interpretation of Article 240 most likely was not states' intended meaning. Berry argues that "Article 240 of the RTC, would greatly hinder, if not prohibit outright, the development of the principle of direct effect."[81] Yet, the CCJ concluded that "Article 240(1) RTC does not require that Member States enact a binding Community decision into domestic law in order to create at the Community level legally binding rights and obligations. The States are merely required to give domestic effect to such a decision *subject to their own relevant constitutional procedures.*"[82] The Court's interpretation of Article 240 advances a position that cannot be clearly discerned from the text of the Treaty. Rather, the CCJ "employed well-crafted legal reasoning ... to cement the Caribbean legal order by roughly establishing the principles of supremacy and the direct effect of CARICOM Community law."[83] Ultimately, due to the implications for supremacy and direct effect, the *Myrie* judgment rejects the states' authority in ways most likely not envisioned by states.

These three pivotal interpretations (special leave, judicial review and remedial powers, and supremacy and direct effect) exemplify the CCJ's nondeference. They defined and expanded the boundaries of the Court's authority, while also rejecting the scope of states' authority and control within areas of Community competence. Beyond these decisions, interviewees describe the CCJ's interpretation and reasoning as generally nondeferential. When asked to characterize the method of treaty interpretation used by the CCJ, interviewees confirmed that the Court tends to use a "purposive" approach.[84] For example, one judge said: "I would say that the Court by and large demonstrates a very big degree of liberal interpretation. And the Court has shown that it is not at all conservative."[85] A lawyer with experience litigating before the Court similarly expressed the view that the CCJ has "definitely, consistently used the

[80] *Myrie v Barbados* [2013] CCJ 3 (OJ), paras. 51–52.
[81] Berry, *Caribbean Integration Law*, 209.
[82] *Myrie v Barbados* [2013] CCJ 3 (OJ), para. 54.
[83] Salvatore Caserta and Mikael Rask Madsen, "Between Community Law and Common Law: The Rise of the Caribbean Court of Justice at the Intersection of Regional Integration and Post-Colonial Legacies," *Law and Contemporary Problems* 79, no. 1 (2016): 110.
[84] Interview 17; Interview 20.
[85] Interview 16.

technique of the purposive construction."[86] No interviewees referred to its interpretation or reasoning as deferential.

However, there is a striking difference in how the Court defers depending on the respondent. The CCJ's interpretation and reasoning reflects more deference when the respondent is CARICOM, as opposed to when a state is the responding party. For instance, the Court expressed that it will be deferential when assessing decisions of CARICOM, giving Community organs a wide margin of discretion. It stated:

> The clear intention of the Court as expressed in this passage is to recognize and retain judicial competence to review decision-making in the organs of the Community where these are capable of legal analysis, whilst reserving the necessary space for policy-making by those organs. The Court will not substitute its own assessment for that of the competent authority but will simultaneously insist that there be adherence to established normative standards. In the modern vernacular, a margin of discretion is reserved to the community actors.[87]

In contrast, the CCJ ruled in *Myrie v Barbados* that a state's rationale for restricting CARICOM nationals' right of definite stay must be "interpreted narrowly and strictly" and that the burden of proof falls upon states seeking to invoke an exemption.[88] In this instance, the Court implies that it will give states a narrow margin of appreciation on exemptions. These two examples are themselves not definitive evidence that the CCJ treats CARICOM differently from states. For example, the Court has not cited these paragraphs in later decisions as precedent (with one exception[89]). Nonetheless, if we combine these examples with the data on case outcomes, there is indication that the CCJ defers more to CARICOM than it does to individual states.

Finally, it should be noted that compared to the earliest decisions of the CCJ, some recent judgments demonstrate greater deference. For instance, the decisions in *Tomlinson*[90] and *Douglas*[91] can be seen as

[86] Interview 25.

[87] *Hummingbird Rice Mills Limited v Suriname & The Caribbean Community* [2012] CCJ 1 (OJ) (February 23, 2012), para. 32 [herein *HRML v Suriname & CARICOM* [2012] CCJ 1 (OJ)]

[88] *Myrie v Barbados* [2013] CCJ 3 (OJ), para. 67.

[89] Paragraph 67 of *Myrie* is cited in *David Bain v The State of Trinidad & Tobago* [2019] CCJ 3 (OJ) (May 29, 2019) [herein *Bain v Trinidad & Tobago* [2019] CCJ 3 (OJ)].

[90] *Maurice Tomlinson v The State of Belize & The State of Trinidad & Tobago* [2016] CCJ 1 (OJ) (June 10, 2016) [herein *Tomlinson v Belize* [2016] CCJ 1 (OJ)].

[91] *Cabral Douglas v The Commonwealth of Dominica* [2017] CCJ 1 (OJ) (February 20, 2017) [herein *Douglas v Dominica* [2017] CCJ 1 (OJ)].

Table 5.2 *Summary of CCJ's remedies (2009–2020)*

Type of remedy	Number of applications
Declaratory judgments	9
• with one additional remedy = 3	
• with two additional remedies = 1	
Reparations	3
Consequential orders	2

Note: The Court has also granted an interim order in one instance: *Trinidad Cement Limited & Arawak Cement Limit v The State of Barbados* [2018] CCJ 1 (OJ) (July 17, 2018).

partially deferential, issued respectively in 2016 and 2017. Berry suggests that *Douglas* might signal a shift to more restrictive interpretations.[92] Similarly, Caserta and Madsen argue that *Tomlinson* reflects a dismissal on narrow factual grounds and an avoidance of human rights matters, despite seemingly bold pronouncements.[93]

Remedies

While the Caribbean Court has exercised the full range of its remedial powers, it defers remedial decisions to states more often than not. Table 5.2 summarizes the Court's use of remedies based on my data. It illustrates that the CCJ has found breaches in nine out of eighteen applications, meaning the Court issued declaratory judgments in half of all its finalized applications. In four of these applications, or in 44 percent of those where a breach was found, the Court ordered at least one remedy in addition to the declaratory judgment. The Court has ordered two

[92] David S. Berry, "The Effect of the Original Jurisdiction of the Caribbean Court of Justice on Regional Integration and National Law," in *The Oxford Handbook of Caribbean Constitutions*, ed. Richard Albert, Derek O'Brien, and Se-shauna Wheatle (Oxford: Oxford University Press, 2020), 536–37.

[93] Salvatore Caserta and Mikael Rask Madsen, "Tomlinson v. Belize; Tomlinson v. Trinidad and Tobago," *American Journal of International Law* 110, no. 3 (2016). The Court's decision to not review human rights claims might be seen as an example of deference. For instance, in *Myrie* Barbados argued that the Court does not have such jurisdiction (paras. 9–10).

remedies in addition to the declaratory judgment in only one case. Interestingly, the Court has issued only declaratory judgments against CARICOM, while states were subject to more intrusive remedies. This is yet another indication that the Court is more deferential toward Community organs than it is toward states.

The Court's merits judgment in *TCL v Guyana* determined that the Court had the power to order compensation (or pecuniary reparations) even though the threshold for giving such orders is high.[94] The Court awarded pecuniary damages (to compensate for material loss) in *TCL v Guyana* as this threshold was met. In *Myrie*, the CCJ went further and determined that it could award both pecuniary damages and nonpecuniary damages (to compensate for moral, nonmaterial loss such as pain and suffering).[95] The Court, however, has found that, in accord with common opinion on punitive damages in international law, it will not order punitive damages.[96] In all, the Court has ordered pecuniary reparations in three cases, representing one-third of the applications where wrongdoing was found.

In addition to reparations, the Court has delivered consequential orders. As discussed earlier, the Court determined in *TCL v CARICOM*, its first merits judgment, that it had the power to deliver coercive remedies.[97] While the Court ultimately did not deliver a consequential order in *TLC v CARICOM*,[98] it has made use of this power in two later instances, or approximately 22 percent of successful applications. These orders required the respondent state(s) to amend their law or policy.[99] Thus, while the Court has asserted its power to deliver intrusive remedies, it typically stops short of ordering changes to law and policy.

That said, the Court does not shy away from recommending reforms. For instance, the Court gave several recommendations in *TLC v CARICOM*, among them "that in the future when the Secretary-General

[94] *Trinidad Cement Limited & TCL Guyana Incorporated v The Co-operative Republic of Guyana* [2009] CCJ 5 (OJ) (August 20, 2009) [herein *TCL v Guyana* [2009] CCJ 5 (OJ)], paras. 23–29.

[95] *Myrie v Barbados* [2013] CCJ 3 (OJ). Both pecuniary and nonpecuniary damages were awarded.

[96] *TCL v Guyana* [2009] CCJ 5 (OJ), paras. 35–40.

[97] *TCL v CARICOM* [2009] CCJ 4 (OJ), para. 43.

[98] Ibid., para. 75.

[99] *Rudisa Beverages & Juices N.V. Caribbean International Distributors Inc. v The Co-operative Republic of Guyana* [2014] CCJ 1 (OJ) (May 8, 2014); *TCL v Guyana* [2009] CCJ 5 (OJ).

takes a decision to authorise a suspension [of the common external tariff] it is a good practice for his authorisation to be supported by a brief statement of the reason or reasons for arriving at his decision."[100] Similar suggestions can be found in the judgment. The Court has also provided extensive policy recommendations in relation to the common external tariff in other applications.[101]

Another important example arose in the case of *Tomlinson*.[102] In this case, Tomlinson claimed that Belize and Trinidad and Tobago "had prejudiced him in the enjoyment of his Community right to enter these countries without hassle or harassment by maintaining an express prohibition on entry of homosexuals in their Immigration Acts."[103] The Court ruled that while the respondent states did keep these incompatible laws on the books, state practice was compatible with Community law and states were legally required by their domestic legal orders to carry out Community law as a result of their Treaty obligation.[104] Moreover, the applicant did not provide evidence that the prohibition was enforced against Community nationals. While the Court dismissed Tomlinson's claim, it stated that its decision

> is not to be taken as condoning the indefinite retention on the statute book of a national law which in appearance seems to conflict with obligations under Community law. Member States should ensure that national laws, subsidiary legislation and administrative practices are transparent in their support of the free movement of all CARICOM nationals. In principle, national legislation should expressly be harmonized with Community law. Any permanent or indefinite discord between administrative practices and the literal reading of legislation is undesirable as the rule of law requires clarity and certainty especially for nationals of other Member States who are to be guided by such legislation and practice.[105]

Thus, the Court formally preserved states' authority to maintain their legislation, but it also strongly suggested what actions would be appropriate for the states to take.

[100] *TCL v CARICOM* [2009] CCJ 4 (OJ), para. 81.

[101] See for example, *Trinidad Cement Limited v The State of Trinidad & Tobago* [2019] CCJ 4 (OJ) (August 6, 2019), paras. 90–95; *TCL v CARICOM* [2009] CCJ 4 (OJ), paras. 76–77.

[102] *Tomlinson v Belize* [2016] CCJ 1 (OJ).

[103] Ibid., para. 2.

[104] Ibid., para. 63.

[105] Ibid., para. 56.

To summarize, the CCJ's deference in terms of case outcomes, interpretation, and remedies varies markedly depending on the respondent: the CCJ defers more to CARICOM than to respondent states. Community organs "win" more frequently than states, and the Court has so far given a wider margin of appreciation to CARICOM than to states. Deference also varies across outcomes, interpretation, and remedies. On the one hand, nondeference is more prominent in outcomes and interpretation, while remedies reflect deference. The Court's decisions have outlined and established an expansion of the Court's authority while rejecting state authority. Also, even though it has shown a willingness to apply intrusive remedies when an infraction is "serious and egregious"[106] or where "there would be grave consequences for the rule of law,"[107] such remedies are minimally applied, even less so for Community organs than for states. On balance, we can therefore describe the CCJ's deference as moderate.

Explaining the Caribbean Court's Deference

What accounts for the Court's moderate deference? By one account, deference depends on the strength and activity of a judicial support network. Alternatively, I have posited that formal independence and political fragmentation shape deference. The following section assesses these accounts in relation to the patterns of (non)deference observed in the case of the CCJ.

The Role of Support Networks

The logic of support networks suggests that the CCJ's moderate deference arises from having a relatively strong and active judicial support network and opportunities for this network to access the Court. At first glance, these conditions apply. From the early days leading to its creation through the beginning of its operations, the Court has enjoyed support from some political and legal elites.[108] Moreover, the Court has several

106 *Myrie v Barbados* [2013] CCJ 3 (OJ), para. 101.

107 *TCL v CARICOM* [2009] CCJ 4 (OJ), para. 43.

108 Joris Kocken and Gerda Roozendaal, "Constructing the Caribbean Court of Justice: How Ideas Inform Institutional Choices," *European Review of Latin American & Caribbean Studies* 93 (2012); Birdsong, "The Formation of the Caribbean Court of Justice"; Pollard, *The Caribbean Court of Justice*; Rawlins, *The Caribbean Court of Justice.*

channels of access for a support network to leverage and utilize. This section examines these access channels, whether the Court has tried to mobilize supporters, whether supporters utilize these points of access, and if there is any evidence that their use aligns with the Court's (non)deference. It shows that even though there are various channels of access, the support network is insufficiently robust or active to account for the observed patterns in deference.

The CCJ features opportunities for private actors (e.g., individuals, for-profit actors, NGOs), subnational actors, and, to a lesser extent, supranational actors to access the Court. Importantly, the CCJ provides direct access for private actors, upon being granted leave according to Article 222 of the RTC. The CCJ has taken both judicial and nonjudicial measures to expand this access and encourage its use. It has adopted several judicial decisions that are pro-private litigant. The CCJ's interpretation of Article 222 has been friendly to private actors and effectively expanded their access to the Court (see also prior discussion about interpretation of Article 222). Article 222 provides that special leave to the Court requires, among other things, that applicants demonstrate (a) a right or benefit is conferred by the Treaty and (b) the enjoyment of that right or benefit was prejudiced. To demonstrate that the Treaty confers a right or benefit, the Court developed a *correlative rights doctrine*, finding that the right or benefit need not be expressly conferred by the Treaty but rather may be derived from and correlated to a state obligation based in the Treaty.[109] Moreover, the CCJ ruled applicants only need to make "an arguable case" that a prejudice has occurred to be granted leave.[110] The Court's approach to Article 222 has thus lowered the threshold for private actors to access to the Court.

The Court's approach to awarding litigation costs is also pro-private litigant. The rules of the Court state that a losing party shall be ordered to pay the costs of the successful party,[111] but where "circumstances are exceptional, the Court may order that the costs be shared or that the parties bear their own costs."[112] The Court has found that "exceptional circumstances" include instances where the application benefits the

[109] *TCL v Guyana* [2009] CCJ 1 (OJ), para. 32. See also Berry, "The Effect of the Original Jurisdiction of the CCJ on Regional Integration and National Law," 533–34.

[110] *TCL v Guyana* [2009] CCJ 1 (OJ), para. 33.

[111] CCJ, *Original Jurisdiction Rules* (Port of Spain: CCJ, 2006). Revised versions of the rules for the Court include similar provisions.

[112] Ibid., Rule 31.1(3). Revised versions of the rules include similar provisions.

Community, for instance by enabling the development of Community law. The Court in *Hummingbird Rice Mills Ltd* v *Suriname & CARICOM* explained that while exceptional circumstances must be determined on a case-by-case basis, "At this nursery stage of the development of Caribbean Community law, it is important that the burden of establishing the basic principles underpinning the Single Market should not weigh too heavily and disproportionately on private entities and thus discourage the bringing of important issues of economic integration law before the Court."[113] With this in mind, the CCJ ordered the Caribbean Community to bear its own costs, even though it was the successful party.

The benefits to the Community also constituted sufficient reason to discharge a private actor from paying the respondent's costs in *TCL v the Competition Commission*, when the CCJ found that the

> Commission and the Community have received benefits from the litigation. To require the Claimant, a private entity to bear the full costs of the proceedings in these circumstances would not be warranted. It would be disproportionate to require it to bear the cost of clarifying the rules and procedures on this important aspect to the Single Market and Economy. At this fledgling stage of the Single Market and Economy, it is important that the private litigants are not discouraged from initiating process.[114]

The Court ordered the complainant to therefore pay 30 percent of the respondent's costs, as opposed to its full costs. The Court has required a losing private litigant to pay partial costs of the responding party in two other instances, both in cement cases where the private litigant was a for-profit actor.[115] In all other applications where the private litigant was unsuccessful, parties were ordered to bear only their own costs – alleviating private litigants of the punishing effects of pursuing litigation.

While the CCJ typically alleviates private litigants from the burden of paying the litigation costs of a successful respondent, the Court has done the same for states and the Community. In fact, the Court has awarded full litigation costs to the successful private litigant in only two cases (as the default rule would require). In all other cases, the Court awarded

[113] *Hummingbird Rice Mills Limited v Suriname & The Caribbean Community* [2012] CCJ 2 (OJ) (April 11, 2012), para. 6.

[114] *Trinidad Cement Limited v The Competition Commission* [2013] CCJ 2 (OJ) (May 29, 2013) [herein *TCL v Competition Commission* [2013] CCJ 2 (OJ)], para. 8.

[115] See *Trinidad Cement Limited & Arawak Cement Limit v The State of Barbados* [2019] CCJ 5 (OJ) (November 28, 2019); *TCL v Competition Commission* [2013] CCJ 2 (OJ).

successful private litigants' only partial costs: meaning that when states and the Community are unsuccessful, typically they do not have to pay the private party's full costs. Nonetheless, the Court has taken a pro-litigant stance by allaying some of the burdens that would otherwise prevent private litigants from filing applications.

The Court has taken several practical steps to facilitate private actors' access to the CCJ. The Court has integrated e-services (e.g., filing of cases and documents) and sub-registries where applications can be filed.[116] These measures allow applicants to access the Court without physically traveling to Port of Spain, which is difficult and expensive due to the geography and nature of transport in the region. The Court also has "off-the-bench" activities through which it informs potential private litigants and their legal counsel about the CCJ and Community law. For example, judges of the Court speak and participate at meetings of regional bar associations, law schools, chambers of commerce, business associations, and more.[117] The Court also hosts events and activities where it disseminates information about the Court and Community law, such as its annual law moot competition for law students.[118]

Despite these significant efforts to mobilize private litigants and inform their potential lawyers, private actors have not widely pursued litigation through the Court's original jurisdiction, as indicated by the relatively small number of applications. When private actors have availed themselves of the CCJ, it has been limited to a narrow set of private actors. Eight out of the eighteen applications originated from a single industry – the cement industry (spearheaded by two companies). Also, a relatively small number of lawyers have been crucial to litigation so far. My data reveal that twelve lawyers (out of thirty-two) have been involved in two-thirds (or twelve) of applications from private actors.[119] While this might be indicative of a burgeoning support network and the centrality of lawyers to the development of Community law, similar to that of the EU,[120] it is doubtful that such a small segment of the Community can account for the nondeference that we observe. The

[116] Sub-registries are offices for the CCJ located at national courts.

[117] See CCJ, "Papers and Speeches," accessed June 25, 2024, https://ccj.org/papers-main/.

[118] See CCJ, "Annual CCJ International Law Moot," accessed June 25, 2024, https://ccj.org/about-the-ccj/annual-ccj-international-law-moot/.

[119] These figures do not consider whether a lawyer was lead counsel or not.

[120] Tommaso Pavone, *The Ghostwriters: Lawyers and the Politics Behind the Judicial Construction of Europe* (Cambridge: Cambridge University Press, 2022); Cichowski, *The European Court and Civil Society*.

relatively small number of applications from private actors within the original jurisdiction may be partially due to private for-profit actors' preferences for mediation or arbitration or, in the worst cases, corruption as opposed to litigation.[121] Also, interregional trade remains comparatively low,[122] which might reduce private actors' functional needs to rely on the CCJ.

Private actors can also participate as a third party to a dispute by acting as an intervener or submitting an amicus curiae brief. The Court has so far entertained either an intervener or an amicus in four applications. An NGO was the third party (amicus) in only one of these instances, while the others were cement companies who intervened in the cement cases.

While the CCJ does have support from a small cross section of private actors, their participation in litigation before the CCJ is associated typically with more, not less, deference. Table 5.3 compares case outcomes and remedial orders against whether applications were represented by a repeat counsel or a private actor participated as a third party.[123] Lawyers who acted as counsel in at least one prior case before the CCJ are counted as repeat counsel. Table 5.3 provides mixed evidence. Two findings from these data match the expectations of a support network logic. First, when looking at case outcomes for all applications, deference occurs less often – in 42 percent of applications – when applicants are represented by repeat counsel than when they are not (67 percent). Second, consequential orders have been delivered, which is indicative of nondeference, only when an applicant is represented by repeat counsel. In contrast, all other findings point to the inadequacy of an explanation based on the strength and activity of a support network, as deference is more common with the participation of a support network than without. For instance, declaratory judgments are less common when a support network participates,

[121] Interview 22; Interview 24.

[122] Abdullah Al Hassan et al., "Is the Whole Greater Than the Sum of Its Parts? Strengthening Caribbean Regional Integration," *IMF Working Paper 20/8* (IMF, 2020). The role of intraregional trade has been an important factor contributing to the CJEU's caseload and the legal construction of the EU; see Stone Sweet and Brunell, "Constructing a Supranational Constitution."

[123] NGO participation in the litigation before the CCJ has been very limited; no NGOs have been applicants, and only one has filed an amicus submission. In contrast to the analysis on the EACJ and ACtHPR, therefore, I include any private actor participating as a third party in this analysis. The Appendix includes a similar assessment including any private or supranational actor participating as a third party (see Table A5.1). It shows their participation more commonly leads to outcomes and remedies that reflect deference.

Table 5.3 *Cross-tabulations of CCJ's deference by support network*

	Repeat counsel		Third-party participation of private actor	
Applicant wins (all applications, N = 18)	No	Yes	No	Yes
No (deferred)	4 (66.67)	5 (41.67)	6 (42.86)	3 (75.00)
Yes	2 (33.33)	7 (58.33)	8 (57.14)	1 (25.00)
	Fisher's Test p-value: 0.620 χ^2 p-value: 0.314		Fisher's Test p-value: 0.576 χ^2 p-value: 0.248	
Violation declared (merits only, N = 13)				
No (deferred)	1 (33.33)	4 (40.00)	2 (22.22)	3 (75.00)
Yes	2 (66.67)	6 (60.00)	7 (77.78)	1 (25.00)
	Fisher's Test p-value: 1.000 χ^2 p-value: 0.834		Fisher's Test p-value: 0.217 χ^2 p-value: 0.070*	
Consequential order (merits only, N = 9)				
No (deferred)	2 (100.00)	5 (71.43)	6 (75.00)	1 (100.00)
Yes	0 (0)	2 (28.57)	2 (25.00)	0 (0.00)
	Fisher's Test p-value: 0.282 χ^2 p-value: 1.000		Fisher's Test p-value: 1.000 χ^2 p-value: 0.464	
Additional remedy (merits only, N = 9)				
No (deferred)	1 (50.00)	4 (57.14)	4 (50.00)	1 (100.00)
Yes	1 (50.00)	3 (42.86)	4 (50.00)	0 (0.00)
	Fisher's Test p-value: 1.000 χ^2 p-value: 0.858		Fisher's Test p-value: 1.000 χ^2 p-value: 0.259	

Note: *p<0.10, ** p<0.05, *** p<0.001. In each cross-tabulation, the first number is the frequency and the second number (in parentheses) is the column percentage.

either as repeat counsel or as a third party, than if it does not. Third-party participation is more often associated with case outcomes or remedies that are deferential than when there is no private actor participating as a third party. Overall, the mix of results suggest that whether the CCJ defers or not cannot be adequately explained by the participation of a support network, especially in terms of lawyers and third parties.

The strength and activity of substate and supranational actors also provide limited evidence of the role of support networks. Substate actors, namely, national courts, could bolster the CCJ by referring cases for preliminary ruling to the Court, which they are required to do when questions of Community law come before them.[124] In the case of the EU, referrals by national courts to the Court of Justice of the EU have been crucial to expansion of judicial power and nondeference.[125] However, this channel of access has yet to bear fruit for the CCJ, as the Court has not received any referrals from national courts as of December 2024. This is not for lack of efforts by the Court to encourage such referrals. The Court has noted in its judgments that national courts should refer questions of Community law to it.[126] The Court's educational arm, the CCJ Academy for Law,[127] informs legal audiences about the referral procedure. For instance, it began organizing lectures in several judiciaries on the Article 214 referral obligation in 2016.[128] More recently, the CCJ Academy developed a referral manual along with an instructional video.[129] Judges also speak at conferences and meetings of national judges and magistrates, which provide opportunities to remind judges of the preliminary reference procedure. Several interviewees suggest that a lack of knowledge contributes to the lack of references.[130] Other factors might contribute to absence of referrals. For example, the referral system requires resources that national courts tend to lack.[131] The administration of justice in many of the national jurisdictions is insufficient,

[124] RTC, Art. 214.

[125] Alter, *Establishing the Supremacy of European Law.*

[126] *HRML v Suriname & CARICOM* [2012] CCJ 1 (OJ), para. 26. See also *Myrie v Barbados* [2013] CCJ 3 (OJ), para. 82.

[127] Formerly the Caribbean Academy for Law and Court Administration (CALCA).

[128] CCJ, *Annual Report 2015–2016* (Port of Spain: CCJ, 2016), 21, accessed June 25, 2024, https://ccj.org/publications/annual-reports/.

[129] See CCJ, "Understanding the Referral Process," accessed June 25, 2024, https://ccj.org/resources/understanding-the-referral-process/?highlight=preliminary.

[130] Interview 19; Interview 20; Interview 25.

[131] Hugh M. Salmon, "The Caribbean Court of Justice: A March with Destiny," *Florida Coastal Law Journal* 2, no. 1 (2000).

according to a 2020 report by the UNDP: "[I]n all jurisdictions the backlog of cases . . . is one of the most challenging issues. The reasons for the backlogs are multifaceted and include primarily the slow pace of investigations by police, inordinate delays in production of depositions, and lack of human and technological resources."[132] There might also be legal reasons or complications that explain the lack of referrals, such as national civil proceeding rules or inadequate incorporation of the RTC obligations into national legislation, which is required in dualist legal systems for the RTC to be enforceable in domestic courts.[133] While additional research is needed to understand the lack of engagement by national courts, the absence of referrals nonetheless casts doubts as to whether the levels of nondeference demonstrated by the CCJ are attributable to support from substate actors, specifically, national courts.

Access and participation of supranational actors is also weak. The opportunities for CARICOM organs (e.g., Secretariat) to access the CCJ are limited; they have minimal capacity to use the CCJ as part of an enforcement mechanism. The Competition Commission is the only supranational organ of CARICOM that has a mandate to enforce compliance in tandem with the Court.[134] For instance, when the Commission finds a company engages in anticompetitive business conduct and fails to comply with actions specified by the Commission, the Commission may seek orders from the CCJ to enforce compliance. The Commission's access to the Court relates only to competition law, and even then, no such requests have yet been made. Aside from the Competition Commission, the only "organ" that has access to the Court and a mandate to monitor compliance is the Community Council of Ministers,[135] which is an intergovernmental organ composed of state representatives.[136] Not only has the Community Council not made any petitions to the Court, but it would be highly irregular for an intergovernmental organ to refer another state to the Court. The only instance of a case arising from a Community organ was an advisory opinion, not a contentious case. As one interviewee explained, "the underlying and associated structures [within CARICOM] to support [the Court] are just

[132] UNDP, *Caribbean Justice*. This report focuses on only nine CARICOM states.

[133] For a discussion of the legal constraints on national court referrals to the CCJ, see Alina Kaczorowska-Ireland and Westmin R.A. James, *Commonwealth Caribbean Law and Procedure: The Referral Procedure under Article 214 RTC in the Light of EU and International Law* (Abingdon: Routledge, 2020).

[134] RTC, Art. 175(11) and 180(3).

[135] RCT, Art. 10 and 211.

[136] Ibid., Art. 13.

not there."[137] Thus, the design of CARICOM limits the likelihood that CARICOM's monitoring and compliance machinery will serve as a crucial access channel through which a supranational contingent of a judicial support network will be able to bolster the Caribbean Court. The CARICOM Secretariat, however, can act as a third party, submitting observations, which it has done on a few occasions.

As this discussion shows, private, substate, and supranational actors, especially the latter two, have yet to realize the full potential of these various access channels through which they can utilize the Court and thereby strengthen its position vis-à-vis states and others who wield power within CARICOM. The general fragility of the CCJ's support network is at odds with the CCJ's moderate deference, as deference is much higher than its support network would imply. The weaknesses of the CCJ's support network may relate to several considerations. Caserta and Madsen argue that Oxbridge legal elites, who have been empowered by colonial legacies, underlie societal reluctance toward the CCJ.[138] In this sense, they might be viewed as an "anti-support" network. Distrust of local justice is deeply engrained in the public consciousness due to centuries of dependence on justice from afar (i.e., the UK), which also contributes to the lack of a robust support network.[139] The CCJ may also be suffering from normal "growing pains," in which only "time builds trust in a court."[140] Moreover, CARICOM is not designed to facilitate supranational enforcement, nor has it developed a practice of doing so, in ways that have been associated with the construction of judicial power in other regional integration organizations, like the EU. The combined effect of these factors, and potentially others, leaves the CCJ without a sufficiently influential and active support network.

The Structural Determinants of the Caribbean Court's Strategic Space

The CCJ's decision-making and tendency toward moderate deference is difficult to understand based on support networks. I have posited that a

137 Interview 26.

138 Caserta and Madsen, "Between Community Law and Common Law."

139 Interview 16; Interview 19. See also Wheatle and Campbell, "Constitutional Faith and Identity in the Caribbean."

140 Lee Cabatingan, "Time and Transcendence: Narrating Higher Authority at the Caribbean Court of Justice," *Law & Society Review* 50, no. 3 (2016), 684.

combination of structural factors – formal independence and political fragmentation – significantly shapes the Court's strategic space. The Court's high level of formal independence alongside the limited political fragmentation of states imposes contrasting pressures on the strategic space of the Court; the former boosts the legitimacy of the Court and hinders possibilities of collective state resistance, while the latter makes collective resistance easier. Combined, these two factors provided intermediate constraints and thus lead to moderate deference. I have also suggested that this strategic space is not static; state preferences can change. Also, past resistance by states can shrink the strategic space. Therefore, these additional considerations help to account for the variation in deference. The following discussion maps out these factors and dynamics in the case of the CCJ.

Formal Independence

The CCJ has an unusual institutional design among international courts. It is the only international court to have dual jurisdiction, and its resource management design[141] and rules on access[142] are unique. Most relevant to the analysis here, the CCJ has a high degree of formal independence, which is the result of several atypical institutional safeguards. The comparative mapping of formal independence in Chapter 3 reveals that the CCJ has the highest independence of all twenty-six international courts. The following section describes the rules that constitute the CCJ's formal independence. Table 5.4 summarizes these rules based on whether they enhance or weaken formal independence. After describing the rules, I evaluate how they affect perceptions of the Court.

Three sets of rules protect the Court from political influence and, thus, enhance its formal independence. The first set of independence enhancing rules relates to the appointment and terms of office for judges, all of which limit states' ability to control the Court through judicial appointments, tenure or similar. The Court is composed of (up to) nine judges and the President of the Court,[143] and they (except the President of the Court) are appointed by the Regional Judicial and Legal Services Commission (RJLSC).[144] The RJLSC is an independent organizational

[141] Theresa Squatrito, "Resourcing Global Justice: The Resource Management Design of International Courts," *Global Policy* 8, no. 5 (2017).

[142] Caserta and Madsen, "Between Community Law and Common Law," 100–101.

[143] CCJ Agreement, Art. 4(1).

[144] Ibid., Art. 4(6–7).

Table 5.4 *Rules constituting the formal independence of the CCJ*

	Independence enhancing	Independence hampering
Appointment and Term of Office	• Judges (except president) elected by independent body • Lifetime (until age 72) appointment • President holds a nonrenewable, seven-year term • Removal of judges decided by RJLSC, with recommendation of tribunal • Oath of office	• President removed by supermajority of states, upon recommendation of RJLSC and tribunal
Managerial autonomy	• Court selects its registrar by RJLSC, includes president • Budget determined by tripartite arrangement between Registry, RJLSC and Trust Fund • Court adopts its rules of procedure	• President selected by supermajority of states
Insulation of Judges	• Secret deliberations • Diplomatic privileges and immunities of office	

body created by the CCJ Agreement composed of public officials, legal professionals and academics, and civil society representatives.[145] Eleven members comprise the RJLSC; they are:

> (a) the President [of the Court] . . .; (b) two persons nominated jointly by the Organisation of the Commonwealth Caribbean Bar Association (OCCBA) and the Organisation of Eastern Caribbean States (OECS) Bar Association; (c) one chairman of the Judicial Services Commission of a Contracting Party selected in rotation. . .; (d) the Chairman of a Public Service Commission of a Contracting Party selected in rotation. . .;

[145] The President of the CCJ influences decisions of the RJLSC. Thus, it is not independent of the Court per se. The key point here, however, is that it is institutionally independent from states.

> (e) two persons from civil society . . . (f) two distinguished jurists. . .; and (g) two persons nominated jointly by the Bar or Law Associations of the Contracting Parties.[146]

The RJLSC elects judges by a majority vote.[147] Judicial commissions are a common model for appointing national judges in the Caribbean and beyond,[148] yet the CCJ is the only international court to have judges selected by an independent body like the RJLSC.

The RJLSC does not select the President of the Court. Rather, the President is appointed by a supermajority (three-fourths) of the member states of CARICOM, upon the recommendation of the RJLSC.[149] The selection of the CCJ's President resembles the selection for judges to most other international courts, who are typically selected by states through an intergovernmental treaty organ or by direct appointment of a state.

Judges are required to take an oath of office, and they hold tenure until the age of seventy-two.[150] The President, however, holds office for a nonrenewable term of seven years, or until he/she attains the age of seventy-two.[151] Lifetime appointments, or similar, are not featured by any other international court. Judges "can be removed from office only for inability to perform the functions of his office, whether arising from illness or any other cause or for misbehavior."[152] Removal of a judge or the President must first be investigated by a tribunal, which is established for this purpose.[153] Following a recommendation by the RJLSC and the advice by the tribunal, the President of the Court can be removed by a three-fourths vote of the Conference of the Heads of Government.[154] All other judges can be removed by majority vote of the RJLSC,[155] on the advice of the tribunal.[156]

[146] Ibid., Art. 5(1).
[147] Ibid., Art. 4(7).
[148] Interview 25. See Nuno Garoupa and Tom Ginsburg, "The Comparative Law and Economics of Judicial Councils," *Berkeley Journal of International Law* 27, no. 1 (2009).
[149] CCJ Agreement, Art. 4(6).
[150] Ibid., Art. 9(3).
[151] Ibid., Art. 9(2). An additional protocol was adopted in 2007 that allowed judges to stay in office until the age of seventy-five (or for seven years, whichever came first) during the "evolutionary phase of the Court." This protocol never entered into force. However, according to Berry this protocol was provisionally applied in June 2007; see Berry, *Caribbean Integration Law*, 385–87. See Table A3.1 for protocol details.
[152] Ibid., Art. 9(4).
[153] Ibid., Art. 9(5–6).
[154] Ibid., Art. 4(6).
[155] Ibid., Art. 4(7).
[156] Ibid., Art. 9(5–6).

The second set of rules that enhance the CCJ's formal independence relate to its managerial autonomy. In short, states have very limited ability to control how the Court is managed. According to the CCJ Agreement, the rules of procedure are developed by the President of the Court in consultation with five other judges.[157] The CCJ has autonomy over the management of its human and monetary resources.[158] The Registrar of the Court is appointed by the RJLSC.[159] Given the structure of the RJLSC, the appointment of the Registrar is selected without any direct role of states.

The monetary resources and the budgetary process of the CCJ are also outside the control of states. The Registry, the RJLSC, and the Trust Fund of the CCJ are all central to the allocation of the CCJ's monetary resources. In order to fund the CCJ, the CARICOM states – with the assistance of the Caribbean Development Bank – established a Trust Fund with an initial capital investment of $100 million.[160] The investment income of the Fund provides the financial resources for the Court. The Trust Fund operates under the direction of a Board of Trustees. The members of the Board of Trustees include: the Secretary-General of CARICOM; the Vice-Chancellor of the University of the West Indies; the President of the Insurance Association of the Caribbean; the Chairman of the Association of Indigenous Banks of the Caribbean; the President of the Caribbean Institute of Chartered Accountants; the President of the Organisation of Commonwealth Caribbean Bar Associations; the Chairman of the Conference of Heads of the Judiciary of Member States of the Caribbean Community; the President of the Caribbean Association of Industry and Commerce; and the President of the Caribbean Congress of Labour.[161] Like the RJLSC, the Trust Fund is directed by individuals representing various sectors, including the banking industry, labor, academia, and the legal profession. None of the trustees are representatives of member states. The Trust Fund, so long as it is properly managed, finances the CCJ in perpetuity and ensures that the CCJ does not rely upon the capacity and willingness of states to adequately provide resources.

157 Ibid., Art. 21(1) and 25(7).
158 Squatrito, "Resourcing Global Justice."
159 CCJ Agreement, Art. 5(3)(1).
160 Simmons, "The Caribbean Court of Justice," 87.
161 CARICOM, *Revised Agreement Establishing the Caribbean Court of Justice Trust Fund* (2004), accessed June 25, 2024, https://ccj.org/wp-content/uploads/2021/02/ccj_rev_trustfund.pdf.

As the Board of Trustees disburses funds to the CCJ, the budget must fall within the limits of what the Trust is able and willing to release to the Court. At the same time, the RJLSC has administrative responsibility over the CCJ. Consequently, the budget process of the CCJ involves the Registry, the RJLSC, and the Trust Fund.[162] Initially the rules governing the adoption of the budget were ambiguous, but after the CCJ became operational a Protocol on the Interfacing and Interaction of the RJLSC, CCJ, and the CCJ Trust Fund was adopted to clarify the procedure.[163] The Protocol states that the budget is prepared by the Court's registry and RJLSC, then discussed with the Executive Officer of the Trust Fund. The budget is then submitted to the RJLSC for approval. After approval, the budget is submitted to the Board of Trustees for comment, and the RJLSC can approve revisions in light of the Board's comments.[164]

A third set of rules enhances formal independence by insulating the judges from political pressure. In particular, judges are granted privileges and immunities of office to protect their independence and impartiality,[165] and deliberations of the Court are to be kept confidential.[166] In sum, the CCJ's design provides extensive institutional safeguards to ensure the Court and its judges are independent, leaving very few formal channels through which states can apply pressure on the Court and its judges.

There are, however, a few rules that hamper the CCJ's independence. These include, as described above, the appointment and terms of office for the President of the Court, which permit a certain degree of state influence. The member states through the CHOG have control over judges' salaries and compensation. Some interviewees identified the rules on the remuneration as the only outstanding rule that potentially weakens the independence of the Court.[167]

On the whole, the design of the CCJ grants the Court robust safeguards to independence, limiting the feasibility and credibility of states to

162 Interview 21.

163 See CCJ, *Annual Report 2006–2007* (Port of Spain: CCJ, 2007), 45, accessed June 25, 2024, https://ccj.org/publications/annual-reports/.

164 The Registrar influences decisions on the CCJ's budget. Thus, the Trust Fund is not independent of the Court per se. The key point here, however, is that it is institutionally independent of states.

165 CCJ Agreement, Art. 30.

166 CCJ, *Original Jurisdiction Rules*. This provision has remained unchanged in later amended versions of the CCJ's rules of procedure.

167 Interview 20; Interview 22.

collectively resist the Court. Moreover, this high level of formal independence endows the CCJ with a reservoir of support that it would otherwise lack at its founding and in its early years. In other words, I expect formal independence to shape stakeholders' and judges' perceptions of the CCJ. In particular, given its high formal independence, the CCJ will be seen as independent.

Interviewees suggest that judges and lawyers alike see the Court as independent. One lawyer, for instance, said, "As I know it, it is purely and fully independent."[168] Another interviewee argued that "I am not aware of any operating factor that exists that hinders the independence of the Court," and any arguments to the contrary are "entirely baseless and in my view ridiculous."[169] Various interviewees attributed the Court's independence to its design. The Court is viewed as independent because "there is little room for any executive government of any of the contracting states to interfere with the appointments to that regional judicial legal services commission."[170] Similarly, another individual explained that the CCJ is independent because "[judges] are not appointed by politicians."[171] Aside from the rules related to the appointment of judges, the unique funding mechanism for the Court has played a role in shaping views of the Court. Interviewees reported that the CCJ's funding mechanism augments its independence.[172] Also speaking of the funding arrangements, another interview argued, "it is impeccable . . . it removes the possibility of political interference . . . and it just guarantees public confidence."[173]

Generally speaking, the formal independence of the Court broadens its strategic space because it reduces the feasibility or credibility of state resistance while also boosting legitimacy perceptions of both judges and its stakeholders. While not all segments of society, or even the legal community, are convinced that the Court is independent, the Court is better situated because of its formal design than it would be otherwise. While the rules are not the end all and be all, they provide the Court and its judges with a greater sense of discretion, or a broader strategic space,

[168] Interview 23. Other interviewees express similar views, including Interview 17; Interview 19; Interview 26.
[169] Interview 25.
[170] Ibid.
[171] Interview 24. Interview 19 expressed similar views.
[172] Interview 20; Interview 23; Interview 25.
[173] Interview 16.

knowing the Court enjoys respect due to its design and that states have less opportunity to restrain or curb the Court through collective means.

Political Fragmentation

While the formal independence of the CCJ expands the CCJ's capacity to not defer, I have also hypothesized that the absence of political fragmentation has the opposite effect. An unfragmented political environment encourages deference because it makes collective resistance more feasible. Put differently, agreement between states narrows the Court's strategic space, making deference more likely (H_2). This logic leads to three observable implications for the CCJ's decision-making: (1) on issues where the Court has deferred, we should observe low fragmentation; (2) an increase in deference should correspond with a decline in observed fragmentation; and (3) on issues where fragmentation has been low, we should observe deference. The following discussion assesses the empirical evidence in relation to each of these observable implications.

First, we would expect low(er) fragmentation on issues where the Court has deferred and high(er) fragmentation when it has not. I consider this implication by comparing fragmentation on two issues over which the CCJ has rendered judgment, one where it deferred and the other not. For this purpose, I select the Court's decisions in *Tomlinson*[174] and *Myrie*,[175] the former representing deference and the latter nondeference.[176] While both applications relate to CARICOM's guarantees to free movement for community nationals (for a definite stay of up to six months) and nondiscrimination on grounds of nationality, they also allude to distinct policy issues. *Myrie* raised rule of law concerns, specifically whether a body cavity search and the conditions of her detention at the port of entry constituted a violation of Community obligations to ensure the right to entry is hassle free or without harassment. In contrast, *Tomlinson* addressed personal autonomy issues, or whether state immigration laws prohibiting entry for "homosexuals" limited Tomlinson's enjoyment of the Community right to entry and definite stay. According to my theoretical expectations, therefore, fragmentation on the rule of law (as in *Myrie*) should be higher than on

174 *Tomlinson v Belize* [2016] CCJ 1 (OJ).
175 *Myrie v Barbados* [2013] CCJ 3 (OJ).
176 There are very few possible cases for this purpose. These were selected because they had some underlying legal similarities, differed in terms of deference, and addressed issues for which there are data to measure preferences.

Table 5.5 *CCJ's deference and CARICOM fragmentation related to* Myrie *and* Tomlinson

	Myrie	*Tomlinson*
CCJ decision	Nondeference • breach declared • reparations granted • legal reasoning based on a standard of reasonableness	Deference • no breach, dismissed • no remedies granted (although states were encouraged to amend law) • legal reasoning based on high threshold and/or restrictive interpretation
Issue	Rule of Law	Personal autonomy
Theoretically expected fragmentation	High	Low
Observed fragmentation	High	Low

Note: For typologies of legal reasoning for deference, see Shirlow, *Judging at the Interface*. Shirlow argues that reasonableness is less deferential than high thresholds or restrictive interpretation.

personal autonomy (addressed in *Tomlinson*). These expectations are summarized in Table 5.5.

I measure fragmentation as the heterogeneity of preference among CARICOM states. To discern state preferences, I rely on Freedom House data, working with the assumption that state practices roughly reflect their preferences.[177] I approximate the issues in *Tomlinson* using Freedom House data on *personal autonomy*, which includes whether persons enjoy social freedoms like same-sex relations.[178] For the issues in *Myrie*, I rely on Freedom House's *rule of law* data, as this incorporates information on due process protections and freedom from inhuman and degrading treatment.[179] I use a statistical measure of data variability – the

[177] Freedom House, "Freedom in the World: Aggregate Category and Subcategory Scores, 2003–2022". I use Freedom House data for the CCJ because it includes most CARICOM member states, unlike alternative data sources. For instance, V-Dem includes only six of the fifteen CARICOM members in its data. Freedom House includes fourteen members, excluding Montserrat only.

[178] Freedom House, "Freedom in the World 2023 Methodology Questions," (2023), accessed April 17, 2023, https://freedomhouse.org/sites/default/files/2023-03/FITW_2023%20MethodologyPDF.pdf.

[179] Ibid.

Figure 5.2 CARICOM political fragmentation on select issues.
Note: Calculations and illustration by author.
Data source: Freedom House, "Freedom in the World: Aggregate Category and Subcategory Scores, 2003–2022,"

coefficient of variation – to assess heterogeneity. The COV indicates the size of a sample's standard deviation in relation to its mean, and therefore, it is a standardized measure of variability that is useful for comparison across indicators. Higher values indicate greater variability in a data sample, and therefore imply greater preference heterogeneity or fragmentation. I calculate the COV for both *personal autonomy* and the *rule of law* among CARICOM member states for the period between 2006 and 2020.[180] Figure 5.2 compares political fragmentation on the *rule of law* to *personal autonomy*. It suggests that fragmentation on the *rule of law* is – across all years – high in comparison to *personal autonomy*. These findings match the theoretical expectations (as shown in Table 5.5) and lend support to H_2.

[180] Freedom House data on personal autonomy and rule of law cover issues not addressed in these two applications.

The second observable implication derived from the hypothesis about political fragmentation is that we would expect declining fragmentation to correspond with increased deference. The contrast between the decision in *Gilbert & others*[181] and *Myrie* speaks to this observable implication. Both of these cases relate to the rule of law, especially inhuman and degrading treatment. Like *Myrie*, the complaint in *Gilbert & others* concerned the applicants' treatment by the Barbadian authorities. The applicants claimed that they were detained and subjected to a humiliating strip search for the alleged theft of a cell phone, which interfered with the right to freely move within and depart Barbados. While *Myrie* related to the treatment of a Community national at the port of border entry, *Gilbert & others* pertained to treatment of Community nationals after their entry and during their stay in Barbados. Despite some differences, these two cases have important similarities. Yet, the Court deferred in *Gilbert & others*, having denied special leave to the applicants as it found they had not made an arguable case that the enjoyment of their Community rights had been prejudiced. Interestingly, states' *rule of law* preferences were more heterogeneous in 2013 when *Myrie* was decided than when *Gilbert* was decided in 2019 (see Figure 5.2). This suggests fragmentation has declined, as expected theoretically given the difference deference.

Third, if political fragmentation is associated with nondeference and vice versa, we would expect to observe low fragmentation on issues where the Court has deferred. Looking at the issue of free movement, this appears to be the case. The Court has, in total, reviewed four[182] cases related to free movement: *Myrie*, *Tomlinson*, *Gilbert & others*, and *Bain*.[183] *Myrie* is the only case in which the Court did not defer along all three dimensions (outcome, interpretation, remedy). At the same time, tracing the history of free movement in CARICOM reveals that states broadly agreed on two core aspects of the right to free moment: (1) it is a limited right, and (2) states will dictate the terms and conditions of the right and its expansion. These two common positions are widely

[181] *Tamika Gilbert, Lynnel Gilbert, Royston Gilbert & Glennor Gilbert v The State of Barbados* [2019] CCJ 2 (OJ) (May 20, 2019).

[182] *Douglas v Dominica* [2017] CCJ 1 (OJ) could potentially be added to this list, also representing deference. See Berry, "The Effect of the Original Jurisdiction of the CCJ on Regional Integration and National Law," 536–37.

[183] *Bain v Trinidad & Tobago* [2019] CCJ 3 (OJ).

known, having clear signals from states, and correspond with the Court's tendency to defer to states on this issue.

From the beginning, states have been reluctant to introduce a broad right to free movement within CARICOM.[184] In fact, the original Treaty of Chaguaramas in 1973 asserted that the Treaty did not impose any obligation on states to grant free movement of persons, including nationals, within the Common Market.[185] In time, however, policymakers and analysts viewed the absence of free movement guarantees as a hindrance to the successful implementation of the Common Market. States consequentially began to integrate a limited principle of free movement. In 1989, they agreed to take steps to ensure passport free travel across CARICOM for its nationals, to enable free movement of skilled and professional personnel and contract workers on a seasonal or project basis, and to eliminate work permits for nationals in the arts, sports, and media for participation at regional events.[186] This agreement was, however, nonbinding, and, with the exception of passport free travel, was limited to the movement of labor. Even the WIC endorsed a *limited* free movement.[187] In 1995, the CHOG agreed to provide for the *free movement of skills*, eliminating the requirement for work permits, for a limited set of professions. These provisions for the free movement of skills were enshrined within the RTC in Article 46.[188]

The RTC reaffirmed that states agreed to keep the right *limited* and *within their control.* Article 45 expressed a broad concept of free movement as merely an aspirational goal, not as a guarantee: Member States "commit[ted] themselves to the goal of free movement of their nationals." Article 46 also suggests that states envisioned an incremental expansion, subject to their determination, of the right to free movement of skill: "The Conference shall keep the provisions of this Article under review in order to: (a) enlarge, as appropriate, the classes of persons entitled to

[184] Jason Haynes, "The Right to Free Movement of Persons in Caribbean Community (CARICOM) Law: Towards 'Juridification'?" *Journal of Human Rights in the Commonwealth* 2, no. 2 (2016): 58.

[185] TOC, Art. 38.

[186] CHOG, *Grand Anse Declaration and Work Programme for the Advancement of the Integration Movement, July 7* (1989), accessed June 25, 2024, https://caricom.org/grand-anse-declaration-and-work-programme-for-the-advancement-of-the-integration-movement-july-1989-grand-anse-grenada/.

[187] WIC, *Time for Action.*

[188] Article 46 provides for the right to seek employment in other member states for specific professions and to establish appropriate legislative, administrative, and procedural arrangements "to provide for movement of Community nationals into and within their jurisdictions without harassment or the imposition of impediments."

move and work."[189] They also retained the responsibility for monitoring its implementation, according to Article 46(b).

States continued to reveal their accord over a *limited* right to free movement for Community nationals. In 2007, the CHOG agreed that "all CARICOM nationals should receive entry for up to six months," but states retained the right to refuse entry for "undesirable persons" and to prevent "persons from becoming a charged on public funds."[190] This decision was not without problems and was a step too far for some members. Antigua and Barbuda entered a reservation to this decision. Moreover, two years after the decision entered into force, CARICOM reported that implementation was problematic. Only two states had amended their legislation to accord with the Community decision, and four states still were not implementing it administratively.[191] More recently in 2018, CHOG decided to expand the free movement of skills to additional professional categories. Yet, Antigua and Barbuda and St Kitts and Nevis opted out of this expansion at the 30th Inter-Sessional Meeting of CHOG.[192] As a result, the Caribbean Community requested an advisory opinion from the CCJ to determine whether the opt-out by these two states violated Article 27(4) of the RTC. The Court concluded that the RTC permitted these opt-outs.[193]

Practical and security concerns shape states' interests in maintaining a limited right within their control. According to the International Organization for Migration (IOM), Caribbean states have significant challenges maintaining their borders. As mostly island nations, their coastal borders are difficult to patrol, which makes them vulnerable to human and drug trafficking as well as trade in illegal arms.[194] They also

[189] RTC, Art. 46(4).

[190] Cited in Berry, *Caribbean Integration Law*, 259. See also *Myrie v Barbados* [2013] CCJ 3 (OJ).

[191] CARICOM, *Report on the Appraisal of the State of the CARICOM Single Market* (Georgetown: CARICOM Secretariat, 2009), paras. 91–94; see also Derek O'Brien, "CARICOM: A New Legal Order?" *UK Constitutional Law Blog*, November 8, 2013, https://ukconstitutionallaw.org/2013/11/08/derek-obrien-caricom-a-new-legal-order/.

[192] CHOG, *Expansion of Categories of Skilled Community Nationals*, Ins/Hgc/2019/30/Dec.5(C), Thirteen Inter-Sessional Meeting, February 26–27, 2019 (Basseterre, St. Kitts and Nevis: CARICOM, 2019) accessed August 25, 2024, https://caricom.org/wp-content/uploads/DECISIONS-30-IS-HGC-FEB-2019.pdf.

[193] Advisory Opinion, requested by the Caribbean Community [2020] CCJ 1 (OJ) (March 18, 2020).

[194] IOM, *Free Movement of Persons in the Caribbean: Economic and Security Dimensions* (San José, Costa Rica: IOM, 2019), 89–91, accessed May 11, 2023, https://publications.iom.int/books/free-movement-caribbean-economic-and-security-dimensions.

lack technical capacity to monitor movement across their borders.[195] For instance, the IOM reports that only four of the CARICOM states have border management systems that are capable of automatically flagging individuals who stay beyond their permitted time.[196] Together, these issues create significant security threats along with challenging circumstances for border control.

Long-standing political sentiments also drive resistance to free movement across the region. While negotiating the West Indies Federation, leaders opposed "divisions of powers which would curtail their ability to prevent immigration from the other [territories]."[197] Larger and more prosperous territories feared they would be stuck supporting poorer Caribbeans. Less densely populated territories were weary of an influx of immigrants from the other territories. Some feared that free movement would threaten the ethnic composition of their territories. For example, Indo-Caribbeans in Trinidad and Guyana were afraid that these territories would become predominately Afro-Caribbean.[198] Similar anxieties and negative perceptions permeate into contemporary political sentiments about free movement protections.[199]

Most states have been reluctant or unable to comply legislatively with their existing commitments to limited free movement rights. Table 5.6 shows that member states, if they do comply, tend to implement provisions through administrative practice, not by legislative reforms. Very few states have codified the various requirements of Community law. No state, as of the end of 2019, had enacted legislation to guarantee spouses and dependents the right to move with their family member who moves on grounds of their Community right to free movement of skills.[200] Member states' broad reliance on administrative implementation as opposed to legislative compliance is significant because it was on this basis that the CCJ ruled in *Tomlinson*: The Court deferred to Belize and Trinidad and Tobago by reasoning that administrative practice was sufficient, irrespective of the incompatibility of the legislation. As one interviewee explained, "to rule on the basis of legislations and to outright say there

195 Ibid., 91.

196 Ibid., 46.

197 Proctor, "The Framing of the West Indian Federal Constitution," 63–64.

198 Ibid.

199 CARICOM, *Report on the Appraisal of the State of the CARICOM Single Market*.

200 Spouses and dependents are also guaranteed free movement when related to the provision of services or establishment.

Table 5.6 *State implementation of CARICOM's free movement requirements*

	Antigua & Barbuda	Barbados	Belize	Dominica	Grenada	Guyana	Jamaica	St Kitts & Nevis	St Lucia	St Vincent & the Grenadines	Suriname	Trinidad & Tobago
Codification of six-month definite entry and stay	No	No	No			Yes					Yes	
Administrative implementation of six-month entry and stay	Yes	Yes	Yes	Yes	Yes	Yes	Yes		Yes	Yes	Yes	Yes
Inconsistent practices reported to CARICOM on six-month entry and entry	Yes	Yes					Yes	Yes	Yes			
Removal of visa requirement in law	No	No	Yes	No	Yes	Yes	No	No	No	N/a	Yes	No
Measures to ensure free movement of ten categories of skilled labor	No	No	No	No	Yes	Yes	Yes	No	No	No	No	No
Codification of right to move with spouse and dependent family	No	No	No	No	No	No	No	No	No	No	No	No
Administrative implementation of right to move with spouse and dependent family	Yes	Yes	Yes	Yes	Yes	Yes	Part	Yes	Yes	Yes	Yes	Yes

Note: No information available for Haiti or Montserrat. Empty cells represent missing information.
Source: IOM, *Free Movement of Persons in the Caribbean: Economic and Security Dimensions.*

was a violation would have had so many potential ramifications."[201] As most member states use administrative implementation, the free movement regime within CARICOM could have been upended if the Court were to use less deferential reasoning and rule on the basis of legislation.

It is fair to say that judges were aware of these dynamics and states' agreement to limit and control free movement. For instance, Judge Winston Anderson spoke on these issues in his address to the OECS Bar Association Meeting in 2013.[202] He elaborated on the historical reluctance on free movement and the context of the "hassle free" principle. The Court itself in *Myrie* noted the historical background of the free movement and relevant CARICOM reports. Thus, as one interviewee explained, it made sense for the Court to keep member states in mind because "to make [RTC] more effective we [the judges] have to consider how slow or fast to try and develop the law. . .And if we move to quickly . . . there could be some problems."[203]

In this broader context, the CCJ's tendency to defer on free movement applications is less surprising. Why then did the Court not defer in *Myrie*, if states were generally unified in their reluctance to extend greater protections to free movement? Most states were in fact dissatisfied with how their nationals were treated and subjected to harassment at ports of entry. A CARICOM report found that

> [o]ne of the strongest and most consistent complaints in every Member State is concerned with hassle free travel and facilitation of travel at ports of entry. The remarkable aspect is that the sharpness of the criticism has come from people at every strata of the Community, government officials - including immigration officials who claim that even on official duties on behalf of their governments there was unwarranted hassle and distrustful treatment. The finger pointing was stronger and more resentful at some Member States. This is a state of affairs that could lead to retaliation, a most undesirable consequence.[204]

The frustration with this state of affairs is probably what led states to agree in 2007 that entry should be "without harassment." All in all, *Myrie* is the only free movement application in which the Court could have

[201] Interview 17.

[202] Winston Anderson, "Free Movement Within CARICOM: Deconstructing the Myrie vs Barbados" (speech, OECS Bar Association Meeting, St George's, Grenada, December 7, 2013).

[203] Interview 17.

[204] CARICOM, *Report on the Appraisal of the State of the CARICOM Single Market*, para. 300.

reasonably inferred that most states would agree with the substantive outcome of the Court's decision to enforce protections on free movement. *Myrie* thus shows that nondeference can arise when most states will generally agree with the Court's position. However, nondeference in the other cases was inhibited by state agreement.

Another example unrelated to free movement, *TCL v the Caribbean Community*, speaks to the third observable implication. In this case, TCL filed a complaint against CARICOM for its decisions to grant a suspension of the common external tariff on cement to seven different states. In reviewing the decision of CARICOM, the Court ruled that there had not been a substantive breach as it was within the discretion of the CARICOM organs to make such a decision, but that CARICOM had procedurally failed by not conducting an adequate assessment. Consequently, the CCJ found that CARICOM had committed a procedural breach but declined to quash the suspension of the CET (deference in terms of remedy). State preferences can help to explain this. Seven states had been granted the suspension (plus Guyana who unilaterally suspended the CET). In essence, eight of the twelve CARICOM Single Market and Economy states supported the suspended CET. The Court could clearly see that if it were to quash the suspension, these eight states would have the necessary votes to override the Court.[205] Therefore, the politically prudent decision for the Court was to shift focus to the procedural issues and to refrain from offering an intrusive remedy. Hence, deference in this case corresponds with a lack of political fragmentation.

As this discussion demonstrates, variation within the CCJ's jurisprudence and the extent to which the Court defers or not correspond with temporal and issue-specific patterns of political fragmentation among member states. It also shows that an international court's strategic space is not static; rather, it is susceptible to fluctuation in political fragmentation.

Past Resistance

Unlike the EACJ, the CCJ has no significant prior experience with collective resistance from states.[206] The Court, however, struggles to gain states' acceptance of its appellate jurisdiction. For instance, the Court's

[205] If states were to overturn the Court, a three-fourths majority vote would be needed. The eight states that already had a suspension of the CET would constitute three-fourths.

[206] To my knowledge, the Court has also not faced much unilateral resistance in the form of noncompliance. Rather, compliance within the CCJ's original jurisdiction is strong.

appellate jurisdiction has been rejected by public referenda on two occasions, and, in total, only five of the fifteen members of CARICOM have acceded to the CCJ's appellate jurisdiction. Arguably, these issues have a minimal impact on the Court's (non)deference in the original jurisdiction. For this reason, I discuss this issue more in relation to public legitimation.

The CCJ's Adaptive Practices

Formal independence and political fragmentation structure the CCJ's strategic space. While these structural constraints are important for understanding the CCJ's moderate deference, I have argued that practices of adaptation can also be employed by a court, especially when these constraints are greater, to enable more nondeference. The following discussion illustrates if and how the CCJ has developed these adaptive practices and considers how they shed light on (non)deference of the CCJ.

Persuasive Argumentation

International courts can potentially broaden their strategic space by fortifying the persuasiveness of their arguments. I have highlighted two potential modes of persuasive argumentation: unanimous decisions and citation practices. The first of these does not apply to the CCJ within its original jurisdiction. According to Rule 3.4(4) of the Court's rules of procedure, the Court cannot issue or publish separate opinions and judgments of the Court do not record or reveal judges' votes.[207] For this reason, we cannot observe persuasive argumentation through voting patterns or separate or dissenting opinions.

However, the Court's citation practices reflect efforts to improve the persuasiveness of its arguments and decisions. Table 5.7 summarizes the Court's citation practices. The table shows that the CCJ cites its own jurisprudence at a relatively high rate, or on average between four and five references to its own judgments per application. Given the Court had only thirty-four judgments in respect of eighteen applications and only one advisory opinion throughout the time period under analysis, this figure is high.

Interview 16; Interview 19; see also Caserta, *International Courts in Latin America and the Caribbean.*

[207] CCJ, *Original Jurisdiction Rules.*

Table 5.7 *Descriptive statistics on CCJ's citation practices*

Types of citation	Mean	Standard deviation	Min	Max
CCJ jurisprudence	4.61	2.36	1	8
External jurisprudence	8.72	8.88	0	36
. *International*	7.44	6.44	0	23
. *Domestic*	1.28	3.02	0	13

Note: All eighteen cases are included. The coding of citation practices is based on citations made by the Court itself in its reasoning. It excludes citations raised by the parties to the dispute (unless it is later cited by the Court) or citations that are referred to as part of the factual background of the application. For some applications, the CCJ issued more than one relevant ruling/judgment. A citation is counted only once, even if it appears more than once in a single judgment or in different judgments related to the same application.

In addition, the CCJ frequently cites external, including international and domestic, jurisprudence. Among external citations, international jurisdictions appear frequently; there are over seven references to international jurisprudence on average in the Court's decisions on any given application. The CCJ cites a wide array of international courts and tribunals, from the ICJ and its predecessor to the Iran–US Claims Tribunal. The Court relies extensively on the jurisprudence of the CJEU, which is an important leader in regional integration law, but it also actively cites other international tribunals, such as WTO panels and the Appellate Body, and human rights bodies (ECtHR, IACtHR, UN human rights treaty bodies). The CCJ cites national courts much less than international courts.[208] When it does cite domestic jurisdictions, it tends to cite common law jurisdictions.

The theoretical argument maintains that persuasive argumentation should be connected to deference, such that it is more prevalent when an IC does not defer. Do the CCJ's citation practices support this proposition? Table 5.8 shows that external references appear less often in case outcomes that reflect deference than in those that reflect non-deference.[209] In fact, in all applications where the applicant wins (or the

[208] As one might expect, domestic jurisprudence is used more in the appellate jurisdiction, Interview 20.

[209] Table A5.2 in the Appendix compares international and domestic references by case outcomes and remedies. It shows that domestic and international citations are more

Table 5.8 *Cross-tabulations of CCJ's citation practices by deference*

	External reference	
Applicant wins	No	Yes
No (defer)	4 (44.44)	5 (55.56)
Yes	0 (0)	9 (100)
Fisher's Test p-value: 0.082*		
χ^2 p-value: 0.010**		

Note: *p<0.10, ** p<0.05, *** p<0.001. All eighteen applications are included. The first number is the frequency and the second number (in parentheses) is the row percentage.

CCJ does not defer), the Court's decision featured at least one reference to an external jurisdiction. Yet, it does so in only about 56 percent of the instances of deference. This pattern extends to deference based on remedies and holds for domestic and international citations (see Table A5.2 in Appendix). The applications in which the Court had made the highest number of external citations were also those in which it used a wider array of remedies. For instance, the application with the highest number of external references had an order for reparations (compensation) alongside the declaratory judgment.[210] All other applications that included a remedial order on top of a declaratory judgment had an above-average number of external citations.

Interviews suggest that the relationship between citations and deference is intentional. Several interviewees claim that writing a high-quality, "well-reasoned" judgment is how judges seek to gain favor with the Court's stakeholders. As one judge explained, respect is gained "by the excellence of your judgment."[211] The Court "focus[es] on . . . produc[ing] really good judgments . . . so as to establish a kind of intellectual legitimacy."[212] Another judge suggested that gaining public confidence and respect requires the Court to "show that we master the law, and that

common when the CCJ does not defer (both in terms of whether a violation is declared and on remedial orders), and that international references are more common.

210 *SM Jaleel & Co Ltd & Guyana Beverages Inc v The Co-operative Republic of Guyana* [2017] CCJ 2 (OJ) (May 9, 2017).

211 Interview 22.

212 Interview 17.

we should not be going our own way . . . we have to look at what earlier courts have said."[213]

Reference to external jurisprudence is critical to producing well-reasoned arguments. One judge explained that the Court cites external jurisprudence to show the CCJ's awareness of how other courts have handled similar issues.[214] Another explained that it is important to look at other jurisdictions "in order to find the best way forward for this society. So that I think there should always be a comparative exercise . . . those are useful. Markers as to what you might consider when considering a problem."[215] Put differently, "outside jurisprudence is not binding, but it can be persuasive."[216] This is not to say that citations are the only way to make arguments compelling. For some judges, reasoning, rather than citations, are most important, which may be a product of the judges coming from different judicial systems (common law versus civil law).[217] Nonetheless, references are an important way in which we can observe the practice of persuasive argumentation and the Court's efforts to make compelling decisions that will be well received.

Public Legitimation

In addition to persuasive argumentation, I have argued that courts will adopt practices of public legitimation to help expand their strategic space or support nondeference, especially when one of two conditions is present: if an IC has low formal independence, or if an IC has low political fragmentation (H_4). The CCJ meets this second condition, as the membership is typically like-minded. I also raised the possibility that public legitimation may be affected by whether states can unilaterally exit (or conversely accede to) aspects of a court's jurisdiction, which applies in the case of the CCJ because states can unilaterally accede to its appellate jurisdiction. As mentioned earlier, only five states have accepted this jurisdiction.[218] The public is especially important for accession to the appellate jurisdiction because several CARICOM states require public referenda to enable the constitutional reform necessary for the CCJ to become their court of last resort. Already, two states (Grenada and

[213] Interview 19.
[214] Interview 20.
[215] Interview 22.
[216] Interview 17.
[217] Interview 19.
[218] For the period under analysis, only four states accepted the appellate jurisdiction. In May 2023, Saint Lucia became the fifth state to join this jurisdiction.

Antigua and Barbuda) have rejected the appellate jurisdiction by public referendum.[219] Thus, I expect to observe extensive practices of public legitimation by the Court, that is, public messaging about the Court's commitment to its political purpose and its people-centeredness. An analysis of the Court's publications, including annual reports[220] and speeches by judges,[221] as well as interview material demonstrate that the Court is concerned with its public image and has utilized a variety of initiatives to (re)construct its public image.

Concern for and a desire to nurture its public image have been a running theme for the Court. When the CCJ began operating in 2005, it was apparent to the Court's leaders that public perceptions were important. In the CCJ's first annual report, it explained: "With the Court still in the early days of its development and with many as yet unfamiliar with its workings, as well as the fact that there has been much misinformation, the Court has to go about gaining the trust and confidence of the people."[222] The Court therefore identified "attaining and preserving public trust and confidence" as one of its key performance standards.[223] It also stated, "[m]uch care has been taken by the Caribbean Court of Justice in ensuring accessibility... The Caribbean Court of Justice is determined to ensure that the people of the Caribbean know their court and have access to the activities and records of the court."[224] It also saw public education as essential to the Court's accountability.

The Court's public image has continued to be an important occupation for the Court, its judges, and personnel. For example, its strategic plan for 2013–17 identified "access to justice" and "attaining and preserving public trust and confidence" among its key strategic themes.[225] Similarly, the last strategic plan applicable to the time period analyzed

[219] Derek O'Brien, "The End of the Caribbean Court of Justice? On Failed Constitutional Referendums in Grenada, and Antigua and Barbuda," *ConstitutionNet*, November 26, 2018, https://constitutionnet.org/news/end-caribbean-court-justice-failed-constitutional-referendums-grenada-and-antigua-and-barbuda.

[220] See CCJ, "Annual Reports," accessed June 25, 2024, https://ccj.org/publications/annual-reports/. All annual reports were extracted from this website for analysis.

[221] CCJ, "Papers and Speeches.". All quoted papers and speeches were extracted from this website.

[222] CCJ, *Annual Report 2005–2006* (Port of Spain: CCJ, 2006), 23.

[223] Ibid., 17.

[224] Ibid., 18.

[225] CCJ, *Strategic Plan 2013–2017: Responsive, Innovative, Inspirational* (Port of Spain: CCJ, 2012), accessed June 25, 2024, https://ccj.org/about-the-ccj/the-ccj-strategic-plan-2013-2017/.

includes "access to justice" as an overarching theme[226] and identifies "inform[ing]and engag[ing] the regional and global community about its role and its work to facilitate greater access to the Court and promote public trust and confidence" as one of its main goals.[227] All in all, the Court expressed concern for its public legitimacy throughout the entire period under examination.

Moreover, the CCJ relied on public-oriented communication, information dissemination, and outreach to nurture its public standing. In its first year of operation, the Court began a "public education and information program," and in conjunction with its "access to justice" initiative, the Court developed a well-functioning website and used technology to make documents, judgments, and audio and video recordings available to the public.[228] Also as part of these programs, the Court's Protocol and Information Division "embarked on the regular provision of information on the Court and the commission through all the media: print, audio and visual."[229] The "Court [undertook] a public outreach programme, through which it interface[d] directly with the Caribbean public, either by inviting groups into the Court for contact sessions, or by taking its message 'on the road' as it were, into the very heart of constituent communities."[230] Judges frequently spoke at various events across the region, for instance, and the Court welcomed and informed visitors such as school groups and guided tours.[231] In 2008, the Public Education and Communication Unit was established, "in keeping with the Court's commitment to Public Education to support access to justice, to build public trusted and confidence and to assist the Court's accountability."[232] This manifested in initiatives like a three-minute video that was featured on Caribbean Airlines' inflight program, and similar video content featured on local television networks across the region.[233]

The Court continued to prioritize public-oriented communication and outreach in the 2010s. For instance, in 2012 it engaged a media

[226] CCJ, *Strategic Plan 2019–2024: Unlocking Potential, Strengthening Caribbean Justice* (Port of Spain: CCJ, 2019), 14, accessed June 25, 2024, https://ccj.org/about-the-ccj/ccj-strategic-plan/.

[227] Ibid., 17.

[228] CCJ, *Annual Report 2005–2006*, 18–19.

[229] Ibid., 22.

[230] Ibid.

[231] Interview 16; Interview 19.

[232] CCJ, *Annual Report 2007–2008* (Port of Spain: CCJ, 2008), 45.

[233] CCJ, *Annual Report 2009–2010* (Port of Spain: CCJ, 2010), 25.

consultant, met with media personnel throughout the region, and relaunched its web presence with an improved website and use of social media platforms.[234] The Court communicated with the public through the press, regularly publishing press releases and engaging with the traditional media. For instance, the Court hosted a Media Day with regional and local media houses in attendance, "during which, judges and external speakers made presentations on the work of the Court and its influence on regional law."[235] In 2019, the Court "disseminat[ed] hundreds of copies of 'Fast Facts about the CCJ' as an insert in a local daily newspaper."[236] Judges represent the Court at various events, meetings, and conferences across the region; between 2005 and 2020 the judges had 154 speaking engagements,[237] or roughly 10 per year. For instance, between July 2018 and July 2019, President Saunders spoke at nine different regional and international meetings.[238] Also important to outreach are its special sittings, when the Court is itinerant. Since its first special sitting in 2010,[239] it has held sessions in Barbados, Guyana, Jamaica, Belize, Antigua, and St Vincent and the Grenadines.

The Court's public communication and outreach, as well as other nonjudicial activities, portray the Court's commitment to its political purpose, especially to strengthening of the rule of law and democracy within the region, community values, and the Caribbean people. On the one hand, the CCJ presents itself as a champion of the rule of law in the region. Since it began operating, the Court envisioned that it would be "worthy of emulation by courts of the region and the trust and confidence of its people."[240] This vision statement was rearticulated in 2018 as "to be a model of judicial excellence."[241] The Court's commitment to the rule of law and democracy is echoed in how the CCJ's President presents the Court: "I am convinced that to gain stronger support in the region, more information must be provided to the Caribbean public about the Court, its institutional architecture, its work over the last 13 years and

234 CCJ, *Annual Report 2011–2013* (Port of Spain: CCJ, 2014), 31; Interview 21.
235 CCJ, *Annual Report 2018–2019* (Port of Spain: CCJ, 2019), 51.
236 Ibid.
237 This count is based on speeches documented on the CCJ's website through the end of 2020. See CCJ, "Papers and speeches."
238 CCJ, *Annual Report 2018–2019*, 43.
239 CCJ, *Annual Report 2011–2013*, 9.
240 CCJ, *Annual Report 2005–2006*, 1.
241 CCJ, *Annual Report 2017–2018* (Port of Spain: CCJ, 2018), 12; CCJ, *Strategic Plan 2019-2024: Unlocking Potential, Strengthening Caribbean Justice.*

what it can do to advance democracy and the rule of law in the Caribbean."[242] Beyond words, the CCJ's vision influences its nonjudicial activities and initiatives. For instance, the CCJ and its judges were part of a project called JURIST, which worked to improve the rule of law and the judiciaries throughout the region.[243] Additionally, the CCJ created the CCJ Academy for Law to "provide informative and innovative perspectives on the rules and the roles of law" and to be "a platform for examining court administration and encouraging best practices in the judicial administration of justice."[244] As Justice Saunders explained at a public gathering, "The Court seeks consciously to develop and adopt effective practices and procedures and assist the courts of the region to strengthen their ability to engage in meaningful judicial reform and enhance justice delivery."[245]

On the other hand, the Court's public messaging and "off-the-bench" activities frequently highlight community values and refer to the community of people it serves. For instance, the main slogan of the Court, as seen on its website, reinforces this image: "Your People. Your Region. Your Court." The CCJ's vision, especially in its early years, included "fostering jurisprudence that is reflective of our history, values and traditions." Similarly, when judges deliver speeches, they often refer to the Caribbean people. For example, Justice Byron, when speaking at the Moot Law ceremony, said: "Culminated in the existence of this Court, your Court, are the aspirations of Caribbean peoples. And it is a hope that the Caribbean Court of Justice by its existences epitomises. The CCJ is currently poised to contribute to positive change in the social order of our Caribbean societies."[246]

Generally, we can see the Court has practiced public legitimation through a variety of actions: It prioritizes reshaping how the Court is perceived through a variety of public-oriented practices that convey messages of the Court's people-centeredness and commitment to its political purpose. Interviews reveal, however, that there is some unease

[242] CCJ, *Annual Report 2017–2018*, 3.

[243] Interview 19. This project was funded by the Government of Canada from 2014 to 2023.

[244] See CCJ Academy for Law, "About Us," accessed August 26, 2024, https://ccjacademy.org/about-us/.

[245] Adrian Saunders, "The Revised Treaty of Chaguaramas: Conflicts and Contradictions for the Island State" (speech, Public Gathering, St Vincent and the Grenadines, May 16, 2017), 15.

[246] Dennis Byron, "Keynote Speech" (speech, CCJ International Law Moot 2018 Award Ceremony, Port of Spain, March 9, 2018).

with the CCJ using these practices. As one judge explained, "we were told by quite a few of our stakeholders that they did not like the idea of the judges doing a lot of what we regarded as public relations work. They did not like the idea of judges debasing themselves as salespersons of the Court."[247] Another judge expressed discomfort with the Court employing some of these methods,[248] while a lawyer suggested that the Court has to be careful with how they promote the Court: "They can't appear to be too strident and too nonjudicial."[249]

The CCJ clearly practices public legitimation. To determine the scale or intensity of these practices and the relative weighting of people-centered and political purpose narratives, I rely on the Court's public communication on social media. Using a web-scraping tool, I extracted the CCJ's Facebook posts from 2018 to 2020.[250] I then conduct a text analysis of its posts, which includes 306 posts in total. Using the words or phrases commonly found in the speeches that frame the Court's political purpose and people-centeredness, I examine the prominence of these narratives in the Facebook posts. Table 5.9 displays the words and phrases used for this purpose, as well as the number and percentage of Facebook posts that feature them. It shows that narratives associated with public legitimation are present in a small portion (approximately 13 percent) of the CCJ's posts. It is difficult to discern any temporal patterns because the CCJ opened a Facebook account after some years of being in operation. However, the data suggest that the CCJ prioritizes people-centered narratives over commitment to its political purpose, as reflected in their relative prominence. The former is present in 10 percent of posts, while the latter is found in 5 percent of posts. The focus on people-centered narratives may be informed by the CCJ's general interest in differentiating itself from British justice, which cannot claim to reflect Caribbean-ness. Given the postcolonial legacies and the generally favorable views toward British justice, if the CCJ is to extend its appellate jurisdiction it will need to differentiate itself from British Privy Council. In other words, portrayals of the Court's Caribbean identity speak to the CCJ's view that the states unilateral acceptance of it plays strongly in how it understands its political constraints, and

[247] Interview 16.
[248] Interview 22.
[249] Interview 25.
[250] The CCJ launched its Facebook page in August 2018. See Facebook, "Page Transparency," accessed November 17, 2023, www.facebook.com/yourCCj/about_profile_transparency.

Table 5.9 *Public legitimation narratives in CCJ's Facebook posts*

Legitimation words and phrases	Number of posts	Percent of total
People-centeredness	32	10.46
community	1	0.33
Caribbean people(s)	0	0
Caribbean public	0	0
citizens	5	1.63
people	7	2.29
region	21	6.86
Caribbean region	3	0.98
Political purpose	15	4.9
integration	1	0.33
justice	7	2.9
rule of law	0	
democracy	0	
rights	7	2.9
judicial excellence	1	0.33
community	1	0.33
People-centeredness or political purpose	39	12.75

Note: All words and phrases are case sensitive.

its public legitimation is oriented toward reshaping its strategic space with this constraint squarely in mind.

In sum, we can see that the CCJ employs both persuasive argumentation and public legitimation. I contend that the Court relies on these practices to boost its strategic space. Nondeference necessitates such practices, even though the institutional safeguards to independence are robust, because the alignment of political preferences effectively lowers the barriers to collective resistance. The way to compensate for the lowered barriers and decrease the feasibility of state override of the Court, or worse, is to raise states' audience costs for doing so. This benefit arises from improving the persuasiveness of judgments and bolstering the Court's public image.

Conclusion

The main findings of this chapter can be summarized in four main points. First, the CCJ is an institution that stemmed from colonial legacies that contributed to prominent political norms of independence and sovereignty and regionalism and unity. These norms historically and currently are in tension. Moreover, the legal culture across CARICOM is characterized by pluralism as well as a lack of faith in the state legal order. This ideational context has important similarities to EACJ and the ACtHPR.

Second, in contrast to the EACJ and ACtHPR, the CCJ demonstrates moderate deference. In some regards, the CCJ is nondeferential. Its legal interpretations, for instance, have paved the way toward establishing principles like the supremacy of Community law and direct effect. In terms of outcomes, states lose more often than they win (by 2:1). On the other hand, the Court defers more to states in terms of how it utilizes its remedial powers. While the CCJ has used its full range of remedial powers, it shows restraint in ordering intrusive remedies. It seems to prefer a subtle approach by recommending, rather than ordering, changes to law and policy. Additionally, the Court defers more toward Community organs than it does to individual respondent states. These patterns generally suggest a Court that operates within a midrange strategic space, which produces a moderate degree of deference.

Third, the observed patterns of deference by the CCJ are difficult to square with the role of its support network. While there are the markings of a burgeoning support network, it remains small and its influence limited, while a subset of the legal elites prefer a weak CCJ. Many channels through which international courts have elsewhere benefited from robust networks remain empty vessels so far. National courts have not referred applications to the CCJ, despite efforts by the Court to encourage national judges and lawyers to pursue this option. The Community institutions are often legally constrained from approaching the CCJ for dispute resolution. CARICOM remains largely state-led and intergovernmental. If they are to avail themselves of the CCJ, they are likely to request advisory opinions rather than use the contentious jurisdiction (if they are able). Private litigants up to this point have been the lifeline of the CCJ's original jurisdiction. In this regard, the Court has benefited enormously from private actors and their lawyers. With that said, their utilization and participation in the judicial process do not align with the patterns of deference. I observe no clear statistical relationship between repeat lawyers or third-party actors and deference. If anything, the Court's nondeference reflects an effort to expand its support network, rather than being a result of it.

Last, the observed deference of the CCJ corresponds with its intermediate constraints. The Court has robust formal safeguards to judicial independence, more than any other international court. The Court's formal independence affects how the institution is perceived: judges and practitioners express confidence in the institutional safeguards protecting the Court from political interference. Formal independence also narrows the options available to states to collectively resist the CCJ, which may account for why the Court has not experienced significant forms of resistance. On the other hand, CARICOM states are minimally fragmented, having homogeneous preferences. This makes potential override of the Court more feasible and credible. It is on this account that the CCJ has deferred both in terms of how it uses remedial orders and when CARICOM is the respondent, whose decisions directly reflect the accord of states. Unlike other regional organizations, CARICOM decisions are taken exclusively by intergovernmental decision-making processes. Thus, while formal independence broadens the CCJ's strategic space, homogeneous preferences narrow it. Additionally, preference homogeneity helps to account for differences in deference depending on the issue at the center of a dispute. To minimize the constraining effects of homogeneous preferences, and thereby expand its strategic space, the Court relies on persuasive argumentation, mostly by situating its decisions in the context of authoritative international jurisprudence, and public legitimation that highlights its Caribbean identity. Thus, the theoretical argument is broadly supported by the case of the CCJ. Chapter 6 assesses the argument in the case of the African Court on Human and Peoples' Rights.

6

The African Court on Human and Peoples' Rights

Subtle Constraints and Minimal Deference

The African Court on Human and Peoples' Rights (also referred to as the African Court) is the third regional court created for the purpose of interpreting and applying international human rights law, and it is an organ of the African Union (AU). The creation and working of the African Court contribute to the development of human rights law on the continent and the broader international justice regime. By examining the ACtHPR, this chapter examines the book's theoretical argument in the case of an international court with a broad strategic space. In contrast to the CCJ, the African Court has subtle constraints because of its moderately high formal independence and politically fragmented membership. Based on the hypotheses presented in Chapter 2, this leads us to expect minimal deference by the ACtHPR.

This chapter analyzes the ACtHPR's decision-making to determine whether this expectation bears out empirically. It reveals that the ACtHPR has proven itself willing to uphold the protection of human rights while deferring to states in limited circumstances. Its decisions frequently reject the states' exercise of authority. This is seen in the Court's tendence to rule in favor of applicants, to embrace legal interpretation that put forward legal standards that most states do not meet and reject respondent's arguments, and by using less deferential modes of reasoning. Moreover, it uses its full range of remedial powers and has not shied away from using intrusive orders, even though it typically opts for the less intrusive remedies. The chapter links these patterns of deference to the African Court's formal independence and the political fragmentation of its membership. Moreover, the Court's minimal deference is facilitated by practices of persuasive argumentation and public legitimation, which help to build and maintain the ACtHPR's strategic space. The Court, however, has shown more deference in the wake of state resistance and as political fragmentation changes.

This chapter begins by providing a brief overview of the creation of the African Court and its ideational setting. Drawing from original data, the chapter then presents the Court's mandate and workload before identifying the extent to which the Court defers to states. The chapter then turns to its explanatory account of the ACtHPR's tendency to not defer. It considers the Court's support networks and illustrates how several impediments hinder the capacity of support networks to adequately strengthen the Court and account for its minimal deference. It then traces the relationship between judicial deference on the one hand and formal independence, political fragmentation, and adaptive practices on the other. Last, the chapter reviews the key findings.

The ACtHPR's Ideational Setting: Colonial Legacies, Political Norms, and Legal Culture

The ideational setting of the ACtHPR has key similarities to that of the EACJ and CCJ. Namely, the origins of the African Court are tied to the colonial past of its member states and the Organization of African Unity (OAU). Inspired by the idea of Pan-Africanism, the OAU was created in 1963 by the newly independent African states. Its founding purposes included the promotion of "African unity and solidarity" and cooperation "to achieve a better life for the peoples of Africa" and "having due regard to the ... Universal Declaration of Human Rights"; at the same time, it aimed "to defend their sovereignty, their territorial integrity and independence."[1] The OAU operated by a strict adherence to the principle of noninterference,[2] and it acted as a "mutual admiration club" where members "were expected to see nothing, hear nothing, and say nothing," especially when it came to human rights.[3] Though its mandate did not include cooperation on and commitments to human rights, beliefs in African solidarity lead to it promote self-determination and the liberation of African peoples' from colonial and white minority rule.[4] This dual set of political norms – noninterference and solidarity – meant the OAU condemned "the abuse of the rights of Africans by non-Africans, such as

[1] Charter of the Organization of African Unity (adopted May 25, 1963, entered into force September 13, 1963), U.N.T.S. 479, at 70–88, Art. 2.

[2] Kofi Oteng Kufuor, "The Collapse of the Organization of African Unity: Lessons from Economics and History," *Journal of African Law* 49, no. 2 (2005): 133.

[3] Nsongurua J. Udombana, "Toward the African Court on Human and Peoples' Rights: Better Late Than Never," *Yale Human Rights & Development Law Journal* 3 (2000): 58.

[4] Frans Viljoen, *International Human Rights Law in Africa*, 2nd ed. (Oxford: Oxford University Press, 2012), 156–57.

in the case of apartheid," but refrained from questioning how African governments treated their own citizens.[5]

External and internal pressures challenged the norm of noninterference in favor of greater commitment to regional cooperation on human rights. Intraregional factors pushed the OAU to address human rights, such as glaring repression and abuse throughout the 1970s, notably in Uganda under Idi Amin, the Central African Empire under Emperor Bokassa, and Equatorial Guinea under Marcia Nguema.[6] There was also Tanzania's invasion of Uganda in 1979, which marked the first time an OAU state invaded another member state. This action set a precedent for interference into domestic affairs for the purpose of human protection, as some accounts suggested that Tanzania acted out of concern for Ugandans facing the repressive rule of Amin.[7] Democratization (even if short-lived) in some African states in the late 1970s, including Ghana and Nigeria, also provided some impetus for cooperation on human rights.[8] Last, in the face of economic turmoil and regime instability, some states desired regional cooperation on human rights to win favor with discontented domestic publics.[9] Pressure came from African transnational civil society actors and epistemic communities, such as African jurists, who actively mobilized for the creation of an African human rights charter and mechanisms for the realization of these rights. These actors participated in several seminars and colloquia spanning the 1960s and 1970s, calling for and offering proposals for an African human rights instrument.[10]

External pressures also challenged commitments to noninterference, calling for African states to improve human rights. By some accounts, the United States and its allies used ideological tools, including human rights, during the Cold War to fight against communism and to maintain American hegemony.[11] Notably, under President Jimmy Carter the

[5] Udombana, "Toward the African Court on Human and Peoples' Rights," 55–56.

[6] Viljoen, *International Human Rights Law in Africa*; Kofi Oteng Kufuor, *The African Human Rights System: Origin and Evolution* (New York: Palgrave Macmillan, 2010).

[7] Kufuor, *The African Human Rights System*; Viljoen, *International Human Rights Law in Africa*.

[8] Viljoen, *International Human Rights Law in Africa*, 159.

[9] Kufuor, *The African Human Rights System*.

[10] Germain Baricako, "The African Charter and African Commission on Human and Peoples' Rights," in *The African Charter on Human and Peoples' Rights: The System in Practice 1986–2006*, ed. Malcolm Evans and Rachel Murray (Cambridge: Cambridge University Press, 2008).

[11] Jack Donnelly, "International Human Rights: A Regime Analysis," *International Organization* 40, no. 3 (1986).

United States placed heightened emphasis on human rights as a requirement for foreign aid.[12] International organizations, especially the UN, and international NGOs like the International Commission of Jurists also put pressure on African states to improve human rights.[13]

Under these pressures, the OAU Assembly of Heads of State and Government in 1979[14] called upon the OAU's Secretary General Edem Kodjo to convene a meeting of African experts to draft a human rights instrument.[15] Kodjo organized a meeting of twenty African experts in Dakar, Senegal in late 1979. Senegalese Supreme Court Judge Kéba Mbaye presided over the meeting, which drafted a proposed charter that was to be reviewed by an intergovernmental conference in March 1980. When it became clear that this conference would not convene, Kodjo called on President Jawara of The Gambia to invite the OAU's Ministers of Justice to Banjul for the purpose of drafting a human rights charter. The Gambia hosted this Ministerial Conference in June 1980, but the draft charter was stalled by its opponents. The OAU Council of Ministers (composed of foreign ministers) called upon the Ministerial Conference of Justice ministers to reconvene. The Ministerial Conference met again in Banjul in January 1981 and adopted the draft charter. The draft was then submitted to the Council of Ministers and the OAU Assembly. The latter adopted the African Charter on Human and Peoples' Rights[16] (often referred to as the Banjul Charter) without debate in 1981.[17]

The Banjul Charter, which entered into force in 1986, was inspired by the European and Inter-American human rights conventions. It nonetheless stands out in some regards. It uniquely articulated duties and obligations. It also espouses both individual and collective rights, and adds a host of economic, social, and cultural rights to the enumerated civil and political rights.[18] More importantly, the Charter represented the

[12] Viljoen, *International Human Rights Law in Africa*, 159.

[13] Baricako, "The African Charter and African Commission on Human and Peoples' Rights."

[14] OAU. Decision AHG/Dec.115 (XVI), rev. 1, July 16–20, 1979, Sixteenth Ordinary Session of the Assembly of Heads of State and Government (Monrovia, Liberia: OAU, 1979).

[15] Baricako, "The African Charter and African Commission on Human and Peoples' Rights," 5.

[16] African Charter of Human and Peoples' Rights (adopted June 27, 1981, entered into force October 21, 1986) U.N.T.S. 1520, at 217–92 [herein "African Charter"].

[17] Baricako, "The African Charter and African Commission on Human and Peoples' Rights," 6–8; Viljoen, *International Human Rights Law in Africa*, 160–61.

[18] Udombana, "Toward the African Court on Human and Peoples' Rights," 60–62; Gino J. Naldi, "The African Union and the Regional Human Rights System," in *The African*

strengthening of a political norm of regional cooperation on human rights, while also affirming the norm of noninterference. As many commentators have noted, the Charter is less intrusive than its European and Inter-American counterparts. First, the Charter has "claw-back" provisions, or escape clauses that effectively weaken the states' human rights obligations while preserving sovereignty. Unlike other human rights instruments which permit derogation of rights under limited circumstances, such as a national emergency, the African Charter allowed states to deviate from rights guarantees so long as it was prescribed by law.[19] For example, Article 6 of the Charter establishes that "Every individual shall have the right to liberty and to the security of his person. *No one may be deprived of his freedom except for reasons and conditions previously laid down by law*" (emphasis added).[20] Several other articles similarly qualify states' obligations. Second, the Charter established the African Commission on Human Rights (ACmHPR) to monitor state compliance,[21] but the ACmHPR was structurally weak and subservient to states.[22] For example, the Commission's judgments could not be publicized without their adoption by the Assembly.[23] Also, the Charter did not include a court.

A court was not realized for nearly two more decades, during which time it became increasingly clear that the ACmHPR was weak and ineffective.[24] Meanwhile, the European human rights system moved away from a dual supervisory mechanism in the 1990s (the European Court entirely replaced the European Commission on Human Rights in 1998), and the Inter-American Court came to overshadow its sister commission. These developments made clear that the African system

Charter on Human and Peoples' Rights: The System in Practice 1986–2006, ed. Malcolm Evans and Rachel Murray (Cambridge: Cambridge University Press, 2008).

19 Udombana, "Toward the African Court on Human and Peoples' Rights," 62–63; Naldi, "The African Union and the Regional Human Rights System," 26–27.

20 For more on the impact of the claw-back provisions, see William Edward Adjei, "Re-Assessment of 'Claw-Back' Clauses in the Enforcement of Human and Peoples' Rights in Africa," *Journal of Legal Studies* 24, no. 38 (2019).

21 By some accounts, the Commission's findings are binding. See Frans Viljoen and Lirette Louw, "The Status of the Findings of the African Commission: From Moral Persuasion to Legal Obligation," *Journal of African Law* 48, no. 1 (2004).

22 Udombana, "Toward the African Court on Human and Peoples' Rights"; Gina Bekker, "The African Court on Human and Peoples' Rights: Safeguarding the Interests of African States," *Journal of African Law* 51, no. 1 (2007).

23 Ibid.

24 Bekker, "The African Court on Human and Peoples' Rights."

was not only out of step with the other regions but that a judicial mechanism could be an effective and respected institutional solution for addressing human rights.[25] At the same time, African states were embracing international courts to facilitate international cooperation. Many states accepted the contentious jurisdiction of the International Court of Justice, and subregional international courts, from SADC to ECOWAS, were established.[26] The newfound reliance on courts among African states is significant because these states previously rejected a human rights court, claiming that African cultural modes of dispute resolution did not resonate with a court.[27]

Democratization following the end of the Cold War gave rise to stronger popular movements calling for state accountability and human rights.[28] NGOs, civil society, and the international community put pressure on leaders to create a human rights court. Pleas for a court were voiced at several conferences in the early 1990s, some coinciding with the ACmHPR's meetings, from organizations like the African Bar Association[29] and the International Commission of Jurists.[30] Some of the calls included detailed proposals, such as a draft protocol commissioned by the International Commission of Jurists in 1993.[31] In fact, the International Commission of Jurists presented a draft protocol to the OAU Secretary General in 1994, requesting the Secretary General add it to the agenda for the Assembly meeting to be held in June 1994.[32] At that meeting, the Assembly adopted a resolution requesting the Secretary General convene a meeting of government experts to consider the creation of an African Court.[33]

Accordingly, a meeting of government experts, held in Cape Town in September 1995, discussed a draft protocol prepared by the Secretary

[25] Ibid., 162; Udombana, "Toward the African Court on Human and Peoples' Rights," 78–79.

[26] Fatsah Ouguergouz, "The Establishment of an African Court of Human and Peoples' Rights: A Judicial Premiere for the African Union," *African Yearbook of International Law* 11, no. 1 (2003): 83–85.

[27] Udombana, "Toward the African Court on Human and Peoples' Rights."

[28] Ibid., 77; Viljoen, *International Human Rights Law in Africa*, 412.

[29] Udombana, "Toward the African Court on Human and Peoples' Rights," 76.

[30] Ibid., 76, 79–80; Viljoen, *International Human Rights Law in Africa*, 412; Ouguergouz, "The Establishment of an African Court of Human and Peoples' Rights," fn. 34.

[31] Udombana, "Toward the African Court on Human and Peoples' Rights."

[32] Ibid., 79–80.

[33] OAU, Resolution AHG/Res.230 (XXX), June 13–15, 1994, Thirtieth Ordinary Session of the Assembly of Heads of State and Government (Tunis, Tunisia: OAU, 1994).

General, the ACmHPR, and International Commission of Jurists.[34] Following the meeting, the "Cape Town draft" was circulated among member states. The Council of Ministers postponed consideration of the Cape Town draft when it met in July 1996 because few member states had commented on the draft. The Council instead invited member states to comment. At its next meeting in February 1997 in Tripoli, the Council of Ministers – again due to the limited responses – renewed its request that states comment on the draft and decided to convene a second meeting of government experts in April 1997. This meeting was held in Nouakchott, Mauritania, and it was attended by delegates from nineteen member states and the ACmHPR. At the meeting, a revised draft protocol called the "Nouakchott Protocol" was adopted, which was supposed to be presented to the Assembly for adoption at its meeting in June 1997. But when the Council of Ministers met at the end of May, it decided to delay the presentation of the Nouakchott Protocol to the Assembly, hoping to obtain more state support for the draft protocol. Consequently, the Council of Ministers called for a third meeting of government experts. Held in Addis Ababa, Ethiopia, in December 1997, this third meeting was open to government experts and diplomats and forty-five OAU member states were represented. The meeting concluded on December 11 with a finalized draft and a unanimous recommendation that the final draft protocol be adopted by the meeting of Ministers of Justice and Attorney Generals. That meeting was held the following day, approved the draft and recommended its final adoption. When the Council of Ministers met in February 1998, it approved the draft protocol and recommended its adoption to the Assembly. The Assembly met in Ouagadougou, Burkina Faso, in June 1998, where it adopted the protocol without discussion and formally approved the protocol establishing the African Court.[35]

The drawn-out process of adopting the African Charter and establishing the African Court represents a persistent tension of political norms: the norm supporting regional cooperation on human rights was long challenged by the strong norm of noninterference or the preservation of sovereignty. Colonialism had fueled a strong norm of noninterference as well as a limited (yet evolving) understanding of how African solidarity translated into a commitment to human rights. The balancing of these two norms tipped in favor of better regional cooperation on human

[34] Ouguergouz, "The Establishment of an African Court of Human and Peoples' Rights," 85.
[35] Ibid., 85–88.

rights, among other things, at the turn of the millennium. This shift can also be seen in the dissolution of the OAU and the constitution of the AU and its norm of "nonindifference."[36]

Another important legacy of colonialism that has bearing on the ACtHPR's ideational setting relates to legal culture. Colonialism contributed to the complex nature of legal pluralism on the continent.[37] Pluralism is reflected in the mix of state legal orders across and within AU member states. Common law, civil law, and hybrid systems were introduced by colonial oppressors and retained during independence. Islamic law is also part of several states legal systems. Additionally, customary or traditional law is an integral part of African legal order(s). State courts are not the sole mode of dispute settlement pursued by local and regional actors; customary modes of dispute settlement are frequently utilized.[38]

Despite variation, legal culture across the region is also often characterized by judicial insecurity. "Judicial insecurity mainly comes from the decay in justice due to the slowness of the cases, the unpredictability of the courts, the corruption of the judicial system, and the difficulty in enforcing the Judgments."[39] Those who wield power often interfere with the judiciary through informal means.[40] Consequently, "African judiciaries – and formal institutions in general – are often considered irrelevant because informality is said to dominate in African politics."[41] There is also a tendency for there to be a poor empirical legitimacy for constitutionalism.[42] For instance, trust in courts, on average among survey respondents across thirty-six African states, is lower than it is for religious leaders, the army, traditional leaders, and the executive.[43]

[36] Tim Murithi, "The African Union's Transition from Non-Intervention to Non-Indifference: An Ad Hoc Approach to the Responsibility to Protect?" *Internationale Politik und Gesellschaft* 1, no. 1 (2009). The AU was established in 2000; see Constitutive Act of the African Union (adopted July 11, 2000, entered into force May 26, 2001) U.N.T.S. 2158, at 3–58 [herein "AU Constitutive Act"].

[37] Kischel, *Comparative Law.*

[38] See, for example, UNDP, *Rule of Law and Access to Justice in Eastern and Southern Africa.*

[39] Salvatore Mancuso, "The New African Law: Beyond the Difference between Common Law and Civil Law," *Annual Survey of International & Comparative Law* 14, no. 1 (2008): 40.

[40] Charlotte Heyl, "The Judiciary and the Rule of Law in Africa," in *Oxford Research Encyclopedia: Politics* (Oxford: Oxford University Press, 2019).

[41] Ibid., 2.

[42] Prempeh, "Marbury in Africa."

[43] Michael Bratton and E. Gyimah-Boadi, "Do Trustworthy Institutions Matter for Development? Corruption, Trust, and Government Performance in Africa,"

To summarize, the ACtHPR's ideational environment should been seen in light of the colonial history of its member states, persistent tensions between noninterference and regional solidarity, and cooperation. Moreover, legal culture is often characterized by complex pluralism, judicial insecurity, and a lack of faith in the state legal order. This setting largely parallels those of the other courts studied in this book.

The African Court at Work

Following the adoption of the African Court Protocol at Ouagadougou, ratifications trickled in, and the Protocol finally entered into force on January 25, 2004, after the requisite fifteen states had ratified it.[44] The ACtHPR officially began operating in Addis Ababa, Ethiopia, in November 2006 and set up its seat in Arusha, Tanzania, in August 2007. Tanzania was likely selected as the seat of the Court in part because the International Criminal Tribunal of Rwanda had been situated there since 1995. As the ACmHPR was located in The Gambia (Banjul) and other AU institutions were in other regions,[45] the Assembly decided the Court should be housed in the Eastern region.[46] The ACtHPR received its first application in 2008 and issued its first decision in 2009. Prior to 2008, the ACtHPR dealt primarily with administrative issues, including developing the structure of the Registrar, hiring staff, formulating staff regulations, and drafting the rules of procedure for the Court.[47]

The African Court Protocol gives the ACtHPR contentious jurisdiction over the interpretation and application of the African Charter, the

Afrobarometer Dispatch 112 (2016), accessed August 30, 2024, www.afrobarometer.org/wp-content/uploads/migrated/files/publications/Dispatches/ab_r6_dispatchno112_trustworthy_institutions_and_development_in_africa.pdf.

[44] Protocol to the African Charter on Human and Peoples' Rights on the Establishment of an African Court on Human and People's Rights (adopted June 10, 1998, entered into force January 25, 2004), accessed August 27, 2024, http://au.int/en/treaties/protocol-african-charter-human-and-peoples-rights-establishment-african-court-human-and [herein "African Court Protocol"].

[45] For example, the AU Commission is in Addis Ababa, Ethiopia, and the Pan-African Parliament is in Johannesburg, South Africa.

[46] Viljoen, *International Human Rights Law in Africa*, 413.

[47] See, for example, ACtHPR, *Report of the African Court on Human and Peoples' Rights to the Budget for Year 2009* (Addis Ababa: ACtHPR, 2009), accessed August 25, 2024, www.african-court.org/wpafc/activity-report/; ACtHPR, *Activities Report for the Court for 2007* (Addis Ababa: ACtHPR, 2008), accessed August 25, 2024, www.african-court.org/wpafc/activity-report/.

African Court Protocol, and any other relevant human rights instruments ratified by the concerned states, for those states that have ratified the African Court Protocol.[48] As of January 2023, thirty-four states have ratified the African Court Protocol.[49] It also has advisory jurisdiction; any AU member state, any AU organ, or any African organization recognized by the African Union can request an advisory opinion of the Court on a legal matter pertaining to the African Charter or any other relevant human rights instruments.[50]

The ACmHPR, state parties to the African Court Protocol, and any African intergovernmental organization may submit applications the African Court. In addition, individuals and NGOs with ACmHPR observer status may file applications against states that have made a declaration, according to Article 34(6), accepting the right of direct access for individuals and NGOs.[51] As of mid-2025, twelve states have made Article 34(6) declarations: Benin, Burkina Faso, Côte d'Ivoire, The Gambia, Ghana, Guinea Bissau, Malawi, Mali, Niger, Rwanda, Tanzania, and Tunisia. As will be discussed in later detail, five of these states have rescinded these declarations (Benin, Côte d'Ivoire, Rwanda, Tanzania, and Tunisia). Consequently, as of May 2025, the Court can accept declarations from seven states: Burkina Faso, The Gambia, Ghana, Guinea Bissau, Malawi, Mali, and Niger.

The empirical analysis that follows is based on an original dataset of the ACtHPR's contentious cases. It includes all cases[52] finalized by the Court from its first decision in 2009 to the end of 2020.[53] Advisory opinions are excluded, but referrals from the ACmHPR are included. As with the EACJ and CCJ, the unit of analysis is cases, not judgments or rulings, because the Court can issue more than one ruling in any given case. For example, sometimes a merits judgment is followed by a separate ruling on reparations. Overall, the data are based on ninety-one finalized

[48] African Court Protocol, Art. 3.

[49] These states are: Algeria, Benin, Burkina Faso, Burundi, Cameroon, Chad, Côte d'Ivoire, Comoros, Congo, Democratic Republic of the Congo, Gabon, The Gambia, Ghana, Guinea-Bissau, Kenya, Libya, Lesotho, Madagascar, Mali, Malawi, Mozambique, Mauritania, Mauritius, Nigeria, Niger, Rwanda, Sahrawi Arab Democratic Republic, South Africa, Senegal, Tanzania, Togo, Tunisia, Uganda, and Zambia.

[50] African Court Protocol, Art. 4.

[51] African Court Protocol, Art. 5(3).

[52] The Court uses the term "application." I use "case" and "application" interchangeably.

[53] See Appendix for a complete list of all applications included in the data. Reparations judgments that were available prior to March 2022 are included, if the merits judgment had been issued in 2020 or earlier.

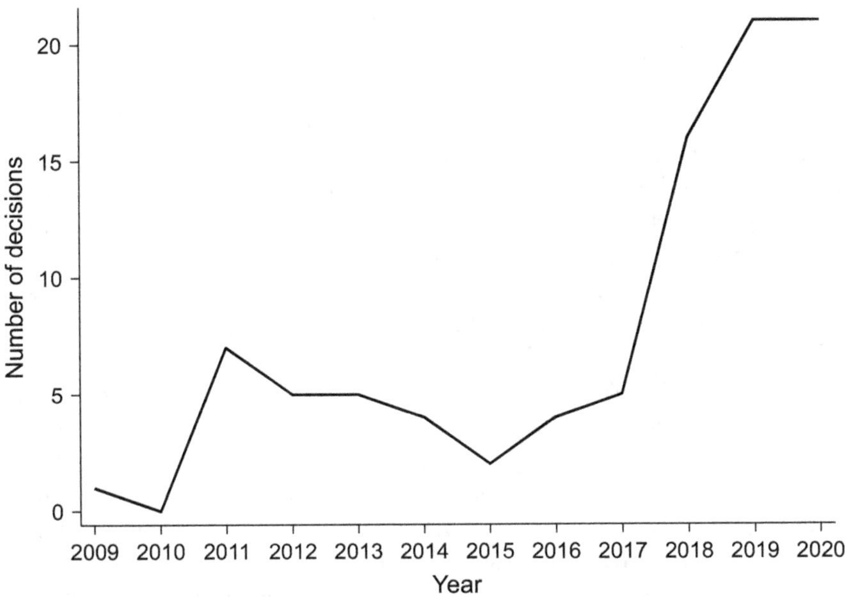

Figure 6.1 Number of ACtHPR finalized cases by year (2009–2020).

cases. I begin by describing some general patterns about the Court's caseload based on this data before exploring deference.

The Court's caseload has steadily increased. Figure 6.1 illustrates the number of finalized cases per year. While the yearly number of judgments pales in comparison to the European Court of Human Rights' current docket, its caseload is sizeable for a nascent court. If we compare the ACtHPR's caseload over the decade following its first decision to that of the ECtHR, the former has been far busier. The ECtHR issued its first judgment in 1961, and by 1971, it had issued decisions in only ten cases.[54] As Madsen describes,

> after ten years of operation, [the ECtHR] had only delivered ten judgments, and of these only a handful found violations of the ECHR. The Court was in fact out of business for a period of five years between 1960 and 1965 after it had been involved in the two cases in 1959 of *Lawless* and *De Becker*, and finding violation in neither.[55]

[54] ECtHR, *Survey: Forty Years of Activity 1959–1998* (Strasbourg: Council of Europe, 1998), 27, accessed January 27, 2022, www.echr.coe.int/Documents/Survey_19591998_BIL.pdf.

[55] Mikael Rask Madsen, "The Protracted Institutionalization of the Strasbourg Court: From Legal Diplomacy to Integrationist Jurisprudence," ed. Jonas Christoffersen and Mikael Rask Madsen (Oxford: Oxford University Press, 2011), 51.

We might also compare the ACtHPR to the Inter-American Court of Human Rights in its early years. The IACtHR opened its doors in 1979 and issued its first contentious judgment in 1988,[56] and by the end of 1998, it had received a total of twenty-seven submissions for contentious cases.[57] Of course, several factors underlie these differences, but they nonetheless help to put the African Court in context. Like its peer institutions, the African Court's early years are defined by a slow, but not insignificant, pace of growth.

For the foreseeable future, the caseload of the Court is likely to remain low. It received seventeen applications in 2021, seven in 2022, ten in 2023, and 15 in 2024 – a substantial decrease from the sixty-six and forty-eight received in 2019 and 2020, respectively.[58] Recent withdrawals of Article 34(6) declarations, especially that of Tanzania, explain much of the decline in applications. Of the cases in the data used here, 44 percent were against Tanzania. Table 6.1 reports the number of cases by respondent. As can be seen, only six states have faced more than two applications. Two of these have been the respondent in more than ten cases (Tanzania and Rwanda), both of which have withdrawn their declarations permitting individual and NGO direct access.

The alleged violations have been diverse to date, covering most rights or obligations included in the African Charter. Table 6.2 summarizes the number of allegations by article of the African Charter. The most frequently alleged violations pertain to Article 7 (due process rights), which has been alleged in a majority of finalized cases. Also frequently alleged are violations of rights to equal protection (Article 3), and freedom from nondiscrimination (Article 2), and freedom from cruel or inhuman or degrading treatment or punishment (Article 5).

As we would expect, not all alleged violations are confirmed by the Court. Article 7 violations have been confirmed by the Court more than any other alleged violation. In many cases this pertained to the right to legal counsel. The other articles with the highest number of confirmed

[56] Alexandra Huneeus, "The Inter-American Court of Human Rights: How Constitutional Lawyers Shape Court Authority," in *International Court Authority*, ed. Karen J. Alter, Laurence R. Helfer, and Mikael Rask Madsen (Oxford: Oxford University Press, 2018), 200.

[57] IACtHR, *2020 Annual Report* (San Jose: IACtHR, 2021), 41, accessed August 25, 2024, www.corteidh.or.cr/informes_anuales.cfm?lang=en. I calculated the total based on provided figure.

[58] See ACtHPR, "AFCHPR Cases: Statistics," accessed June 25, 2024, www.african-court.org/cpmt/statistic.

Table 6.1 *Number of ACtHPR cases by respondent (2009–2020)*

Respondent	Number of finalized cases	Percent of finalized cases
African Commission on Human Rights	1	1.10
African Union	2	2.20
Algeria	1	1.10
Benin	5	5.49
Burkina Faso	2	2.20
Cameroon and Nigeria	1	1.10
Côte d'Ivoire	4	4.40
Gabon	1	1.10
Ghana	3	3.30
Kenya	1	1.10
Libya	2	2.20
Malawi	2	2.20
Mali	7	7.69
Morocco	1	1.10
Mozambique	1	1.10
Pan African Parliament	1	1.10
Republic of Sudan	1	1.10
Rwanda	11	12.09
Senegal	1	1.10
South Africa	2	2.20
Tanzania	40	43.96
Tunisia	1	1.10
Total	91	100.00

violations are related to Articles 1, 5, and 13 (right to freely participate in government). We might also consider the percentage of allegations confirmed by the Court. The most frequently confirmed violations are not necessarily the ones that have been alleged the most. The Court has tended to rule in favor of applicants on the right to economic, social, and cultural development and the right to free movement, residence, and asylum, despite having been alleged in only a small number of cases. Another important pattern we can observe is that the most commonly alleged violations are confirmed most of the time, with the exception of Article 5. There are also a number of rights that have been alleged more

Table 6.2 *Alleged and confirmed African Charter violations (2009–2020)*

Charter article	Rights or obligations	Number of applications which allege violation	Number of violations confirmed by ACtHPR	Percent of allegations confirmed
1	Give effect to Charter rights	20	10	50.0
2	Freedom from discrimination	27	4	14.8
3	Equal protection	43	3	7.0
4	Right to life and dignity	15	4	26.7
5	Freedom from slavery and cruel, inhuman or degrading punishment and treatment	26	7	26.9
6	Right to liberty and security of person	19	4	21.1
7	Right to due process (to have one's cause heard, to appeal, presumption of innocence, defense, timely time by impartial court, no retroactive punishment)	58	30	51.7
8	Freedom of conscience and religion	2	1	50.0
9	Right to receive information and expression.	10	3	30.0
10	Right to free association	4	2	50.0
11	Right to assemble	2	0	0
12	Right to freedom of movement and residence, asylum	4	3	75
13	Right to participate freely in government and access to public services and property	12	7	58.3
14	Right to property	10	2	20
15	Right to work, satisfactory conditions, and equal pay for equal work	9	0	0
16	Right to health	4	0	0

Charter article	Rights or obligations	Number of applications which allege violation	Number of violations confirmed by ACtHPR	Percent of allegations confirmed
17	Right to education and cultural life;	3	1	33.3
18	Right to family life; freedom from discrimination against women and equal rights of women and children; right to special protections for the aged and disabled	6	1	16.7
19	Equality of persons	4	0	0
21	Right to freely dispose of one's wealth and natural resources	1	1	100
22	Right to economic, social and cultural development	3	2	66.7
23	Right to national and international peace and security	3	1	33.3
24	Right to development	2	0	0
26	Guarantee the independence of courts	12	3	25.0
28	Every individual shall have the duty to respect and consider his fellow beings without discrimination, and to maintain relations aimed at promoting, safeguarding and reinforcing mutual respect and tolerance	3	0	0
Total		302	89	29.5

Note: Articles that have not been alleged are not included in this table. Figures are based on a simple count of whether an article is alleged to have been violated or a violation of the article is found. It does not count based on rights (e.g., Article 7 is counted only once when it is cited for the right to counsel and right to appeal).

than ten times, yet confirmed by the Court less than a third of those times. These include Articles 2, 3, 4, 5, 6, and 26.

Judicial Deference by the African Court

How has the Court responded to its applications so far? Does it tend to defer to states or not? In what ways does deference manifest in the Court's decisions? The data reveal that the ACtHPR decisions are characterized by minimal deference. This can be seen in case outcomes, legal interpretation and reasoning, and remedial orders. In this section, I detail each of these.

Case Outcomes

The ACtHPR's case outcomes indicate its tendency to not defer. Table 6.3 summarizes case outcomes. As described in Chapter 2, deference is conceived as the acceptance of the state's exercise of authority and can take the form of abstention by the ACtHPR or its validation of the state's exercise of authority. Deference is therefore represented by case outcomes in which the Court (1) dismisses the application as inadmissible or outside its jurisdiction (i.e., abstention), or (2) the merits of the application are reviewed but no violation is found (i.e., validation). The *total deference rate* includes all outcomes falling within either of these two categories. The ACtHPR's total deference rate is 54 percent. The total deference rate, however, misrepresents deference because many dismissals, especially in the first five years, arose from poor quality applications. They therefore do not indicate abstention by the Court but rather a simple, straightforward application of the rules. Viljoen claims, "no fewer than 55 per cent of the cases submitted in the first five years have been submitted manifestly without any legal basis."[59] In fact, Justice Fatsah Ouguergouz filed separate opinions in several of these early rulings, arguing that the lack of jurisdiction or admissibility was so clear cut that the Court need not have deliberated over them, but the applications instead should have been administratively dismissed.[60]

[59] Frans Viljoen, "Understanding and Overcoming Challenges in Accessing the African Court on Human and Peoples' Rights," *International and Comparative Law Quarterly* 67, no. 1 (2018): 68.

[60] See, for example, *Femi Falana v African Commission on Human and Peoples' Rights* (Separate opinion of Judge Fatsah Ouguergouz), Application No. 19/2015, ACtHPR (November 20, 2015).

Table 6.3 *Summary of ACtHPR's case outcomes (2009–2020)*

Outcome	Number of cases	Percent of category
Admissibility/Jurisdiction only		
. *Inadmissible*	18	45.00
. *No jurisdiction*	22	55.00
Merits		
. *No violation*	9	17.65
. *At least one violation*	42	82.35
	Deference rate (percent)	
Total (N = 91)	53.85	
Merits (N = 51)	17.65	

Note: Total deference rate = *(no violation + inadmissible + no jurisdiction)* ÷ Total N. Merits deference rate = *no violation* ÷ Merits N.

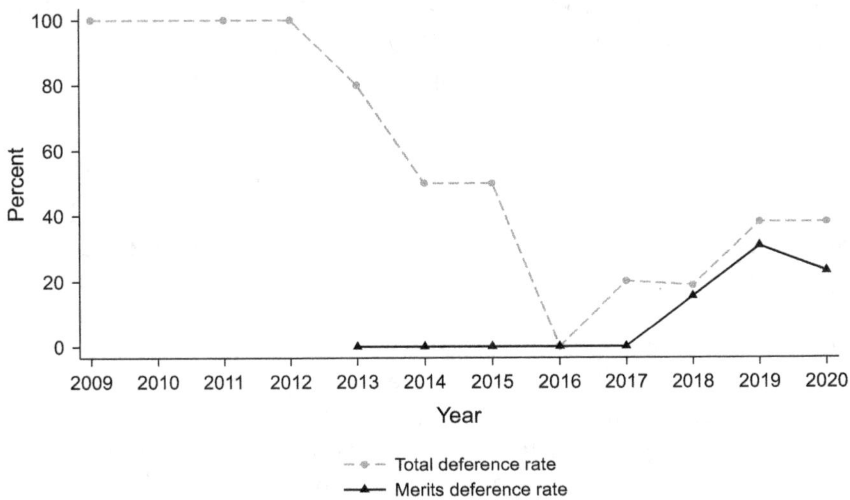

Figure 6.2 ACtHPR's deference rate by year (2009–2020).

Fifty-one applications (or 56 percent) were assessed on the merits. The Court declared at least one violation in 82 percent of these. In other words, the Court deferred in only 18 percent of merits judgments.

The picture becomes slightly different when we look at the yearly deference rate (Figure 6.2). As mentioned, the first few years are misleading due to the early rulings on jurisdiction and admissibility. Nevertheless, Figure 6.2 shows that merits deference rate has changed over time. In the first five years of issuing merits judgments, the Court ruled against states in all cases and therefore had a 0 percent merits deference rate. This rate, however, increased beginning in 2018. Being cautious not to over interpret these numbers, they nonetheless suggest the Court tends not to defer, even though deference increased in the few years leading up to 2020.

Legal Interpretations and Reasoning

A more complete picture of deference requires us to look beyond case outcomes and to examine the ACtHPR's legal interpretation and reasoning. Like case outcomes, the ACtHPR's legal interpretations reflect minimal deference. Three key aspects of its jurisprudence illustrate non-deference. First, the Court has eschewed restrictive, "work-to-rule" interpretations of its material and temporal jurisdiction, typically rejecting what respondent parties have argued. The African Court Protocol gives the ACtHPR jurisdiction over the African Charter, the Court Protocol "and any other relevant Human Rights instrument ratified by the States concerned."[61] The Court determined the meaning of this last clause in the case of *APDH v Côte d'Ivoire*.[62] It decided that the African Charter on Democracy[63] and the ECOWAS Democracy Protocol[64] are "human rights instruments" within its jurisdiction. This interpretation was broad as neither instrument is restricted to human rights, nor do they apply to all states subject to the Court. In the case of the ECOWAS Democracy Protocol, it also falls within the jurisdiction of another international court. Consequently, the interpretation adopted by the ACtHPR effectively expanded its jurisdiction to cover any legal instrument that has bearing on human rights or contains provisions relevant to human rights, regardless of its principal focus, so long as it had been ratified by the respondent state, irrespective of its status among other member states or

[61] African Court Protocol, Art. 3(1). This is a unique feature of the ACtHPR.

[62] *Actions pour la protection des droits de l'homme v Republic of Côte d'Ivoire*, Application No. 1/2014, ACtHPR (November 18, 2016) [herein *APHD v Côte d'Ivoire*, App. 1/2014].

[63] African Charter on Democracy, Elections and Governance (adopted January 30, 2007, entered into force February 15, 2012), https://au.int/en/treaties/african-charter-democracy-elections-and-governance.

[64] Protocol A/SP1/12/01 on Democracy and Good Governance Supplementary to the Protocol Relating to the Mechanism for Conflict Prevention, Management, Resolution, Peacekeeping and Security (adopted December 21, 2001), www2.ohchr.org/english/law/compilation_democracy/ecowasprot.htm.

whether the instrument itself recognizes the Court as the relevant judicial authority over that instrument.

On this question, restrictive interpretations that would better preserve state sovereignty were plausible. For example, Heyns argued that Article 3 could be interpreted as only those "treaties that make express provision for adjudication by the African Human Rights Court."[65] Viljoen suggests that stricter interpretation of Article 3 would take "the term 'states concerned' as *all the state parties to the Protocol*, and not only the state against which the complaint is brought."[66] Thus, while the Court could have availed itself of these possible interpretations, it rejected them and took a broader approach, proving "itself willing to exercise its material jurisdiction to the fullest possible extent."[67] As one former judge explained, the Court's approach on these questions should be viewed as broad, liberal, and purposive.[68]

Similarly on jurisdiction, the African Court's addressed a crucial question about its temporal jurisdiction in *Mtikila v Tanzania*: Was the Court's jurisdiction for any given state determined by the date upon which that state ratified the African Charter or the date upon which the African Court Protocol entered into force for said state?[69] In *Mtikila*, the alleged violation began in 1993. Meanwhile Tanzania acceded to the African Charter in 1986 and to the African Court Protocol in 2006. If the Court interpreted its temporal jurisdiction based on the date of accession to the Court Protocol, the alleged violations would have been outside the Court's jurisdiction. The Court, however, decided that the temporal jurisdiction was based on the date of ratification of the African Charter, contrary to the position put forward by the respondent state. Tanzania took the view that the jurisdiction was based on its ratification of the Protocol in 2006.[70] The judges themselves were divided on this issue. The written separate opinions contended a narrower, more sovereignty preserving, interpretation was not only feasible but also more

[65] Christof Heyns, "The African Regional Human Rights System: In Need of Reform," *African Human Rights Law Journal* 1, no. 2 (2001): 168.

[66] Viljoen, *International Human Rights Law in Africa*, 438.

[67] Rachovitsa, "On New 'Judicial Animals'," 256.

[68] Gérard Niyungeko, "The African Charter on Democracy, Elections and Governance as a Human Rights Instrument," *Journal of African Law* 63, no. S1 (2019).

[69] *Tanganyika Law Society and the Legal and Human Rights Centre & Reverend Christopher Mtikila v United Republic of Tanzania*, Application Nos. 9 and 11/2011, ACtHPR (June 14, 2013) [herein *Mtikila v Tanzania*, Apps. 9 and 11/2011].

[70] Ibid., para. 80.3.

sound. In his separate opinion, Justice Ouguergouz argued that the Court had erred, as the temporal jurisdiction when addressing an individual petition should be the date upon which the state made its Article 34(6) declaration.[71] Justice Niyungeko's separate opinion said the Court's interpretation of its temporal jurisdiction was "difficult to grasp" and "simply inconceivable."[72] The ACtHPR rejected a narrow, restrictive interpretation of its temporal jurisdiction, effectively enabling applicants to petition for allegations that occurred prior to a state's accession to the African Court Protocol.

Second, the ACtHPR has adopted broad interpretations of admissibility requirements, expanding applicants' access to justice. These interpretations went beyond a work-to-rule or restrictive approach. The Court often refuses to validate states' preferred interpretations and does not abstain in effect from "making law." The African Court Protocol requires applicants to exhaust domestic remedies, unless those remedies are unduly prolonged, for an application to be admissible.[73] States in various cases have argued that nonjudicial remedies should apply. The Court has rejected this position and found that the Protocol is concerned with ordinary, judicial remedies that are available, effective, and sufficient.[74] States have also argued that applicants must have personally exhausted remedies, even if previous litigation has proven remedies are ineffective. The Court rejected this argument also. Chenwi confirms this finding, arguing that the ACtHPR's has taken a "flexible approach" that facilitates victims' access to justice.[75]

To be admissible, applications must be submitted to the ACtHPR within a "reasonable" time following the exhaustion of domestic remedies. The African Court interprets this requirement broadly, determining that a case-by-case assessment is necessary to determine whether the applicant seized the Court within a "reasonable" time. Rather than declare a fixed time

71 Ibid., Separate opinion of Judge Fatsah Ouguergouz.

72 Ibid., Separate opinion of Judge Gérard Niyungeko, paras. 11–16. See also Oliver Windridge, "A Watershed Moment for African Human Rights: Mtikila & Others v Tanzania at the African Court on Human and Peoples' Rights," *African Human Rights Law Journal* 15, no. 2 (2015).

73 African Court Protocol, Art. 6(2) in conjunction with African Charter, Art. 56(5).

74 This excludes remedies that are "discretionary" and "extraordinary" remedies, such as constitutional review, administrative or parliamentary remedies. For example, see *Mtikila v Tanzania*, Apps. 9 and 11/2011.

75 Lilian Chenwi, "Exhaustion of Local Remedies Rule in the Jurisprudence of the African Court on Human and Peoples' Rights," *Human Rights Quarterly* 41, no. 2 (2019).

limit,[76] the Court considers factors such as applicants' education, imprisonment, indigence, and access to a lawyer to determine whether the application was filed within a reasonable timeframe. This puts the Court at odds with other human rights courts, which have fixed-time limits of six months.[77] In fact, respondent states have argued for a six-month time limit.[78] The Court has deemed applications admissible in instances where filing occurred more than three years after exhausting domestic remedies.[79] Overall, the Court abstained from a work-to-rule approach.

Third, the African Court's interpretation on substantive rights has eschewed conservative or restrictive interpretations. These interpretations signaled the Court's refusal to validate states' preferred interpretations: meaning their laws would not pass muster with the Court. The Court has also applied more intense scrutiny, such as balancing, finding that states have not met its criteria necessary for upholding their actions or laws. This can be observed in several areas. One such area relates to due process rights of Article 7, which has been among the most frequently claimed rights before the African Court (see Table 6.2). As Makunya argues, the Court has played a "continuous role. . .in 'humanising' criminal law and procedures."[80] For instance, the Court has found violations for failures to provide legal aid and for unreasonable delays in criminal proceedings.[81] When reviewing the Court's case law, Mujuzi concludes that "the Court is expanding the elements of the right to a fair trial under Article 7 of the African Charter."[82] The Court has also

[76] African Court Protocol, Art. 6(2) in conjunction with African Charter, Art. 56(6).

[77] See European Convention for the Protection of Human Rights and Fundamental Freedoms (adopted November 4, 1950, entered into force September 3, 1953). U.N.T.S. 213, at 221–70: Art. 35(1); American Convention on Human Rights (adopted November 22, 1969, entered into force July 18, 1978) U.N.T.S. 1144, at 143–212: Art. 46 (1)(d).

[78] See, for example, *Peter Joseph Chacha v United Republic of Tanzania*, Application No. 3/2012, ACtHPR (March 28, 2014).

[79] See, for example, *Kennedy Owino Onyachi & Others v United Republic of Tanzania*, Application No. 3/2015, ACtHPR (September 28, 2017).

[80] Trésor Muhindo Makunya, "Decisions of the African Court on Human and Peoples' Rights During 2020: Trends and Lessons," *African Human Rights Law Journal* 21, no. 2 (2021): 1238.

[81] See, for example, *Alex Thomas v United Republic of Tanzania*, Application No. 5/2013, ACtHPR (November 20, 2015) [herein *Thomas v Tanzania*, App. 5/2013]; *Wilfred Onyango Nganyi & 9 Others v United Republic of Tanzania*, Application No. 6/2013, ACtHPR (March 18, 2016) [herein *Nganyi & Ors. v Tanzania*, App. 6/2013].

[82] Jamil Ddamulira Mujuzi, "The African Court on Human and Peoples' Rights and Its Protection of the Right to a Fair Trial," *Law & Practice of International Courts and Tribunals*, no. 2 (2017): 222.

advanced protections for speech. For example, in *Konaté v Burkina Faso* the Court examined whether criminal charges and sentencing were proportionate to the state's interests to regulate against defamation of public officials.[83] The Court found that custodial measures were not proportionate. In *Umuhoza v Rwanda*, the Court came to a similar conclusion, finding that criminal sanctions for speech violated the African Charter.[84] While this interpretation may be in line with international human rights jurisprudence elsewhere, the judgment was the first time the African Court ruled on free speech. Moreover, several AU states have criminal defamation laws that are actively in force.[85] Thus, with this interpretation, the Court implies that it would refuse to validate laws that exist in a large share of states. The ACtHPR also applied balancing in these decisions to determine whether a state's action or law is acceptable.

The African Court, along with other subregional courts, has become an important venue for opposition politicians and activists to challenge ruling governments,[86] reflecting the African Court's role in the judicialization of mega politics.[87] It has addressed several issues at the core of domestic governance and politics, including electoral management, the process for constitutional amendment, and the independence of domestic judiciaries. The Court took nondeferential approaches on these issues.

The Court has addressed domestic election management in several cases. The Court's first case to assess laws on electoral management was *Mtikila v Tanzania*,[88] and it determined that laws barring independents from running for political office do not serve a legitimate aim. The Court's decision rested in part on a broad reading of the freedom of association, arguing that right of association is negated by a law which indirectly mandates an individual associate or belong to a political party

83 *Lohé Issa Konaté v Burkina Faso*, Application No. 4/2013, ACtHPR (December 5, 2014) [*Konaté v Burkina Faso*, App. 4/2013].

84 *Ingabire Victoire Umuhoza v Republic of Rwanda*, Application No. 3/2014, ACtHPR (November 24, 2017) [herein *Umuhoza v Rwanda*, App. 3/2014].

85 Jennifer Dunham, Bret Nelson, and Elen Aghekyan, "Harsh Laws and Violence Drive Global Decline: Freedom of the Press 2015" (Washington D.C.: Freedom House, 2015), accessed April 4, 2022, https://freedomhouse.org/report/freedom-press/2015/harsh-laws-and-violence-drive-global-decline. The authors report that restrictions on press freedom, including criminal defamation laws, are in force in several African states.

86 Olabisi D. Akinkugbe, "Houngue Éric Noudehouenou v. Republic of Benin," *American Journal of International Law* 115, no. 2 (2021).

87 Ran Hirschl, "The Judicialization of Mega-Politics and the Rise of Political Courts," *Annual Review of Political Science* 11, no. 1 (2008).

88 *Mtikila v Tanzania*, Apps. 9 and 11/2011.

in order to enjoy another right.[89] *Mtikila* represents nondeference because it withheld validation of Rwanda's law, and more importantly signaled to other states with similar laws barring nonpartisans from running for public office that their laws would not pass muster.[90] In other words, the Court's decision resembled an encroachment into the lawmaking authority of states.

The African Court has also considered the independence of election management bodies (EMB). In *APDH v Côte d'Ivoire*,[91] the Court was asked whether the state's national electoral commission accorded with the state's obligation to maintain an independent and impartial EMB, as guaranteed by Article 17 of the African Charter on Democracy and Article 3 of the ECOWAS Democracy Protocol. The Court ruled that the composition of Côte d'Ivoire's EMB was imbalanced in favor of the government and therefore contravened its human rights obligations. Following legal reforms in 2019, the Court revisited Côte d'Ivoire's EMB in *Suy Bi Gohore Emile & Others*.[92] At that time, the Court found that the national electoral commission was adequately balanced, but Côte d'Ivoire violated its obligations because the local election commissions remained imbalanced in their composition. Benin's electoral laws, which were amended after President Patrice Talon took power in 2016, have also been considered by the African Court. As in the cases dealing with Côte d'Ivoire, the African Court addressed the composition of the state's EMB in *XYZ (59) v Benin*.[93] It determined that one of Benin's election bodies, the *Conseil d'orientation et de supervision de la Liste électorale permanent informatisée*, was composed in favor of the government in contravention of Article 17 of the African Charter on Democracy and Article 3 of the ECOWAS Democracy Protocol. The Court reiterated this finding in *Ajavon (62) v Benin*.[94] The Court's decisions on EMBs

[89] Windridge, "A Watershed Moment for African Human Rights," 311–12.

[90] The ACE Project reports that twenty-four of fifty-four African states (data are missing for Western Sahara) bar independent candidates from running in either legislative or presidential elections, or both. See ACE Project, "Comparative Data: Independent Candidates," accessed June 25, 2024, http://aceproject.org/epic-en/CDMap?question=PC008&f=e.

[91] *APHD v Côte d'Ivoire*, Application No. 1/2014.

[92] *Suy Bi Gohore Emile & Others v Republic of Côte d'Ivoire*, Application No. 44/2019, ACtHPR (July 15, 2020).

[93] *XYZ v Republic of Benin*, Application No. 59/2019, ACtHPR (November 27, 2020).

[94] *Sébastien Germain Marie Aikoue Ajavon v Republic of Benin*, Application No. 62/2019, ACtHPR (December 4, 2020) [herein *Ajavon v Benin*, App. 62/2019]. Also in response to the application by Mr. Ajavon, who is a prominent critic of the government and did not

represent nondeference because, like *Mtikila*, it adopted a legal standard that many African states would not meet,[95] and therefore would appear to encroach on the lawmaking authority of states. At the same time, these decisions do not resemble a work-to-rule approach, which would entail taking the strictest, most sovereignty preserving reading of the law to resolve ambiguity.

The African Court has also addressed domestic judicial independence. In *Ajavon (62) v Benin*, the Court ruled that the composition of Benin's High Judicial Council, a body which disciplines judges, violated Article 26 of the African Charter on the duty to guarantee an independent judiciary.[96] According to legal reforms in 2018, Benin's president is a member of the judicial council, along with two members of government, and appoints an additional six members by his/her sole discretion. The Court found that the president's authority to directly appoint individuals to the judicial council constitutes executive interference with the judiciary. It further argued that the fact that the president sits on the council alongside members of government is "clear proof that the judiciary is not independent."[97] This decision followed an earlier judgment in 2019 by the African Court, in which it ruled that the executive had interfered in the functioning of the judiciary in a criminal case against Mr. Ajavon.[98] The Court went further in *XYZ (10) v Benin*, ruling that Benin had violated Article 26 of the African Charter because the president and the Bureau of the National Assembly had sole discretion to renew the terms of judges to the Constitutional Court.[99] Like the previous examples, these

reside in Benin, the Court found several aspects of Benin's electoral laws violated the African Charter. The violations included restrictions on nonresident citizens from running for office (Article 13(1)) and electoral alliances from listing candidates in elections (Article 10), as well as requirements that those standing for election have membership in a political party (Article 13(1)).

95 Comparative research on African electoral commissions suggests that a significant share of AU member states' commissions would not be independent according to the Court's interpretation. See, for example, Jørgen Elklit, "The Structure and Performance of African Electoral Commissions," *Oxford Research Encyclopedia of Politics* (Oxford: Oxford University Press, 2019).

96 *Ajavon v Benin*, App. 62/2019.

97 Ibid., para 322. The African Commission reached a similar conclusion for similar compositions of judicial councils in Cameroon and the DRC. *Kevin Mgwanga Gunme et al. v Cameroon*, Communication 266/03, ACmHPR (May 2009); *Jose Alidor Kabambi and Others v DRC*, Communication 408/11, ACmHPR (November 15, 2016).

98 *Sébastien Germain Ajavon v Republic of Benin*, Application No. 13/2017, ACtHPR (March 29, 2019) [herein *Ajavon v Benin*, App. 13/2017].

99 *XYZ v Republic of Benin*, Application No. 10/2020, ACtHPR (November 27, 2020).

interpretations by the African Court indicate nondeference because many AU member states would not meet the Court's standards on judicial independence.[100]

The Court has also addressed the process of amending national constitutions. Namely, in *XYX (10) v Benin*, the Court ruled that Benin had violated the principle of "national consensus," as espoused in Article 10 (2) of the African Charter on Democracy, when amending its constitution.[101] Benin's National Assembly, according to the ACtHPR, did not include opposition voices as it was not constituted through free and fair elections, nor was the public directly or indirectly consulted; consequently, the impugned constitutional amendment was contrary to Benin's obligations. The Court reaffirmed this position in *Houngue Eric Noudehouenou v Benin*[102] and its 2020 judgment in *Ajavon (62) v Benin*;[103] jointly these cases raised the bar for states when amending constitutions. Along with other decisions in which the African Court has assessed the compatibility of constitutional provisions with human rights law, these decisions are noteworthy indications of nondeferential legal interpretation because they reflect the Court's refusal to abstain and its willingness to assess the legality of state constitutions – a power not always granted to domestic constitutional courts.[104]

The Court's interpretations on the so-called "claw-back clauses" also represent nondeference by effectively expanding human rights protections. "Through its case-law, the Court has mitigated some of the starker deficiencies of the African Charter (compared to the American and European human rights conventions). Most notably, beginning with its first merits judgment in *Mtikila*, the Court has softened the impact of so-called 'clawback clauses' in the African Charter through recourse to proportionality analysis – effectively establishing a 'restriction on

[100] Charles Manga Fombad, "A Comparative Overview of Recent Trends in Judicial Appointments: Selected Cases from Africa," *Canadian Journal of African Studies* 55, no. 1 (2021); Heyl, "The Judiciary and the Rule of Law in Africa"; VonDoepp and Ellett, "Reworking Strategic Models of Executive-Judicial Relations."

[101] *XYZ (10) v Benin* 2020. Article 10(2) of the African Charter on Democracy provides that "State Parties shall ensure that the process of amendment or revision of their constitution reposes on national consensus, obtained if need be, through referendum."

[102] *Houngue Eric Noudehouenou v Republic of Benin*, Application No. 3/2020, ACtHPR (December 4, 2020).

[103] *Ajavon v Benin*, App. 62/2019.

[104] Adem Kassie Abebe, "Taming Regressive Constitutional Amendments: The African Court as a Continental (Super) Constitutional Court," *International Journal of Constitutional Law* 17, no. 1 (2019).

restrictions'."[105] The Court's treatment of these clauses reduces states' discretion to derogate from their human rights obligations and thereby expands human rights protections for ordinary citizens. In other words, it rejects unfettered exercise of state authority when it comes to derogation.

In sum, the ACtHPR has tended toward nondeference in its legal interpretations. This tendency pervades its decisions on jurisdiction, on admissibility, and on the merits. Its interpretations are often in contrast to restrictive, work-to-rule approaches that would better preserve sovereignty, go against interpretations that respondent states argue for, and set higher legal standards than many member states otherwise have. This is not to say that the Court's rulings are broad for international human rights law in general. Rather, they represent nondeference because they resemble an encroachment into states' authority to make law and clearly signal the Court's refusal to abstain from exercising its own authority.

There are exceptions to the Court's tendency not to defer. For example, the Court has raised the bar on admissibility criteria, requiring applicants to provide more robust evidence on admissibility. In *Anthony & Kisite v Tanzania*, the Court ruled the application was not admissible because it had not been filed in a reasonable time. Diverging from its earlier jurisprudence, which did not require substantial evidence of an applicant's inability (e.g., illiteracy, indigency) to seize the Court in a timely manner, the Court argued in *Anthony* "that although the Applicants are also incarcerated and thus restricted in their movement, they have not asserted or provided any proof that they are illiterate, lay, or had no knowledge of the existence of the Court. The Applicants have simply described themselves as 'indigent'."[106] While the Court tried to reconcile this position with its earlier rulings, the decision in *Anthony* is less pro-private litigant than previous decisions, restricts access to the Court, and ultimately abstains from intervening into the case. Moreover, *Anthony* was not a one-off. A further three applications against Tanzania were rejected for similar reasons – the applicants had not adequately proven their indigency.[107] Instances like these are "wins" for states and

[105] Tom Gerald Daly and Micha Wiebusch, "The African Court on Human and Peoples' Rights: Mapping Resistance Against a Young Court," *International Journal of Law in Context* 14, no. 2 (2018): 305.

[106] *Godfred Antony & Ifunda Kisite v United Republic of Tanzania*, Application No. 15/2015, ACtHPR (September 26, 2019), para. 48.

[107] *Livinus Daudi Manyuka v United Republic of Tanzania*, Application No. 20/2015, ACtHPR (November 28, 2019); *Chananja Luchagula v United Republic of Tanzania*,

Table 6.4 *Summary of ACtHPR's remedies (2009–2020)*

Type of remedy	No. of instances
Declaratory judgments	42
Reparations	48
• Compensation = 29	
• Restitution = 19	
Publish judgment	10
Consequential orders	14
Total (excluding declaratory judgments)	72

Note: Judgments can have more than one remedy type. The coding included up to four per case. Reparation rulings were pending in two cases and therefore are excluded in the data. These figures exclude the Court's decisions on whether costs are awarded. Typically, the Court orders that parties bear their own costs of the litigation.

help to illustrate the differences between deference and nondeference. Even though instances of the former do exist, the Court's legal interpretations by and large reflect the latter.

Remedies

Remedial orders also shed light on deference. The African Court Protocol provides that "[i]f the Court finds that there has been violation of a human or peoples' rights, it shall make appropriate orders to remedy the violation, including the payment of fair compensation or reparation."[108] Based on this provision, the ACtHPR frequently grants remedies to wronged parties. Table 6.4 summarizes the Court's remedial orders. In particular, the data reveal three main patterns to its remedial orders.

First, the Court relies more on nonintrusive remedies than on intrusive remedies. Nonintrusive remedies, like declaratory judgments and to a lesser extent reparations, represent deference because the Court shows more acceptance of the state's authority to determine how to right wrongs. Declaratory orders by themselves reflect a court's abstention from the determination of remedies. In contrast, intrusive remedies such as consequential orders are nondeferential because they reject the state's

Application No. 39/2016, ACtHPR (September 25, 2020); *Hamad Mohamed Lyambaka v United Republic of Tanzania*, Application No. 10/2016, ACtHPR (September 25, 2020).

108 African Court Protocol, Art. 27(1).

authority to decide on remedies and can go so far as to mandate changes in law or policy. As Table 6.4 shows, excluding declaratory judgments, the ACtHPR has granted seventy-two different remedial orders, and several judgments include more than one remedy. Reparations have been ordered the greatest number of times and represent two-thirds of all remedies. Compensation is the most common order for reparations (and comprises 40 percent of all remedies). In its first opportunity to rule on remedies, the Court denied compensation to the victims, arguing that applicants must demonstrate a causal link between a violation and damages.[109] This judgment, however, expressed the ACtHPR's openness to granting compensation in the future. It "may, therefore, be seen as a positive step in the development of the award of damages by the African Court, as seen in *Zongo*, where the African Court took the foundations laid in *Mtikila* to proceed to award damages to the applicants – the first such award by the African Court."[110] Since these early decisions, compensation has been applied for pecuniary damages (i.e., economic losses) and nonpecuniary damages (pain and suffering, mental anguish, etc.) for both direct and indirect victims.[111]

Reparations also include orders of restitution. Restitution has been ordered in nineteen cases (26 percent of all remedies), including orders to release a victim from prison,[112] to reopen trials or investigations,[113] to expunge convictions,[114] and more. Nonintrusive remedies also include orders for states to publish the Court's judgment in official legal publications.

Second, the African Court orders intrusive remedies but when it does so, it grants some discretion to states on the precise nature of the remedy.

[109] *Mtikila v Tanzania*, Apps. 9 and 11/2011. See Windridge, "A Watershed Moment for African Human Rights," 319–26.

[110] Ibid., 325. See also *Beneficiaries of the Late Norbert Zongo, Abdoulaye Nikiema alias Ablassé, Ernest Zongo & Blaise Ilboudo & Burkinabè Human and Peoples' Rights Movement v Burkina Faso*, Application No. 13/2011, ACtHPR (March 28, 2014) [herein *Zongo v Burkina Faso*, App. 13/2011].

[111] See *Umuhoza v Rwanda*, App. 3/2014; *Lucien Ikili Rashidi v United Republic of Tanzania*, Application No. 9/2015, ACtHPR (March 28, 2019) [herein *Rashidi v Tanzania*, App. 9/2015].

[112] See, for example, *Mgosi Mwita Makungu v United Republic of Tanzania*, Application No. 6/2016, ACtHPR (December 7, 2018); *Thomas v Tanzania*, Application No. 5/2013 (Interpretation, September 28, 2017); *Mohamed Abubakari v United Republic of Tanzania*, Application No. 7/2013, ACtHPR (Interpretation, September 28, 2017).

[113] *Zongo v Burkina Faso*, App. 13/2011 (Reparations, June 5, 2015).

[114] *Konaté v Burkina Faso*, App. 4/2013 (Reparations, June 3, 2016).

The ACtHPR issued consequential orders in fourteen different cases, or in one-third of all cases where a violation was found. These orders typically require the state to change the law. In *Konaté v Burkina Faso* the Court ordered Burkina Faso to amend its law to remove criminal sanctions for libel.[115] This case involved Konaté, an editor of a newspaper, who was criminally charged for libel and defamation against public officials. Konaté alleged that this violated the freedom of speech as provided by, inter alia, Article 9 of the African Charter. The Court found that custodial sentences for libel, except in exceptional circumstances, violate free speech and ordered Burkina Faso to amend its law accordingly. Similarly, in *Mtikila v Tanzania* the Court determined that Tanzania's law, which barred individuals from running for public office as independents, violated the right to free participation in government, the freedom of association, and equality.[116] The Court ordered Tanzania, "to take constitutional, legislative and all other necessary measures within a reasonable time to remedy the violations found by the Court."[117] Another example where the Court ordered the respondent state to revise its law occurred in *APDH v Côte d'Ivoire*.[118] In this case, the Court found that Côte d'Ivoire's law pertaining to its Independent Election Commission violated its obligations to establish an independent and impartial electoral body and to ensure equal protection of citizens' rights to participate freely in government. The state was ordered to make the law compliant with these obligations. Other examples include orders for Mali to amend its Persons and Family Code[119] and Tanzania to amend legislation to provide individuals with judicial remedies in citizenship disputes.[120] Finally, in all the cases reviewed, the Court ordered provisional measures in seven cases.

The Court couples its intrusive remedies with subtle deference by giving states discretion to determine the exact nature of the solution. As Mbori states, "the remedial orders of the African Court have tended to be limited in scope, finding human rights violations but leaving a wide margin of appreciation for states to determine how best to remedy these

[115] *Konaté v Burkina Faso*, App. 4/2013.
[116] *Mtikila v Tanzania*, Apps. 9 and 11/2011.
[117] Ibid., para. 126(3).
[118] *APHD v Côte d'Ivoire*, App. 1/2014.
[119] *ADPF & IHRDA v Mali*, App. 46/2016.
[120] *Anudo Ochieng Anudo v United Republic of Tanzania*, Application No. 12/2015, ACtHPR (March 22, 2018).

violations."[121] One interviewee confirmed the Court tries to show some deference or to partially abstain even on consequential orders, saying, "we must not unduly direct states to do this or that, without giving them an opportunity to seek for themselves other ways to address the situation."[122] The coupling of subtle deference with intrusive remedies is best exemplified in *Thomas v Tanzania*.[123] In 1998, Thomas was convicted of armed robbery and sentenced to thirty years' imprisonment. The Court found Thomas' rights to defense, to legal counsel, and a fair trial were violated. Thomas pleaded with the Court to order his immediate release from prison. The Court refused (by a split decision), finding that orders to release prisoners could only occur under very specific and/or compelling circumstances, which had not been demonstrated by Thomas. The Court found that the typical recourse for the violations of the kind Thomas experienced was to reopen the case or a retrial, but as the sentence "served so far has been about 20 years out of 30 years, both remedies would result in prejudice and occasion a miscarriage of justice."[124] At the same time, the Court ordered Tanzania to "take appropriate measures to remedy the violations taking into account the above factors."[125] Thus, while the Court did not order his release, it barred the state from retrying Thomas, effectively leaving the state no option but to release him.[126] The Court took a similar approach in *Abubakari v Tanzania*.[127]

Third, the ACtHPR frequently combines different types of remedy in any given case. In forty-one of the forty-two applications where the Court found violation(s), it issued at least one remedy in addition to the declaratory judgment. In half of all cases where violation(s) are identified, the Court awarded two remedies in addition to the declaratory judgment. In ten of the cases (or 24 percent) where it declared violation(s), the Court ordered three additional types of remedies. Decisions that

121 Harrison Mbori, "Ingabire Victoire Umuhoza v. The Republic of Rwanda," *American Journal of International Law* 112, no. 4 (2018): 718.

122 Interview 7.

123 *Thomas v Tanzania*, App. 5/2013.

124 Ibid., para 158.

125 Ibid., para 159.

126 The Court later clarified that its judgment should be interpreted to mean that Thomas should be released; see *Thomas v Tanzania*, App. 5/2013 (Interpretation, September 28, 2017).

127 *Mohamed Abubakari v United Republic of Tanzania*, Application No. 7/2013, ACtHPR (June 3, 2016).

combine remedies are generally less deferential than when there are lone remedies.

In sum, we can see that the African Court balances deference and nondeference in its remedial order. While it has not cowered from using intrusive remedies, it applies them with caution and instead prefers nonintrusive remedies, often through a combination of remedies. Given the Court's tendencies toward nondeference on legal interpretation and case outcomes, remedial orders that are nonintrusive enable the Court to reconcile decision-making that favors applicants' access to justice and the protection of human rights while acknowledging its political context.

Explaining the African Court's Decision-Making

The ACtHPR's decision-making is characterized by minimal deference, as seen in case outcomes, legal interpretation and reasoning, and, to a lesser degree, remedies. What accounts for the Court's tendency toward minimal deference?

The Role of Support Networks

The logic of support networks suggests that nondeference arises from the strength, opportunities, and activity of a court's support network. More specifically, this theoretical account would expect minimal deference to follow from broad opportunities for supporters to access to the Court, efforts by the Court to mobilize its supporters, and/or an active use of the Court by its proponents. In this section, I look at whether the empirical evidence corresponds to this expectation. It reveals that access opportunities, while available and despite efforts of the Court, are limited in important ways and a variety of barriers prevent would-be supporters from actively realizing these opportunities. Consequently, the African Court's tendency to not defer is difficult to reconcile with the logic of a support network.

From the beginning, a host of civil society and professional organizations have been proponents of the Court. Some of these actors were influential in its creation, while others have developed since the adoption of the African Court Protocol, like the African Court Coalition.[128] Other

[128] The African Court Coalition formed in 2003 as an umbrella organization for NGOs and independent national human rights institutions. See African Court Coalition, "Background & Structure," accessed June 25, 2024, www.africancourtcoalition.org/background-structure/.

important support comes from the Pan-African Lawyers' Union and the East African Law Society.

The Court features various channels of access for would-be supporters, and it actively encourages such supporters to utilize these channels. Importantly, the ACtHPR features direct access for private actors. Individuals and NGOs (with ACmHPR observer status) can directly petition the Court, so long as the state has ratified the Court Protocol and declared its acceptance of the right of direct petition, according to Article 34(6). The African Court openly urges states to submit Article 34 (6) declarations. Also, as described earlier, the Court's jurisprudence on jurisdiction and admissibility is generally pro-private litigant and expands opportunities of direct access. The Court has also developed a legal aid scheme to support direct access. The scheme includes a roster of pro-bono counsel and a legal aid fund, which provides legal representation and aid to applicants.[129] In several instances, the Court has called upon its partners in the legal aid scheme to act as legal counsel for an applicant. I have recorded fifteen instances of this occurring, or 16 percent of all cases in the data.[130] Moreover, a large portion of the Court's cases are litigated with the help of NGOs, such as PALU or the EALS. My data reveal that NGOs have acted as legal representation in about one-third of all cases (see Table 6.5).

Despite these points for optimism, "the Court does not provide an avenue for a large number of human rights and civil liberties NGOs across Africa to challenge rights violations."[131] Direct access has significant limitations. It depends on states' willingness to accept direct access through an Article 34(6) declaration. In mid 2025, only seven states out of the thirty-four that had ratified the Court Protocol have Article 34(6) declarations in force. Also, not all decisions by the Court encourage potential applicants to seek recourse through the Court. For example, the ACtHPR has generally refrained from awarding costs to successful litigants. My data reveal that the Court has awarded costs to only four out of forty-two successful applicants, but the African Court's legal aid

[129] See ACtHPR, "Statute on the Establishment of Legal Aid Fund," accessed August 20, 2024, www.african-court.org/wpafc/wp-content/uploads/2020/10/22-STATUTE-ON-THE-ESTABLISHMENT-OF-LEGAL-AID-FUND.pdf; ACtHPR, "Legal Aid Policy 2016," accessed August 20, 2024, www.african-court.org/wpafc/wp-content/uploads/2020/12/English_version_Legal_Aid_Policy_From_2016.pdf.

[130] This figure captures only those instances that are mentioned in the Court's judgments.

[131] Daly and Wiebusch, "The African Court on Human and Peoples' Rights," 303.

Table 6.5 *Legal representation of applicants before ACtHPR, by type*

Type of legal representation	Number of cases	Percent of total
Self-representation	33	36.3
Private counsel	19	20.9
Unknown	11	12.1
NGO*	28	30.8
• *PALU*	13	14.3
• *EALS*	5	5.5
• *Other NGO*	10	11.0

* These figures include representation as part of the Court's legal aid scheme.
Note: Legal representation is coded based on information provided in the Court's judgments.

scheme does partially make up for this shortcoming. In addition, broader legal and societal factors constrain the support that the Court might otherwise derive from private actors. Cases making their way to the African Court face three critical obstacles: For most Africans, conceiving grievances as a legal dispute is remote, access to justice domestically is limited for many Africans because proximity to lawyers and courts as well as high costs can be prohibitive, and the structural deficiencies of domestic judiciaries (poor resources, weak independence, corruption, etc.) impair litigation as a means of redress.[132] These obstacles make access to domestic justice "illusory," in Viljoen's terms, and by extension access to the African Court because domestic remedies must be exhausted. Added to this, the Court is not widely known or understood even among the legal community.[133] While applications by private actors have so far been the lifeline of the ACtHPR, the full potential of direct access to empower the Court is a long way off.

Another channel of access for would-be supporters is through referrals from and interactions with supranational actors. Most relevant is the ACmHPR. The Court has sought to strengthen its ties with the Commission. For example, the two institutions have tried to harmonize their rules of procedure, and in 2010 they agreed to hold a

[132] Viljoen, "Understanding and Overcoming Challenges in Accessing the African Court," 74.

[133] Interview 10; Interview 2.

joint annual meeting,[134] the first of which was held in July 2012.[135] They also collaborate on some of their promotional and educational activities.[136]

The ACmHPR can lend support to the Court through its ability to refer cases to the Court. The Commission can refer its merits decisions to the Court if a state fails to comply.[137] This essentially enables the Commission to convert its nonbinding recommendations into a binding decision.[138] As of mid-2024, the Court had not yet received any referrals of this nature.[139] The ACmHPR has political and legal reasons to be reluctant to refer its merits decisions to the Court. First, it is not clear whether such referrals would result in the Court's de novo review of the complaint, whereby the Court would de facto assess the Commission's decisions and risk delegitimizing the ACmHPR.[140] Second, once a case is referred to the Court, the disputing parties become the Commission and the respondent state, leaving the original complainant (i.e., the victim) as a nonparty to the dispute. Thus, the victim could be denied due representation and participation in contravention of the principle of equality of arms.[141]

The Commission can also refer its requests for interim measures to the Court.[142] Complainants to the Commission can seek interim measures, where the ACmHPR would request the state to suspend action while the

[134] ACtHPR, *2010 Activity Report of the African Court on Human and Peoples' Rights* (Addis Ababa: ACtHPR, 2011), 9–10, accessed August 25, 2024, www.african-court.org/wpafc/activity-report/.

[135] ACtHPR, *Report of the 2012 Activities of the African Court on Human and Peoples' Rights* (Addis Ababa: ACtHPR, 2013), para. 95, accessed August 25, 2024, www.african-court.org/wpafc/activity-report/.

[136] See, for example, ACtHPR, *Activity Report of the African Court on Human and Peoples' Rights: 1 January – 31 December 2020* (Addis Ababa: ACtHPR, 2021), 11–12, accessed August 25, 2024, www.african-court.org/wpafc/activity-report/.

[137] ACmHPR, *Rules of Procedure of the ACmHPR*, Rule 118(1) (Banjul: ACmHPR, 2020), https://achpr.au.int/sites/default/files/files/2021-04/rulesofprocedure2020eng1.pdf.

[138] Viljoen, "Understanding and Overcoming Challenges in Accessing the African Court," 75.

[139] See ACtHPR, "AFCHPR Cases"; see also Frans Viljoen, "Forging a Credible African System of Human Rights Protection by Overcoming State Resistance and Institutional Weakness: Compliance at a Crossroads," in *Research Handbook on Compliance in International Human Rights Law*, ed. Rainer Grote, Mariela Morales Antoniazzi, and Paris Davide (Cheltenham: Edward Elgar Publishing, 2021), 375.

[140] Viljoen, "Understanding and Overcoming Challenges in Accessing the African Court," 78–79.

[141] Ibid., 79–80.

[142] ACmHPR, *Rules of Procedure of the ACmHPR*, Rule 118(2).

matter is reviewed. The Commission can only issue nonbinding interim measures. If states do not implement these measures, the Commission can refer it to the Court, essentially asking the Court to transform its nonbinding interim measures into binding provisional orders. The Commission has previously made two such referrals.[143] In both instances, the Court first ruled on the provisional measure and subsequently examined the merits of the cases. The Commission can also refer situations to the Court which the former views as a serious or massive violation of human rights,[144] or at any stage of its proceedings.[145] Under this latter provision, the Commission has referred one additional case.[146]

Across the board, ACmHPR referrals to the ACtHPR have thus far been rare. This rarity speaks to the Commission's limited capacity to act as a strong interlocutor for the Court. In part, this is because the ACmHPR can only refer cases against states that have ratified the African Court Protocol. Moreover, the Commission faces its own constraints, including limited autonomy and scarce resources.[147]

A final channel of access that might be utilized by court supporters is the Court's advisory jurisdiction. AU member states, AU organs, or "any African organization recognized by the African Union" may request an advisory opinion on "any legal matter relating to the African Charter or any other relevant human right instrument."[148] By mid-2024, the Court had received and finalized fifteen requests for advisory opinions.[149] Of these, one was withdrawn, ten were dismissed for not properly falling within the Court's advisory jurisdiction, and the Court delivered opinions in four.[150] This

[143] Viljoen, "Understanding and Overcoming Challenges in Accessing the African Court," 80–81. These two referrals are: *African Commission (Al-Islam Gaddafi) v Libya* (Provisional Measures), Application No. 2/2013, ACtHPR (March 15, 2013); *African Commission (Ogiek) v Kenya* (Provisional Measures), Application 6/2012, ACtHPR (March 15, 2013). The Court considered the merits of these cases, presumably as they constituted serious human rights violations.

[144] ACmHPR, *Rules of Procedure of the ACmHPR*, Rule 118(3).

[145] Ibid., Rule 118(4).

[146] Viljoen, "Understanding and Overcoming Challenges in Accessing the African Court," 83–84. See also *African Commission on Human and Peoples' Rights v Great Socialist People's Libyan Arab Jamahiriya*, Application No. 4/2011, ACtHPR (March 15, 2013). The Court issued a provisional measure in this case but did not consider the merits.

[147] Ibid., 77.

[148] African Court Protocol, Art. 4(1).

[149] See ACtHPR, "AFCHPR Cases."

[150] Lilian Chenwi, "The Advisory Proceedings of the African Court on Human and Peoples' Rights," *Nordic Journal of Human Rights* 38, no. 1 (2020): 65. Two opinions followed after Chenwi's article was published.

number is low, especially of delivered opinions, in comparison to the IACtHR.[151] Standing for advisory jurisdiction has been called into question in two regards. First, what constitutes an "African organization," and second, what constitutes recognition. On the first question, the Court has determined that an organization can be intergovernmental or nongovernmental if it is registered in at least one African state. As for "recognition," the African Court interpreted this to mean that recognition is conferred by the AU itself, not by any organ of the AU. This excludes NGOs that have observer status with the ACmHPR, unless they have also been recognized by the broader AU, from the African Court's advisory jurisdiction. In the end, this view significantly narrows the number of NGOs that can utilize the Court's advisory jurisdiction,[152] at least in the short term.

Overall, legal and practical factors limit the opportunities for private and supranational actors to access and support the ACtHPR. Consequently, the activity of would-be supporters is lower than would be expected by the support network logic, given the Court's minimal deference. However, their activity is not negligible. Indeed, as shown above, roughly one-third of cases involve NGOs. This raises the question of whether cases involving the support networks are more commonly associated with nondeference, as the support network explanation would expect. I assess this by examining whether there is systematic difference in case outcomes and remedies depending on whether the applicant's legal representation has repeated experience at the ACtHPR or an NGO participates in the litigation. Repeat counsel is defined as lawyer or legal association (e.g., firm) who served as legal counsel in at least one prior case before the ACtHPR; most repeat counsel are NGOs. NGO participation includes any case where an NGO is the applicant, serves as legal counsel (e.g., PALU), or submits an amicus curiae brief in the dispute. The findings are mixed (Table 6.6). In terms of case outcomes, applicants receive favorable outcomes (reflecting nondeference) more often when their case is presented by a repeat lawyer or if an NGO participates in some capacity. For instance, applicants represented by repeat lawyers won 90 percent of the time in contrast to 34 percent when not represented by a repeat lawyer. Similarly, applicants won on the merits more often if their case was argued by a repeat lawyer or if an NGO participated in the case. These differences correspond with theoretical expectations about the role of support networks.

[151] Ibid.

[152] Ibid. Daly and Wiebusch, "The African Court on Human and Peoples' Rights," 303.

	Repeat counsel		NGO participation	
Applicant wins (N = 91)	No	Yes	No	Yes
No (defer)	47 (66.20)	2 (10.00)	38 (69.09)	11 (30.56)
Yes	24 (33.80)	18 (90.00)	17 (30.91)	25 (69.44)
	Fisher's Test p-value: 0.000*** χ^2 p-value: 0.000***		Fisher's Test p-value: 0.000*** χ^2 p-value: 0.001***	
Violation declared, if merits decision (N = 51)				
No (defer)	8 (25.00)	1 (5.26)	7 (29.17)	2 (7.41)
Yes	24 (75.00)	18 (94.74)	17 (70.83)	25 (92.59)
	Fisher's Test p-value: 0.128 χ^2 p-value: 0.054*		Fisher's Test p-value: 0.066* χ^2 p-value: 0.038**	
Consequential order, if violation declared (N = 42)				
No (defer)	13 (54.17)	15 (83.33)	11 (64.71)	17 (68.00)
Yes	11 (45.83)	3 (16.67)	6 (35.29)	8 (32.00)
	Fisher's Test p-value: 0.057* χ^2 p-value: 0.042**		Fisher's Test p-value: 1.000 χ^2 p-value: 0.824	
Additional remedy, if violation declared (N = 42)				
No (defer)	0 (0)	2 (11.11)	0 (0)	2 (8.00)
Yes	24 (100.00)	16 (88.89)	17 (100)	23 (92.00)
	Fisher's Test p-value: 0.178 χ^2 p-value: 0.061*		Fisher's Test p-value: 0.506 χ^2 p-value: 0.143	

Note: *p<0.10, ** p<0.05, *** p<0.001. In each cross-tabulation, the first number is the frequency and the second number (in parentheses) is the column percentage.

The data on remedies, however, do not align with the support network logic. According to this logic, consequential orders or any remedy in addition to a declaratory judgment should be more common when a repeat lawyer represents the applicant or an NGO participates than if these actors are not involved. Table 6.6 depicts the relationship between remedial orders and the involvement of repeat lawyers or NGOs. Consequential orders and additional remedies are less frequently issued when repeat counsel or an NGO participates. For instance, consequential orders were delivered in 17 percent of cases argued by repeat lawyers in contrast to 46 percent where there was no repeat lawyer. This finding is important because case outcomes are an insufficient measure of deference. Rather, when deference is measured by remedial orders, the data suggest that deference occurred more often – not less – when a support network was involved in the legal cases.

In sum, private actors and NGOs have been crucial to litigation before the African Court. Yet, the ACtHPR's minimal deference, or its tendency to reject the state's exercise of authority, cannot be adequately explained by its support networks. Case outcomes are more often favorable to applicants when supporters participate in litigation, but remedies that are more intrusive, such as consequential orders, are less common when supporters participate. Additionally, there are significant barriers to the support network's ability to access and use the Court. Given these impediments that the Court's support network faces, we would expect the Court to defer more often than it does.

The Structural Determinants of the African Court's Strategic Space

The previous discussion shows the limitations of the support networks logic as an account of the observed minimal deference in the case of the ACtHPR. In contrast, I have posited that two structural factors – formal independence and political fragmentation – shape the Court's strategic space. Combined, these two factors produce a broad strategic space for the ACtHPR, enabling minimal deference.

Formal Independence

As Chapter 3 illustrated, the ACtHPR's formal independence is above the average of all international courts. In this section, I review the rules that constitute the Court's formal independence. I also show how these rules affect the perceived legitimacy of the Court and reduce the credibility and

Table 6.7 *Rules constituting the formal independence of the ACtHPR*

	Independence enhancing	Independence hampering
Appointment and Term of Office	• Judges elected by supermajority • Six-year term • Removal of judges decided by court • Oath of office	• Reappointment possible
Managerial autonomy	• Court recommends its budget • Court selects its registrar and president • Court adopts its rules of procedure	• States decide on budget
Insulation of Judges	• Secret deliberations • Diplomatic privileges and immunities of office	

plausibility of collective state resistance. Table 6.7 summarizes the rules that enhance independence as well as those that hamper it.

Several rules governing the appointment and terms of office of judges enhance the ACtHPR's formal independence. The Court is composed of eleven judges.[153] They are nominated by state parties to the African Court Protocol. To be qualified, a nominee must be a national of an AU member state and "of high moral character and of recognized practical, judicial or academic competence and experience in the field of human and peoples' rights."[154] Each state may propose up to three candidates, at least two of whom must be nationals of that state.[155] The Assembly of the AU votes by secret ballot on all of the nominees.[156] Judges are elects by a two-thirds supermajority when consensus cannot be reached.[157] In practice, the two-thirds rule applies.[158] Selection by a supermajority, compared to unanimity, prevents any one state from

[153] African Court Protocol, Art. 11.
[154] Ibid.
[155] Ibid., Art. 12.
[156] Ibid., Art. 13–14.
[157] AU Constitutive Act, Art. 7(1).
[158] Interview 6.

vetoing appointments (meaning judges do not have to win the approval of all states). Judges serve a six-year term, which is the same as the average term length for all ICs and thus is neither particularly short nor inordinately long. The process for removing judges from office also enhances independence, as it prevents states from punishing judges through removal. Rather, the African Court on its own initiative can remove or suspend a judge by a unanimous decision.[159] The Assembly of the AU, however, can set aside this decision.[160] To date, no judge has been successfully removed from the Court. To my knowledge, there have been two instances where the Court reviewed allegations against a judge. In one instance, the Court found there had been no breach of the terms of office, and in the other, the judge resigned before a determination was made.[161] Last, judges must take an oath of office declaring to perform their duties faithfully and impartially.[162]

On the other hand, independence is weakened because judges may be reelected to serve a second term.[163] The possibility of reelection reduces formal independence because it may cause judges to make decisions favorable to states to guarantee reappointment.[164] In practice, several judges have been reappointed to the ACtHPR. Interviewees suggest that reappointment decisions, even if affected by the votes and opinions of individual judges, are influenced by other factors, such as change in government, judges' decisions to not stand for reelection, as well as the requirement that overall composition of the Court represent all legal traditions and regions of the AU and reflect a gender balance.[165]

The African Court's formal independence is enhanced by rules that provide it with managerial autonomy. In particular, the Court has control over the selection of its registrar,[166] president, and vice-president.[167] The

159 African Court Protocol, Art. 19(1).
160 Ibid., Art. 19(2).
161 Interview 6.
162 African Court Protocol, Art. 16; see also ACtHPR, *Rules of Court* (Arusha: ACtHPR, 2010), Rule 4, www.african-court.org/en/images/Basic%20Documents/Final_Rules_of_Court_for_Publication_after_Harmonization_-_Final__English_7_sept_1_.pdf.
163 African Court Protocol, Art. 15(1).
164 Some may argue that judges will have similar incentives if there are no reappointment possibilities and terms are short, as judges will still be motivated by their employability after their tenure.
165 Interview 6; Interview 2.
166 African Court Protocol, Art. 24.
167 Ibid., Art. 21.

Court also determines its own rules of procedure.[168] States, however, maintain control over the Court's budget, and judges express concern that this limits the Court's independence.[169] The Assembly of the AU approves the budget of the Court, so states have the final say on both the size and allocation of resources. While the Court does not have final control over its resources, formal rules do require that it is at least consulted by the AU.[170] The Court prepares a preliminary budget and presents it to the AU,[171] and in practice, the AU controls the size of the budget but reserves decisions on the allocation of resources for the Court.[172]

Rules that insulate judges from political pressure also enhance the ACtHPR's independence. On the one hand, judges "enjoy, from the moment of their election and throughout their term of office, the immunities extended to diplomatic agents in accordance with international law" and "at no time shall the judges of the Court be held liable for any decision or opinion issued in the exercise of their functions."[173] Likewise, deliberations of the Court are to remain private.[174]

While this is distinct from independence, I note safeguards to impartiality. Judges are barred from participating in activities that are incompatible with the independence or impartiality of their office,[175] including holding "political, diplomatic or administrative positions functions or government legal advisers."[176] Judges must recuse themselves from hearing cases in which they were previously involved or in which they have a conflict of interest.[177] Also, judges are not allowed to hear cases if they are a national of the respondent state.[178] On the other hand, the AU Assembly determines the remuneration of judges,[179] which can be viewed as an independence hampering rule because salaries of judges could become a potential avenue for states to punish judges.

[168] Ibid., Art. 33.
[169] Interview 7; Interview 6.
[170] Ibid., Art. 32.
[171] Interview 1.
[172] Interview 9.
[173] African Court Protocol, Art. 17 (3–4).
[174] ACtHPR, *Rules of Court*, Rule 60.
[175] African Court Protocol, Art. 18.
[176] ACtHPR, *Rules of Court*, Rule 5(2).
[177] African Court Protocol, Art. 17(2).
[178] Ibid., Art. 22.
[179] Ibid., Art. 32.

Overall, there are several independence-enhancing safeguards. These provisions are more numerous than those that reduce independence. They also cover the main aspects of the Court's governance – the selection and tenure of judges, their terms of office, and managerial autonomy. Together they make collective state resistance politically challenging to implement. Moreover, they have an impact on how the Court is perceived. Several interviewees confirm that they view the Court as independent. One interviewee stated that "the integrity of the judges and their willingness and commitment to remain independent . . . to not be influenced" has been crucial to the Court's operation.[180] Some interviewees pointed to specific provisions as ensuring greater independence. For example, one judge felt that the independence benefited from the requirement that judges not preside over cases in which their national state was the respondent.[181] Largely, interviewees view the Court as able to operate independently, without fear of political retribution from states. As one interviewee explains, the Court generally "does not care about the states when giving a legal decision."[182] This is not to say that judges are not cognizant of politics. The judges know that fellow international courts – like the SADC Tribunal – have faced political backlash from states. For example, one judge explains, states "are the ones that set us up and may decide to shut us down; it's a possibility, one of these examples is SADC. So that lays back in the mind of judges; you have to be careful."[183] Formal independence is generally high for the Court, but, as this quote illustrates, it does not completely alleviate political constraints. Rather, it seems to supply it with a certain reservoir of legitimacy that helps to broaden its strategic space and therefore impacts its decision-making.

Political Fragmentation

As I have argued, political fragmentation also shapes a court's strategic space and, therefore, its decision-making. H_2 implies that we would observe minimal deference when a court's membership is politically fragmented. The AU fits this characterization. Most importantly, the AU members are divided on the jurisdiction of the Court itself. For example, only thirty-four (out of fifty-five) AU member states have ratified the African Court Protocol.

[180] Interview 9.
[181] Interview 6.
[182] Interview 10.
[183] Interview 6.

A second implication of H_2 is that we should observe higher than normal political fragmentation on issues where the Court has been nondeferential. I assess this implication by comparing political fragmentation on human rights *overall* against fragmentation on specific rights where the Court did not defer. As in the previous chapters, I measure fragmentation as the heterogeneity of member states' preference. I infer preferences from state practice based on V-Dem data.[184] Heterogeneity is measured by calculating the coefficient of variation for all AU member states in any given year. The COV is a statistical measure of variability, which is standardized as a percentage (0–100) to compare across indicators.[185] Higher values indicate greater heterogeneity of preferences.

I selected six issues on which the Court has been nondeferential, albeit to varying degrees. They are *rule of law*, *high court independence*, *election management body autonomy*, *access to justice*, *free expression*, and *electoral democracy*.[186] These issues are among the more commonly litigated rights before the African Court (see Table 6.2). I compare fragmentation on these rights issues against fragmentation on civil liberties overall. I use the V-Dem *civil liberties index* to capture overall human rights preferences; this index is an aggregate measure of physical violence, political civil liberties, and private civil liberties.[187]

Figure 6.3 depicts the coefficients of variation for the *civil liberties index* alongside the six selected rights. It shows that heterogeneity for all six selected rights where the Court has been nondeferential is higher compared to heterogeneity on civil liberties overall. This corresponds with the observable implication mentioned above: Political fragmentation is higher than normal on issues where the ACtHPR has not deferred.

To elaborate with an example, the African Court has found violations in 52 percent of cases alleging violations of due process rights (see Table 6.2). Two indicators in Figure 6.3 relate to due process rights, namely, the *rule of law* and *access to justice*. Fragmentation on the rule of law and access to justice across all years is higher than it is for *civil liberties* overall, suggesting

[184] Coppedge et al., "V-Dem [Country-Year] Dataset V12." I infer preferences from practices because the codified law may not reflect a current government's position as much as its behavior does.

[185] The COV is calculated as the standard deviation of a sample divided by the sample mean.

[186] Coppedge et al., "V-Dem Codebook V12." For each of these issues, I use the corresponding V-Dem indicator.

[187] Ibid.

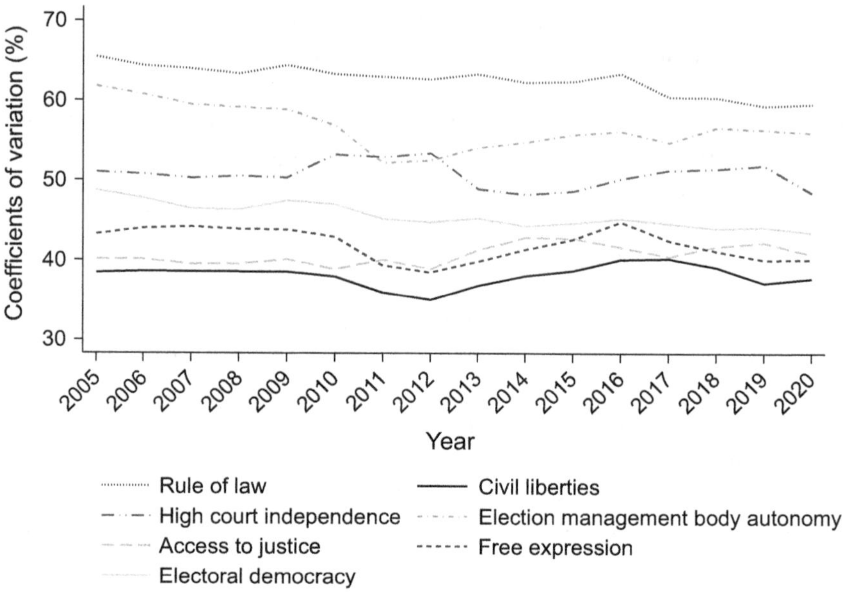

Figure 6.3 AU political fragmentation on select issues.
Note: Calculations and illustration by author.
Data source: Coppedge et al., "V-Dem [Country-Year] Dataset V12."

that nondeference arises when states are more fragmented than normal. The difference is especially large when comparing the rule of law and civil liberties. As another example, we can see a similar pattern related to election management and Article 13 (right to freely participate in government). On Article 13, the Court found violations in 58 percent of the instances where it was invoked by applicants. At the same time, fragmentation on *electoral democracy*[188] and *electoral management body autonomy*, especially the latter, is markedly higher than it is for *civil liberties* overall. Thus, this evidence supports H_2 as preference heterogeneity is higher for issues where the Court has been less inclined to defer.

H_2 has a third observable implication: When fragmentation decreases, we should see an increase in deference. Temporal patterns on deference

[188] This index is based on measures of the freedom of association, free and fair elections, freedom of expression and alternative information, whether the executive and legislature are selected by popular elections, and the degree of suffrage. For a description of these indicators, see Ibid.

are consistent with this observable implication. Figure 6.2 shows that civil liberty heterogeneity peaked in 2016, then decreased slightly. The rule of law and freedom of expression did the same. At the same time, the ACtHPR began to defer more since 2016–17 (see Figure 6.2). Taken together, the evidence supports the proposition that political fragmentation enables nondeference.

Past Resistance

The ACtHPR's strategic space benefits from robust formal safeguards to independence alongside political fragmentation, which together help to explain the Court's minimal deference. I have also argued that past resistance can narrow a court's strategic space and lead to more deference (H_5). The ACtHPR has faced instances of unilateral state resistance, shedding further light on temporal dynamics in the Court's decision-making. Namely, the ACtHPR's deference rose soon after an episode of exit. Rwanda withdrew its Article 34(6) declaration granting direct access to the Court for individuals and NGOs on February 24, 2016.[189] The withdrawal notice was received by the Court while prehearing procedures were ongoing in the *Umuhoza v Rwanda*.[190] The applicant, Umuhoza, is a leader of an opposition party who on various occasions made public comments allegedly denying or downplaying the Rwandan genocide. She was prosecuted and convicted in 2012 for, among other crimes, "minimizing" the genocide. She petitioned the ACtHPR, claiming she was denied a fair trial. As it became clear that the Court would proceed with the application, Rwanda withdrew its declaration.[191] The withdrawal notice stated that the Government "never envisaged" that a "[g]enocide convict who is a fugitive from justice" would be able to secure the right to be heard by virtue of its declaration. In parallel, the Court had other high-profile applications against Rwanda on its docket, which likely factored into Rwanda's decision also.[192]

Despite Rwanda's exit, the Court declared that Rwanda violated Umuhoza's right to a defense and that even if the state had a legitimate purpose in restricting free expression, criminal conviction was not

[189] The Court has ruled that withdrawals enter into force after one year.

[190] *Umuhoza v Rwanda*, App. 3/2014 (Jurisdiction, June 3, 2016).

[191] Oliver Windridge, "Assessing Rwexit: The Impact and Implications of Rwanda's Withdrawal of Its Article 34(6) Declaration Before the African Court on Human and Peoples' Rights," *African Human Rights Yearbook* 2, no. 1 (2018).

[192] Viljoen, "Understanding and Overcoming Challenges in Accessing the African Court," 66.

proportionate as the state "could have adopted other less restrictive measures to attain the same objectives."[193] The Court demonstrated some restraint, however, ruling against Umuhoza on some claims and exercising restraint on remedies as it did not mandate a change in the law.[194] Also, Rwanda has shown resistance by not participating in some of the proceedings of the Court, leading to default judgments.[195] This episode, along with slight decreases in preference heterogeneity, coincides with the upward trend in the ACtHPR's deference in 2016–17 (Figure 6.2).

Four other states followed Rwanda and submitted withdrawal notices.[196] Tanzania submitted on November 14, 2019, followed by Benin in March 2020, and Côte d'Ivoire in April 2020. These withdrawals significantly reduce direct access. While these unilateral forms of state resistance arose for slightly different reasons, they nonetheless have harmed the Court's legitimacy.[197] In other words, it has narrowed the Court's otherwise broad strategic space and encouraged greater caution by the Court. Yet, it is also notable that while these exits have no doubt been harmful to the Court, some states have submitted declarations after others rescinded theirs, namely The Gambia, Niger, and Guinea-Bissau.

The ACtHPR's Adaptive Practices

As I have shown, the African Court's minimal deference has been aided by its safeguards to independence and political fragmentation, which together endow the Court with a broad strategic space and subtle constraints. Past resistance and some decline in political fragmentation overlap with increases in deference. However, deference is not the Court's only response to its constraints. The theoretical argument

[193] *Umuhoza v Rwanda*, App. 3/2014 (Jurisdiction, June 3, 2016), para 162.

[194] The Court ordered compensation but dismissed requests for consequential orders.

[195] *Mulindahabi Fidèle v Republic of Rwanda*, Application No. 6/2017, ACtHPR (July 4, 2019); *Mulindahabi Fidèle v Republic of Rwanda*, Application No. 9/2017, ACtHPR (July 4, 2019); *Leon Mugesera v Republic of Rwanda*, Application No. 12/2017, ACtHPR (November 27, 2020).

[196] Four other states have submitted withdrawal notices. Tanzania submitted on November 14, 2019, followed by Benin in March 2020, Côte d'Ivoire in April 2020, and Tunisia in March 2025. See ACtHPR, "Declarations," accessed June 8, 2025, www.african-court.org/wpafc/declarations/.

[197] Sègnonna Horace Adjolohoun, "A Crisis of Design and Judicial Practice? Curbing State Disengagement from the African Court on Human and Peoples' Rights," *African Human Rights Law Journal* 20, no. 1 (2020).

presented by this book suggests that courts can adopt practices that help to reconstitute their strategic space. I find that the African Court employs persuasive argumentation and public legitimation to boost its nondeferential decision-making. Yet, these practices take on unique forms due to the Court's broad strategic space and subtle constraints.

Persuasive Argumentation

The ACtHPR uses persuasive argumentation, but it relies more on its citation practices than it does speaking with a single voice to boost the persuasiveness of its judgments. Table 6.8 summarizes the African Court's citation practices. It shows that among the ACtHPR's citations, it places greater emphasis on its own jurisdiction. On average, the Court cites 4.96 external references in its judgments compared to 8.59 references to its own judgments. Put differently, the Court cites on average slightly more than one external judgment for every two of its own. This general pattern resonates with the theoretical argument, which claims that courts with broad strategic space will be less reliant on persuasive argumentation in the form of external citations (H_3). It also suggests that armed with a broad strategic space, the Court is able to focus more on constructing compelling arguments through references to its own jurisprudence.

Despite this general trend, external references are featured in half of all the ACtHPR's judgments (not shown). The Court relies on external jurisprudence especially when it ventures into new territory or makes a far-reaching

Table 6.8 *Descriptive statistics on ACtHPR's citation practices*

Type of citation	Mean	Standard deviation	Min	Max
ACtHPR jurisprudence	8.59	7.09	0	25
External jurisprudence	4.96	9.08	0	47
• *International*	4.52	8.45	0	47
• *Domestic*	0.44	1.37	0	10

Note: All ninety-one cases are included. The coding records citations made by the Court itself in its reasoning. It excludes citations raised by the parties to the dispute (unless it is later cited by the Court) or citations that are referred to as part of the factual background of the application, such as domestic proceedings concerning the application. Some applications have more than one relevant ruling/judgment. A citation is counted only once, even if it appears more than once in a single judgment or in different judgments related to the same application.

decision. The two judgments with the highest number of external citations are *Zongo v Burkina Faso*[198] (forty-seven citations) and *Thomas v Tanzania*[199] (thirty-five citations). Both decisions are noteworthy for their nondeference. Other judgments with many external references are: *Rashidi v Tanzania* (nineteen citations),[200] *Rajabu v Tanzania* (twenty citations),[201] *Nganyi v Tanzania* (twenty-one),[202] *Konaté v Burkina Faso* (twenty-seven),[203] *Ajavon (13) v Benin* (twenty-eight),[204] *Mtikila v Tanzania* (twenty-nine),[205] and *Ajavon (62) v Benin* (thirty-two).[206] These judgments are also notable for their nondeference. For example, in *Rashidi*, the Court addressed whether a body-cavity search, conducted in the presence of the applicant's children, violated the right to integrity of person and dignity.[207] By drawing up the ECtHR's jurisprudence, the Court determined the search was degrading and an affront to dignity. Further, the ACtHPR relied on decisions of the Inter-American Commission of Human Rights to argue that the search was inappropriate because it was not necessary for achieving the state's interest as less invasive alternatives were available. *Rashidi* was the first case where the ACtHPR addressed this issue, ruling that the body-cavity search was a violation of not only Article 5 (which the applicant alleged) but also Article 4 of the African Charter (which the applicant did not allege). Moreover, the judgment included an intrusive remedy, ordering the state to reform its policies on body-cavity searches to avoid any future violations. *Rajabu* similarly suggests that external references are more common when the Court rejects the state's exercise of authority.[208] In this case, the Court found that a mandatory death sentence for the crime of murder is an arbitrary deprivation of the right to life (Article 4) and death by hanging is cruel and degrading (Article 5). *Rajabu* was the first case in which the Court assessed a death penalty on the merits.[209] The Court ordered that the state repeal the

198 *Zongo v Burkina Faso*, App. 13/2011.

199 *Thomas v Tanzania*, App. 5/2013.

200 *Rashidi v Tanzania*, App. 9/2015.

201 *Ally Rajabu & Others v United Republic of Tanzania*, Application No. 7/2015, ACtHPR (November 28, 2019) [herein *Rajabu v Tanzania*, App. 7/2015].

202 *Nganyi & Ors. v Tanzania*, App. 6/2013.

203 *Konaté v Burkina Faso*, App. 4/2013.

204 *Ajavon v Benin*, App. No. 13/2017.

205 *Mtikila v Tanzania*, Apps. 9 and 11/2011.

206 *Ajavon v Benin*, App. 62/2019.

207 *Rashidi v Tanzania*, App. 9/2015.

208 *Rajabu v Tanzania*, App. 7/2015.

209 The Court, however, had previously issued provisional measures enjoining the execution of the death penalty.

relevant penal code. In constructing its decision, the Court cited jurisprudence of the European and Inter-American human rights courts. It also cited human rights bodies, including the UN Human Rights Committee and the African and Inter-American human rights commissions. The Court argued, "there is extensive and well-established international human rights case-law on the criteria to apply in assessing arbitrariness of a sentence of death."[210] It drew on this case law to establish its position on how arbitrariness was to be determined. The Court later argued that its reasoning on arbitrariness "is affirmed by relevant international case law. Furthermore, domestic courts in some African countries have adopted the same interpretation in finding the mandatory imposition of the death penalty arbitrary and in violation of due process."[211] In addition to rooting its findings in international law, it argued that its interpretation was consistent with that of other member states' judiciaries, having cited high courts from Kenya, Malawi, and Uganda.

Table 6.8 shows that the Court cites domestic jurisprudence less than international jurisprudence. The *Ajavon (62)* judgment in 2020 stands out because it features a high number of references to international and domestic jurisprudence. The African Court pointed to rulings of Benin's Constitutional Court which had similarly determined the amendment to the composition of the higher judicial council violated principles of judicial independence,[212] and it based its interpretation of the national consensus on the Constitutional Court's own interpretation and application of national consensus.[213]

While the Court relies more on its own jurisprudence, the above examples give some indication that persuasive argumentation, especially by citing international jurisprudence, might be more common when the Court's does not defer to states. Table 6.9 takes a closer look at the relationship between deference and the Court's citations practices. It reveals that external references are more commonly found in decisions that reflect nondeference, in terms of both case outcomes and remedies, than in decisions of deference. This relationship is stronger for international references than domestic references. For example, the Court's decisions featured at least one international citation in 44 percent of cases in which the Court found no violation (deferral) in contrast to 74 percent when it did find a violation. The contrast is less stark for domestic references, which were included in 22 percent of

[210] Ibid., para. 99.
[211] Ibid., para. 110.
[212] *Ajavon v Benin*, App. 62/2019, paras. 316–17.
[213] Ibid., para. 338.

Table 6.9 *Cross-tabulation of ACtHPR's citation practices by deference (merits only)*

	Domestic references		International references	
Declared violation	No	Yes	No	Yes
No (deferred)	7 (77.78)	2 (22.22)	5 (55.56)	4 (44.44)
Yes	30 (71.43)	12 (28.57)	11 (26.19)	31 (73.81)
	Fisher's Test p-value: 1.000 χ^2 p-value: 0.693		Fisher's Test p-value: 0.118 χ^2 p-value: 0.095*	
Consequential order				
No (deferred)	29 (78.38)	8 (21.62)	15 (40.54)	22 (59.46)
Yes	8 (57.14)	6 (42.86)	1 (7.14)	13 (92.86)
	Fisher's Test p-value: 0.166 χ^2 p-value: 0.139		Fisher's Test p-value: 0.039** χ^2 p-value: 0.012**	
Additional remedy				
No (deferred)	8 (72.73)	3 (27.27)	5 (45.45)	6 (54.55)
Yes	29 (72.50)	11 (27.50)	11 (27.50)	29 (72.50)
	Fisher's Test p-value: 1.000 χ^2 p-value: 0.988		Fisher's Test p-value: 0.288 χ^2 p-value: 0.266	

Note: N = 51. *p<0.10, ** p<0.05, *** p<0.001. In each cross-tabulation, the first number is the frequency and the second number (in parentheses) is the row percentage.

declarations of no violation but 29 percent of declared violations. The patterns are similar for remedies. An international reference can be found in 93 percent of decisions with consequential orders compared to 60 percent of decisions without consequential orders. A domestic reference is also found in a larger portion of decisions with consequential orders compared to those without consequential orders. An international or domestic reference was included in 73 and 28 percent, respectively, of decisions with any remedy in addition to a declaratory order. External references are featured less often when there is no additional remedy (55 percent for international and 27 percent for domestic references). Thus, while the Court shows less persuasive argumentation through external citations than the CCJ (which will be discussed further in Chapter 7), it does use external citations more when it does not defer than when it does. These findings align with the theoretical arguments developed in Chapter 2 – persuasive argumentation through external citations facilitates nondeference.

Also, the Court does not rely heavily on unanimous decisions as a means of persuasive argumentation. In other words, the Court openly expresses disagreement on the bench, reflecting its broad strategic space. According to my data, one-quarter of the Court's judgments have been non-unanimous. Also, judges write separate and dissenting opinions.[214] Twenty-one cases in my data have written dissents, and separate opinions were published in thirty-nine cases. Similarly, there is little evidence that unanimous judgments are systematically used to bolster nondeference. My data reveal no strong relationship between unanimous decisions and deference (see Table A6.1). These findings are not surprising because the Court enjoys a broad strategic space (H_3). Overall, the broad strategic space corresponds with the Court's high use of its own jurisprudence to reason its judgments and is willingness to express dissent and disagreement. Nonetheless, the evidence does show that external jurisprudence is instrumental to nondeference, especially when the Court ventures into new territory.

Public Legitimation

An examination of the Court's strategic plans, annual activity reports,[215] "off-the-bench" activities like speeches and presentations by the judges,[216] as well as the Court's public communication (e.g., press releases) and interview material, reveals that the African Court has developed practices of *public legitimation* to construct its strategic space. Specifically, the Court engages in a range of activities that target its public audience with portrayals of its rightfulness.

The Court is attuned to the public's awareness of it. For example, one interviewee explained: "we are sensitive to the public's perception about the Court, especially the image of the Court."[217] Poor public knowledge of the Court has been an ongoing concern. Its strategic plan for 2011–14 pointed to the lack of awareness as one of its weaknesses.[218] In 2011,

214 Separate opinions reflect agreement with the outcome but express reasoning that differs from the decision of the Court. Dissents show disagreement on reasoning and outcome.

215 See ACtHPR, "Activity report," accessed August 30, 2024, www.african-court.org/wpafc/activity-report/. All cited activity reports can be found on this webpage.

216 See ACtHPR, "Speeches," accessed August 30, 2024, www.african-court.org/wpafc/category/speeches/. All speeches were extracted from this website and examined. Cited speeches can be found on this webpage.

217 Interview 9.

218 ACtHPR, *Strategic Plan 2011–2014* (Arusha: ACtHPR, 2011).

during a "sensitization" visit – when representatives of the Court travel to member states to pay courtesy calls, speak with national leaders, civil society, and human rights communities – the then President of the Court, Justice Gérard Niyungeko explained to his audience in Ghana that the Court "is not well known by the African people."[219] Similarly, Justice Akuffo's report on the Court to a summit of constitutional, regional, and supreme court justices noted, "there is an overall lack of awareness about the very existence of the Court among Africans across the board."[220] These concerns also received attention in the Court's 2016–20 Strategic Plan, seeing the lack of public awareness as a "threat" to the Court. The most recent strategic plan repeats this concern.

The Court recognizes its own ability to shape its public image. As one interviewee expressed, "The Court must take care of its own public relations. . .we've come along to accept that."[221] This has been the Court's view from its early days. During the Court's 2011 sensitization visit to Ghana, Judge Gérard Niyungeko, for example, explained that "It is precisely to raise awareness about itself that the Court decided to embark on a series of promotional activities, comprising the organization of sensitization seminars in a number of countries, with a view to popularize the Court."[222] Judge Akuffo's 2012 report on the ACtHPR similarly illustrated the Court's agency in addressing its public image, claiming, "the Court has taken the unusual policy decision to strategically improve its visibility and accessibility to all relevant stakeholders by undertaking activities that inform them of its existence, its mandate and how it may be utilized."[223]

More recently, President Judge Sylvain Oré urged the Court's staff to use publicity to counter existing negative impressions made by states and improve public opinion.[224] Accordingly, the Court adopted "outreach and coordination" as one of its four main goals for its 2016–20 Strategic Plan, with the aim of "build[ing] the Court's reputation and profile as a

[219] Gérard Niyungeko, "National Sensitization Seminar" (speech, National Sensitization Seminar of the African Court on Human and Peoples' Rights, Accra, Ghana, December 12, 2011).

[220] Sophia Akuffo, "Report of the ACtHPR on the Relevant Aspects Regarding the Judiciary in the Protection of Human Rights in Africa" (speech, First Summit of Constitutional, Regional and Supreme Court Justices, Mexico City, November 8–9, 2012), para. 20.

[221] Interview 7.

[222] Niyungeko, "National Sensitization Seminar."

[223] Akuffo, "Report of the ACtHPR on the Relevant Aspects Regarding the Judiciary in the Protection of Human Rights in Africa," para. 21.

[224] Sylvain Oré, "Opening Statement by the President" (speech, 48th Ordinary Session of the ACtHPR, Arusha, Tanzania, February 26, 2018), 3–4.

veritable pillar in the African Human Rights architecture and improve awareness of the Court by engaging stakeholders."[225] When announcing this strategic plan, President Oré claimed, "We have to intensify our efforts to increase the visibility of the Court so that more people and stakeholders understand the existence of the Court and hope that in return they will presurize [*sic*] their States to ratify and or deposit declarations."[226] The 2021–25 Strategic Plan similarly made greater awareness a central goal and identified several strategic actions to carry out for this purpose.[227]

The Court has adopted a range of public-oriented "off-the-bench" activities. "Sensitization" visits are one such activity. Among the objectives stated for sensitization are "raising public awareness about the Court . . . [and] encouraging the public to utilise the Court in settling human rights disputes."[228] Other activities range from essay contests,[229] participating in various regional events, like the 2010 Decade of the African Women[230] and the commemoration of African Human Rights Day.[231] The Court also relies on media and technology to "reach out to those people who are not here [in Arusha]."[232] The Court has provided media training on how to cover the Court. In 2013, for instance, the Court organized a conference for the media. It "was attended by a total of 67 journalists and media practitioners from thirty (30) African countries and 10 Judges of the African Court. At the end of the two-day conference, the participants adopted conclusions on how to work to enhance the visibility of the Court in particular and promote human rights as a

225 ACtHPR, *2016–2020 Strategic and Implementation Plan* (Arusha: ACtHPR, 2016).

226 Augustino Ramadhani, "Statement" (speech, Opening of the Validation of the African Court's Strategic Plan, Arusha, Tanzania, March 5, 2016).

227 ACtHPR, *2021–2025 Strategic Plan: Deepening Trust in the African Court by Enhancing Its Efficiency and Effectiveness* (Arusha: ACtHPR, 2021), accessed July 10, 2025, www.african-court.org/wpafc/african-court-on-human-and-peoples-rights-strategic-plan-2021-2025/.

228 ACtHPR, "African Court Successfully Concludes Three Day Sensitization Mission to Cape Verde," Press release, December 18, 2017, www.african-court.org/wpafc/african-court-successfully-concludes-three-day-sensitisation-mission-to-cape-verde/. Sensitization is also part of the Court's efforts to strengthen its support network through outreach to legal practitioners, civil society organizations, and national judges.

229 ACtHPR, *Report of the African Court on Human and Peoples' Rights: 2011* (Addis Ababa: AU, 2012), 11.

230 ACtHPR, *2010 Activity Report of the African Court on Human and Peoples' Rights*, 8.

231 ACtHPR, *Activity Report of the African Court on Human and Peoples' Rights*, 12.

232 Interview 10.

whole."[233] Also, the Court distributes promotional materials (posters, pamphlets, videos, etc.),[234] and it maintains a website and social media profiles (e.g., Twitter, Facebook) to have a public presence.

The Court's outreach and communication not only target a public audience, but also convey norm-referential and value-laden narratives. For example, the Court advertises that one of its core values is "fair and impartial application and interpretation" of human rights law.[235] The Court conveys or displays these values through its off-the-bench activities.[236] When Judge Niyungeko spoke to the Pan-African Parliament, he explained, "the Court pledges to discharge its role as the judicial pillar of the African Union with independence, justice and fairness."[237] The Court makes other norm-referential representations, like how its adheres to rules of admissibility and the exhaustion of local remedies. For example, during the moot court competition, the Court emphasized its respect for these rules.[238]

A prominent narrative signals the Court's commitment to its founding political purpose: the protection of human rights and effective justice for these rights. For example, the theme of the Court's 2011 sensitization visit to Ghana was: "Your new partner in the reinforcement of the protection of human rights in Africa."[239] At the Third Continental Judicial Dialogue, President Oré explained: "to render a more effective justice in Africa is no longer an option. It is imperative!"[240] The Court's promotion of other human rights institutions helps to portray its commitment to human rights, putting it before institutional allegiance. When addressing audiences where the Court does not have jurisdiction, one

[233] ACtHPR, *Activity Report of the African Court for the Year 2013* (Addis Ababa: AU, 2014), 21.

[234] These activities are supported by external funders, but the funders do not determine what activities the ACtHPR conducts. Interview 3; Interview 4; Interview 9.

[235] See ACtHPR, "Basic Information," accessed April 4, 2022, www.african-court.org/wpafc/basic-information/#corevalues.

[236] Participant observation, Remarks by Registrar Robert Eno and Justice Duncan Tambala, Arusha, November 30, 2015.

[237] Gérard Niyungeko, "The African Court on Human and Peoples' Rights and the Possible Role of the Pan-African Parliament in Promoting the Court" (speech, Fifth Ordinary Session of the Second Parliament of the Pan African Parliament, Midrand, South Africa, October 6, 2011).

[238] Participant observation, Remarks by Registrar Robert Eno and Justice Duncan Tambala, Arusha, November 30, 2015.

[239] Niyungeko, "National Sensitization Seminar."

[240] Sylvain Oré, "Presidential Speech" (speech at Opening Ceremony of the Third Continental Judicial Dialogue, Arusha, Tanzania, November 9, 2017), 3.

interviewee explained that efforts are made to point to other institutional opportunities for the protection of human rights, such as the ACmHPR or Court of Justice for ECOWAS.[241] The Court also highlights its complementarity with the ACmHPR.[242] The prominence of parallel human rights institutions in the Court's outreach and communication signals its broad commitment to human rights and its overall political purpose.

The Court's messaging is also people-centered, frequently speaking to its promotion of the African people and their values and aspirations. When addressing the ACmHPR, Justice Augustino Ramadhani said, "The noble mission of our two sister organs is to serve the common man and woman of Africa . . .. So, let us make his and her life better in so doing we are making sure that our tomorrow will be better also."[243] In another statement, Oré expressed how human rights reflect a common African goal: "it is our struggle, our common responsibility for an Africa which places human rights at the heart of the African Union reforms and as the key to socio-economic and human development."[244] On another occasion, Oré asserted how the Court is "neither a Court for the States nor a Court of the Judges, but rather a Court for all African citizens."[245] He claimed that "to build a more worthy, more humane and more prosperous Africa" is a "common struggle."[246]

Thus, the ACtHPR practices public legitimation. Many of its "off-the-bench" activities and communications are public-oriented and feature narratives of the Court's respect for its political purpose and its people-centeredness. To examine the intensity of these narratives in the Court's public communication, I look at the Court's Facebook profile. Using a web-scraping tool, I extract the ACtHPR's Facebook posts from 2012 to 2020.[247] A total of 897 posts were extract. Using the words or phrases commonly found in the Court's political purpose and people-centeredness

241 Interview 6.

242 Participant observation, Remarks by Registrar Robert Eno and Justice Duncan Tambala, Arusha, November 30, 2015.

243 Augustino Ramadhani, "Statement to ACmHPR" (speech, Opening of the Fifty-Sixth Ordinary Session of the ACmHPR, Banjul, The Gambia, April 21, 2015).

244 Oré, "Opening Statement by the President," 3.

245 *Business Ghana*, "African Court Rejuvenated for the Next 10 Years," November 23, 2016, www.businessghana.com/site/news/business/138199/African-Court-rejuvenated-for-the-next-10-yrs.

246 Ibid.

247 The Court launched its Facebook page in January 2012. See Facebook, "Page Transparency," accessed November 17, 2023, www.facebook.com/afchpr/about_profile_transparency.

Table 6.10 *Public legitimation narratives in ACtHPR's Facebook posts*

	Number of posts	Percent of total
People-centeredness	39	4.39
Africa	32	3.75
Africans	2	0.22
African peoples	0	0
people(s)	6	0.67
people of Africa	1	0.11
citizens	4	0.45
Political purpose	27	3.01
justice	8	0.89
rule of law	1	0.11
protection	8	0.89
respect	12	1.34
People-centered or political purpose	59	6.58

Notes: Additional terms – e.g., democracy, fair(ness), equality, dignity – were checked but were absent. "Public" is excluded because it is often used to announce that hearings are public. Equivalent French terms are also included, although very few posts are in French. All terms and phrases are case sensitive.

narratives, I identify their prominence in Facebook posts. Table 6.10 displays the words and phrases used for this analysis, as well as the number and percentage of posts that feature them. It illustrates that these narratives are minimally present on the African Court's Facebook page, suggesting a relatively limited degree of public legitimation through social media. In fact, many posts have short texts and instead rely on visual imagery, like photos and videos. Less than 7 percent of posts feature narratives about the Court's people-centeredness or political purpose. People-centeredness appears more than messaging about its political purposes, although the difference is modest.

The public legitimation narratives declined beginning in 2017 (see Table A6.2). This decline coincides with a decrease in deference (see Figure 6.2). Based on the logic of H_4, we would expect public legitimation to decline as nondeference declines. While the temporal data are limited and should be read with caution, the observed pattern is congruent with the theoretical expectation.

To briefly summarize the African Court's adaptive practices, the analysis reveals that the Court has adopted practices of persuasive argumentation and public legitimation. However, these practices take on a unique form due to the Court's broad strategic space. Its persuasive argumentation is focused more on making the Court's jurisprudence coherent as external references have been less prominent in its decisions, and it does not systematically rely on unanimous judgments to bolster nondeferential decisions. Public legitimation can also be seen through its "off-the-bench" activities and outreach. These activities are frequently public-oriented and norm referential. The messages appear to place more emphasis on the Court's people-centeredness than on its commitment to its political purpose.

Conclusion

Four main findings emerge from this analysis of the ACtHPR. First, the ACtHPR, much like the EACJ and CCJ, evolved from and operates within the context of colonial legacies. Importantly, a lasting impact of colonialism is a dualism of a norm of political independence and noninterference alongside a norm embracing regional cooperation on human rights. Additionally, the African Court's ideational setting includes a legal culture defined by complex legal pluralism, judicial insecurity, and a lack of confidence in state legal order.

Second, the African Court defers to a limited extent, showing a willingness to reject states' exercise of authority in case outcomes, interpretation and reasoning, and through remedies. More than the other courts studied in this book, the ACtHPR declares states to be in violation of their obligations. Its legal interpretations frequently reject states preferred interpretations and encroach on states' authority to make law by establishing legal standards that would otherwise not be met by many member states. The Court's interpretations and legal reasoning, in other words, demonstrate the Court's refusal to abstain from exercising its own authority. The Court has, however, exercised more caution in its remedial orders; it generally reserves intrusive remedies for a limited number of applications, but it readily provides for reparations to victims. The ACtHPR's decision-making, therefore, can be described as minimally deferential, even though deference increased toward the end of the time under analysis (2017 onward).

Third, the Court's tendency to not defer is difficult to explain based on the role of its support network. While there is a support network from which the Court draws strength, it is wanting in several ways and faces impediments. The key channels through which support networks would be able to preserve the Court are troubled. Supranational actors, namely, the ACmHPR, have made limited use of their capacity to refer applications to the Court. Private actors also face legal and practical barriers to accessing the Court. Moreover, when the support network is involved in litigation, the Court may be less likely to defer on the merits, but it is more likely to abstain from ordering intrusive remedies.

Fourth, the ACtHPR's nondeference and rejection of states' exercise of authority are significantly shaped by its high formal independence and political fragmentation, which endows it with a broad strategic space. Interview material supports the proposition that the Court's formal independence contributes to stakeholders' views of the Court. Where political fragmentation is greater, we see the Court favoring nondeference. Also, nondeference lessened as the Court experienced a wave of unilateral exits. Even with this resistance, however, the African Court retains a relatively broad strategic space. This broad strategic space sheds light on the Court's adaptive practices. Specifically, the African Court's persuasive argumentation does not hinge on having unanimous judgments and external citations. Rather, it appears to focus its reasoning on the internal coherence of its jurisprudence. In addition, while the Court works to legitimate itself publicly, the Court appears to be less dependent on narratives about its respect for its political purpose and opts for more messaging about its people-centeredness. Overall, the analysis reveals the Court is minimally deferential because it faces only subtle constraints. Chapter 7 revisits these findings once more while exploring how the EACJ, CCJ, and ACtHPR compare.

7

Conclusion

International courts have risen in prominence over the past few decades. Their numbers have increased, and their jurisprudence has expanded. Many current regional and global problems find their way onto the dockets of these institutions. The ECtHR, for example, has been asked to weigh in on climate change.[1] The ICC and ICJ have been ports of call following the outbreak of war and conflict, like in Ukraine and Gaza. The CJEU has been called upon to consider whether practices of some of the world's largest companies, including Google (Alphabet), Microsoft, and Facebook (Meta), undermine business competition. Closer to the focus on this book, the EACJ has considered whether presidents can run for reelection, and the ACtHPR has been asked to rule on state responsibility for corporate-based human rights abuses. Faced with these questions, among many others, ICs decide whether to accept a state's (or an international organization's) exercise of authority and thereby defer.

This book has examined what factors shape deference by international courts. It has argued that deference is determined by an IC's strategic space – understood as the scope of possible decisions that a court could deliver that would satisfy both legal and political imperatives. The broader this strategic space is, the less inclined a court will be to defer. Moreover, I have hypothesized that two structural factors constitute a court's key political constraints and, thus, its strategic space. These are: (1) *formal independence*, or the formal rules that safeguard a court's isolation from political interference; and (2) *political fragmentation*, conceived of as the heterogeneity in member states' preferences. These two factors have the capacity to alter an international court's strategic space because they condition a court's legitimacy and the feasibility and credibility of collective state resistance. Both are expected to have a

[1] The IACtHR, ITLOS, and ICJ have been asked to address climate change within their advisory jurisdiction.

positive effect on a court's strategic space, and therefore a negative relationship with deference. I have also suggested that additional factors play a role over time, including past episodes of resistance and the practices that courts develop.

The previous three chapters explored deference by the EACJ, CCJ, and ACtHPR. They revealed each court defers to varying degrees and in different ways. Moreover, the chapters analyzed the evidence in support of the argument. They showed that each court has a unique set of formal rules that enhance or hamper independence, which together affect how stakeholders view the courts and the potential of collective state resistance. These chapters also showed how each court's temporal and cross-sectoral variation in deference corresponds with patterns in political fragmentation among member states – the more homogeneous states' preferences are at any given time or on any given issue, the more deference is observed. Additionally, deference increased following episodes of resistance when they occurred. The analysis also indicates that each court relies on practices of persuasive argumentation and public legitimation to expand their strategic space and enable nondeference, but these practices differ depending on each court's political constraints. Overall, the previous three chapters rely on within-case comparison and empirically support the core argument of the book.

This chapter shifts gears and has two aims. First, it puts the EACJ, CCJ, and ACtHPR into dialogue with each other. Specifically, it draws on the findings of the previous three chapters for the purpose of a cross-case comparison. This provides an opportunity to review the main findings and to offer a final empirical test of the argument. Second, this chapter situates the argument and findings within broader scholarly debates and identifies potential avenues for future research.

Comparing the EACJ, CCJ, and ACtHPR

Chapters 4–6 provided empirical support for the core argument based on within-case comparison. The theoretical framework, however, purports not only to explain variation in deference within a single court's jurisprudence but to also provide an account of how deference varies across courts. This section therefore compares the EACJ, CCJ, and ACtHPR by drawing on the empirical findings of the previous chapters to assess whether the explanation developed in this book accounts for the differences observed in these courts' deference.

In view of this aim, I recall that the book's core argument consists of five theoretical expectations, which are summarized by the following hypotheses.

H_1: The higher an IC's formal independence is, the less it will defer.
H_2: The more politically fragmented the membership of an IC is, the less it will defer.
H_3: The narrower an IC's strategic space is (as a result of either formal independence or political fragmentation), the more it will rely on persuasive argumentation to facilitate nondeference.
H_4: The narrower an IC's strategic space is (as a result of either formal independence or political fragmentation), the more it will rely on public legitimation to facilitate nondeference.
H_5: All else equal, an international court will defer more when it has experienced past resistance.

I also speculated – although more tentatively – two additional expectations. First, persuasive argumentation may depend more on domestic citations when an international court has a relatively narrow strategic space. Second, ICs to which states can unilaterally exit or enter a court's jurisdiction (or part thereof) may be especially inclined to rely on people-oriented public legitimation narratives.

To determine whether the evidence is congruent with these expectations, I develop observable implications – or claims about what we can expect to see if the hypotheses hold – to guide the comparison of the three ICs. For this purpose, I begin by describing each court's relative level of formal independence and political fragmentation. Chapter 3 measured formal independence and showed that among the three courts analyzed here the EACJ has the lowest formal independence followed by the ACtHPR, while the CCJ has the highest.

To measure political fragmentation, I look at the variability in the EAC, AU, and CARICOM member states' preferences using Freedom House data – assuming state practices reveal preferences.[2] I then calculated the coefficient of variation for each court's membership from 2005 to 2020 on three indicators relating to issues covered within the courts' jurisprudence.[3] Higher values imply greater preference heterogeneity or fragmentation. Figure 7.1 depicts the yearly coefficient of

[2] I use Freedom House because V-Dem includes only six of fifteen CARICOM members. Freedom House includes all members except Montserrat.

[3] The COV is a standardized measure of variability, and it reflects the size of a sample's standard deviation in relation to its mean.

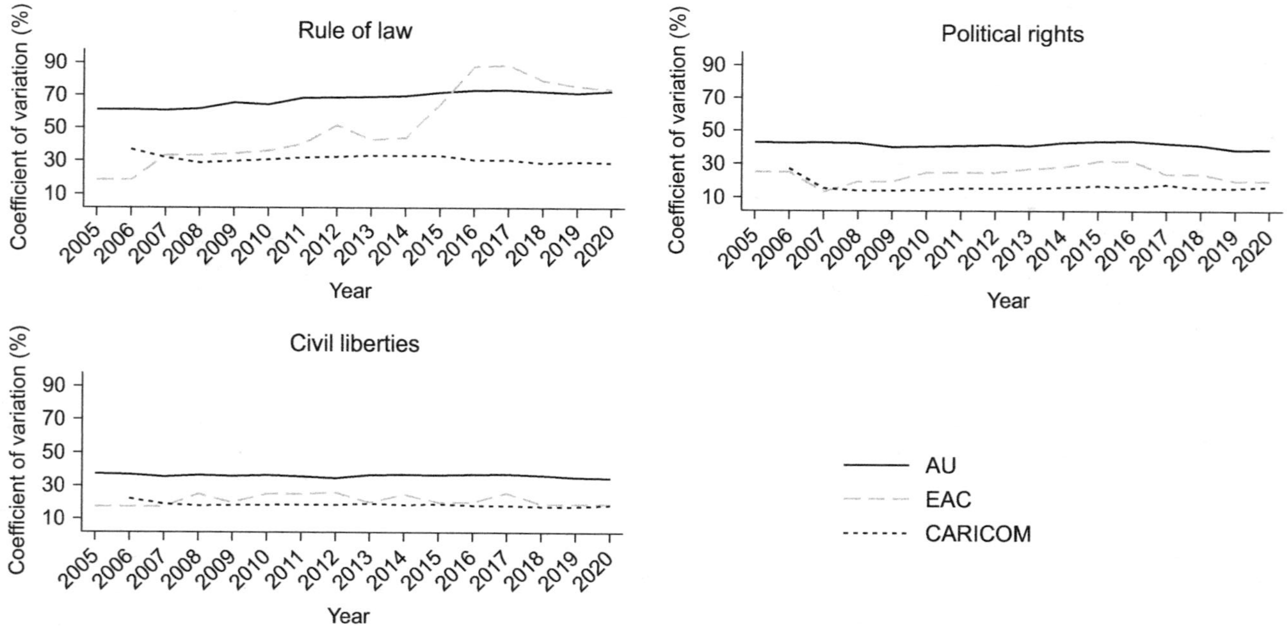

Figure 7.1 Political fragmentation of EAC, CARICOM, and AU.
Note: Calculations and illustration by author.
Data source: Coppedge et al., "V-Dem [Country-Year] Dataset V12."

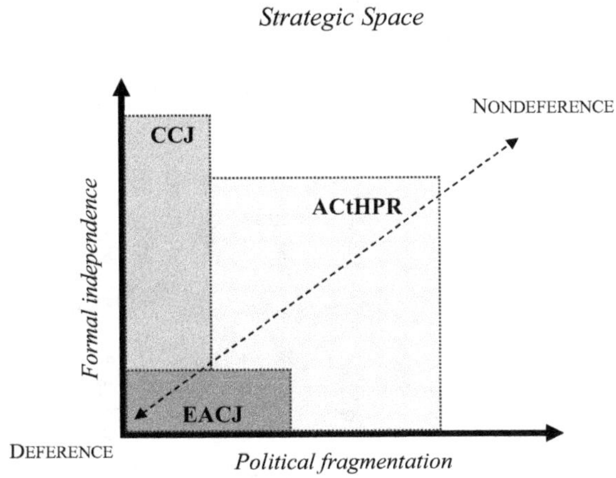

Figure 7.2 Visualization of the strategic space for the EACJ, CCJ, and ACtHPR.

variation for the memberships on the *rule of law*, *civil liberties*, and *political rights*. It reveals that the AU tends to have the highest levels of fragmentation, while CARICOM has the lowest and the EAC lies between.

Taking this information together, Figure 7.2 positions the three ICs within a two-dimensional space to reflect where they reside based on their formal independence and political fragmentation. Each IC's strategic space roughly corresponds to its surrounding shaded box. The EACJ has the smallest strategic space because of its comparatively low formal independence and low-to-midrange political fragmentation. The CCJ has the next largest strategic space, which is a product of high formal independence alongside homogenous preferences among CARICOM states. In contrast, the ACtHPR has both relatively high formal independence and political fragmentation, and consequently has the largest strategic space. The smaller the shaded box, the more deference we expect to observe. This provides the first observable implication. We expect *the EACJ to defer the most, followed by the CCJ, and the ACtHPR to defer the least.*

The empirical findings closely align with the first observable implication. Table 7.1 summarizes the aggregate patterns of deference of each court, presented in Chapters 4–6. During the period under analysis, the EACJ's case outcomes display more deference than the other two courts. It ruled in favor of states in 54 percent of its merits judgments. The CCJ found in favor of states in 33 percent of cases, while the ACtHPR decided

Table 7.1 *Comparison of deference by the EACJ, CCJ, and ACtHPR*

Deference	EACJ	CCJ	ACtHPR
Case outcomes Percentage of merits judgments in favor of state (higher percent = more deference)	54%	33%	18%
Interpretation and reasoning	• "work-to-rule" or restrictive interpretations are *commonplace* • limited scrutiny	• "work-to-rule" or restrictive interpretations are *rare* • heightened scrutiny	• "work-to-rule" or restrictive interpretations are *rare* • heightened scrutiny
Remedies Percentage of merits judgments (lower percent = more deference)	• 46 % with consequential orders • 8% with two additional remedies	• 25 %with consequential orders • 13% with two additional remedies	• 33 % with consequential orders • 50 % with two additional remedies

Note: Percentages exclude cases where EAC organs or CARICOM organs are the respondents.

in favor of states the least, or in 18 percent of its merits judgments. This pattern matches the observable implication.

Case outcomes provide an imperfect picture of deference, and a more complete picture of an international court's acceptance of the state's exercise of authority would also include the court's legal interpretation and reasoning and remedial orders. However, comparing courts' interpretation and reasoning is challenging. I have not proposed a quantitative indicator of deference based on interpretation and reasoning. My qualitative assessment of the courts' jurisprudence, however, found that typically (or despite some notable exceptions) the EACJ adopts "work-to-rule" or restrictive interpretations, and it applies limited scrutiny when accessing states' actions or decisions. The CCJ and ACtHPR are the opposite: work-to-rule or restrictive interpretations and limited scrutiny tend to be the exception, not the rule, with these two courts. The observed patterns in interpretation and reasoning, as with case outcomes, closely align with my argument's first observable implication.

The courts' remedial orders also shed light on deference. Deference based on remedies is high when a court abstains from delivering a consequential order. Conversely, it is low when consequential orders are issued. Table 7.1 shows that the CCJ and ACtHPR's deference based on consequential remedies conforms to expectations: The ACtHPR issued consequential orders more often than the CCJ. However, 46 percent of the EACJ judgments include a consequential order, which is higher than both the CCJ and ACtHPR and therefore is at odds with the first observable implication. That said, as Chapter 4 discussed, many of the EACJ's consequential orders intruded less on state sovereignty than would seem at first glance, suggesting that the percentage of decisions with consequential orders overestimates the EACJ's nondeference. Also, deference as seen by consequential orders of the CCJ and ACtHPR might underestimate nondeference as these two courts often make strong recommendations or tie the hands of states without explicitly issuing a consequential order (see discussion on remedies in Chapters 5 and 6).

For these reasons, I also consider how the courts combine remedies. Chapter 2 suggested that nondeference is greater when there is a combination of remedies, as opposed to a single remedy, within a decision. For example, if a court orders both restitution and compensation, it defers less than if it were to only require compensation. Table 7.1 provides data on the portion of disputes that included at least two orders in addition to the declaratory judgment. Based on these data, the empirical results align with the first observable implication. The EACJ rarely issues multiple remedies in cases. Only 8 percent of its judgments extended two remedies after declaring a violation by a state. This contrasts with the CCJ which combined remedies slightly more often (in 13 percent of its cases), and the ACtHPR which combined remedies the most. Half of all ACtHPR's decisions included at least two remedies in addition to a declaratory judgment.

In sum, across all three measures of deference, the ACtHPR defers the least, followed by the CCJ, and the EACJ the most. These findings are congruent with the first observable implication (which corresponds to H_1 and H_2). They also align with H_5, as the EACJ is the only court to have previously faced collective resistance and it displays the most deference.

Adaptive Practices

I have also argued that over time ICs can exercise agency over their strategic space by adopting practices that help to improve their legitimacy while reducing the plausibility of state resistance. I have focused on two adaptive practices: persuasive fragmentation and public legitimation. According to H_3 and H_4, when a strategic space is narrower, these adaptive practices are likely to be more prominent. I measured persuasive argumentation as unanimous judgments and references to external jurisprudence. A second and third observable implication is thus derived from H_3. I begin with the second observable implication, specifically *the EACJ should issue more unanimous judgments than the ACtHPR*. The evidence is congruent with this expectation. Ninety-eight percent of the EACJ's judgments were unanimous, in contrast to 75 percent of the ACtHPR's judgment. Of the two instances of expressed dissent by the EACJ, one included a dissent by the national judge of the respondent state, which was found by the majority to be in violation of its obligations. On the face of it, this dissent reflects strategic voting on the part of the dissenting judge. The ACtHPR did not have such striking examples of strategic voting because the African Court's judges are required to recuse themselves from presiding over disputes involving their national state. The CCJ is not permitted to issue split decisions (within its original jurisdiction), so there are no expectations for the CCJ related to unanimous judgments.

A court's citations practices can also reveal persuasive argumentation. While all courts will cite authoritative sources to make their judgments compelling, a court's strategic space will inform what types of sources will boost legitimacy and mitigate state resistance. I have argued that

Table 7.2 *Descriptive statistics on citation practices by court*

	EACJ		CCJ		ACtHPR	
Type of citation	Mean	Standard deviation	Mean	Standard deviation	Mean	Standard deviation
Internal jurisprudence	4.71	4.01	4.61	2.36	8.59	7.09
External jurisprudence	3.84	4.42	8.72	8.88	4.96	9.08
. *International*	1.36	1.92	7.44	6.44	4.52	8.45
. *Domestic*	2.48	3.51	1.28	3.01	0.44	1.37

external citations, especially references to domestic jurisdictions, will be more central to judicial decisions the narrower an IC's strategic space is. This leads to the third observable implication: *the EACJ should cite external jurisprudence the most, followed by CCJ and then the ACtHPR.* Table 7.2 summarizes the descriptive statistics for each court's citation practices. It confirms that each court's practice of citing domestic jurisprudence corresponds to the respective size of their strategic space. On average, the EACJ cites domestic jurisprudence the most often, while the ACtHPR does the least. This suggests that the EACJ boosts the persuasiveness of its judgments by signaling its respect for domestic law. It cites domestic jurisprudence nearly twice as often as the CCJ and nearly five times that of the ACtHPR. One might speculate that this has something to do with the nature of the EACJ's jurisdiction as a regional integration court, where domestic law may be more central to resolving disputes. If this were the case, the EACJ's and CCJ's citation practices should be similar. Yet, not only does the CCJ cite domestic jurisprudence much less than the EACJ, but the CCJ cites international jurisprudence more than the other two courts. This suggests that domestic jurisprudence is not inherently more central to disputes relating to regional integration than international jurisprudence. Looking at domestic and international citations combined, the EACJ cites external jurisprudence the least (as expected). However, the CCJ cites external jurisprudence on average more than the ACtHPR. The ACtHPR might cite external jurisprudence less than the CCJ because the former has much more internal jurisprudence upon which to construct its arguments. Regardless, it seems that references to domestic jurisprudence appear to be the type of persuasive argumentation most closely aligned with the courts' respective strategic spaces. Also, it is worth recalling that Chapters 4–6 showed that when a judgment represents either a loss for state(s) or includes intrusive remedies, external jurisprudence is typically cited. This suggests that references to external jurisdictions are associated with less deference, as expected. Interviews also confirmed that judges view the quality of their judgments, including how they are reasoned and embedded within broader jurisprudence, as essential to having well-regarded decisions that will be respected. In other words, citation patterns are determined not only by a court's legal constraints, but its political constraints also play a role in shaping how a court presents persuasive arguments.

Last, H_4 expected more public legitimation the narrower a court's strategic space is. This leads to a fourth observable implication: *the EACJ presents public legitimation the most, followed by CCJ and then the ACtHPR*. I also posited that unilateral exit options might impact the use of public legitimation, leading to a preference for people-centered narratives.

Interview material, official publications, and speeches for each court make clear that all three courts show concern for their public image, and they have adopted many initiatives to build public awareness and confidence. Most of the data I presented on public legitimation is qualitative. Quantitatively comparing the courts' "off-the-bench" activities is not useful because many of these activities are contingent on financial resources (sometimes from external donors). Moreover, some activities are by invitation (e.g., a judge might be invited as a keynote speaker), and thus are not entirely within the control of the courts themselves. All three courts, however, use social media as part of their public communication strategies. I therefore compare public legitimation based on the courts' communication over Facebook. As described in Chapters 4–6, I used a web-scraping tool to extract each court's posts on their own Facebook pages and then analyzed the texts of the posts for key words and phrases that reflect their respective *people-centered* and *political purpose* narratives.[4] With this data I compare the relative prominence of these narratives in the courts' public communication.[5]

[4] I included all posts from the date the courts opened their Facebook page to the end of 2020. I use Facebook because it was among the first social media outlet these courts used. Also, Facebook does not limit the number of characters or word per post, which could otherwise constrain public legitimation via social media.

[5] The courts opened their Facebook pages in different years. I therefore compare the percentage of posts, as the absolute numbers vary significantly (but the number of posts per year is roughly comparable).

Table 7.3 *Prominence of public legitimation narratives on courts' Facebook pages*

	EACJ	CCJ	ACtHPR
Narrative(s)	Percent of posts with narrative(s)	Percent of posts with narrative(s)	Percent of posts with narrative(s)
People-centeredness	4.73	10.46	4.39
Political purpose	12.31	4.9	3.01
People-centeredness or political purpose	12.88	12.75	6.58
N =	528	306	897

Table 7.3 depicts the extent to which the courts' social media posts feature either of the public legitimation narratives. The findings corroborate H_4. The EACJ presents either of the public legitimation narratives slightly more than the CCJ. In contrast, the ACtHPR conveys one of the two narratives the least.

While the EACJ and CCJ are roughly similar in the overall portion of their communication that features public legitimation narratives, they favor different narratives. The EACJ emphasizes its political purpose while the CCJ, as well as the ACtHPR, highlights its people-centeredness. These differences reflect the varied sources of political constraints. The CCJ and ACtHPR are both constrained by the politics of states' unilateral acceptance (or withdrawal) to parts of their jurisdiction. In contrast, the EACJ places greater emphasis on its political purpose – unilateral exit is not an option as the EACJ's jurisdiction is compulsory for EAC members, and it has a narrow strategic space. Thus, the EACJ focuses on portraying itself as central to the process of integration, while the CCJ and ACtHPR signal their ties to the Caribbean peoples and African peoples, respectively.

Alternative Accounts

The above comparison shows that the evidence is largely consistent with the theoretical framework advanced by this book. The argument was developed against the backdrop of two other perspectives – support networks, and political norms and legal culture. The preceding chapters also assessed these two perspectives within the context of each court. In the following, I briefly apply them comparatively.

Existing literature attributes aspects of judicial decision-making to ideational factors, especially political norms and legal culture. As illustrated in Chapters 4–6, the EACJ, ACtHPR, and CCJ share important similarities regarding their ideational setting. Colonial legacies shaped the normative environments in which these courts were created and operate. First, the origins for the EACJ, ACtHPR, and CCJ are connected to the colonial pasts of their member states. Impulses toward regional unity, regionalism, and cooperation existed alongside strong norms of noninterference and sovereignty. Both the EAC and CARICOM were rooted in failed experiments of integration under their colonial oppressors. In the case of the OAU, colonialism spurred sentiments of solidarity and cooperation, but largely led states to favor norms of noninterference. For all three of these ICs, they were created at a time when ideas supportive of regional cooperation were spreading but coexisting with principles of sovereignty and noninterference. This tension has had lasting impacts on the courts and broader regional organizations within which they are embedded.

Also related to their colonial histories, the EACJ, CCJ, and ACtHPR function within legal cultures that are characterized by pluralism and fragile faith in state (or formal) law and courts. Pluralism arises from the mix of civil and common law systems both within and across the members of all three courts. In addition, customary and religious law operates alongside state law, and alternative dispute resolution is widespread. Legal culture in most member states is also shaped by public distrust or a lack of faith in state law and courts. Finally, as newer courts, their sui generis legal cultures are mutable and evolving.

A comparison of these three courts, therefore, reveals strong similarities based on ideational factors. In methodological terms, the research design and selection of ICs aimed to hold these considerations constant. Thus, my argument complements theoretical perspectives that highlight the role of ideational factors, and it suggests additional factors are instrumental to international judicial deference. Also, the analysis revealed that colonial legacies had both political and legal impacts. This sits comfortably with the view that a court's decision-making will be informed by both political and legal imperatives.

Previous research has pointed to the pivotal role of judicial support networks. If a strong and active support network were crucial to explaining why an international court forgoes deference, we would expect ICs that typically defer to feature few channels of access for its supporters, to minimally mobilize its supporters, or for its support network to be inactive or lack political influence. Conversely, ICs that demonstrate less deference would have various opportunities for access and demonstrate efforts to mobilize their supporters and for the support network to be strong and active. Knowing that the EACJ is the most deferential court of the three ICs studied, while the ACtHPR is the least deferential followed by CCJ, we would expect the EACJ to have a weak or inactive support network. Conversely, the ACtHPR should have the most active and strongest support. Similarly, we should also observe variation in access opportunities and efforts to mobilize supporters.

Chapters 4–6 demonstrated that the EACJ, CCJ, and ACtHPR alike have established practical (legal aid schemes, sub-registries, etc.) and extensive "off-the-bench" activities to mobilize their would-be supporters. Moreover, the three courts feature access for private actors, substate actors, and/or supranational actors. Substate actors (i.e., national courts) and supranational actors have been reluctant supporters of all three courts as they have rarely made use of their available access channels. National courts can refer cases to the EACJ and the CCJ, but except for one referral to the EACJ, this channel has not been utilized. Supranational actors can make referral in all three courts, although this is more limited in the case of the CCJ, but this opportunity has not generated much, if any, litigation for the EACJ, CCJ, or ACtHPR. Thus, these courts are roughly similar in their opportunities and use by substate and supranational actors.

Private actors, whether individual, NGOs, or for-profit organizations, can access all three courts. Nonetheless, private access varies to some degree among the EACJ, CCJ, and ACtHPR. For example, the hurdles for private access to the ACtHPR are significant because many states have not submitted Article 34(6) declarations and the two-month time limit on filing makes a successful petition to the EACJ challenging. The restrictiveness of access to these two courts is difficult to reconcile with their very different approaches to deference.

Also, the strength and activeness of private actors does not align with how much each court defers. Table 7.4 summarizes the empirical findings on support networks. It shows that the ACtHPR has had the fewest portion of its cases represented by repeat lawyers, as one measure of the strength and activity of a judicial support network, yet it has been the least deferential of the three courts. On the other hand, the most deferential court, the EACJ, has a large portion of applications represented by repeat lawyers. Also, the CCJ had the largest portion of cases represented by repeat lawyers, yet deference by this court has not been the lowest.

Table 7.4 *Summary of findings on support networks by court*

	EACJ	CCJ	ACtHPR
Cases represented by repeat lawyers	54 %	67 %	22 %
Cases involving an NGO	28 %	6 %	40 %
Statistical findings			
Are violations declared, if merits consider, more often with repeat counsel?	No	Yes*	Yes*
Are violations more often declared when NGO participates?	No	No	Yes*
Are consequential orders more frequent with repeat counsel?	Yes*	Yes*	No
Are consequential orders more frequent when NGO participates?	Yes*	No	No
Are additional remedies issued more often with repeat counsel?	Yes*	No	No
Are additional remedies applied more often when NGO participates?	Yes*	No	No

* Findings are congruent with theoretical expectations of the support network logic.

A second measure for the relative strength and activity of a support network is the proportion of cases involving an NGO. As the support network logic would expect, the ACtHPR is the least deferential court and had the largest portion of cases with NGO participation. However, the EACJ had a relatively high portion of cases involving NGOs, even though it was the most deferential among the three courts. Also, NGO participation at the CCJ has been limited, yet this court is less deferential than the EACJ.[6]

Last, Table 7.4 summarizes the findings related to whether deference in legal outcomes and remedies is associated with the involvement of repeat

[6] NGO participation occurred in only one case before the CCJ. Considering alternative measures of support network activity for the CCJ does not better align with the expectations of the support network logic. For example, 22 percent of cases involved a private actor as a third party, which is still below the 28 percent for the EACJ, or 56 percent included either a private actor or supranational actors as a third party, which is higher than the ACtHPR. Regardless of measure, the level of participation does not align with the expectation that the CCJ should fall between the EACJ and ACtHPR if activity of supporters accounted for deference.

lawyers or NGOs. This shows that these relationships are not systematically congruent with the expectations of the support network logic. For instance, the EACJ does not declare violations more often when repeat lawyers or NGOs are involved in disputes than when they are not. Similarly, nondeferential remedies occur less often in the CCJ and ACtHPR when these actors are involved in the litigation.

Overall, the analysis suggests that support networks provide an incomplete account – a court's supporters do not systematically predict deference. This is not to say they are insignificant to the development of international courts. Indeed, individuals, NGOs, and lawyers have been essential to the litigation before the EACJ, CCJ, and ACtHPR. Thus, my argument and findings do not reject that support networks have an important function for international courts and their performance. Rather, it complements this perspective in a few ways. First, my argument assumes that court's need proponents to ensure a broad strategic space. This includes litigants – as would be the case for the support network logic – but it also includes the broader public, as I have argued. Second, I have focused on two adaptive practices that ICs employ to expand their strategic space. An IC's mobilization of its support networks is another type of adaptive practice that could have bearing on a court's strategic space. Third, *time* is an important element of my argument. That is, the structural factors I have highlighted are crucial in the early years of a court, or at t_0 (see Figure 2.3). A court's support network – even if civil society and the legal profession were key to its creation – is likely to also be in a nascent stage at t_0. My argument does not exclude the possibility that support networks may be capable of empowering a court, and thus altering its strategic space, with time.

Summarizing the Argument

Taken together, the empirical record supports the core argument advanced in this book. Judicial deference is shaped by an international court's strategic space. Two political constraints – formal independence and political fragmentation – are key to structuring this strategic space. Formal independence and political fragmentation have bearing on how a court takes decisions because they interact to shape a court's legitimacy, or how it is perceived by stakeholders, and affect the plausibility of state resistance. Higher formal independence and a more fragmented membership provide ICs with a broader strategic space, leading them to defer less. However, even with a generous strategic space, ICs will defer at times, often due to legal constraints. To extend the strategic space and enable nondeference that a court might not otherwise feel secure in executing, it will lean into practices of persuasive argumentation and public legitimation. These will take unique forms depending on the nature of the court's underlying political constraints. Courts with narrower strategic space will favor unanimous judgments and highlight the compatibility of their decisions with external (especially domestic) jurisprudence. They will also be more inclined to integrate legitimation narratives into their public communications, especially by conveying commitment to their political purpose if there are no unilateral exit options for states. Those with a broader space will be more at ease expressing dissent on the bench (when permitted by the formal rules) and external jurisprudence will be less central to the reasoning of their decisions. While not neglectful of public perceptions, their public communications will focus less on legitimation narratives.

The empirical findings are congruent with this argument. Namely, I have shown that the EACJ has the narrowest strategic space of the three ICs studied, due to *pervasive constraints* arising from its low formal independence and moderate political fragmentation among the EAC members. At the same time, it has been the most deferential. Unlike the other courts, the EACJ's strategic space has also been affected by past collective resistance. Given its narrow strategic space, the EACJ leans into the practice of publishing unanimous judgments and citing domestic law to construct compelling arguments. Also, its public communication portrays the Court as dutiful to its intended political purpose, signaling the Court's respect for state sovereignty and the limits of its mandate. These practices help to buttress the Court's nondeference. Even with these practices in place, however, the EACJ overall displays *substantial deference.*

The CCJ's strategic space is larger than the EACJ's. It enjoys high formal independence yet minimal political fragmentation, constituting *intermediate constraints* and leading the CCJ to be *moderately deferential.* The CCJ defers especially when it perceives states as likeminded and likely to reject its preferred position. Regardless, to make nondeference palatable to states and other audiences, the CCJ cites external jurisprudence (especially international case law) to make arguments compelling. Public legitimation also benefits nondeference and helps the Court to gain public acceptance of its appellate jurisdiction. Given past reluctance of states (and their voting public) to join the appellate jurisdiction, the CCJ's public communication emphasizes legitimation narratives that illustrate its people-centeredness and representation of the Caribbean people.

Of the three courts, the ACtHPR has the broadest strategic space, due to its robust formal safeguards to independence and marked political divisions among member states, and it deferred the least among the three courts studied. In other words, the ACtHPR's *subtle constraints* enable *minimal deference*. The Court's nondeference has been facilitated additionally by persuasive argumentation that emphasizes international jurisprudence as well as its own case law, and public legitimation that highlights people-centered narratives. Yet, state resistance, especially their reluctance to accept private actors' right to petition the Court and withdrawals of Article 34(6) declarations, has affected the Court's strategic space. This is made evident by an increase in deference.

Scope of the Argument

While my theoretical framework may generalize to a broad set of ICs, the argument was developed and tested within a specific set of conditions. First, this argument is a story of *new* international courts and the early years of their development. In the early years of an institution, institutional design is likely to have a heightened importance as relationships between states, societal actors, the public, and courts are in formation. Appearances make stronger impressions on legitimacy beliefs in the absence of prior performance, states have not yet shown resistance, and the resilience of a court is not yet proven. In other words, courts and their judges are growing into their relationship with states, and states are navigating new terrain. The early years for international courts are not necessarily determinative of their future trajectories. While there is some evidence from previous scholarship that sui generis cultures, practices, and path dependencies can set in, for which formative years may be pivotal, the argument assumes that the political environment can change, and the empirical evidence supports this assumption. Political fragmentation is not static. Fragmentation fluctuates due to factors such as changes in memberships and governments. Also, resistance, if it arises, can also alter the strategic space. In the end, additional research is needed to understand if and how an international court's early years are formative and constrain their future trajectories. Put differently, looking back at the nascent stages of older courts – like the ECtHR – could offer new perspectives on where they are today.

Second, the argument has been evaluated in the context of international courts that operate in the Global South and mostly low- and middle-income countries. The relationship between development and how international courts engage with their stakeholders is not entirely clear. Socioeconomic considerations have previously been shown to have an impact on engagement with international courts and tribunals. For instance, development has been the focus of research on legal outcomes in international investment arbitration,[7] legal representation before the ICJ,[8] and whether states launch litigation at the WTO,[9] to name a few. Development and wealth could have a range of potential effects, including state legal capacity and expertise, and societal access to courts and capacity to litigate. It might also affect legal consciousness, and therefore how courts perceive their political constraints. Moreover, research that questions the impact of formal independence of domestic judiciaries finds a contrast between developing and developed states.[10] Yet, this study has by and large set these issues aside by looking only at courts among primarily low- and middle-income countries. Thus, the argument is linked to this context, even though the book may raise questions about how far the argument travels beyond these boundaries.

Third, the argument has not been developed to apply to interstate jurisdictions and disputes. Admittedly, other factors might affect an international court's legitimacy and the credibility of state resistance within its interstate jurisdiction. For example, the distribution of power may affect deference in interstate disputes. Also, the threefold measure of deference used here may not fit interstate disputes. Thus, further

7 Daniel Behn, Tarald Laudal Berge, and Malcolm Langford, "Poor States or Poor Governance? Explaining Outcomes in Investment Treaty Arbitration," *Northwestern Journal of International Law & Business* 38, no. 3 (2018); Sergio Puig and Anton Strezhnev, "The David Effect and ISDS," *European Journal of International Law* 28, no. 3 (2017).

8 Shashank P. Kumar and Cecily Rose, "A Study of Lawyers Appearing Before the International Court of Justice, 1999–2012," *European Journal of International Law* 25, no. 3 (2014).

9 Andrew Guzman and Beth A. Simmons, "Power Plays and Capacity Constraints: The Selection of Defendants in World Trade Organization Disputes," *Journal of Legal Studies* 34, no. 2 (2005); Thomas Sattler and Thomas Bernauer, "Gravitation or Discrimination? Determinants of Litigation in the World Trade Organisation," *European Journal of Political Research* 50, no. 2 (2011).

10 Hayo and Voigt, "The Long-Term Relationship between De Jure and De Facto Judicial Independence."

theoretical and empirical analysis would most likely be necessary to modify the approach presented by this book for it to apply to interstate adjudication.

Thus, the generalizability of the argument beyond these conditions requires further research. Many readers, nonetheless, will want an indication of how my argument applies to the international courts they know best. Thus, I offer a brief interpretation of the WTO Appellate Body (AB) and the ECtHR, but with two important caveats. First, I have not measured deference for these courts and can only rely on previous scholarly descriptions of their jurisprudence and existing data as a preliminary indicator of their deference. Second, these interpretations are tentative.

The WTO AB seemingly presents a challenging case for my argument. It began operating within a midrange strategic space, due to its limited formal independence (see Figure 3.2) and a politically fragmented membership.[11] Yet, by many accounts the WTO AB has typically been non-deferential. Many scholars suggest that "it has shown a strong inclination for gap-filling and ambiguity clarification, which is often achieved through considerable judicial creativity."[12] Also, most cases (or 89 percent of disputes) resulted in a finding of at least one violation.[13] Does this undermine my argument, as the WTO AB deferred less than we would expect? I would suggest that the WTO AB needs to be interpreted in light of its predecessor – the General Agreement on Tariffs and Trade (GATT) dispute settlement system. In contrast to the WTO, GATT's dispute settlement system was less independent and the membership less fragmented.[14] The WTO AB's strategic space was broader than under GATT

[11] See Joseph Jupille, Walter Mattli, and Duncan Snidal, *Institutional Choice and Global Commerce* (Cambridge: Cambridge University Press, 2013), 100. The authors describe preference heterogeneity as very high at the WTO's founding and during the Doha Round.

[12] Gao and Zhou, "'Overreaching' or 'Overreacting'?" 959; Robert Howse, "The World Trade Organization 20 Years On: Global Governance by Judiciary," *European Journal of International Law* 27, no. 1 (2016); Judith L. Goldstein and Richard H. Steinberg, "Regulatory Shift: The Rise of Judicial Liberalization at the WTO," in *The Politics of Global Regulation*, ed. Walter Mattli and Ngaire Woods (Princeton: Princeton University Press, 2009); Steinberg, "Judicial Lawmaking at the WTO."

[13] Simon Lester, "U.S. "Wins" and "Losses" in WTO Disputes," *International Economic Law and Policy Blog*, March 15, 2020, https://ielp.worldtradelaw.net/2020/03/us-wins-and-losses-in-wto-disputes.html. This figure includes all WTO disputes (panels and AB).

[14] Jupille, Mattli, and Snidal, *Institutional Choice and Global Commerce*, 100. Jupille et al. describe heterogeneity as moderate during GATT.

and its creation an endorsement of a stronger dispute settlement system. Armed then with a broader strategic space, the WTO AB demonstrated more "judicial lawmaking," "filling of gaps," or "agent slack" than had been seen under GATT's dispute settlement.[15] Thus, seen in this light, the shift from the GATT to the WTO corresponds to my expectations: the expansion in formal independence and fragmentation meant that the WTO AB has comparatively wider strategic space, giving rise to less deference. Moreover, as fragmentation continued to grow with the expansion of membership, for example, with the membership of China, the WTO AB continued to not defer.

My argument brings out two additional points about the WTO Appellate Body. First, episodes of resistance are important. The WTO Dispute Settlement Understanding (DSU) did face attempted collective resistance in its first decade of operation. Member states tried to reform the WTO DSU when the AB determined that it would accept amicus submission.[16] This attempted reform signaled to the AB that collective resistance was unlikely to be successful as states could not find enough agreement.[17] In other words, these events effectively green-lighted non-deference. Second, courts can misread their political environment and miscalculate the plausibility of resistance as well as their legitimacy. That is, they may perceive their strategic space to be different from what it is. This would seem to have been the case for the WTO AB. The WTO AB did not anticipate the United States would use appointment procedures to paralyze it, even if the United States had previously blocked reappointments.[18] The WTO AB did not appear to appreciate that international courts could indeed fall victim to such a strategy. Although under very different circumstances, the SADC Tribunal was also paralyzed through an intentional strategy of refusing to appoint judges.[19] It does not appear

[15] Goldstein and Steinberg, "Regulatory Shift"; see also Howse, "The World Trade Organization 20 Years On."

[16] Theresa Squatrito, "Opening the Doors to the WTO Dispute Settlement: State Preferences on Ngo Access as Amici," *Swiss Political Science Review* 18, no. 2 (2012). Some states wanted to permit amicus curiae submissions, while others wanted to prohibit them.

[17] Howse, "The World Trade Organization 20 Years On," 28.

[18] Elsig and Pollack, "Agents, Trustees, and International Courts"; Mark A. Pollack, "International Court Curbing in Geneva: Lessons from the Paralysis of the WTO Appellate Body," *Governance* 36, no. 1 (2023).

[19] The SADC Tribunal's fate is well-known story to international jurists today. For a detailed account of what transpired, see, for example, Nathan, "The Disbanding of the SADC Tribunal"; Alter, Gathii, and Helfer, "Backlash Against International Courts in West, East and Southern Africa," 306–14.

that the AB adopted practices to help alleviate political constraints either. For example, the WTO AB did little in the way of public legitimation,[20] even though it undoubtedly had developed a relationship with the legal community.[21] Thus, the WTO AB for all intents and purposes miscalculated or undervalued its evolving political environment and failed to recognize how intricacies of its institutional design, like the rules related to the selection and tenure of its judges, could be significant.

The ECtHR also presents an interesting case for my argument. Over the years, the ECtHR has seen many changes. The formal independence of the ECtHR increased at two points, first in 1998 when Protocol 11[22] entered into force; and again in 2010 when Protocol 14[23] entered into force. Political fragmentation has fluctuated over the years. It was moderate to high until the early 1970s, then declined and remained low until the early 1990s. It increased markedly in the mid-1900s and was relatively high. Since the early 2000s, fragmentation has increased modestly (see Figure A7.1). Based on my argument, we therefore expect the first ten to fifteen years of the Court to show some deference, the early 1970s until the early 1990s to be a period of relatively high deference, and for deference to decrease in the mid-to-late 1990s onward. Madsen's summary of the ECtHR's authority roughly corresponds to these expectations, although he does not speak in terms of deference. He argues that, even though the Court had few cases in its first decade, from its inception until the mid-to-late 1970s the Court "deploy[ed] a relatively restrictive and often state-friendly interpretation of the Convention."[24] The first time it declared a violation was in 1968.[25] In the period of 1970 to 1990, he describes the ECtHR as having "narrow and

[20] See WTO, "Appellate Body Annual Reports," accessed August 4, 2024, www.wto.org/english/tratop_e/dispu_e/ab_an_rep_e.htm.

[21] Gregory Shaffer, Manfred Elsig, and Sergio Puig, "The Extensive (But Fragile) Authority of the WTO Appellate Body," *Law and Contemporary Problems* 79, no. 1 (2016).

[22] Protocol No. 11 to the Convention for the Protection of Human Rights and Fundamental Freedoms of 4 November 1950, restructuring the control machinery established thereby (adopted May 11, 1994, entered into force November 1, 1998), U.N.T.S. 2061, at 7–24. In relation to formal independence, Protocol 11 changed the length of a judicial term from nine to six years, modified rules on the selection of the registrar so the Court did not have to consult with the Secretary-General and introduced a rule on the removal of judges.

[23] ECHR Protocol No. 14. In relation to formal independence, the Protocol changed the term length from six to nine years and removed the possibility of reappointment.

[24] Madsen, "The European Court of Human Rights," 244.

[25] Ibid., 250.

intermediate authority, with flashes of expansive authority."[26] These flashes were mostly in relation to the United Kingdom, and expansive authority toward other states did not arise until the 1990s.[27] The 1990s marked a new era for the Court, in which it spun "an expansive and tighter normative web of European human rights."[28] Another measure of deference, which I have used in the previous chapters, is the portion of cases in which the respondent was found to have committed at least one treaty violation. Figure A7.2 depicts the ECtHR's annual deference rate on merits judgments. This figure roughly corresponds to Madsen's characterization of ebbs and flows in the ECtHR's jurisprudence. Deference in the first fifteen years fluctuated significantly, but also there were few merits decisions. From the late 1970s to early 1980s, a clear pattern evolves. Deference was relatively high and steadily declined until the late 1990s. In the 2000s, deference steeply declined and was at an all-time low. This pattern also roughly aligns with the expectation mentioned above.

The ECtHR, however, has been more deferential throughout the 2010s, in what has been called its "procedural turn."[29] Can my theoretical framework account for the procedural turn, viewed as deference? The Court's formal independence was at its highest point from 2010 onward, and its fragmentation increased modestly, both of which are at odds with increased deference. I would suggest that the procedural turn and uptick in deference reflects how episodes of state resistance can affect a court's strategic space, all else equal. Discontent was a growing reality for the ECtHR in the 2000s, ranging from outrage at the backlog to pesky noncompliance and pushback by key states, like the UK and Russia. The resistance came to a head around the Brighton Declaration of 2012, which incorporated a principle of subsidiarity and effectively narrowed the Court's authority.[30] Thus, in the case of the ECtHR, resistance played an important role in shrinking the Court's strategic space to affect its deference. At the same time, it was not until this time that the

[26] Ibid. 257.
[27] Ibid., 251–57.
[28] Ibid., 259.
[29] Oddný Mjöll Arnardóttir, "The 'Procedural Turn' Under the European Convention on Human Rights and Presumptions of Convention Compliance," *International Journal of Constitutional Law* 15, no. 1 (2017); Miles Jackson, "Judicial Avoidance at the European Court of Human Rights: Institutional Authority, the Procedural Turn, and Docket Control," *International Journal of Constitutional Law* 20, no. 1 (2022).
[30] Madsen, "The European Court of Human Rights."

ECtHR became more attentive to its public legitimacy in my estimation. For instance, the Court's 2013 Annual Report was the first to note its outreach activities.[31]

As these two brief illustrations suggest, my argument has broader applications and could shed light on older and more widely known international courts. That said, a test of the generalizability outside the conditions outlined above requires analysis beyond what I can do here.

Implications for Scholarship on International Courts and International Organizations

This book contributes to interdisciplinary scholarship on international courts. It also offers new insights for IR research on international organizations in contemporary world politics. I conclude with a brief discussion of these implications.

Interdisciplinary Approaches to International Courts

This book contributes empirically to interdisciplinary research on international courts. While I am not the first to research the EACJ, CCJ, and ACtHPR, this book has uniquely presented the most comprehensive data to date on the judgments of these courts, as well as their broader political and normative context and practices. The book also introduced original data on the formal independence of twenty-six international courts, which revealed two important findings about the judicialization of world politics and the proliferation of ICs. First, the independence of these courts on average has declined over time. This contrasts with other trends in the design of international courts, which reflect a progression or expansion of liberal design elements. For example, elsewhere it has been shown that the expansion of private actor access has been part and parcel with the proliferation of courts.[32] Formal independence bucks this generally progressive trend. Second, rules defining the appointment and terms of office for international judges as well as the managerial autonomy of ICs drive most of the observed variation in formal independence. This finding is significant because comparative judicial politics research has shown these are the elements of de jure independence that have the

[31] See ECtHR, "Reports," accessed August 4, 2024, www.echr.coe.int/annual-reports.

[32] Theresa Squatrito, "The Democratizing Effects of Transnational Actors' Access to International Courts," *Global Governance* 24, no. 4 (2018): 600–601.

largest impact on de facto independence.[33] It also supports the move toward better understanding the managerial aspects of international courts, ranging from the funding and control over resources as well as the influence of their registries and secretariats.[34]

The book also contributes theoretically to literature on the performance of international courts, seen as the extent to which and how they resolve disputes, clarify law, and facilitate compliance in discrete instances as well as their broader impacts on peaceful settlement, a rule-based order, and international cooperation.[35] Some might refer to some of these broader impacts as judicial power.[36] This book shows that two factors interact to play a crucial role in understanding the performance or power of ICs: institutional design and preferences of states. Elsewhere it has been shown that the institutional rules by which an international court is governed affect various aspects of judicial performance, including capacity to generate compliance,[37] early dispute settlement,[38] and legal clarification (e.g., judicial activism or restraint).[39] Design has also been found to have links to the politicization of international courts as well as state exit,[40] both of which are likely to have profound consequences for if and how courts impact peaceful settlement, the rule-based order, and international cooperation. I add to this

[33] Melton and Ginsburg, "Does De Jure Judicial Independence Really Matter?"

[34] Squatrito, "Resourcing Global Justice"; Baetens, *Legitimacy of Unseen Actors in International Adjudication*; Thordis Ingadottir, "The Financing of International Adjudication," in *The Oxford Handbook of International Adjudication*, ed. Cesare Romano, Karen Alter, and Yuval Shany (Oxford: Oxford University Press, 2014); Jonathan O'Donohue, "Financing the International Criminal Court," in *The Realities of International Criminal Justice*, ed. Dawn L. Rothe, James Meernik, and Þórdís Ingadóttir (Leiden: Brill, 2013); Stéphanie Cartier and Cristina Hoss, "The Role of Registries and Legal Secretariats in International Judicial Institutions," in *The Oxford Handbook of International Adjudication*, ed. Karen Alter, Cesare Romano, and Yuval Shany (Oxford: Oxford University Press, 2014); Pauwelyn and Pelc, "Who Guards the 'Guardians of the System'?"

[35] Squatrito et al., "A Framework for Evaluating the Performance of International Courts and Tribunals."

[36] Staton and Moore, "Judicial Power in Domestic and International Politics."

[37] Tallberg and McCall Smith, "Dispute Settlement in World Politics"; Helfer and Slaughter, "Towards a Theory of Effective Supranational Adjudication"; Leslie Johns, *Strengthening International Courts: The Hidden Costs of Legalization* (Ann Arbor: University of Michigan Press, 2015).

[38] Johns, *Strengthening International Courts.*

[39] Stiansen, "(Non)Renewable Terms and Judicial Independence in the ECtHR."

[40] Johns, *Strengthening International Courts*; Elsig and Pollack, "Agents, Trustees, and International Courts."

literature by highlighting formal independence as a design feature – distinct from de facto independence and other design elements like access – which has not been underscored by previous research. The book establishes that the formal independence of ICs contributes to their deference. While I did not examine if and how formal independence has bearing on other aspects of IC performance, such as compliance, this book provides the conceptual and empirical tools for future exploration into how sweeping the effects of formal independence are.

In addition, I have shown that state preferences, namely, in terms of how aligned states' preferences are, have bearing on how international courts judge. While previous research suggests that preference heterogeneity among states affects international organizations, including their policy agendas[41] and autonomy,[42] it has received less attention by scholars of ICs.[43] This book gives credence to its impact on adjudication. At the same time, it leaves room for future theoretical advances. However, it remains unclear exactly how courts ascertain states' preferences. I have assumed that courts gather information from various sources, like existing domestic law and practices, intergovernmental decisions, or states' third-party participation during legal proceedings (e.g., observations). If political fragmentation is indeed important to understanding international judicial decisions, additional research is needed to understand how courts come to know of their political environments, especially the preferences of states. Participation in legal proceedings, which is relatively common in the WTO dispute settlement or before the CJEU, is not necessarily widespread practice in other courts. In these circumstances, researchers might ask what information on states' preferences is available to courts, what information do they regard as credible information, and under what conditions are courts likely to misread information signals.

The empirical analysis reveals two additional implications for future research. First, I observed a somewhat surprising lack of engagement by

[41] Magnus Lundgren, Theresa Squatrito, and Jonas Tallberg, "Stability and Change in International Policy-Making: A Punctuated Equilibrium Approach," *Review of International Organizations* 13, no. 4 (2018).

[42] Heldt, "Regaining Control of Errant Agents?"

[43] For notable exceptions, see, for example, Stone Sweet and Brunell, "Trustee Courts and the Judicialization of International Regimes"; Garrett, Kelemen, and Schulz, "The European Court of Justice, National Governments, and Legal Integration in the European Union"; Larsson and Naurin, "Judicial Independence and Political Uncertainty."

national courts and supranational organs. I speculated that the absence of these partners is not reducible to legal constraints – substate and supranational actors face their own political constraints.[44] For example, the underusage of the preliminary references to the EACJ could reflect the vulnerabilities of domestic courts to their executives. Referring cases to the EACJ could exacerbate these vulnerabilities, rather than empower them in the absence of strong domestic political opposition. Similarly, delegation to CARICOM organs is minimal and intergovernmentalism is the modus operandi. CARICOM organs formally have limited capacity to refer cases to the CCJ and their inclination to act independently of states is restricted. The African Commission on Human Rights also has its own constraints that make it less likely to refer cases to the ACtHPR. Thus, the extent to which substate and supranational actors do make referrals is likely shaped by political constraints that are not yet fully understood, opening new avenues for research: under what conditions are national courts or supranational institutions likely to engage with international courts? Recent research on the European Commission and its referrals (infringement proceedings) to the CJEU suggest that the Commission's relationship with national governments, and its efforts to stand in their good graces and maintain intergovernmental support, affect how the Commission acts as an enforcer and its referrals to the CJEU.[45] These dynamics are more likely when pressures against supranationalism are greater. The cases examined here suggest that such dynamics may extend to other international courts.

Moreover, the case studies raise questions about the role of hierarchy in international judicial politics. Some scholars have argued that hierarchy, not anarchy, structures international judicial politics, much like domestic judicial politics.[46] They claim that judicial politics is best understood through the perspective of a separation of power and call for researchers to avoid imposing strict divisions between domestic and international courts. I take the view that one can find traces of both anarchy and hierarchy,[47] and I draw from studies on comparative judicial

[44] Alter also recognizes that such actors can have their own political constraints; see Alter, *The New Terrain of International Law*.

[45] Kelemen and Pavone, "Where Have the Guardians Gone?"

[46] Staton and Moore, "Judicial Power in Domestic and International Politics."

[47] Some IR scholarship rejects the validity of a strict dichotomy between anarchy and hierarchy and suggests that both shape international relations; see, for example, David A. Lake, *Hierarchy in International Relations* (Ithaca: Cornell University Press, 2009); Helen Milner, "The Assumption of Anarchy in International Relations Theory:

politics and international relations. My examination of the EACJ, CCJ, and ACtHPR, however, points to another dynamic – the potential effects of "global hierarchies."[48] Global hierarchies are akin neither to the separation of power nor to anarchy. Rather, they refer to informal inequalities that often crosscut interstate boundaries and are distinct from sights of formal political authority (e.g., legislature, executives, judiciaries).

I observed impacts on the creation of ICs, on their judicial decisions and practices, and the accessibility of international justice. In terms of creation, legacies of colonialism and the inequalities they imbue shaped the origins of these courts. Inequalities enabled external actors to influence decision to create new courts.[49] The EACJ, CCJ, and ACtHPR cite external jurisprudence, especially the European courts and courts from the Global North – although there are also citations from other regions. In terms of public legitimation, while there is a history of African domestic courts engaging in such efforts,[50] foreign funders enable the EACJ, CCJ, and ACtHPR to engage in public legitimation. Both the German and Canadian development agencies, for example, have been crucial funders for the off-the-bench activities. Hierarchies and inequalities also seem to affect the accessibility of ICs. Most litigation before the EACJ, CCJ, and ACtHPR benefits from epistemic resources, common to repeat lawyers and NGOs. These actors have literacy and skills about how to translate grievances into legal complaints, and they have knowledge about the competencies and procedures of the relevant international court. All of this suggests that the accessibility of international justice is contingent not only on formal access but also on access to epistemic resources. In other words, global inequalities in terms of socioeconomic conditions play a role in whether individuals access justice mechanisms.[51] It further speaks to a broader understanding of how international law can be exclusionary and institutionalize global inequalities.[52] Overall,

A Critique," *Review of International Studies* 17, no. 1 (1991). Additionally, principal-agent theory arguably assumes both are at work; see, for example, Hawkins et al., *Delegation and Agency in International Organizations*; Pollack, *The Engines of European Integration*. I embrace these perspectives.

48 Mattern and Zarakol, "Hierarchies in World Politics."

49 Lenz, *Interorganizational Diffusion in International Relations*; Karen J. Alter, "The Global Spread of European Style International Courts," *West European Politics* 35, no. 1 (2012).

50 Widner, *Building the Rule of Law*; Trochev and Ellett, "Judges and Their Allies."

51 Steinert, "Elitist Remedies?"

52 Viola, *The Closure of the International System.*

these findings point to a need to explore the processes through which global hierarchies and inequalities affect international law and courts.[53]

International Organizations in Contemporary World Politics

This book also contributes to literature on international organizations in contemporary world politics. In recent years, observers of IOs, including international courts, point to two key developments. First, there is a heightened recognition that IOs are publicly salient and that IOs are aware of their public perceptions. Second, many are concerned that IOs are facing hard times, experiencing waves of noncooperation and contestation, and we are witnessing a crisis of multilateralism or the end of the liberal international order. International courts are part of these dynamics. This book contributes to IR literature by integrating these two realities of contemporary world politics into how we think about IOs.

There is a growing sense that the public is more attuned to international organizations, including international courts, and vice versa. This has led to an extensive body of literature on the legitimacy and legitimation of IOs.[54] This book has integrated the concepts of legitimacy and legitimation into theorizing the relationship between IOs and states. In other words, it adds an important nuance to rational institutionalist perspectives, especially in the tradition of principal-agent (PA) theory.[55] While I do not use the terminology common to PA theory, I draw extensively from it. Like PA theory, my argument assumes that states delegate responsibilities to international courts and that both ICs (agents) and states (principals) are self-interested actors. Moreover, the interests

[53] TWAIL scholars have elucidated how colonialism has had lasting impacts on international law (and international organizations); see, for example, Anghie, *Imperialism, Sovereignty and the Making of International Law*; Anghie, "Rethinking International Law"; Gathii, "Promise of International Law."

[54] Tallberg and Zürn, "The Legitimacy and Legitimation of International Organizations"; Imerman, "Contested Legitimacy and Institutional Change"; Hurd, *After Anarchy*; Ian Hurd, "Legitimacy and Authority in International Politics," *International Organization* 53, no. 2 (1999); Buchanan and Keohane, "The Legitimacy of Global Governance Institutions"; Follesdal, "Survey Article: The Legitimacy of International Courts"; Dellmuth and Tallberg, *Legitimacy Politics*; Zaum, *Legitimating International Organizations*; Tobias Lenz and Henning Schmidtke, "Agents, Audiences and Peers: Why International Organizations Diversify Their Legitimation Discourse," *International Affairs* 99, no. 3 (2023); Dingwerth et al., *International Organizations Under Pressure*.

[55] Hawkins et al., *Delegation and Agency in International Organizations*.

of states and ICs diverge. Institutional design, including the nature of institutional safeguards to independence, provides mechanisms of control that can disincentivize agency slack (or the agent's pursuit of her interests that are contrary to the principal's interests). Moreover, it is feasible for principals to utilize mechanisms to regain their control, but this may depend on fragmentation in instances of multiple principals. My framework, however, incorporates legitimacy into a theoretical account of how agents and principals interact, suggesting that legitimacy serves as a crucial mechanism shaping the behavior of agents.[56] In particular, I have argued that legitimacy can empower agents vis-à-vis their principals by making it politically costly for the latter to utilize the mechanism of controls available to them, and that agents can exercise agency over their legitimacy. Thus, my argument diverges from traditional PA theory and contributes more broadly to our understanding of the relationship between IOs and states because it conceives of legitimacy as the main source of power available to international organizations.[57] This not only distinguishes my argument from traditional PA theory, but it also suggests future research might explore which IO practices have the capacity to change public opinion[58] and under what conditions public opinion alters states' preferences and their willingness to utilize mechanisms of control.

Second, the book contributes to current debates related to contestation and noncooperation, including backlash, pushback, delegitimation, and other forms of resistance. In recent years, observers of IOs have been struck by a wide range of examples of noncooperation and contestation, ranging from the paralysis of the WTO AB, protests against other international economic organizations or UN peacekeepers, or exit from key international institutions, like Brexit or the withdrawals from the ICC by Burundi and the Philippines. Scholars have developed conceptual tools for defining the various forms of contestation and noncooperation that have been observed in contemporary world politics. This research

[56] Mark Pollack argues that principal-agent theory does not fully capture the dynamics of legitimacy concerns; see Pollack, *The Engines of European Integration*. The trustee model integrates the concept of legitimacy but not in relation to public beliefs per se; see Alter, "Agents or Trustees?"

[57] Hurd, "Legitimacy and Authority in International Politics"; Franck, *The Power of Legitimacy Among Nations*.

[58] Chapman, "Audience Beliefs and International Organization Legitimacy"; Greenhill, "How Can International Organizations Shape Public Opinion?"; Grieco et al., "Let's Get a Second Opinion."

offers a variety of theoretical accounts about the causes and consequences of noncooperation and contestation. Among the causal explanations that have been offered are the role of ideology, like nationalism and populism,[59] geopolitical factors,[60] the expansion of authority,[61] the power and influence of institutional proponents or conversely institutional opponents,[62] and the domestic distributional impacts of IOs,[63] to mention some. Others have suggested that the consequences of noncooperation and contestation might include institutional death or paralysis, creation, and adjustments,[64] or contagion effects.[65] Yet, we know much less about how noncooperation and contestation affect the performance of IOs. In other words, how do they respond? Do they alter their decisions and policy outputs that they produce? Do we see impacts on legitimation practices? What factors condition their reactions to backlash, resistance, delegitimation, or politicization?

This book suggests that IOs might respond in terms of their decisions, outputs and practices, yet not always in expected ways. For instance, following the backlash experienced by the EACJ, deference increased. In the face of withdrawals of Article 34(6) declarations, the ACtHPR also seems to defer more frequently. This suggests that resistance can affect IOs' decisions and outputs. The case studies reveal resilience and reactions we might not expect. For instance, the EACJ, CCJ, and ACtHPR's legitimation practices do not necessarily become defensive in reaction to

59 Jack Snyder, "The Broken Bargain: How Nationalism Came Back," *Foreign Affairs* 98, no. 2 (2019); Erik Voeten, "Populism and Backlashes Against International Courts," *Perspectives on Politics* 18, no. 2 (2020).

60 von Borzyskowski and Vabulas, "Hello, Goodbye"; Kruck and Zangl, "The Adjustment of International Institutions to Global Power Shifts."

61 Michael Zürn, Martin Binder, and Matthias Ecker-Ehrhardt, "International Authority and Its Politicization," *International Theory* 4, no. 1 (2012).

62 Alter, Gathii, and Helfer, "Backlash Against International Courts in West, East and Southern Africa"; Gonzalez-Ocantos and Sandholtz, "The Sources of Resilience of International Human Rights Courts."

63 Hillebrecht, *Saving the International Justice Regime*; Stephen Chaudoin, "How Contestation Moderates the Effects of International Institutions: The International Criminal Court and Kenya," *Journal of Politics* 78, no. 2 (2016); Tabea Palmtag, Tobias Rommel, and Stefanie Walter, "International Trade and Public Protest: Evidence from Russian Regions," *International Studies Quarterly* 64, no. 4 (2020).

64 Kruck and Zangl, "The Adjustment of International Institutions to Global Power Shifts"; Morse and Keohane, "Contested Multilateralism"; von Borzyskowski and Vabulas, "Hello, Goodbye."

65 Stefanie Walter, "Brexit Domino? The Political Contagion Effects of Voter-Endorsed Withdrawals from International Institutions," *Comparative Political Studies* 54, no. 13 (2021).

resistance or politicization. I observe no significant shift in how the three courts analyzed here portray themselves or the initiatives they adopt to gain additional support from stakeholders. This suggests that legitimation may be ordinary practices for institutions, and that explicitly defending them against attacks is rare – international judges and IO bureaucrats may think defensive legitimation is risky. Some previous work suggests that resilience comes from external factors.[66] The case studies here, however, suggest resilience may also come from within an IO. Changes in IO decision-making behavior and other practices may contribute to institutional resilience. While the jury is out on what factors determine IO resilience, this book contributes by looking at ICs in their early years to reveal aspects of how IOs navigate hard times.

[66] Gonzalez-Ocantos and Sandholtz, "The Sources of Resilience of International Human Rights Courts"; Alter, Gathii, and Helfer, "Backlash Against International Courts in West, East and Southern Africa."

Appendix

EACJ Cases Included in Analysis [Short Name]

Note: First Instance and Appellate cases listed separately. Interim proceeding not listed.

Abdu Katuntu v The Attorney General of the Republic of Uganda & The Secretary General of the East African Community, Reference No. 5/2012, EACJ (November 25, 2013)

African Network for Animal Welfare v The Attorney General of the United Republic of Tanzania, Reference No. 9/2010, EACJ (June 20, 2014), [*ANAW v Tanzania*, Ref. 9/2010]

Alcon International Limited v Standard Chartered Bank of Uganda & 2 Others, Appeal No. 3/2013, EACJ (July 27, 2015)

Alcon International Limited v Standard Chartered Bank of Uganda & 2 Others, Reference No. 6/2010, EACJ (September 2, 2013)

Among A. Anita v The Attorney General of the Republic of Uganda & The Secretary General of The East African Community, Reference No. 6/2012, EACJ (November 29, 2013), [*Anita v Uganda & EAC*, Ref. 6/2012]

Anthony Calist Komu v The Attorney General of the United Republic of Tanzania, Reference No. 7/2012, EACJ (September 26, 2014)

Audace Ngendakumana v The Attorney General of the Republic of Burundi, Reference No. 11/2014, EACJ (November 27, 2015)

Baranzira Raphael & Ntakiyiruta Joseph v The Attorney General of the Republic of Burundi, Reference No. 15/2014, EACJ (March 22, 2016), [*Raphael & Anor v Burundi*, Ref. 15/2014]

Benoit Ndorimana v The Attorney General of the Republic of Burundi, Reference No. 2/2013, EACJ (November 28, 2014)

Bonaventure Gasutwa & 2 Others v The Attorney General of the Republic of Burundi, Reference No. 13/2014, EACJ (November 26, 2015)

British American Tobacco (U) Ltd v The Attorney General of the Republic of Uganda, Reference No. 7/2017, EACJ (March 26, 2019), [*BAT Ltd v Uganda*, Ref. 7/2017]

Burundi Journalists Union v The Attorney General of the Republic of Burundi, Reference No. 7/2013, EACJ (May 15, 2015), [*Burundi Journalist Union v Burundi*, Ref. 7/2013]

Calist Andrew Mwatela & 2 Others v The East African Community, Application No. 1/2005 (arising from Reference No. 1/2005), EACJ (October 1, 2006), [*Mwatela & Ors. v EAC*, App. 1/2005]

Christopher Mtikila v The Attorney General of the United Republic of Tanzania & The Secretary General of the East African Community, Reference No. 2/2007, EACJ (April 24, 2007)

Democratic Party & Mukasa Mbidde v The Secretary General of the East African Community & The Attorney General of the Republic of Uganda, Reference No. 6/2011, EACJ (May 9, 2012), [*Democratic Party & Mbidde v EAC & Uganda*, Ref. 6/2011]

Democratic Party v The Secretary General of the East African Community & 4 Others, Appeal No. 1/2014, EACJ (July 28, 2015)

Democratic Party v The Secretary General of the East African Community & 4 Others, Reference No. 2/2012, EACJ (November 29, 2013)

East African Centre for Trade Policy & Law v The Secretary General of the East African Community, Reference No. 9/2012, EACJ (May 10, 2013)

East African Civil Society Organizations' Forum v The Attorney General of the Republic of Burundi & 2 Others, Appeal No. 4/2016, EACJ (May 24, 2018)

East African Civil Society Organizations' Forum v The Attorney General of the Republic of Burundi & 2 Others, Reference No. 2/2015 (de novo), EACJ (December 3, 2019)

East African Civil Society Organizations' Forum v The Attorney General of the Republic of Burundi & 2 Others, Reference No. 2/2015, EACJ (September 29, 2016)

East African Law Society & 4 Others v The Attorney General of the Republic of Kenya & 3 Others, Reference No. 3/2007, EACJ (August 31, 2008), [*EALS & Ors. v Kenya & Ors.*, Ref. 3/2007]

East African Law Society v The Attorney General of the Republic of Burundi & The Secretary General of the East African Community, Reference No. 1/2014, EACJ (May 15, 2015), [*EALS v Burundi & EAC*, Ref. 1/2014]

East African Law Society v The Attorney General of the Republic of Uganda & The Secretary General of the East African Community, Reference No. 2/2011, EACJ (March 28, 2018), [*EALS v Uganda & EAC*, Ref. 2/2011]

East African Law Society v The Attorney General of the United Republic of Tanzania & The Secretary General of the East African Community, Reference No. 1/2019, EACJ (November 25, 2020)

East African Law Society v The Secretary General of The East African Community, Reference No. 1/2011, EACJ (February 14, 2013)

East African Law Society vs The Secretary General of the East African Community, Reference No. 7/2014, EACJ (March 22, 2016), [*EALS v EAC*, Ref. 7/2014]

Emmanuel Mwakisha Mjawasi & 748 Others v The Attorney General of the Republic of Kenya, Reference No. 2/2010, EACJ (September 28, 2011)

Emmanuel Mwakisha Mjawasi & 748 Others vs The Attorney General of the Republic of Kenya, Appeal No. 4/2011, EACJ (April 27, 2012)

Eric Kabalisa Makala v The Attorney General of the Republic of Rwanda, Reference No. 1/2017, EACJ (June 18, 2020), [*Makala v Rwanda*, Ref. 1/2017]

Georges Ruhara v The Attorney General of the Republic of Burundi, Reference No. 4/2014, EACJ (August 7, 2015)

Godfrey Magezi v The Attorney General of the Republic of Uganda, Appeal No. 3/2015, EACJ (May 26, 2016)

Godfrey Magezi v The Attorney General of the Republic of Uganda, Reference No. 5/2013, EACJ (May 14, 2015)

Grands Lacs Suppliers S.A.R.L. & Others v The Attorney General of the Republic of Burundi, Reference No. 6/2016, EACJ (June 19, 2018), [*Grands Lacs Suppliers & Ors. v Burundi*, Ref. 6/2016]

Hassan Basajjabalaba & Another v The Attorney General of the Republic of Uganda, Reference No. 8/2018, EACJ (July 22, 2020)

Henry Kyarimpa v The Attorney General of the Republic of Uganda, Appeal No. 6/2014, EACJ (February 19, 2016)

Henry Kyarimpa v The Attorney General of the Republic of Uganda, Reference No. 4/2013, EACJ (November 28, 2014)

Hilaire Ndayizamba v The Attorney General of the Republic of Burundi & The Secretary General of the East African Community, Reference No. 3/2012, EACJ (March 28, 2014)

Hon. Dr. Margaret Zziwa v The Secretary General of the East African Community, Appeal No. 2/2017, EACJ (May 25, 2018)

Hon. Dr. Margaret Zziwa v The Secretary General of the East African Community, Reference No. 17/2014, EACJ (February 3, 2017)

Hon. Justice Malek Mathiang Malek v The Attorney General of the Republic of South Sudan & The Secretary General of the East African Community, Reference No. 9/2017, EACJ (July 24, 2020)

Hon. Sitenda Sebalu v The Secretary General of the East African Community & 2 Others, Reference No. 1/2010, EACJ (June 29, 2011)

Hon. Sitenda Sebalu v The Secretary General of The East African Community, Reference No. 8/2012, EACJ (December 22, 2013)

Human Rights Awareness and Promotion Forum v The Attorney General of the Republic of Uganda, Reference No. 6/2014, EACJ (September 27, 2016)

Independent Medical Legal Unit v The Attorney General of the Republic of Kenya & 4 Others, Reference No. 3/2010, EACJ (July 20, 2011), [*IMLU v Kenya*, Ref. 3/2010]

Ismael Dabule & 1004 Others v The Attorney General of the Republic of Uganda, Reference No. 5/2016, EACJ (November 28, 2018)

Ismael Dabule & 1004 Others v The Attorney General of the Republic of Uganda, Appeal No. 1/2018, EACJ (February 25, 2020)

James Alfred Koroso v The Attorney General of the Republic of Kenya & Another, Reference No. 12/2014, EACJ (March 24, 2016)

James Katabazi & 21 Others v The Secretary General of the East African Community & The Attorney General of the Republic of Uganda, Reference No. 1/2007, EACJ (October 31, 2007), [*Katabazi v EAC & Uganda*, Ref. 1/2007]

Le Forum pour le Renforcement de la Société Civile & 4 Others v The Attorney General of the Republic of Burundi & The Secretary General of the East African Community, Reference No. 12/2016, EACJ (December 4, 2019), [*FORSC & Ors. v Burundi & EAC*, Ref. 12/2016]

Legal Brains Trust Limited v Attorney General of the Republic of Uganda, Appeal 4/2012, EACJ (May 19, 2012)

Legal Brains Trust Limited v The Attorney General of the Republic of Uganda, Reference No. 10/2011, EACJ (March 30, 2012)

M/S Quick Telecommunications Services v The Attorney General of the United Republic of Tanzania, Reference No. 10/2016, EACJ (July 3, 2019), [*M/S Quick Telecommunications v Tanzania*, Ref. 10/2016]

Malcom Lukwiya v The Attorney General of the Republic of Uganda & The Attorney General of the Republic of Kenya, Reference No. 6/2015, EACJ (November 27, 2018)

Male H. Mabirizi K. Kiwanuka v The Attorney General of the Republic of Uganda, Reference No. 6/2019, EACJ (September 30, 2020)

Manariyo Desire v The Attorney General of the Republic of Burundi, Appeal No. 1/2017, EACJ (November 28, 2018)

Manariyo Desire v The Attorney General of the Republic of Burundi, Reference No. 8/2015, EACJ (December 2, 2016)

Martha Wangari Karua v The Attorney General of the Republic of Kenya, Reference No. 20/2019, EACJ (November 30, 2020)

Mary Ariviza & Another v the Attorney General of Kenya & The Secretary General of the East African Community, Reference No. 7/2010, EACJ (November 30, 2011)

Mary Ariviza v The Attorney General of the Republic of Kenya & The Secretary General of the East African Community, Appeal No. 3/2012, EACJ (November 8, 2013)

Mbugua Mureithi Wa Nyambura v The Attorney General of the Republic of Uganda & The Attorney General of the Republic of Kenya, Reference No. 11/2011, EACJ (February 24, 2014)

Media Council of Tanzania & 2 Others v The Attorney General of the United Republic of Tanzania, Application No. 5/2019 (in an intended appeal), EACJ (June 9, 2020)

Media Council of Tanzania & 2 Others v The Attorney General of the United Republic of Tanzania, Reference No. 2/2017, EACJ (March 28, 2019), [*Media Council of Tanzania v Ors. v Tanzania*, Ref. 2/2017]

Modern Holdings (EA) Limited v Kenya Ports Authority, Reference No. 1/2008, EACJ (February 11, 2009)

Mpozayo Christophe v The Attorney General of the Republic of Rwanda, Reference No. 10/2014, EACJ (September 28, 2018), [*Christophe v Rwanda*, Ref. 10/2014]

Mseto & Another v The Attorney General of the United Republic of Tanzania, Consolidated Applications Nos. 3 and 4/2019 (in an intended appeal), EACJ (June 2, 2020)

Mseto & Another v The Attorney General of the United Republic of Tanzania, Reference No. 7/2016, EACJ (June 21, 2018), [*Mseto & Anor. v Tanzania*, Ref. 7/2016]

Patrick Ntege Walusimbi & 2 Others v The Attorney General of the Republic of Uganda & 5 Others, Reference No. 8/2013, EACJ (February 27, 2015)

Paul John Mhozya v The Attorney General of the United Republic of Tanzania, Reference No. 2/2016, EACJ (June 27, 2018)

Plaxeda Rugumba v The Secretary General of the East African Community & the Attorney General of the Republic of Rwanda, Reference No. 8/2010, EACJ (November 30, 2011), [*Rugumba v EAC & Rwanda*, Ref. 8/2010]

Preliminary Ruling in the case of the Attorney General of the Republic of Uganda v Tom Kyahurwenda, Case Stated 1/2014, EACJ (July 31, 2015)

Prof. Nyamoya Francois v The Attorney General of the Republic of Burundi & The Secretary General of the East African Community, Reference No. 8/2011, EACJ (March 28, 2014)

Prof. Peter Anyang' Nyong'o & 10 Others v The Attorney General of Kenya & 5 Others, Reference No. 1/2006, EACJ (March 29, 2007), [*Anyang' Nyong'o v Kenya & Ors.*, Ref. 1/2006]

Rashid Salim Adiy & 39,999 Others v The Attorney General of the United Republic of Tanzania, Reference No. 9/2016, EACJ (September 29, 2020)

Ronald Ssembuusi v The Attorney General of the Republic of Uganda, Reference No. 16/2014, EACJ (November 23, 2020), [*Ssembuusi v Uganda*, Ref. 16/2014]

Rwenga Etienne & Another vs The Secretary General of the East African Community, Reference No. 5/2015, EACJ (March 23, 2016)

Samuel Mukira Mohochi v The Attorney General of the Republic of Uganda, Reference No. 5/2011, EACJ (May 17, 2013), [*Mohochi v Uganda*, Ref. 5/2011]

Simon Peter Ochieng & Another v The Attorney General of the Republic of Uganda, Appeal No. 4/2015, EACJ (November 24, 2016)

Simon Peter Ochieng & Another v The Attorney General of the Republic of Uganda, Reference No. 11/2013, EACJ (August 7, 2015)

Steven Deniss v The Attorney General of the Republic of Burundi & 5 Others, Reference No. 3/2015, EACJ (March 31, 2017)

The Attorney General of the Republic of Burundi v The Secretary General of the East African Community, Appeal No. 2/2019, EACJ (June 4, 2020), [*Burundi v EAC*, Appeal 2/2019]

The Attorney General of the Republic of Burundi v The Secretary General of the East African Community, Reference No. 2/2018, EACJ (July 2, 2019)

The Attorney General of the Republic of Kenya v Independent Medical Legal Unit, Appeal No. 1/2011, EACJ (March 15, 2012), [*Kenya v IMLU*, Appeal 1/2011]

The Attorney General of the Republic of Rwanda v Plaxeda Rugumba, Appeal No. 1/2012, EACJ (June 21, 2012), [*Rwanda v Rugumba*, Appeal 1/2012]

The Attorney General of the Republic Uganda v Omar Awadh & 6 Others, Appeal No. 2/2012, EACJ (April 15, 2013)

The Attorney General of the United Republic of Tanzania v African Network for Animal Welfare, Appeal No. 3/2014, EACJ (July 29, 2015), [*Tanzania v ANAW*, Appeal 3/2014]

The Attorney General of the United Republic of Tanzania v Anthony Calist Komu, Appeal No. 2/2015, EACJ (November 25, 2016)

Theodore Niyongabo & 2 Others v The Attorney General of the Republic of Burundi, Reference No. 4/2017, EACJ (June 16, 2020)

Timothy Alvin Kahoho v The Secretary General of The East African Community, Appeal No. 2/2013, EACJ (November 28, 2014)

Timothy Alvin Kahoho v The Secretary General of the East African Community, Reference No. 1/2012, EACJ (May 17, 2013)

Union Trade Centre v The Attorney General of the Republic of Rwanda, Reference No. 10/2013, EACJ (November 27, 2014)

Union Trade Centre v The Attorney General of the Republic of Rwanda, Appeal No. 1/2015, EACJ (November 20, 2015)

Union Trade Centre v The Attorney General of the Republic of Rwanda, Reference No. 10/2013 (denovo), EACJ (November 26, 2020)

Venant Masenge v The Attorney General of the Republic of Burundi, Reference No. 9/2012, EACJ (June 18, 2014)

CCJ Cases Included in Analysis, by Application [Short Name]

In Respect to Application No. AR 1 of 2008 & OA 2 of 2009 (Relating to Common External Tariff)

Trinidad Cement Limited & TCL Guyana Incorporated v The Co-operative Republic of Guyana, [2008] CCJ 1 (OJ) (July 22, 2008)

Trinidad Cement Limited & TCL Guyana Incorporated v The Co-operative Republic of Guyana, [2009] CCJ 1 (OJ) (January 15, 2009), [*TCL v Guyana* [2009] CCJ 1 (OJ)]

Trinidad Cement Limited & TCL Guyana Incorporated v The Co-operative Republic of Guyana, [2009] CCJ 5 (OJ) (August 20, 2009), [*TCL v Guyana* [2009] CCJ 5 (OJ)]

Trinidad Cement Limited & TCL Guyana Incorporated v The Co-operative Republic of Guyana, [2009] CCJ 6 (OJ) (October 27, 2009)

Trinidad Cement Limited & TCL Guyana Incorporated v The Co-operative Republic of Guyana, [2010] CCJ 1 (OJ) (March 29, 2010)

In Respect to Application No. AR 3 of 2008 & OA 1 of 2009 (Relating to Common External Tariff)

Trinidad Cement Limited v The Caribbean Community, [2009] CCJ 2 (OJ) (February 5, 2009)

Trinidad Cement Limited v The Caribbean Community, [2009] CCJ 4 (OJ) (August 10, 2009), [*TCL v CARICOM* [2009] CCJ 4(OJ)]

In Respect to Application No. AR 2 of 2008 (Relating to Jurisdiction Over Community Institutions)

Doreen Johnson v Caribbean Centre for Development Administration, [2009] CCJ 3 (OJ) (March 2, 2009)

In Respect to Application No. OA 1 of 2011 (Relating to Common External Tariff)

Hummingbird Rice Mills Limited v Suriname & The Caribbean Community, [2011] CCJ 1 (OJ) (June 27, 2011)

Hummingbird Rice Mills Limited v Suriname & The Caribbean Community, [2012] CCJ 1 (OJ) (February 23, 2012), [*HRML v Suriname & CARICOM* [2012] CCJ 1 (OJ)]

Hummingbird Rice Mills Limited v Suriname & The Caribbean Community, [2012] CCJ 2 (OJ) (April 11, 2012)

In Respect to Application No. OA 1 of 2012 (Relating to Competition)

Trinidad Cement Limited v The Competition Commission, [2012] CCJ 4 (OJ) (November 12, 2012)
Trinidad Cement Limited v The Competition Commission, [2013] CCJ 2 (OJ) (May 29, 2013), [*TCL v Competition Commission* [2013] CCJ 2 (OJ)]

In Respect to Application No. OA 2 of 2012 (Relating to Freedom of Movement)

Shanique Myrie v The State of Barbados, [2013] CCJ 3 (OJ) (October 4, 2013), [*Myrie v Barbados* [2013] CCJ 3 (OJ)]
Shanique Myrie v The State of Barbados, [2013] CCJ 1 (OJ) (March 19, 2013)
Shanique Myrie v The State of Barbados, [2012] CCJ 3 (OJ) (September 27, 2012)

In Respect to Application No. OA 1 of 2013 (Relating to Import Duties)

Rudisa Beverages & Juices N.V. Caribbean International Distributors Inc. v The Co-operative Republic of Guyana, [2014] CCJ 1 (OJ) (May 8, 2014)

In Respect to Applications No. OA 1 of 2013 and OA 2 of 2013 (Relating to Freedom of Movement)

Maurice Tomlinson v The State of Belize & The State of Trinidad & Tobago, [2016] CCJ 1 (OJ), (June 10, 2016), [*Tomlinson v Belize* [2016] CCJ 1 (OJ)]
Maurice Tomlinson v The State of Belize & The State of Trinidad & Tobago, [2014] CCJ 2 (OJ) (May 8, 2014)

In Respect to Application No. DMOJ2016/001 (Relating to Freedom of Services)

Cabral Douglas v The Commonwealth of Dominica, [2017] CCJ 1 (OJ) (February 20, 2017), [*Douglas v Dominica*, [2017] CCJ 1 (OJ)]

In Respect to Application No. TTOJ2016/001 (Relating to Import Duties)

SM Jaleel & Co Ltd & Guyana Beverages Inc v The Co-operative Republic of Guyana, [2017] CCJ 2 (OJ) (May 9, 2017)

In Respect to Application No. GDOJ2018/001 (Relating to Freedom of Movement)

Tamika Gilbert, Lynnel Gilbert, Royston Gilbert & Glennor Gilbert v The State of Barbados, [2019] CCJ 2 (OJ) (May 20, 2019)

In Respect to Application No. GDOJ2018/002 (Relating to Freedom of Movement)

David Bain v The State of Trinidad & Tobago, [2019] CCJ 3 (OJ) (May 29, 2019), [*Bain v Trinidad & Tobago* [2019] CCJ 3 (OJ)]

In Respect to Application No. TTOJ2018/002 (Relating to Common External Tariff)

Trinidad Cement Limited & Arawak Cement Limited v The State of Barbados, [2018] CCJ 1 (OJ) (July 17, 2018)
Trinidad Cement Limited & Arawak Cement Limited v The State of Barbados, [2018] CCJ 4 (OJ) (December 11, 2018)
Trinidad Cement Limited & Arawak Cement Limited v The State of Barbados, [2018] CCJ 5 (OJ) (December 11, 2018)
Trinidad Cement Limited & Arawak Cement Limited v The State of Barbados, [2019] CCJ 4 (OJ) (August 6, 2019)
Trinidad Cement Limited & Arawak Cement Limited v The State of Barbados, [2019] CCJ 1 (OJ) (April 17, 2019)
Trinidad Cement Limited & Arawak Cement Limited v The State of Barbados, [2019] CCJ 5 (OJ) (November 28, 2019)

In Respect to Application No. TTOJ2018/003 (Relating to Jurisdiction Over Community Institutions)

Jason Jones v Council of Legal Education & Council for Human and Social Development & Council for Trade and Economic Development, [2018] CCJ 2 (OJ) (November 9, 2018)

In Respect to Application No. SLUOJ2018/001 (Relating to Common External Tariff)

Rock Hard Distribution Limited v The State of Trinidad & Tobago & The Caribbean Community, [2018] CCJ 3 (OJ) (December 11, 2018)
Rock Hard Distribution Limited v The State of Trinidad & Tobago & The Caribbean Community, [2019] CCJ 4 (OJ) (August 6, 2019)

Rock Hard Distribution Limited v The State of Trinidad & Tobago & The Caribbean Community, [2019] CCJ 5 (OJ) (November 28, 2019)

In Respect to Application No. TTOJ2018/001 (Relating to Common External Tariff)

Trinidad Cement Limited v The State of Trinidad & Tobago, [2018] CCJ 4 (OJ) (December 11, 2018)
Trinidad Cement Limited v The State of Trinidad & Tobago, [2019] CCJ 4 (OJ) (August 6, 2019)
Trinidad Cement Limited v The State of Trinidad & Tobago, [2019] CCJ 5 (OJ) (November 28, 2019)

In Respect to Application No. BBOJ2018/001 (Relating to Common External Tariff)

Rock Hard Cement Limited v The State of Barbados & The Caribbean Community, [2019] CCJ 4 (OJ) (August 6, 2019)
Rock Hard Cement Limited v The State of Barbados & The Caribbean Community, [2019] CCJ 1 (OJ) (April 17, 2019)
Rock Hard Cement Limited v The State of Barbados & The Caribbean Community, [2019] CCJ 5 (OJ) (November 28, 2019)

In Respect to Application No. BBOJ2019/001 (Relating to Common External Tariff)

Rock Hard Cement Limited v The State of Barbados & The Caribbean Community, [2020] CCJ 2 (OJ) (June 10, 2020)

ACtHPR Cases Included in Analysis [Short Name]

Note: When the case has more than one ruling or judgment (e.g., jurisdiction, merits, reparations), I list the merits judgment.

Actions pour la protection des Droits de l'Homme v Republic of Côte d'Ivoire, Application No. 1/2014, ACtHPR (November 18, 2016), [*APHD v Côte d'Ivoire*, App. 1/2014]
African Commission on Human and Peoples' Rights v Great Socialist People's Libyan Arab Jamahiriya, Application No. 4/2011, ACtHPR (March 15, 2013)
African Commission on Human and Peoples' Rights v Libya, Application No. 2/2013, ACtHPR (June 3, 2016)

African Commission on Human and Peoples' Rights v Republic of Kenya, Application No. 6/2012, ACtHPR (May 26, 2017)

Akwasi Boateng & 351 Others v Republic of Ghana, Application No. 59/2016, ACtHPR (November 27, 2020)

Alex Thomas v United Republic of Tanzania, Application No. 5/2013, ACtHPR (November 20, 2015), [*Thomas v Tanzania*, App. 5/2013]

Alfred Agbes Woyome v Republic of Ghana, Application No. 1/2017, ACtHPR (June 28, 2019)

Ally Rajabu & Others v United Republic of Tanzania, Application No. 7/2015, ACtHPR (November 28, 2019), [*Rajabu v Tanzania*, App. 7/2015]

Amir Adam Timan v Republic of Sudan, Application No. 5/2012, ACtHPR (March 30, 2012)

Amir Ramadhani v United Republic of Tanzania, Application No. 10/2015, ACtHPR (May 11, 2018)

Anaclet Paulo v United Republic of Tanzania, Application No. 20/2016, ACtHPR (September 21, 2018)

Andrew Ambrose Cheusi v United Republic of Tanzania, Application No. 4/2015, ACtHPR (June 26, 2020)

Anudo Ochieng Anudo v United Republic of Tanzania, Application No. 12/2015, ACtHPR (March 22, 2018)

Armand Guehi v United Republic of Tanzania, Application No. 1/2015, ACtHPR (December 7, 2018)

Association des Juristes d'Afrique pour la Bonne Gouvernance v Republic of Côte d'Ivoire, Application No. 6/2011, ACtHPR (June 16, 2011)

Association pour le Progrès et la Défense des Droits des Femmes Maliennes & The Institute for Human Rights and Development v Republic of Mali, Application No. 46/2016, ACtHPR (May 11, 2018), [*ADPF & IHRDA v Mali*, App. 46/2016]

Atabong Denis Atemnkeng v African Union, Application No. 14/2011, ACtHPR (March 15, 2013)

Baghdadi Ali Mahmoudi v Republic of Tunisia, Application No. 7/2012, ACtHPR (June 26, 2012)

Benedicto Daniel Mallya v United Republic of Tanzania, Application No. 18/2015, ACtHPR (September 26, 2019)

Beneficiaries of the Late Norbert Zongo, Abdoulaye Nikiema alias Ablassé, Ernest Zongo & Blaise Ilboudo & Burkinabè Human and Peoples' Rights Movement v Burkina Faso, Application No. 13/2011, ACtHPR (March 28, 2014)

Boubacar Sissoko & 74 Others v Republic of Mali, Application No. 37/2017, ACtHPR (September 25, 2020)

Chananja Luchagula v United Republic of Tanzania, Application No. 39/2016, ACtHPR (September 25, 2020)

Christopher Jonas v United Republic of Tanzania, Application No. 11/2015, ACtHPR (September 28, 2017)

Collectif des Anciens Travailleurs de la Semico Tabakoto v Republic of Mali, Application No. 9/2018, ACtHPR (November 27, 2020)

Collectif des Anciens Travailleurs du Laboratoire v Republic of Mali, Application No. 42/2016, ACtHPR (March 28, 2019)

Daniel Amare & Mulugeta Amare v Republic of Mozambique, Application No. 5/2011, ACtHPR (June 16, 2011)

Delta International Investments S.A., Mr and Mrs A.G.L. De Lange v Republic of South Africa, Application No. 2/2012, ACtHPR (March 30, 2012)

Dexter Eddie Johnson v Republic of Ghana, Application No. 16/2017, ACtHPR (March 28, 2019)

Diocles William v United Republic of Tanzania, Application No. 16/2016, ACtHPR (September 21, 2018)

Dismas Bunyerere v United Republic of Tanzania, Application No. 31/2015, ACtHPR (November 28, 2019)

Efoua Mbozo'o Samuel v Pan-African Parliament, Application No. 10/2011, ACtHPR (September 30, 2011)

Ekollo Moundi Alexandre v Republic of Cameroon & Federal Republic of Nigeria, Application No. 8/2011, ACtHPR (September 23, 2011)

Emmanuel Joseph Uko & Others v Republic of South Africa, Application No. 4/2012, ACtHPR (March 30, 2012)

Ernest Francis Mtingwi v Republic of Malawi, Application No. 1/2013, ACtHPR (March 15, 2013)

Femi Falana v African Commission on Human and Peoples' Rights, Application No. 19/2015, ACtHPR (November 20, 2015)

Femi Falana v African Union, Application No. 1/2011, ACtHPR (June 26, 2012)

Frank David Omary & Others v United Republic of Tanzania, Application No. 1/2012, ACtHPR (March 28, 2014)

George Maili Kemboge v United Republic of Tanzania, Application No. 2/2016, ACtHPR (May 11, 2018)

Godfred Antony & Ifunda Kisite v United Republic of Tanzania, Application No. 15/2015, ACtHPR (September 26, 2019)

Gombert Jean-Claude Roger v Republic of Côte d'Ivoire, Application No. 38/2016, ACtHPR (March 22, 2018)

Hamad Mohamed Lyambaka v United Republic of Tanzania, Application No. 10/2016, ACtHPR (September 25, 2020)

Houngue Eric Noudehouenou v Republic of Benin, Application No. 3/2020, ACtHPR (December 4, 2020)

Ingabire Victoire Umuhoza v Republic of Rwanda, Application No. 3/2014, ACtHPR (November 24, 2017), [*Umuhoza v Rwanda*, App. 3/2014]

James Wanjara & 4 Others v United Republic of Tanzania, Application No. 33/2015, ACtHPR (September 25, 2020)

Jebra Kambole v United Republic of Tanzania, Application No. 18/2018, ACtHPR (July 15, 2020)

Jibu Amir alias Mussa & Saidi Ally alias Mangaya v United Republic of Tanzania, Application No. 14/2015, ACtHPR (November 28, 2019)

Job Mlama & 2 Others v United Republic of Tanzania, Application No. 19/2016, ACtHPR (September 25, 2020)

Kalebi Elisamehe v United Republic of Tanzania, Application No. 28/2015, ACtHPR (June 26, 2020)

Kenedy Ivan v United Republic of Tanzania, Application No. 25/2016, ACtHPR (March 28, 2019)

Kennedy Gihana & Others v Republic of Rwanda, Application No. 17/2015, ACtHPR (November 28, 2019)

Kennedy Owino Onyachi & Others v United Republic of Tanzania, Application No. 3/2015, ACtHPR (September 28, 2017)

Kijiji Isiaga v United Republic of Tanzania, Application No. 32/2015, ACtHPR (March 21, 2018)

Leon Mugesera v Republic of Rwanda, Application No. 12/2017, ACtHPR (November 27, 2020)

Livinus Daudi Manyuka v United Republic of Tanzania, Application No. 20/2015, ACtHPR (November 28, 2019)

Lohé Issa Konaté v Burkina Faso, Application No. 4/2013, ACtHPR (December 5, 2014), [*Konaté v Burkina Faso*, App. 4/2013]

Lucien Ikili Rashidi v United Republic of Tanzania, Application No. 9/2015, ACtHPR (March 28, 2019), [*Rashidi v Tanzania*, App. 9/2015]

Majid Goa alias Vedatus v United Republic of Tanzania, Application No. 25/2015, ACtHPR (September 26, 2019)

Mamadou Diakite & Diakite Habibata B. Guindo v Republic of Mali, Application No. 9/2016, ACtHPR (September 28, 2017)

Mariam Kouma & Another v Republic of Mali, Application No. 40/2016, ACtHPR (March 21, 2018)

Mgosi Mwita Makungu v United Republic of Tanzania, Application No. 6/2016, ACtHPR (December 7, 2018)

Michelot Yogogombaye v Republic of Senegal, Application No. 1/2008, ACtHPR (December 15, 2009)

Minani Evarist v United Republic of Tanzania, Application No. 27/2015, ACtHPR (September 21, 2018)

Mohamed Abubakari v United Republic of Tanzania, Application No. 7/2013, ACtHPR (June 3, 2016)

Mulindahabi Fidèle v Republic of Rwanda, Application No. 4/2017, ACtHPR (June 26, 2020)

Mulindahabi Fidèle v Republic of Rwanda, Application No. 5/2017, ACtHPR (June 26, 2020)
Mulindahabi Fidèle v Republic of Rwanda, Application No. 6/2017, ACtHPR (July 4, 2019)
Mulindahabi Fidèle v Republic of Rwanda, Application No. 7/2017, ACtHPR (July 4, 2019)
Mulindahabi Fidèle v Republic of Rwanda, Application No. 9/2017, ACtHPR (July 4, 2019)
Mulindahabi Fidèle v Republic of Rwanda, Application No. 10/2017, ACtHPR (June 26, 2020)
Mulindahabi Fidèle v Republic of Rwanda, Application No. 11/2017, ACtHPR (June 26, 2020)
National Convention of Teachers Trade Union v Republic of Gabon, Application No. 12/2011, ACtHPR (December 15, 2011)
Nguza Viking & Johnson Nguza v United Republic of Tanzania, Application No. 6/2015, ACtHPR (March 23, 2018)
Oscar Josiah v United Republic of Tanzania, Application No. 53/2016, ACtHPR (March 28, 2019)
Peter Joseph Chacha v United Republic of Tanzania, Application No. 3/2012, ACtHPR (March 28, 2014)
Ramadhani Issa Malengo v United Republic of Tanzania, Application No. 30/2015, ACtHPR (July 4, 2019)
Robert John Penessis v United Republic of Tanzania, Application No. 13/2015, ACtHPR (November 28, 2019)
Rutabingwa Chrysanthe v Republic of Rwanda, Application No. 22/2015, ACtHPR (May 11, 2018)
Sébastien Germain Ajavon v Republic of Benin, Application No. 13/2017, ACtHPR (March 29, 2019)
Sébastien Germain Marie Aikoue Ajavon v Republic of Benin, Application No. 62/2019, ACtHPR (December 4, 2020), [*Ajavon v Benin*, App. 62/2019]
Shukurani Mango & Others v United Republic of Tanzania, Application No. 8/2015, ACtHPR (September 26, 2019)
Soufiane Ababou v People's Democratic Republic of Algeria, Application No. 2/2011, ACtHPR (June 16, 2011)
Suy Bi Gohore Emile & Others v Republic of Côte d'Ivoire, Application No. 44/2019, ACtHPR (July 15, 2020)
Tanganyika Law Society and The Legal and Human Rights Centre & Reverend Christopher Mtikila v United Republic of Tanzania, Application Nos. 9 and 11/2011, ACtHPR (June 14, 2013), [*Mtikila v Tanzania*, Apps. 9 and 11/2011]
Thobias Mango & Another v United Republic of Tanzania, Application No. 5/2015, ACtHPR (May 11, 2018)

Urban Mkandawire v Republic of Malawi, Application No. 3/2011, ACtHPR (June 21, 2013)

Werema Wangoko Werema & Another v United Republic of Tanzania, Application No. 24/2015, ACtHPR (December 7, 2018)

Wilfred Onyango Nganyi & 9 Others v United Republic of Tanzania, Application No. 6/2013, ACtHPR (March 18, 2016), [*Nganyi & Ors. v Tanzania*, App. 6/2013]

XYZ v Republic of Benin, Application No. 10/2020, ACtHPR (November 27, 2020)

XYZ v Republic of Benin, Application No. 59/2019, ACtHPR (November 27, 2020)

Yacouba Traore v Republic of Mali, Application No. 10/2018, ACtHPR (September 25, 2020)

Youssef Ababou v Kingdom of Morocco, Application No. 7/2011, ACtHPR (September 2, 2011)

Table A1.1 *Interviews*

Interview number	Date	Location of interview	Relevant court
1	November 24, 2015	Arusha	ACtHPR
2	November 25, 2015	Arusha	ACtHPR, EACJ
3	November 26, 2015	Arusha	ACtHPR, EACJ
4	November 26, 2015	Arusha	ACtHPR, EACJ
5	November 26, 2015	Arusha	ACtHPR
6	November 28, 2015	Arusha	ACtHPR
7	November 30, 2015	Arusha	ACtHPR, EACJ
8	December 1, 2015	Arusha	ACtHPR
9	December 1, 2015	Arusha	ACtHPR
10	December 3, 2015	Arusha	ACtHPR
11	December 1, 2015	Arusha	ACtHPR, EACJ
12	December 1, 2015	Arusha	ACtHPR, EACJ
13	December 1, 2015	Arusha	ACtHPR, EACJ
14	November 26, 2015	Arusha	EACJ
15	December 1, 2015	Arusha	EACJ
16	March 21, 2016	Port of Spain	CCJ
17	April 4, 2016	Port of Spain	CCJ
18	March 24, 2016	Port of Spain	CCJ
19	March 24, 2016	Port of Spain	CCJ
20	April 6, 2016	Port of Spain	CCJ
21	April 1, 2016	Port of Spain	CCJ
22	April 4, 2016	Port of Spain	CCJ
23	March 29, 2016	Georgetown	CCJ

Table A1.1 (*cont.*)

Interview number	Date	Location of interview	Relevant court
24	March 29, 2016	Georgetown	CCJ
25	April 6, 2016	Port of Spain	CCJ
26	May 18, 2023	Virtual	CCJ
27	September 26, 2023	Virtual	ACtHPR, EACJ
28	October 6, 2023	Virtual	EACJ

Note: In total ten judges, ten lawyers with direct experience before the courts, six registry staff members, and two staff members from external funders were formally interviewed.

Table A3.1 *Sources for coding of formal independence by international court*

African Court on Human and Peoples' Rights
Constitutive Act of the African Union (adopted July 11, 2000, entered into force May 26, 2001), U.N.T.S. 2158, at 3–58.
Rules of Court. Arusha: ACtHPR, 2010. african-court.org/en/images/Basic%20Documents/Final_Rules_of_Court_for_Publication_after_Harmonization_-_Final__English_7_sept_1_.pdf.
Protocol to the African Charter on Human and Peoples' Rights on the Establishment of an African Court on Human and People's Rights (adopted June 10, 1998, entered into force January 25, 2004). OAU Doc. AU/LEG/EXP/AFCHPR/PROT (III). au.int/en/treaties/protocol-african-charter-human-and-peoples-rights-establishment-african-court-human-and.
Andean Community Tribunal of Justice (ATJ)
Protocol of Cochabamba amending the Treaty Creating the Court of Justice of the Cartagena Agreement (adopted May 28, 1996, entered into force August 25, 1999). www.tribunalandino.org.ec/transparencia/normatividad/Tratado_Creaci%C3%B3n_TJCA.pdf.
Statute of the Court of Justice of the Cartagena Agreement, Decision No. 184. Quito: Commission of the Cartagena Agreement, 1983. www.comunidadandina.org/normativa-andina/decisiones/page/76/
Statute of the Court of the Andean Community, Decision No. 500. Council of Ministers: Valencia, 2001. www.tribunalandino.org.ec/transparencia/normatividad/EstatutoTJCA.pdf.
Treaty Creating the Court of Justice of the Cartagena Agreement (adopted May 28, 1979, entered into force May 19, 1983). *International Legal Materials* 18, no. 5 (1979): 1203–10.

Table A3.1 (*cont.*)

Arab Investment Court
Pact of the League of Arab States (adopted March 22, 1945, entered into force May 10, 1945), U.N.T.S. 7, at 237–63. Unified Agreement for the Investment of Arab Capital in the Arab States (adopted November 26, 1980, entered into force September 7, 1981). https://investmentpolicy.unctad.org/international-investment-agreements/treaty-files/2394/download. Statute of the Arab Investment Court (entered into force February 2, 1985; amended 2009). www.lasportal.org/en/legalnetwork/Pages/Investment_CourtSystems.aspx. Arab Investment Court's Internal Rules (adopted March 3, 1986). www.lasportal.org/en/legalnetwork/Pages/Investment_CourtSystems.aspx. Hamida, Walid Ben. "The First Arab Investment Court Decision." *Journal of World Investment & Trade* 7, no. 5 (2006): 699–721. Hamida, Walid Ben. "Arab Investment Court." In *Max Planck Encyclopedia of International Procedural Law*. Oxford: Oxford University Press, 2018.
Benelux Court of Justice (BCJ)
Treaty concerning the Establishment and the Statute of a Benelux Court of Justice (adopted March 31, 1965, entered into force January 1, 1974; amended by Protocols of June 10, 1981 and November 23, 1984), U.N.T.S. 924, at 42–60; U.N.T.S. 1402, at 362–63; U.N.T.S. 1458, at 355–59. Treaty Instituting the Benelux Economic Union (adopted February 3, 1958, entered into force November 1, 1960), U.N.T.S. 381, at 260–304. Treaty Revising the Treaty Instituting the Benelux Economic Union (adopted June 17, 2008, entered into force January 1, 2012), U.N.T.S. 2868, at 107–38.
Central American Court of Justice (CACJ)
Convention on the Statute of the Central American Court of Justice (adopted December 10, 1992, entered into force February 2, 1994), U.N.T.S. 1821, at 292–303. Tegucigalpa Protocol to the Charter of the Organization of Central American States (adopted December 13, 1991, entered into force July 23, 1992), U.N.T.S. 1695, at 400–10. Reglamento General (adopted October 1995). In *Regimen Juridico*, 2nd ed., 79–102. Managua: Central American Court of Justice, 2007. http://portal.ccj.org.ni/CCJ2/Default.aspx?tabid=102.
Caribbean Court of Justice (CCJ)
Agreement establishing the Caribbean Court of Justice (adopted February 14, 2001, entered into force July 23, 2002), U.N.T.S. 2255, at 319–41. Revised Treaty of Chaguaramas establishing the Caribbean Community including the CARICOM Single Market and Economy (adopted July 5, 2001, entered into force February 4, 2002), U.N.T.S. 2259, at 293–443.

Table A3.1 (*cont.*)

Protocol to the Agreement Establishing the Caribbean Court of Justice relating to the Tenure of Judges, Rules of Court, Financial Arrangements and withdrawal from Agreement, as well as the relationship between Provisions on the Original Jurisdiction of the Caribbean Court of Justice and the Constitutions of States Parties, Paramaribo Suriname, February 17, 2005, entered into force March 6, 2006). https://caricom.org/treaties/protocol-to-the-agreement-establishing-the-ccj-relating-to-the-tenure-of-judges-rules-of-court-financial-arrangements-and-withdrawal/
Revised Agreement establishing the Caribbean Court of Justice Trust Fund (adopted January 12, 2004, entered into force January 27, 2004), U.N.T.S. 2324, at 231–43.
Protocol for the Interfacing and Interaction of the Regional Judicial and Legal Services Commission, The Caribbean Court of Justice and the Caribbean Court of Justice Trust Fund (adopted and entered into force January 25, 2007)
Protocol to the Agreement Establishing the Caribbean Court of Justice Relating to the Tenure of Office of Judges of the Court (adopted May 26, 2007, not yet in force but provisionally applied since June 7, 2007).
Central African Economic and Monetary Community Court of Justice (CEMAC CJ)
Convention regissant la Cour de Justice de CEMAC (adopted July 5, 1996). www.cemac.int/textes-officiels.
Convention révisé regissant la Cour de Justice de CEMAC (adopted January 30, 2009). www.cemac.int/textes-officiels.
Statut de la Chambre Judiciaire de la Cour de Justice (adopted December 14, 2000). Acte Additionnel N° 06/00/CEMAC-041-CCE-CJ-02. www.cemac.int/textes-officiels.
Traité révisé de la Communauté Economique et Monétaire de l'Afrique Centrale (CEMAC) (adopted June 25, 2008). www.cemac.int/textes-officiels.
Traité instituant la Communauté Économique et Monétaire de l'Afrique Centrale (adopted March 16, 1994, entry into force June 25, 1999). www.wipo.int/wipolex/fr/text/201451.
Règles de procédure de la Chambre Judiciaire de la Cour de Justice (adopted December 14, 2000). Acte Additionnel N° 4/00/CEMAC-041-CCE-CJ-02. www.cemac.int/textes-officiels.
Court of Justice of the European Union (CJEU)
Consolidated Version of the Treaty on European Union, 2010 O.J. C 83/01. See https://eur-lex.europa.eu/homepage.html for early versions of treaties.
Protocol No 3 to the Treaty of European Union on the Statute of the Court of Justice of the European Union, Consolidated Version of the Treaty on European Union, 2010 O.J. C 83/01.

Table A3.1 (*cont.*)

Common Market for Eastern and Southern Africa Court of Justice (COMESA CJ)
Treaty establishing the Common Market for Eastern and Southern Africa (adopted November 5, 1993, entered into force December 8, 1994) U.N.T.S. 2314, at 265–385. Rules of the Court of the Court of Justice of the Common Market for Eastern and Southern African. Lusaka: COMESA CJ, 2006. Accessed July 26, 2024. https://web.archive.org/web/20131220114112/http://comesacourt.org/en/rules-of-the-court/.
East African Court of Justice (EACJ)
Treaty for the establishment of the East African Community (adopted November 30, 1999, entered into force July 7, 2000) U.N.T.S. 2144, at 255–327. Revised Treaty for the establishment of the East African Community (as amended December 14, 2006 and August 20, 2007). Arusha: EAC. www.eac.int/documents/category/key-documents.
Economic Court of the Commonwealth of Independent States (ECCIS)
Agreement on the Statute of the Commonwealth of Independent States Economic Court (adopted and entered into force July 6, 1992). Moscow: Council of Heads of State of the Commonwealth of Independent States. https://cis.minsk.by/reestrv2/doc/123 Regulations on the Economic Court of the Commonwealth of Independence States (adopted July 6, 1992). Moscow: Council of Heads of State of the Commonwealth of Independent States. https://sudsng.org/download_files/statdocs/agr_eccis.pdf.
Economic Community of West African States Court of Justice (ECOWAS CJ)
Protocol A/P.l/7/91 on the Community Court of Justice (adopted July 6, 1991). Accra: ECOWAS: Abuja, 1991. www.courtecowas.org/basic-texts/. Supplementary Protocol A/SP.1/01/05 amending Protocol A/P.1/7/91 relating to the Community Court of Justice (adopted January 19, 2005). Accra: ECOWAS, 2005. www.courtecowas.org/basic- texts/. Rules of the Community Court of Justice of the Economic Community of West African States. Abuja: ECOWAS CJ, 2002. www.courtecowas.org/basic-texts/.
Eurasian Economic Union Court (EAEU CT)
Treaty on the Eurasian Economic Union (adopted May 29, 2014, entered into force January 1, 2015), U.N.T.S. 3049–50. Statute of the Court of the Eurasian Economic Union (adopted May 29, 2014, entered into force January 1, 2015), U.N.T.S. 3049, at 167–88.
European Court of Human Rights (ECtHR)
European Convention for the Protection of Human Rights and Fundamental Freedoms (adopted November 4, 1950, entered into force September 3, 1953),

Table A3.1 (*cont.*)

U.N.T.S. 213, at 221–70; as amended by Protocol Nos. 11 and 14, see E.T.S. No. 5, see https://rm.coe.int/1680063765 Statute of the Council of Europe, as amended (adopted May 5, 1949, entered into force August 3, 1949), U.N.T.S. 87, at 103–29. Rules of Court (adopted June 29, 2009, entered into force July 1, 2009). European Court of Human Rights. www.echr.coe.int/documents/d/echr/Library_2020_RoC_ENG.
European Free Trade Agreement Court (EFTAC)
Agreement between the EFTA States on the Establishment of a Surveillance Authority and a Court of Justice (adopted May 2, 1992, entered into force January 1, 1993; amended March 17, 1993), *Official Journal of the EU*, 1994 (L 344), at 3–13. Protocol 5 to the ESA/Court Agreement on the Statute of the EFTA Court (adopted May 2, 1992, entered into force January 1, 1993; amended August 10, 1996, March 25, 1999, December 8, 2010), *Official Journal of the EU*, 1994 (L 344), at 68–71. Rules of Procedure (adopted January 4 and February 1, 1994; amended August 22, 1996, September 20, 2007, November 10, 2010). https://eftacourt.int/the-court/rules-of-procedure/.
Inter-American Court of Human Rights (IACtHR)
American Convention on Human Rights (adopted November 22, 1969, entered into force July 18, 1978), U.N.T.S. 1144, at 143–212. Statute of the Inter-American Court on Human Rights, OAS Res 448 (IX-0/79), OAS Official Records OEA/Ser P/IX.0.2/80, Vol. 1, pp. 98–108. Rules of Procedure of the Inter-American Court on Human Rights (adopted August 9, 1980; amended January 18, 1991, September 20, 1996, November 25, 2000, December 4, 2004, January 31, 2009). San Jose: IACtHR. www.corteidh.or.cr/reglamento.cfm?lang=en#_ftn2.
International Criminal Court ICC
Rome Statute of the International Criminal Court (adopted July 17, 1998, entered into force July 1, 2002; amended November 30, 1999, May 8, 2000, January 17, 2001, January 16, 2002), U.N.T.S. 2187, at 90–158. Financial Regulations and Rules (adopted September 9, 2002; amended December 3, 2005, December 14, 2007, November 21, 2008) ICC-ASP/1/3 (Part. II-D). The Hague: ICC, 2002. www.icc-cpi.int/news/financial-regulations-and-rules.
International Court of Justice (ICJ)
Statute of the International Court of Justice (adopted June 26, 1945, entered into force October 24, 1945), UNCIO XV, at 355–64. Financial Regulations and Rules of the United Nations (adopted July 1, 2013). ST/SGB/2013/4. New York: UN, 2013. https://policy.un.org/policy-doc/29543.

Table A3.1 (*cont.*)

International Criminal Tribunal for Rwanda (ICTR)
Statute of the International Criminal Tribunal for Rwanda (adopted November 8, 1994; last amended December 16, 2009). UN DocS/Res955. New York: UN, 1994. https://unictr.irmct.org/sites/unictr.org/files/legal-library/100131_Statute_en_fr_0.pdf. Rules of Procedure and Evidence (adopted June 29, 1995, last amended May 13, 2015). Arusha: ICTR, 2015. http://unictr.unmict.org/sites/unictr.org/files/legal-library/150513-rpe-en-fr.pdf.
International Criminal Tribunal of the Former Yugoslavia (ICTY)
Statute of the International Criminal Tribunal for the former Yugoslavia (adopted May 25, 1993; last amended July 7, 2009), UN DocS/Res 827. New York: UN, 1993. www.icty.org/x/file/Legal%20Library/Statute/statute_sept09_en.pdf. Rules of Procedure and Evidence (adopted February 11, 1994, last amended July 10, 2015). The Hague: ICTY, 1994. www.icty.org/en/documents/rules-procedure-evidence.
International Tribunal for the Law of the Sea (ITLOS)
Statute of the International Tribunal for the Law of the Sea (Annex IV of UN Convention on the Law of the Sea) (adopted December 10, 1982, entered into force November 16, 1994), U.N.T.S. 1833, at 561–70. Financial Regulations and Rules (adopted June 15, 2004, entered into force January 1, 2005). SPLOS/120. New York: LOS Meeting of State Parties, 2004. www.itlos.org/fileadmin/itlos/documents/basic_texts/Financial.Regs.Rules.E.pdf. Rules of Procedure for Meetings of States Parties (adopted June 24, 2005), SPLOS/2/Rev.4. New York: LOS Meeting of State Parties, 2005. https://digitallibrary.un.org/record/542002/files/SPLOS_2_Rev.4-EN.pdf?ln=ru.
Mercosur Permanent Review Tribunal (PRT)
Olivos Protocol for the Settlement of Disputes in Mercosur (adopted on February 18, 2002; entered into force January 1, 2004), U.N.T.S. 2251, at 288–303. Additional Protocol to the Asunción Treaty on the institutional structure of Mercosur (adopted December 17, 1994; entered into force December 15, 1995), U.N.T.S. 2145, at 346–59. Secretaría del Tribunal Permanente de Revisión, Reglamentación del Artículo 35 de la Decisión, Resolución GMC N° 66/05. (Montevideo: Secretaría del Mercosur, 2005), pp: 88–93. www.tprmercosur.org/es/docum/adm/RES_66_05_es_Secretaria_TPR.pdf.
OHADA Common Court of Justice and Arbitration (CCJA)
Treaty on the Harmonisation of Business Law in Africa (adopted October 17, 1993). www.ohada.com/traite/10/treaty-on-the-harmonisation-of-business-law-in-africa.html.

Table A3.1 (*cont.*)

Treaty related to the Revisions to the Treaty on the Harmonisation of Business Law in Africa (adopted October 17, 2008). www.ohada.com/traite.html Rules of Procedure of the Common Court of Justice and Arbitration (adopted April 18, 1996). OHADA Official Journal No. 4 of November 1, 1997. www.ohada.com/textes-ohada/reglements-d-application.html
Southern African Development Community Tribunal (SADC T)
Treaty of the Southern African Development Community (adopted August 17, 1992, entered into force October 5, 1993). *International Legal Material* 32, no. 1 (1993): 116–35. Protocol on Tribunal in the Southern African Development Community (adopted August 7, 2000). www.sadc.int/sites/default/files/2021-08/Protocol_on_the_Tribunal_and_Rules_thereof2000.pdf. Rules of Procedure of the Southern African Development Community Tribunal (adopted August 7, 2000). www.sadc.int/sites/default/files/2021-08/Protocol_on_the_Tribunal_and_Rules_thereof2000.pdf.
West African Economic and Monetary Union Court of Justice (WAEMU CJ)
Revised Treaty on the West African Economic and Monetary Union (adopted January 10, 1994, entered into force August 1, 1994; amended January 29, 2003). www.uemoa.int/traite-modifie. Protocole Additionnel No. 1 relatif aux Organes de contrôle de l'UEMOA. www.uemoa.int/sites/default/files/bibliotheque/pages_-_protocole_additionnel_i.pdf. Acte additionnel n°10/96 du 10 mai 1996 de la Conférence des Chefs d'État et de Gouvernement portant Statuts de la Cour de Justice de l'UEMOA. https://courdejusticeuemoa.org/wp-content/uploads/2019/12/Statuts-CJ.pdf. Règlement n° 1/96/CM portant Règlement des procédures de la Cour de Justice de l'UEMOA. https://courdejusticeuemoa.org/wp-content/uploads/2019/12/R%C3%A8glement-de-proc%C3%A9dure-Cour-de-Justice.pdf.
World Trade Organization Appellate Body (WTO AB)
Marrakesh Agreement Establishing the World Trade Organization (adopted April 15, 1994; entered into force January 1, 1995), U.N.T.S. 1867–69. Understanding on Rules and Procedures Governing the Settlement of Disputes (Annex 2 to the Agreement Establishing the World Trade Organization) (adopted April 15, 1994; entered into force January 1, 1995), U.N.T.S. 1869, at 401–25. Establishment of the Appellate Body, decision of the Dispute Settlement Body (adopted February 10, 1995), WT/DSB/1. Working Procedures for Appellate Review (adopted August 16, 2010), WT/AB/WP/6.

Table A3.1 (*cont.*)

Rules of conduct for the understanding on rules and procedures governing the settlement of disputes (adopted December 11, 1996), WT/DSB/RC/1.
Financial Regulation of the WTO (adopted February 27, 2015). WT/L/156/Rev. 3.

Note: This table includes founding treaties and statutes that were used to code formal independence. Amendments to founding treaties and statutes are noted when relevant, if in force prior to 2015. Rules of procedure or regulations that were in force in 2015 are included above, if relevant for the coding. Earlier versions of rules of procedure (where relevant) were used for the coding but are not listed. English language texts were coded when available. French language texts listed above were coded by author. Spanish texts were coded by Spanish-speaking research assistants. Russian texts were coded by a Russian-speaking research assistant (although I list the text in English above). Secondary materials were used to code aspects of the Arab Investment Court, when Arabic-only texts could be identified. Founding treaties and statutes are listed first, followed by rules of procedure or other relevant regulations.

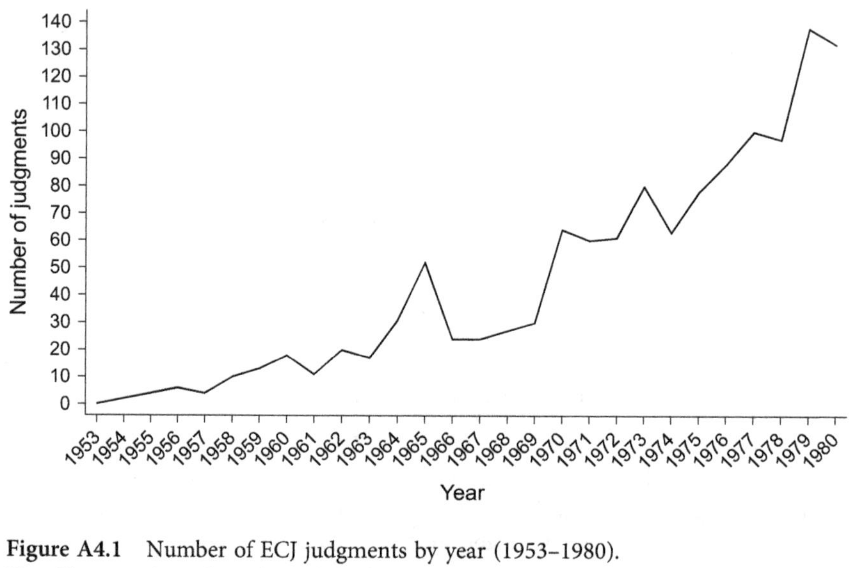

Figure A4.1 Number of ECJ judgments by year (1953–1980).

Note: Illustration by author. The total number of judgments from 1953 to 1967 is 236. The total for 1953–72 is 478.

Data source: ECJ. *Annual Report 1997: Synopsis of the Work of the Court of Justice and the Court of First Instance of the European Communities* (Luxembourg: ECJ, 1997): 183, accessed June 23, 2024. https://curia.europa.eu/jcms/upload/docs/application/pdf/2017-07/rapportannuel1997en.pdf.

Table A4.1 *Cross-tabulations of EACJ citation practices by deference (all cases)*

	Domestic references		International references	
Declared violation	No	Yes	No	Yes
No	29 (49.15)	30 (50.85)	31 (52.54)	28 (47.46)
Yes	7 (23.33)	23 (76.67)	10 (33.33)	20 (66.67)
	Fisher's Test p-value: 0.023** χ^2 p-value: 0.017**		Fisher's Test p-value: 0.116 χ^2 p-value: 0.083*	
Consequential order				
No	34 (45.95)	40 (54.05)	37 (50.00)	37 (50.00)
Yes	2 (14.29)	12 (85.71)	3 (21.43)	11 (78.57)
	Fisher's Test p-value: 0.037** χ^2 p-value: 0.019**		Fisher's Test p-value: 0.077* χ^2 p-value: 0.042**	
Additional remedy				
No	33 (47.83)	36 (52.17)	35 (50.72)	34 (49.28)
Yes	3 (15.79)	16 (84.21)	5 (26.32)	14 (73.68)
	Fisher's Test p-value: 0.017** χ^2 p-value: 0.008***		Fisher's Test p-value: 0.072* χ^2 p-value: 0.054**	

Note: N = 88. This excludes cases where jurisdiction is affirmed or the case is remanded to the FI. In each cross-tabulation, the first number is the frequency and the second number (in parentheses) is the row percentage.

Table A4.2 *Annual percent of EACJ's Facebook posts with at least one public legitimation narrative (people-centered or political purpose)*

At least one narrative is present	2013	2014	2015	2016	2017	2018	2019	2020
No	98.1	93.0	93.5	100	92.3	61.0	66.7	82.3
Yes	1.9	7.0	6.5	0	7.7	39.0	33.3	17.7
N =	52	143	46	51	52	64	24	96

Table A5.1 *Cross-tabulations of CCJ's deference by support network (private or supranational actor)*

	Participation of private or supranational actor	
Applicant wins, all decisions (N = 18)	No	Yes
No (deferred)	3 (37.50)	6 (60.00)
Yes	5 (62.50)	4 (40.00)
	Fisher's Test p-value: 0.637 χ^2 p-value: 0.341	
Violation declared (merits only, N = 13)		
No (deferred)	0 (0)	5 (55.56)
Yes	5 (100.00)	4 (44.44)
	Fisher's Test p-value: 0.015** χ^2 p-value: 0.086*	
Consequential order (merits only, N = 9)		
No (deferred)	4 (80.00)	3 (75.00)
Yes	1 (20.00)	1 (25.00)
	Fisher's Test p-value: 1.000 χ^2 p-value: 0.858	
Additional remedy (merits only, N = 9)		
No (deferred)	3 (60.00)	2 (50.00)
Yes	2 (40.00)	2 (50.00)
	Fisher's Test p-value: 1.000 χ^2 p-value: 0.764	

Note: In each cross-tabulation, the first number is the frequency and the second number (in parentheses) is the column percentage.

Table A5.2 *Cross-tabulation of CCJ citation practices by deference, including remedies (merits only)*

	Domestic references		International references	
Declared violation	No	Yes	No	Yes
No (defer)	2 (40.00)	3 (60.00)	1 (20.00)	4 (80.00)
Yes	3 (33.33)	6 (66.67)	0 (0)	9 (100.00)
	Fisher's Test p-value: 1.000 χ^2 p-value: 0.804		Fisher's Test p-value: 0.357 χ^2 p-value: 0.138	

Table A5.2 (*cont.*)

	Domestic references		International references	
Declared violation	No	Yes	No	Yes
Consequential order				
No (defer)	4 (33.33)	8 (66.67)	1 (8.33)	11 (91.67)
Yes	1 (50.00)	1 (50.00)	0 (0)	2 (100.00)
	Fisher's Test p-value: 1.000 χ^2 p-value: 0.655		Fisher's Test p-value: 1.000 χ^2 p-value: 0.571	
Additional remedy				
No (defer)	4 (40.00)	6 (60.00)	1 (10.00)	9 (90.00)
Yes	1 (25.00)	3 (75.00)	0 (0)	4 (100.00)
	Fisher's Test p-value: 1.000 χ^2 p-value: 0.590		Fisher's Test p-value: 1.000 χ^2 p-value: 0.402	

Note: N = 14. In each cross-tabulation, the first number is the frequency and the second number (in parentheses) is the row percentage.

Table A6.1 *Cross-tabulation of ACtHPR's unanimous decisions by deference*

	Unanimous decision	
Declared violation	No	Yes
No (defer)	3 (33.33)	6 (66.67)
Yes	13 (30.95)	29 (69.05)
	Fisher's Test p-value: 1.000 χ^2 p-value: 0.889	
Consequential order		
No (defer)	11 (29.73)	26 (70.27)
Yes	5 (35.71)	9 (64.29)
	Fisher's Test p-value: 0.742 χ^2 p-value: 0.683	

Note: In each cross-tabulation, the first number is the frequency and the second number (in parentheses) is the row percentage.

Table A6.2 *Annual percent of ACtHPR's Facebook posts with at least one public legitimation narrative (people-centered or political purpose)*

At least one narrative is present	2012	2013	2014	2015	2016	2017	2018	2019	2020
No	90	84.8	89.3	100	89.3	97.3	92.8	94.0	98.8
Yes	10	15.3	10.7	0	10.7	2.7	7.2	6.0	1.2
$N =$	40	59	28	16	112	185	222	151	84

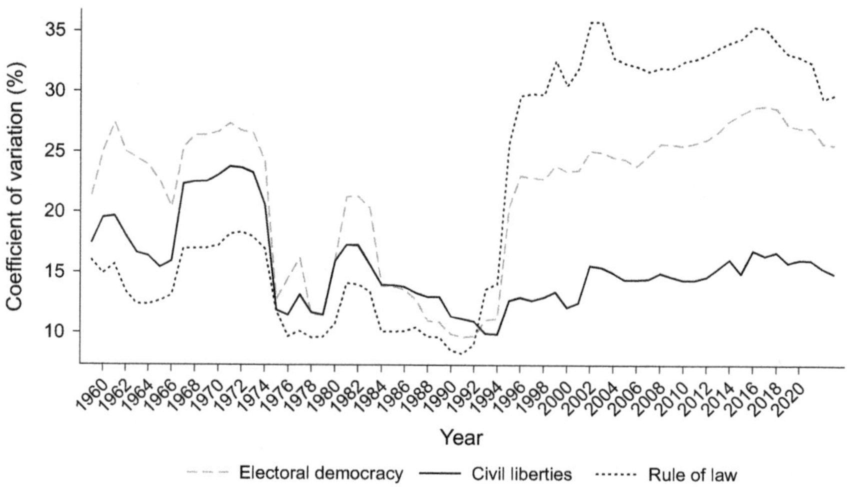

Figure A7.1 Council of Europe political fragmentation (1959–2023).
Note: Calculations and illustration by author.
Data source: Coppedge et al., "V-Dem [Country-Year] Dataset V12."

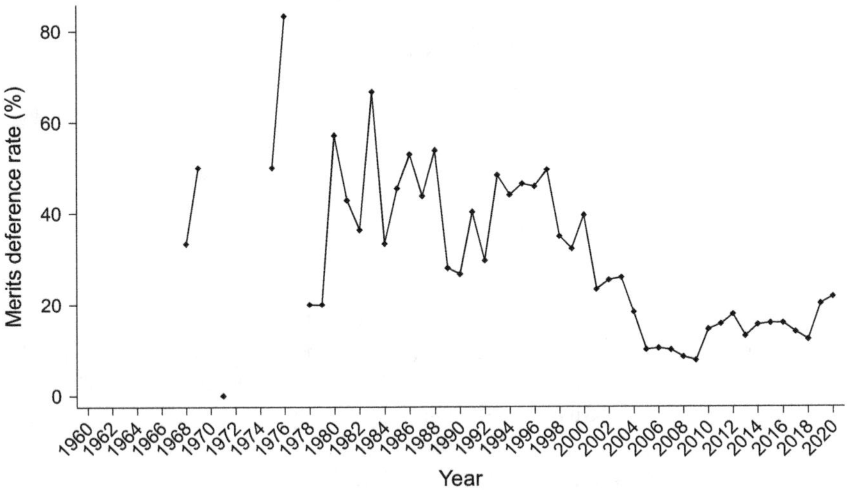

Figure A7.2 ECtHR merits deference rate by year (1960–2020).
Note: Illustration by author. Data based on all judgments by a Chamber, Grand Chamber, Plenary Court (before 1998) or a committee (after 2010). Line gaps are due to the absence of merits judgments in relevant year.
Acknowledgment: I thank Øyvind Stiansen for assistance with these data.
Data source: Stiansen, Øyvind, and Erik Voeten, "ECtHR Judgments." Georgetown/PluriCourts European Court of Human Rights Database (2019). Harvard Dataverse. https://doi.org/10.7910/DVN/OBYUO5.

REFERENCES

Abebe, Adem Kassie. "Taming Regressive Constitutional Amendments: The African Court as a Continental (Super) Constitutional Court." *International Journal of Constitutional Law* 17, no. 1 (2019): 89–117.

ACE Project. "Comparative Data: Independent Candidates." Accessed June 25, 2024. http://aceproject.org/epic-en/CDMap?question=PC008&f=e.

ACmHPR. *Rules of Procedure of the ACmHPR*. Banjul: ACmHPR, 2020. https://achpr.au.int/sites/default/files/files/2021-04/rulesofprocedure2020eng1.pdf.

ACtHPR. *2010 Activity Report of the African Court on Human and Peoples' Rights*. Addis Ababa: ACtHPR, 2011. www.african-court.org/wpafc/activity-report/.

2016–2020 Strategic and Implementation Plan. Arusha: ACtHPR, 2016.

2021–2025 Strategic Plan: Deepening Trust in the African Court by Enhancing Its Efficiency and Effectiveness. Arusha: ACtHPR, 2021. www.african-court.org/wpafc/african-court-on-human-and-peoples-rights-strategic-plan-2021-2025/.

Activities Report for the Court for 2007. Addis Ababa: ACtHPR, 2008. www.african-court.org/wpafc/activity-report/.

Activity Report of the African Court for the Year 2013. Addis Ababa: ACtHPR, 2014. www.african-court.org/wpafc/activity-report/.

Activity Report of the African Court on Human and Peoples' Rights: 1 January – 31 December 2020. Addis Ababa: ACtHPR, 2021. www.african-court.org/wpafc/activity-report/.

"AFCHPR Cases: Statistics." Accessed June 25, 2024. www.african-court.org/cpmt/statistic.

"African Court Successfully Concludes Three Day Sensitization Mission to Cape Verde." Press release. December 18, 2017. www.african-court.org/wpafc/african-court-successfully-concludes-three-day-sensitisation-mission-to-cape-verde/.

"Declarations." Accessed July 10, 2024. www.african-court.org/wpafc/declarations/.

"Legal Aid Policy 2016." Accessed August 20, 2024. www.african-court.org/wpafc/wp-content/uploads/2020/12/English_version_Legal_Aid_Policy_From_2016.pdf.

Report of the 2012 Activities of the African Court on Human and Peoples' Rights. Addis Ababa: ACtHPR, 2013. www.african-court.org/wpafc/activity-report/.

Report of the African Court on Human and Peoples' Rights to the Budget for Year 2009. Addis Ababa: ACtHPR, 2009. www.african-court.org/wpafc/activity-report/.

Report of the African Court on Human and Peoples' Rights: 2011. Addis Ababa: ACtHPR, 2012. www.african-court.org/wpafc/activity-report/.

Rules of Court. Arusha: ACtHPR, 2010. www.african-court.org/en/images/Basic % 20Documents/Final_Rules_of_Court_for_Publication_after_Harmonization_-_Final__English_7_sept_1_.pdf.

"Speeches." Accessed August 30, 2024. www.african-court.org/wpafc/category/speeches/.

"Statute on the Establishment of Legal Aid Fund." Accessed August 20, 2024. www.african-court.org/wpafc/wp-content/uploads/2020/10/22-STATUTE-ON-THE-ESTABLISHMENT-OF-LEGAL-AID-FUND.pdf.

Strategic Plan 2011–2014. Arusha: ACtHPR, 2011.

Adan, Jibril. "EALA Nominees Contest Ruling." *The East African Standard,* December 12, 2006.

Adjei, William Edward. "Re-Assessment of 'Claw-Back' Clauses in the Enforcement of Human and Peoples' Rights in Africa." *Journal of Legal Studies* 24, no. 38 (2019): 1–22.

Adjolohoun, Sègnonna Horace. "A Crisis of Design and Judicial Practice? Curbing State Disengagement from the African Court on Human and Peoples' Rights." *African Human Rights Law Journal* 20, no. 1 (2020): 1–40.

African Court Coalition. "Background & Structure." Accessed June 25, 2024. www.africancourtcoalition.org/background-structure/.

Akinkugbe, Olabisi D. "Houngue Éric Noudehouenou v. Republic of Benin." *American Journal of International Law* 115, no. 2 (2021): 281–87.

Akuffo, Sophia. "Report of the ACtHPR on the Relevant Aspects Regarding the Judiciary in the Protection of Human Rights in Africa." Speech at the First Summit of Constitutional, Regional and Supreme Court Justices. Mexico City. November 8–9, 2012.

Al Hassan, Abdullah, Mary Burfisher, Julian Chow, Ding Ding, Fabia Di Vittorio, Dmitriy Kovtun, Arnold McIntyre, *et al.* "Is the Whole Greater Than the Sum of Its Parts? Strengthening Caribbean Regional Integration." In *IMF Working Paper 20/8*, 2020.

Alter, Karen J. "Agents or Trustees? International Courts in Their Political Context." *European Journal of International Relations* 14, no. 1 (2008): 33–63.

Establishing the Supremacy of European Law: The Making of an International Rule of Law in Europe. Oxford: Oxford University Press, 2001.

"The Global Spread of European Style International Courts." *West European Politics* 35, no. 1 (2012): 135–54.

"The Multiple Roles of International Courts and Tribunals: Enforcement, Dispute Settlement, Constitutional and Administrative Review." In *Interdisciplinary Perspectives on International Law and International Relations*, edited by Jeffrey Dunoff and Mark Pollack, 345–70. Cambridge: Cambridge University Press, 2013.

The New Terrain of International Law: Courts, Politics, Rights. Princeton: Princeton University Press, 2014.

Alter, Karen J., James T. Gathii, and Laurence R. Helfer. "Backlash Against International Courts in West, East and Southern Africa: Causes and Consequences." *European Journal of International Law* 27, no. 2 (2016): 293–328.

Alter, Karen J., and Laurence Helfer. "Nature or Nurture? Judicial Lawmaking in the European Court of Justice and the Andean Tribunal of Justice." *International Organization* 64, no. 4 (2010): 563–92.

Alvarez, José. "What Are International Judges For? The Main Functions of International Adjudication." In *The Oxford Handbook of International Adjudication*, edited by Cesare Romano, Karen Alter and Yuval Shany, 159–78. Oxford: Oxford University Press, 2014.

Anderson, Winston. "Free Movement Within CARICOM: Deconstructing the Myrie vs Barbados." Speech at OECS Bar Association Meeting. St George's, Grenada. December 7, 2013.

Anghie, Antony. *Imperialism, Sovereignty and the Making of International Law.* Cambridge: Cambridge University Press, 2007.

"Rethinking International Law: A TWAIL Retrospective." *European Journal of International Law* 34, no. 1 (2023): 7–112.

Antoine, Rose-Marie B. *Commonwealth Caribbean Law and Legal Systems.* 2nd ed. New York: Routledge-Cavendish, 2008.

"Waiting to Exhale: Commonwealth Caribbean Law and Legal Systems." *Nova Law Review* 29, no. 2 (2005): 142.

Arnardóttir, Oddný Mjöll. "The 'Procedural Turn' Under the European Convention on Human Rights and Presumptions of Convention Compliance." *International Journal of Constitutional Law* 15, no. 1 (2017): 9–35.

Arusha Times. "Wagging Tongues Over EALA Ruling 'Is Contempt of Court'." December 11, 2006. [Freedom House access date: We can put August 25, 2024.]

Axelrod, Robert, and Robert O. Keohane. "Achieving Cooperation Under Anarchy: Strategies and Institutions." *World Politics* 38, no. 1 (1985): 226–54.

Baetens, Freya, ed. *Legitimacy of Unseen Actors in International Adjudication.* Cambridge: Cambridge University Press, 2019.

Bahri, Amrita. "Appellate Body Held Hostage: Is Judicial Activism at Fair Trial?" *Journal of World Trade* 53, no. 2 (2019): 293–315.

Bailliet, Cecilia. "Measuring Compliance with the Inter-American Court of Human Rights: The Ongoing Challenge of Judicial Independence in Latin America." *Nordic Journal of Human Rights* 31, no. 4 (2013): 477–95.

Baricako, Germain. "The African Charter and African Commission on Human and Peoples' Rights." In *The African Charter on Human and Peoples' Rights: The System in Practice 1986–2006*, edited by Malcolm Evans and Rachel Murray, 1–19. Cambridge: Cambridge University Press, 2008.

Barnett, Michael N., and Martha Finnemore. *Rules for the World: International Organizations in Global Politics.* Ithaca: Cornell University Press, 2004.

Beach, Derek, and Rasmus Brun Pedersen. *Causal Case Study Methods: Foundations and Guidelines for Comparing, Matching, and Tracing.* Ann Arbor: University of Michigan Press, 2016.

Behn, Daniel, Tarald Laudal Berge, and Malcolm Langford. "Poor States or Poor Governance? Explaining Outcomes in Investment Treaty Arbitration." *Northwestern Journal of International Law & Business* 38, no. 3 (2018): 333–89.

Bekker, Gina. "The African Court on Human and Peoples' Rights: Safeguarding the Interests of African States." *Journal of African Law* 51, no. 1 (2007): 151–72.

Benvenisti, Eyal, and George W. Downs. "Prospects for the Increased Independence of International Tribunals." *German Law Journal* 12, no. 5 (2011): 1057–82.

Berry, David S. *Caribbean Integration Law.* Oxford: Oxford University Press, 2014.

"The Effect of the Original Jurisdiction of the Caribbean Court of Justice on Regional Integration and National Law." In *The Oxford Handbook of Caribbean Constitutions*, edited by Richard Albert, Derek O'Brien and Se-shauna Wheatle, 529–54. Oxford: Oxford University Press, 2020.

"The Original Jurisdiction Jurisprudence of the Caribbean Court of Justice: Promoting Regional Integration." *Social and Economic Studies* 61, no. 2 (2012): 27–49.

Birdsong, Leonard. "The Formation of the Caribbean Court of Justice: The Sunset of British Colonial Rule in the English Speaking Caribbean." *University of Miami Inter-American Law Review* 36, no. 2/3 (2005): 197–227.

Blatter, Joachim, and Markus Haverland. *Designing Case Studies Explanatory Approaches in Small-N Research.* Basingstoke, UK: Palgrave Macmillan, 2012.

Blauberger, Michael, Anita Heindlmaier, Dion Kramer, Dorte Sindbjerg Martinsen, Jessica Sampson Thierry, Angelika Schenk, and Benjamin Werner. "ECJ Judges Read the Morning Papers. Explaining the Turnaround of European Citizenship Jurisprudence." *Journal of European Public Policy* 25, no. 10 (2018): 1422–41.

Bourdieu, Pierre. "The Force of Law: Toward a Sociology of the Juridical Field." *Hastings Law Journal* 38, no. 5 (1987): 805–13.

Bratton, Michael, and E. Gyimah-Boadi. "Do Trustworthy Institutions Matter for Development? Corruption, Trust, and Government Performance in Africa." *Afrobarometer* Dispatch No. 112 (2016): 1–17. Accessed August 30, 2024. www.afrobarometer.org/wp-content/uploads/migrated/files/publications/Dispatches/ab_r6_dispatchno112_trustworthy_institutions_and_development_in_africa.pdf.

Brems, Eva, and Laurens Lavrysen. "Procedural Justice in Human Rights Adjudication: The European Court of Human Rights." *Human Rights Quarterly* 35, no. 1 (2013): 177–200.

Brinks, Daniel. "Judicial Reform and Independence in Brazil and Argentina: The Beginning of a New Millennium?" *Texas International Law Journal* 40, no. 3 (2005): 595–622.

Brown, Chester. *A Common Law of International Adjudication*. Oxford: Oxford University Press, 2007.

Buchanan, Allen, and Robert Keohane. "The Legitimacy of Global Governance Institutions." *Ethics and International Affairs* 20, no. 4 (2006): 405–37.

Burihabwa, Ntagahoraho Z., and Devon E. A. Curtis. "Postwar Statebuilding in Burundi: Ruling Party Elites and Illiberal Peace." *International Affairs* 97, no. 4 (2021): 1221–38.

Burley, Anne-Marie, and Walter Mattli. "Europe Before the Court: A Political Theory of Legal Integration." *International Organization* 47, no. 1 (1993): 41–76.

Business Ghana. "African Court Rejuvenated for the Next 10 Years." November 23, 2016. www.businessghana.com/site/news/business/138199/African-Court-rejuvenated-for-the-next-10-yrs.

Byron, Dennis. "Keynote Speech." Speech at CCJ International Law Moot 2018 Award Ceremony. Port of Spain. March 9, 2018.

Cabatingan, Lee. "Time and Transcendence: Narrating Higher Authority at the Caribbean Court of Justice." *Law & Society Review* 50, no. 3 (2016): 674–702.

Cali, Başak, Anne Koch, and Nicola Bruch. "The Legitimacy of Human Rights Courts: A Grounded Interpretivist Analysis of the European Court of Human Rights." *Human Rights Quarterly* 35, no. 4 (2013): 955–84.

CARICOM. *Report on the Appraisal of the State of the Caricom Single Market*. Georgetown: CARICOM Secretariat, 2009.

Revised Agreement Establishing the Caribbean Court of Justice Trust Fund. 2004. Accessed June 25, 2024. https://ccj.org/wp-content/uploads/2021/02/ccj_rev_trustfund.pdf.

Carrubba, Clifford. "A Model of the Endogenous Development of Judicial Institutions in Federal and International Systems." *Journal of Politics* 71, no. 1 (2009): 55–69.

Carrubba, Clifford J., Matthew Gabel, and Charles Hankla. "Judicial Behavior Under Political Constraints: Evidence from the European Court of Justice." *American Political Science Review* 102, no. 4 (2008): 435–52.

Carrubba, Clifford J., and Matthew J. Gabel. *International Courts and the Performance of International Agreements: A General Theory with Evidence from the European Union.* Cambridge: Cambridge University Press, 2014.

Cartier, Stéphanie, and Cristina Hoss. "The Role of Registries and Legal Secretariats in International Judicial Institutions." In *The Oxford Handbook of International Adjudication*, edited by Cesare Romano, Karen J. Alter and Yuval Shany, 712–33. Oxford: Oxford University Press, 2014.

Caserta, Salvatore. *International Courts in Latin America and the Caribbean: Foundations and Authority.* Oxford: Oxford University Press, 2020.

Caserta, Salvatore, and Mikael Rask Madsen. "Between Community Law and Common Law: The Rise of the Caribbean Court of Justice at the Intersection of Regional Integration and Post-Colonial Legacies." *Law and Contemporary Problems* 79, no. 1 (2016): 88–115.

"Tomlinson v. Belize; Tomlinson v. Trinidad and Tobago." *American Journal of International Law* 110, no. 3 (2016): 533–40.

Castanha, Tony. *The Myth of Indigenous Caribbean Extinction: Continuity and Reclamation in Borikén (Puerto Rico).* New York: Palgrave Macmillan, 2011.

CCJ. "Annual CCJ International Law Moot." Accessed June 25, 2024. https://ccj.org/about-the-ccj/annual-ccj-international-law-moot/.

Annual Report 2005–2006. Port of Spain: CCJ, 2006. Accessed June 25, 2024. https://ccj.org/publications/annual-reports/.

Annual Report 2006–2007. Port of Spain: CCJ, 2007.

Annual Report 2007–2008. Port of Spain: CCJ, 2008.

Annual Report 2009–2010. Port of Spain: CCJ, 2010.

Annual Report 2011–2013. Port of Spain: CCJ, 2014.

Annual Report 2015–2016. Port of Spain: CCJ, 2016.

Annual Report 2017–2018. Port of Spain: CCJ, 2018.

Annual Report 2018–2019. Port of Spain: CCJ, 2019.

"Annual Reports." Accessed June 25, 2024. https://ccj.org/publications/annual-reports/.

Original Jurisdiction Rules. Port of Spain: CCJ, 2006.

"Papers and Speeches." Accessed June 25, 2024. https://ccj.org/papers-main/.

Strategic Plan 2013–2017: Responsive, Innovative, Inspirational. Port of Spain: CCJ, 2012. Accessed June 25, 2024. https://ccj.org/about-the-ccj/the-ccj-strategic-plan-2013-2017/.

Strategic Plan 2019–2024: Unlocking Potential, Strengthening Caribbean Justice. Port of Spain: CCJ, 2019. Accessed June 25, 2024. https://ccj.org/about-the-ccj/ccj-strategic-plan/.

"Understanding the Referral Process." Accessed June 25, 2024. https://ccj.org/resources/understanding-the-referral-process/?highlight=preliminary.

CCJ Academy for Law. "About Us." Accessed August 26, 2024. https://ccjacademy.org/about-us/.

Chapman, Terrence L. "Audience Beliefs and International Organization Legitimacy." *International Organization* 63, no. 4 (2009): 733–64.

Chaudoin, Stephen. "How Contestation Moderates the Effects of International Institutions: The International Criminal Court and Kenya." *Journal of Politics* 78, no. 2 (2016): 557–71.

Chavez, Rebecca Bill. *The Rule of Law in Nascent Democracies: Judicial Politics in Argentina.* Stanford: Stanford University Press, 2004.

Checkel, Jeffrey T. "Why Comply? Social Learning and European Identity Change." *International Organization* 55, no. 3 (2001): 553.

Chenwi, Lilian. "The Advisory Proceedings of the African Court on Human and Peoples' Rights." *Nordic Journal of Human Rights* 38, no. 1 (2020): 61–77.

"Exhaustion of Local Remedies Rule in the Jurisprudence of the African Court on Human and Peoples' Rights." *Human Rights Quarterly* 41, no. 2 (2019): 374–98.

Cheyne, Ilona. "Deference and the Use of the Public Policy Exception in International Courts and Tribunals." In *Deference in International Courts and Tribunals: Standard of Review and Margin of Appreciation*, edited by Lukasz Gruszczynski and Wouter Werner, 38–57. Oxford: Oxford University Press, 2014.

CHOG. "Communiqué of the Eighth Meeting of the Conference of Heads of Government of the Caribbean Community, June 29 – July 3, 1987, Castries, Saint Lucia." CARICOM, July 4, 1987. Accessed August 25, 2024. https://caricom.org/communique-of-the-eighth-meeting-of-the-conference-of-heads-of-government-of-the-caribbean-community-29-june-3-july-1987-castries-saint-lucia/.

"Communiqué Issued at the Conclusion of the Nineteenth Meeting of the Conference of Heads of Government of the Caribbean Community, June 30 – July 4, 1998, Castries, Saint Lucia." CARICOM, July 5, 1998. Accessed August 25, 2024. https://caricom.org/communique-issued-at-the-conclusion-of-the-the-nineteenth-meeting-of-the-conference-of-heads-of-government-of-the-caribbean-community-30-june-4-july-1998-castries-saint-lucia/.

"Communiqué Issued at the Conclusion of the Tenth Meeting of the Conference of Heads of Government of the Caribbean Community, July 3 –7, 1989, Grande Anse, Grenada." CARICOM, July 8, 1989. Accessed August 25, 2024. https://caricom.org/communique-issued-at-the-conclusion-of-the-tenth-meeting-of-the-conference-of-heads-of-government-of-the-caribbean-community-3-7-july-1989-grand-anse-grenada/.

"Expansion of Categories of Skilled Community Nationals. Ins/Hgc/2019/30/ Dec.5(C)." In *Thirteen Inter-Sessional Meeting*. Basseterre, St. Kitts and Nevis: CARICOM, February 26–27, 2019. Accessed August 25, 2024. https://caricom.org/wp-content/uploads/DECISIONS-30-IS-HGC-FEB-2019.pdf.

"Grand Anse Declaration and Work Programme for the Advancement of the Integration Movement, July 7, 1989, Grande Anse, Grenada." CARICOM, July 31, 1989. Accessed June 25, 2024. https://caricom.org/grand-anse-declaration-and-work-programme-for-the-advancement-of-the-integration-movement-july-1989-grand-anse-grenada/.

Cichowski, Rachel A. *The European Court and Civil Society: Litigation, Mobilization and Governance.* Cambridge: Cambridge University Press, 2007.

Congressional Research Service. *The World Trade Organization's Appellate Body: Key Disputes and Controversies, R46852.* 2021. Accessed August 24, 2024. https://crsreports.congress.gov/.

Coppedge, Michael, John Gerring, Carl Henrik Knutsen, Staffan I. Lindberg, Jan Teorell, Nazifa Alizada, Nazifa Altman, *et al.* "V-Dem [Country-Year] Dataset V12." Varieties of Democracy (V-Dem) Project, 2022. Accessed August 25, 2024. www.v-dem.net/data/dataset-archive/.

Coppedge, Michael, John Gerring, Carl Henrik Knutsen, Staffan I. Lindberg, Jan Teorell, David Altman, Michael Bernhard, *et al.* "V-Dem Codebook V12." Varieties of Democracy (V-Dem) Project, 2022. Accessed August 25, 2024. www.v-dem.net/static/website/img/refs/codebookv12.pdf.

Corley, Pamela C., and Justin Wedeking. "The (Dis)Advantage of Certainty: The Importance of Certainty in Language." *Law & Society Review* 48, no. 1 (2014): 35–62.

Couso, Javier, Alexandra Huneeus, and Rachel Sieder, eds. *Cultures of Legality: Judicialization and Political Activism in Latin America.* Cambridge: Cambridge University Press, 2010.

Dai, Xinyuan. "Why Comply? The Domestic Constituency Mechanisms." *International Organization* 59, no. 2 (2005): 363–98.

Daly, Tom Gerald, and Micha Wiebusch. "The African Court on Human and Peoples' Rights: Mapping Resistance Against a Young Court." *International Journal of Law in Context* 14, no. 2 (2018): 294–313.

Dancy, Geoff, Yvonne Marie Dutton, Tessa Alleblas, and Eamon Aloyo. "What Determines Perceptions of Bias Toward the International Criminal Court? Evidence from Kenya." *Journal of Conflict Resolution* 64, no. 7–8 (2019): 1443–69.

Davies, Gareth. "Activism Relocated: The Self-Restraint of the European Court of Justice in Its National Context." *Journal of European Public Policy* 19, no. 1 (2012): 76–91.

Deitelhoff, Nicole. "The Discursive Process of Legalization: Charting Islands of Persuasion in the ICC Case." *International Organization* 63, no. 1 (2009): 33–65.

Dellmuth, Lisa, and Jonas Tallberg. *Legitimacy Politics: Elite Communication and Public Opinion in Global Governance*. Cambridge: Cambridge University Press, 2023.

"The Social Legitimacy of International Organisations: Interest Representation, Institutional Performance, and Confidence Extrapolation in the United Nations." *Review of International Studies* 41, no. 3 (2015): 451–75.

De Mestral, Armand. "The Constitutional Functions of the Caribbean Court of Justice." *McGill Journal of Dispute Resolution* 1, no. 2 (2015): 43–75.

Derlén, Mattias, and Johan Lindholm. "Characteristics of Precedent: The Case Law of the European Court of Justice in Three Dimensions." *German Law Journal* 16, no. 5 (2015): 1073–98.

De Vries, Catherine E., Sara B. Hobolt, and Stefanie Walter. "Politicizing International Cooperation: The Mass Public, Political Entrepreneurs, and Political Opportunity Structures." *International Organization* 75, no. 2 (2021): 306–32.

De Witte, Bruno, Elise Muir, and Mark Dawson. *Judicial Activism at the European Court of Justice*. Cheltenham: Edward Elgar, 2013.

Deya, Donald. "Why Undermining EA Court Is Sheer Folly." *The East African*, December 12, 2006.

Dezalay, Yves. *Dealing in Virtue: International Commercial Arbitration and the Construction of a Transnational Legal Order*. Chicago: University of Chicago Press, 1996.

Dingwerth, Klaus, and Antonia Witt. "Legitimation Contests: A Theoretical Framework." In *International Organizations Under Pressure: Legitimating Global Governance in Challenging Times*, edited by Klaus Dingwerth, Antonia Witt, Ina Lehmann, Ellen Reichel, and Tobias Weise, 29–61. Oxford: Oxford University Press, 2019.

Dingwerth, Klaus, Antonia Witt, Ina Lehmann, Ellen Reichel, and Tobias Weise, eds. *International Organizations Under Pressure: Legitimating Global Governance in Challenging Times*. Oxford: Oxford University Press, 2019.

Donnelly, Jack. "International Human Rights: A Regime Analysis." *International Organization* 40, no. 3 (1986): 599–642.

Dothan, Shai. "Judicial Tactics in the European Court of Human Rights." *Chicago Journal of International Law* 12, no. 1 (2011): 115–42.

Dunham, Jennifer, Bret Nelson, and Elen Aghekyan, "Harsh Laws and Violence Drive Global Decline: Freedom of the Press 2015." Washington D.C.: Freedom House, 2015. Accessed April 4, 2022. https://freedomhouse.org/report/freedom-press/2015/harsh-laws-and-violence-drive-global-decline.

Dunoff, Jeffrey L., and Mark A. Pollack. "The Judicial Trilemma." *American Journal of International Law* 111, no. 2 (2017): 225–76.

EAC. *Annual Report: Financial Year 2016/2017*. Arusha: EAC Secretariat, 2018.

Annual Report: Financial Year 2017/2018. Arusha: EAC Secretariat, 2019.

Bills Supplement. No. 9 of November 18, 2016. Arusha: EAC, 2016. Accessed June 18, 2024. www.eala.org/uploads/EACJ_bill2.pdf.

EAC Development Strategy: 2006–2010. Arusha: EAC, 2006. Accessed June 18, 2024. http://repository.eac.int/bitstream/handle/11671/214/3rd-EAC-Development-Strategy.pdf?sequence=1&isAllowed=y.

EACJ Rules of Procedure 2004. Arusha: EAC, 2004.

EACJ Rules of Procedure 2013. Legal Notices Supplement No. 1 to the East African Community Gazette No. 7. Arusha: EAC, 2013.

Joint Communiqué of the Eighth Summit of EAC Heads of State, November 30, 2006. Arusha: EAC, 2006.

EACJ. *Court Manual: A Practical Guide to the Law and Practice of the East African Court of Justice*. Arusha: EACJ, 2020. Accessed August 18, 2024. www.eacj.org/wp-content/uploads/2023/02/EACJ-Manual.pdf.

"EACJ President Calls Upon the Stakeholders to Strengthen Their Cooperation & Relationship with the Court." Press release. June 21, 2018.

"EACJ to Develop Five-Year Strategic Plan to Guide Its Operations." Press release. February 23, 2010.

"EACJ Workshop for Judges of the National Courts & Civil Society Workshop Officially Open in Kigali, Rwanda." Press release. September 24, 2014.

"President of the Court Attends the Conference on Requirements for an Independent and Effective Judiciary in Nairobi." Press release. February 17, 2016.

Strategic Plan: 2010–2015. Arusha: EACJ, 2010.

Strategic Plan: 2018–2023. Arusha: EACJ, 2018. Accessed June 18, 2024. www.eacj.org/?page_id=1359.

ECJ. *Annual Report 1997: Synopsis of the Work of the Court of Justice and the Court of First Instance of the European Communities*. Luxembourg: ECJ, 1997. Accessed June 23, 2024. https://curia.europa.eu/jcms/upload/docs/application/pdf/2017-07/rapportannuel1997en.pdf.

Ecker-Ehrhardt, Matthias. "Self-Legitimation in the Face of Politicization: Why International Organizations Centralized Public Communication." *Review of International Organizations* 13, no. 4 (2018): 519–46.

ECtHR. "Reports." Accessed August 4, 2024. www.echr.coe.int/annual-reports.

Survey: Forty Years of Activity 1959–1998. Strasbourg: Council of Europe, 1998. Accessed January 27, 2022. www.echr.coe.int/Documents/Survey_19591998_BIL.pdf.

Efrat, Asif, and Abraham L. Newman. "Deciding to Defer: The Importance of Fairness in Resolving Transnational Jurisdictional Conflicts." *International Organization* 70, no. 2 (2016): 409–41.

Elklit, Jørgen. "The Structure and Performance of African Electoral Commissions." In *Oxford Research Encyclopedia of Politics*. Oxford: Oxford University Press, 2019. Accessed August 25, 2024. https://doi.org/10.1093/acrefore/9780190228637.013.987

Elsig, Manfred, and Mark Pollack. "Agents, Trustees, and International Courts: The Politics of Judicial Appointment at the World Trade Organization." *European Journal of International Relations* 20, no. 2 (2014): 391–415.

Epp, Charles. *The Rights Revolution: Lawyers, Activists, and Supreme Courts in Comparative Perspective*. Chicago: University Press of Chicago, 1998.

Epstein, Lee, and Jack Knight. *The Choices Justices Make*. Washington, DC: Congressional Quarterly Press, 1998.

Facebook. "Page transparency." Accessed November 17, 2023. www.facebook.com/afchpr/about_profile_transparency.

"Page Transparency." Accessed November 17, 2023. www.facebook.com/yourCCj/about_profile_transparency.

"Page Transparency." Accessed November 14, 2023. www.facebook.com/eacjcourt/about_profile_transparency.

Fahner, Johannes Hendrik. *Judicial Deference in International Adjudication: A Comparative Analysis. Studies in International Law*. Oxford: Hart Publishing, 2020.

"*In Dubio Mitius*: Advancing Clarity and Modesty in Treaty Interpretation." *European Journal of International Law* 32, no. 3 (2021): 835–62.

Feld, Lars P., and Stefan Voigt. "Economic Growth and Judicial Independence: Cross-Country Evidence Using a New Set of Indicators." *European Journal of Political Economy* 19, no. 3 (2003): 497–527.

Fenrich, Jeanmarie, Paolo Galizzi, and Tracy E. Higgins, eds. *The Future of African Customary Law*. Cambridge: Cambridge University Press, 2011.

Ferejohn, John A., and Larry D. Kramer. "Independent Judges, Dependent Judiciary: Institutionalizing Judicial Restraint." *New York University Law Review* 77, no. 4 (2002): 962–1039.

Finnemore, Martha, and Kathryn Sikkink. "International Norm Dynamics and Political Change." *International Organization* 52, no. 4 (1998): 887–917.

Follesdal, Andreas. "Survey Article: The Legitimacy of International Courts." *Journal of Political Philosophy* 28, no. 4 (2020): 476–99.

Forte, Maximilian C. "Extinction: Ideologies Against Indigeneity in the Caribbean." *Southern Quarterly* 43, no. 4 (2006): 46–69.

Franck, Thomas M. *The Power of Legitimacy Among Nations*. Oxford: Oxford University Press, 1990.

Frankenreiter, Jens. "The Politics of Citations at the ECJ – Policy Preferences of E.U. Member State Governments and the Citation Behavior of Judges at the European Court of Justice." *Journal of Empirical Legal Studies* 14, no. 4 (2017): 813–57.

Freedom House. "Freedom in the World 2023 Methodology Questions." 2023. Accessed April 17, 2023. https://freedomhouse.org/sites/default/files/2023-03/FITW_2023%20MethodologyPDF.pdf.

"Freedom in the World: Aggregate Category and Subcategory Scores, 2003–2022." 2023. Accessed August 25, 2024. https://freedomhouse.org/report/freedom-world.

Gao, Henry, and Weihuan Zhou. "'Overreaching' or 'Overreacting'? Reflections on the Judicial Function and Approaches of WTO Appellate Body." *Journal of World Trade* 53, no. 6 (2019): 951–78.

Gardiner, Richard K. *Treaty Interpretation.* 2nd ed. Oxford: Oxford University Press, 2015.

Garoupa, Nuno, and Tom Ginsburg. "The Comparative Law and Economics of Judicial Councils." *Berkeley Journal of International Law* 27, no. 1 (2009): 53–83.

Garrett, Geoffrey, R. Daniel Kelemen, and Heiner Schulz. "The European Court of Justice, National Governments, and Legal Integration in the European Union." *International Organization* 52, no. 1 (1998): 149–76.

Gathii, James Thuo. "International Courts as Coordination Devices for Opposition Parties: The Case of the East African Court of Justice." In *The Performance of Africa's International Courts: Using Litigation for Political, Legal, and Social Change*, edited by James Thuo Gathii, 35–87. Oxford: Oxford University Press, 2020.

"Mission Creep or a Search for Relevance: The East African Court of Justice's Human Rights Strategy." *Duke Journal of Comparative & International Law* 24, no. 2 (2013): 249–96.

The Performance of Africa's International Courts: Using International Litigation for Political, Legal, and Social Change. Oxford: Oxford University Press, 2020.

"Promise of International Law: A Third World View (Including a Twail Bibliography 1996–2019 as an Appendix)." *American Society of International Law, Proceedings of the Annual Meeting* 114 (2020): 165–87.

"Saving the Serengeti: Africa's New International Judicial Environmentalism." *Chicago Journal of International Law* 16, no. 2 (2016): 386–438.

"Variation in the Use of Subregional Integration Courts between Business and Human Rights Actors: The Case of the East African Court of Justice." *Law and Contemporary Problems* 79, no. 1 (2016): 37–62.

Gayoye, Martha. "'Constitutions without Constitutionalism' and Judicial Leadership in Kenya." *Journal of Eastern African Studies* 18, no. 3 (2024): 345–65.

Gebeye, Berihun A. "Decoding Legal Pluralism in Africa." *Journal of Legal Pluralism and Unofficial Law* 49, no. 2 (2017): 228–49.

George, Alexander L., and Andrew Bennett. *Case Studies and Theory Development in the Social Sciences.* Cambridge, MA: MIT Press, 2005.

Gerring, John. *Case Study Research: Principles and Practices.* 2nd ed. Cambridge: Cambridge University Press, 2016.

Ghany, Hamid A. *Constitutional Development in the Commonwealth Caribbean.* Kingston, Jamaica: Ian Randle Publishers, 2018.

Ginsburg, Tom. "Bounded Discretion in International Judicial Lawmaking." *Virginia Journal of International Law* 45, no. 3 (2005): 631–73.

"Political Constraints on International Courts." In *The Oxford Handbook of International Adjudication*, edited by Cesare Romano, Karen Alter and Yuval Shany, 483–502. Oxford: Oxford University Press, 2014.

Gloppen, Siri. "The Accountability Function of the Courts in Tanzania and Zambia." *Democratization* 10, no. 4 (2003): 112–36.

Goldstein, Judith, and Robert O. Keohane. *Ideas and Foreign Policy: Beliefs, Institutions and Political Change.* Ithaca: Cornell University Press, 1993.

Goldstein, Judith L., and Richard H. Steinberg. "Regulatory Shift: The Rise of Judicial Liberalization at the WTO." In *The Politics of Global Regulation*, edited by Walter Mattli and Ngaire Woods, 211–41. Princeton: Princeton University Press, 2009.

Gonzalez-Ocantos, Ezequiel, and Wayne Sandholtz. "The Sources of Resilience of International Human Rights Courts: The Case of the Inter-American System." *Law & Social Inquiry* 47, no. 1 (2022): 95–131.

Gori, Gisella. "Compliance." In *The Oxford Handbook of International Human Rights Law*, edited by Dinah Shelton, 893–920. Oxford: Oxford University Press, 2013.

Gourevitch, Peter. "The Second Image Reversed: The International Sources of Domestic Politics." *International Organization* 32, no. 4 (1978): 881–912.

Gray, Christine. "Remedies." In *The Oxford Handbook of International Adjudication*, edited by Cesare Romano, Karen Alter and Yuval Shany, 871–97. Oxford: Oxford University Press, 2014.

Green, Craig. "An Intellectual History of Judicial Activism." *Emory Law Journal* 58, no. 5 (2009): 1195.

Greenhill, Brian. "How Can International Organizations Shape Public Opinion? Analysis of a Pair of Survey-Based Experiments." *Review of International Organizations* 15, no. 1 (2020): 165–88.

Grieco, Joseph M., Christopher Gelpi, Jason Reifler, and Peter D. Feaver. "Let's Get a Second Opinion: International Institutions and American Public Support for War." *International Studies Quarterly* 55, no. 2 (2011): 563–83.

Grimmel, Andreas. "Judicial Interpretation or Judicial Activism? The Legacy of Rationalism in the Studies of the European Court of Justice." *European Law Journal* 18, no. 4 (2012): 518–35.

Grobe, Christian. "The Power of Words: Argumentative Persuasion in International Negotiations." *European Journal of International Relations* 16, no. 1 (2010): 5–29.

Grossman, Nienke. "Legitimacy and International Adjudicative Bodies." *George Washington International Law Review* 41, no. 1 (2009): 107–80.

Gruber, Lloyd. *Ruling the World Power Politics and the Rise of Supranational Institutions.* Princeton: Princeton University Press, 2000.

Gruszczynski, Lukasz, and Wouter Werner. *Deference in International Courts and Tribunals: Standard of Review and Margin of Appreciation.* Oxford: Oxford University Press, 2014.

Guillaume, Gilbert. "Some Thoughts on Independence of International Judges." *The Law & Practice of International Courts and Tribunals* 2, no. 1 (2003): 163–68.

Gutmann, Jerg, and Stefan Voigt. "The Rule of Law: Measurement and Deep Roots." *European Journal of Political Economy* 54 (2018): 68–82.

Gutner, Tamar, and Alexander Thompson. "The Politics of IO Performance: A Framework." *Review of International Organizations* 5, no. 3 (2010): 227–48.

Guzman, Andrew, and Beth A. Simmons. "Power Plays and Capacity Constraints: The Selection of Defendants in World Trade Organization Disputes." *Journal of Legal Studies* 34, no. 2 (2005): 557–98.

Guzman, Andrew T. "International Tribunals: A Rational Choice Analysis." *University of Pennsylvania Law Review* 157, no. 1 (2008): 171–236.

Haddad, Heidi Nichols. *The Hidden Hands of Justice: NGOs, Human Rights, and International Courts.* Cambridge: Cambridge University Press, 2018.

Haftel, Yoram, and Alexander Thompson. "The Independence of International Organizations: Concept and Applications." *Journal of Conflict Resolution* 50, no. 2 (2006): 253–75.

Hagan, John, Ron Levi, and Gabrielle Ferrales. "Swaying the Hand of Justice: The Internal and External Dynamics of Regime Change at the International Criminal Tribunal for the Former Yugoslavia." *Law & Social Inquiry* 31, no. 3 (2006): 585–616.

Haggard, Stephan, and Lydia Tiede. "The Rule of Law and Economic Growth: Where Are We?" *World Development* 39, no. 5 (2011): 673–85.

Halliday, Terence C., Lucien Karpik, and Malcolm M. Feeley. *Fighting for Political Freedom: Comparative Studies of the Legal Complex and Political Liberalism.* Oxford: Hart Publishing, 2007.

Harsch, Michael F., and Vladislav Maksimov. "International Courts and Public Opinion: Explaining the CJEU's Role in Protecting Terror Suspects' Rights." *Journal of Common Market Studies* 57, no. 5 (2019): 1091–1110.

Hawkins, Darren G., David A. Lake, Daniel L. Nielson, and Michael J. Tierney. *Delegation and Agency in International Organizations.* Cambridge: Cambridge University Press, 2006.

Hawkins, Darren, and Wade Jacoby. "Agent Permeability, Principal Delegation and the European Court of Human Rights." *Review of International Organizations* 3, no. 1 (2008): 1–28.

Haynes, Jason. "The Right to Free Movement of Persons in Caribbean Community (CARICOM) Law: Towards 'Juridification'?" *Journal of Human Rights in the Commonwealth* 2, no. 2 (2016): 57–66.

Hayo, Bernd, and Stefan Voigt. "Explaining De Facto Judicial Independence." *International Review of Law & Economics* 27, no. 3 (2007): 269–90.

"The Long-Term Relationship between De Jure and De Facto Judicial Independence." *Economics Letters* 183 (2019): 108603.

Hazlewood, Arthur. "The End of the East African Community: What Are the Lessons for Regional Integration Schemes?" *Journal of Common Market Studies* 18, no. 1 (1979): 40–58.

Heinrich, Andrew. "Sub-Regional Courts as Transitional Justice Mechanisms: The Case of the East African Court of Justice in Burundi." In *The Performance of Africa's International Courts: Using Litigation for Political, Legal, and Social Change*, edited by James Thuo Gathii, 88–105. Oxford: Oxford University Press, 2020.

Heldt, Eugénia. "Regaining Control of Errant Agents? Agency Slack at the European Commission and the World Health Organization." *Cooperation and Conflict* 52, no. 4 (2017): 469–84.

Helfer, Laurence, and Anne-Marie Slaughter. "Towards a Theory of Effective Supranational Adjudication." *Yale Law Journal* 107, no. 2 (1997): 273–391.

"Why States Create International Tribunals: A Response to Professors Posner and Yoo." *California Law Review* 93, no. 3 (2005): 899–956.

Helmke, Gretchen. *Courts Under Constraints: Judges, Generals, and Presidents in Argentina*. Cambridge: Cambridge University Press, 2005.

Hermansen, Silje Synnøve Lyder. "Building Legitimacy: Strategic Case Allocations in the Court of Justice of the European Union." *Journal of European Public Policy* 27, no. 8 (2020): 1215–35.

Heyl, Charlotte. "The Judiciary and the Rule of Law in Africa." In *Oxford Research Encyclopedia: Politics*. Oxford: Oxford University Press, 2019. Accessed August 25, 2024. https://10.1093/acrefore/9780190228637.013.1352.

Heyns, Christof. "The African Regional Human Rights System: In Need of Reform." *African Human Rights Law Journal* 1, no. 2 (2001): 155–74.

Hilbink, Lisa. *Judges Beyond Politics in Democracy and Dictatorship: Lessons from Chile*. Cambridge: Cambridge University Press, 2007.

Hillebrecht, Courtney. *Saving the International Justice Regime: Beyond Backlash Against International Courts*. Cambridge: Cambridge University Press, 2021.

Hirschl, Ran. "The Judicialization of Mega-Politics and the Rise of Political Courts." *Annual Review of Political Science* 11, no. 1 (2008): 93–118.

Hirschman, Albert O. *Exit, Voice, and Loyalty Responses to Decline in Firms, Organizations, and States.* Cambridge, MA: Harvard University Press, 1970.

Holland, Kenneth, ed. *Judicial Activism in Comparative Perspective.* New York: St. Martin's Press, 1991.

Hönnige, Christoph. "The Electoral Connection: How the Pivotal Judge Affects Oppositional Success at European Constitutional Courts." *West European Politics* 32, no. 5 (2009): 963–84.

Hooghe, Liesbet, and Gary Marks. "Delegation and Pooling in International Organizations." *Review of International Organizations* 10, no. 3 (2015): 305–28.

Howse, Robert. "The World Trade Organization 20 Years On: Global Governance by Judiciary." *European Journal of International Law* 27, no. 1 (2016): 9–77.

Hume, Robert J. "The Use of Rhetorical Sources by the U.S. Supreme Court." *Law & Society Review* 40, no. 4 (2006): 817–44.

Huneeus, Alexandra. "The Inter-American Court of Human Rights: How Constitutional Lawyers Shape Court Authority." In *International Court Authority*, edited by Karen J. Alter, Laurence R. Helfer and Mikael Rask Madsen, 196–220. Oxford: Oxford University Press, 2018.

Huneeus, Alexandra, and René Urueña. "Treaty Exit and Latin America's Constitutional Courts." *AJIL Unbound* 111 (2017): 456–60.

Hurd, Ian. *After Anarchy: Legitimacy and Power in the United Nations Security Council.* Princeton: Princeton University Press, 2007.

"Legitimacy and Authority in International Politics." *International Organization* 53, no. 2 (1999): 379–408.

IACtHR. *2020 Annual Report.* San Jose: IACtHR, 2021. Accessed August 25, 2024. www.corteidh.or.cr/informes_anuales.cfm?lang=en.

Ibhawoh, Bonny. *Imperial Justice: Africans in Empire's Court.* Oxford: Oxford University Press, 2013.

Imerman, Dane. "Contested Legitimacy and Institutional Change: Unpacking the Dynamics of Institutional Legitimacy." *International Studies Review* 20, no. 1 (2018): 74–100.

Ingadottir, Thordis. "The Financing of International Adjudication." In *The Oxford Handbook of International Adjudication*, edited by Cesare Romano, Karen Alter and Yuval Shany, 594–615. Oxford: Oxford University Press, 2014.

Ingram, Matthew C. "Crafting Courts in New Democracies: Ideology and Judicial Council Reforms in Three Mexican States." *Comparative Politics* 44, no. 4 (2012): 439–58.

IOM. *Free Movement of Persons in the Caribbean: Economic and Security Dimensions.* San José, Costa Rica: IOM, 2019. Accessed May 11, 2023. https://publications.iom.int/books/free-movement-caribbean-economic-and-security-dimensions.

Jackson, Miles. "Judicial Avoidance at the European Court of Human Rights: Institutional Authority, the Procedural Turn, and Docket Control." *International Journal of Constitutional Law* 20, no. 1 (2022): 112–40.

Johns, Leslie. *Strengthening International Courts: The Hidden Costs of Legalization.* Ann Arbor: University of Michigan Press, 2015.

Johnson, Tana. "Guilt by Association: The Link between States' Influence and the Legitimacy of Intergovernmental Organizations." *Review of International Organizations* 6, no. 1 (2011): 57–84.

Johnston, Alastair Iain. "Treating International Institutions as Social Environments." *International Studies Quarterly* 45, no. 4 (2001): 487–515.

Jupille, Joseph, Walter Mattli, and Duncan Snidal. *Institutional Choice and Global Commerce.* Cambridge: Cambridge University Press, 2013.

Kaczorowska-Ireland, Alina, and Westmin R. A. James. *Commonwealth Caribbean Law and Procedure: The Referral Procedure Under Article 214 RTC in the Light of EU and International Law.* Abingdon: Routledge, 2020.

Kamotho, Joseph. "Changes to the EAC Treaty Unwise." *The Nation*, January 25, 2007.

Kapiszewski, Diana. "How Courts Work: Institutions, Culture, and the Brazilian Supremo Tribunal Federal." In *Cultures of Legality: Judicialization and Political Activism in Latin America*, edited by Alexandra Huneeus, Javier Couso and Rachel Sieder, 51–77. Cambridge: Cambridge University Press, 2010.

Kapiszewski, Diana, Gordon Silverstein, and Robert A. Kagan, eds. *Consequential Courts: Judicial Roles in Global Perspective.* Cambridge: Cambridge University Press, 2013.

Katende, J. W., and George W. Kanyeihamba. "Legalism and Politics in East Africa: The Dilemma of the Court of Appeal for East Africa." *Transition*, 43 (1973): 43–54.

Kato, L. L. "The Court of Appeal for East Africa: From a Colonial Court to an International Court." *East African Law Journal* 7, no. 1 (1971): 1–31.

Keith, Linda Camp. "Judicial Independence and Human Rights Protection Around the World." *Judicature* 85, no. 4 (2002): 194–200.

Kelemen, Daniel. "The Limits of Judicial Power: Trade-Environment Disputes in the GATT/WTO and the EU." *Comparative Political Studies* 34, no. 6 (2001): 622–50.

Kelemen, R. Daniel. "The Court of Justice of the European Union: Changing Authority in the Twenty-First Century." In *International Court Authority*, edited by Karen J. Alter, Laurence Helfer and Mikael Rask Madsen, 223–42. Oxford: Oxford University Press, 2018.

"The Political Foundations of Judicial Independence in the European Union." *Journal of European Public Policy* 19, no. 1 (2012): 43–58.

Kelemen, R. Daniel, and Tommaso Pavone. "Where Have the Guardians Gone? Law Enforcement and the Politics of Supranational Forbearance in the European Union." *World Politics* 75, no. 4 (2023): 779–825.

Keohane, Robert O. *After Hegemony Cooperation and Discord in the World Political Economy*. Princeton: Princeton University Press, 1984.

Keohane, Robert O., Andrew Moravcsik, and Anne-Marie Slaughter. "Legalized Dispute Resolution: Interstate and Transnational." *International Organization* 54, no. 3 (2000): 457–88.

Kischel, Uwe. *Comparative Law*. Oxford: Oxford University Press, 2019.

Kmiec, Keenan D. "The Origin and Current Meanings of 'Judicial Activism'." *California Law Review* 92, no. 5 (2004): 1441–77.

Koch, Alexander, Chris Brierley, Mark M. Maslin, and Simon L. Lewis. "Earth System Impacts of the European Arrival and Great Dying in the Americas after 1492." *Quaternary Science Reviews* 207 (2019): 13–36.

Kocken, Joris, and Gerda Roozendaal. "Constructing the Caribbean Court of Justice: How Ideas Inform Institutional Choices." *European Review of Latin American & Caribbean Studies* 93 (2012): 95–112.

Kolb, Robert. *The Elgar Companion to the International Court of Justice*. Cheltenham: Edward Elgar, 2014.

Kombo, Brenda K. "Napoleonic Legacies, Postcolonial State Legitimation, and the Perpetual Myth of Non-Intervention: Family Code Reform and Gender Equality in Mali." *Social & Legal Studies* 30, no. 5 (2021): 704–25.

Krebs, Ronald R., and Patrick Thaddeus Jackson. "Twisting Tongues and Twisting Arms: The Power of Political Rhetoric." *European Journal of International Relations* 13, no. 1 (2007): 35–66.

Kruck, Andreas, and Bernhard Zangl. "The Adjustment of International Institutions to Global Power Shifts: A Framework for Analysis." *Global Policy* 11, no. S3 (2020): 5–16.

Kufuor, Kofi Oteng. *The African Human Rights System: Origin and Evolution*. New York: Palgrave Macmillan, 2010.

"The Collapse of the Organization of African Unity: Lessons from Economics and History." *Journal of African Law* 49, no. 2 (2005): 132–44.

Kumar, Shashank P., and Cecily Rose. "A Study of Lawyers Appearing Before the International Court of Justice, 1999–2012." *European Journal of International Law* 25, no. 3 (2014): 893–917.

Kuyper, Jonathan W., and Theresa Squatrito. "International Courts and Global Democratic Values: Participation, Accountability, and Justification." *Review of International Studies* 43, no. 1 (2017): 152–76.

Lake, David A. *Hierarchy in International Relations*. Ithaca: Cornell University Press, 2009.

Lake, David A., and Robert Powell. *Strategic Choice and International Relations*. Princeton: Princeton University Press, 1999.

Larsson, Olof, and Daniel Naurin. "Judicial Independence and Political Uncertainty: How the Risk of Override Affects the Court of Justice of the EU." *International Organization* 70, no. 2 (2016): 377–408.

Larsson, Olof, Daniel Naurin, Mattias Derlén, and Johan Lindholm. "Speaking Law to Power: The Strategic Use of Precedent of the Court of Justice of the European Union." *Comparative Political Studies* 50, no. 7 (2017): 879–907.

Legro, Jeffrey W. "Culture and Preferences in the International Cooperation Two-Step." *American Political Science Review* 90, no. 1 (1996): 118–37.

Lenz, Tobias. *Interorganizational Diffusion in International Relations: Regional Institutions and the Role of the European Union.* Oxford: Oxford University Press, 2021.

Lenz, Tobias, and Mariel Reiss. "Globalising the Study of Diffusion: Multiple Sources and the East African Community." *Journal of European Public Policy* 31, no. 11 (2024): 3703–31.

Lenz, Tobias, and Henning Schmidtke. "Agents, Audiences and Peers: Why International Organizations Diversify Their Legitimation Discourse." *International Affairs* 99, no. 3 (2023): 921–40.

Lester, Simon. "U.S. 'Wins' and 'Losses' in WTO Disputes." *International Economic Law and Policy Blog*, March 15, 2020. Accessed August 25, 2024. https://ielp.worldtradelaw.net/2020/03/us-wins-and-losses-in-wto-disputes .html.

Lewis, Patsy. *Caribbean Regional Integration: A Critical Development Approach.* London: Routledge, 2022.

Lieberman, Evan S. "Nested Analysis as a Mixed-Method Strategy for Comparative Research." *American Political Science Review* 99, no. 3 (2005): 435–52.

Lindquist, Stefanie A., and Frank B. Cross. *Measuring Judicial Activism.* Oxford: Oxford University Press, 2009.

López-Medina, Diego. "The Latin American and Caribbean Legal Traditions: Repositioning Latin America and the Caribbean on the Contemporary Maps of Comparative Law." In *The Cambridge Companion to Comparative Law*, edited by Mauro Bussani and Ugo Mattei, 344–67. Cambridge: Cambridge University Press, 2012.

Lundgren, Magnus, Theresa Squatrito, and Jonas Tallberg. "Stability and Change in International Policy-Making: A Punctuated Equilibrium Approach." *Review of International Organizations* 13, no. 4 (2018): 547–72.

Lupu, Yonatan, and James H. Fowler. "Strategic Citations to Precedent on the U.S. Supreme Court." *Journal of Legal Studies* 42, no. 1 (2013): 151–86.

Lupu, Yonatan, and Erik Voeten. "Precedent in International Courts: A Network Analysis of Case Citations by the European Court of Human Rights." *British Journal of Political Science* 42, no. 2 (2012): 413–39.

Mackenzie, Ruth, Kate Malleson, Penny Martin, and Philippe Sands. *Selecting International Judges: Principle, Process, and Politics*. Oxford: Oxford University Press, 2010.

Mackenzie, Ruth, and Philippe Sands. "International Courts and Tribunals and the Independence of the International Judge." *Harvard International Law Journal* 44, no. 1 (2003): 271–85.

Madsen, Mikael Rask. "The European Court of Human Rights: From the Cold War to the Brighton Declaration and Backlash." In *International Court Authority*, edited by Karen J. Alter, Laurence R. Helfer and Mikael Rask Madsen, 243–74. Oxford: Oxford University Press, 2018.

"From Cold War Instrument to Supreme European Court: The European Court of Human Rights at the Crossroads of International and National Law and Politics." *Law & Social Inquiry* 32, no. 1 (2007): 137–59.

"The Protracted Institutionalization of the Strasbourg Court: From Legal Diplomacy to Integrationist Jurisprudence." In *The European Court of Human Rights between Law and Politics*, edited by Jonas Christoffersen and Mikael Rask Madsen, 43–60. Oxford: Oxford University Press, 2011.

Madsen, Mikael Rask, Pola Cebulak, and Micha Wiebusch. "Backlash Against International Courts: Explaining the Forms and Patterns of Resistance to International Courts." *International Journal of Law in Context* 14, no. 2 (2018): 197–220.

Majone, Giandomenico. "Two Logics of Delegation: Agency and Fiduciary Relations in EU Governance." *European Union Politics* 2, no. 1 (2001): 103–21.

Makunya, Trésor Muhindo. "Decisions of the African Court on Human and Peoples' Rights During 2020: Trends and Lessons." *African Human Rights Law Journal* 21, no. 2 (2021): 1230–64.

Mancuso, Salvatore. "The New African Law: Beyond the Difference between Common Law and Civil Law." *Annual Survey of International & Comparative Law* 14, no. 1. (2008): 39–60.

Manga Fombad, Charles. "A Comparative Overview of Recent Trends in Judicial Appointments: Selected Cases from Africa." *Canadian Journal of African Studies* 55, no. 1 (2021): 161–82.

Mansfield, Edward D., and Eric Reinhardt. "Multilateral Determinants of Regionalism: The Effects of GATT/WTO on the Formation of Preferential Trading Arrangements." *International Organization* 57, no. 4 (2003): 829–62.

Martin, Lisa L., and Beth A. Simmons. "International Organizations and Institutions." In *Handbook of International Relations*, edited by Walter Carlsnaes, Thomas Risse and Beth A. Simmons, 326–351. London: Sage, 2012.

Martinsen, Dorte Sindbjerg. "Conflict and Conflict Management in the Cross-Border Provision of Healthcare Services." *West European Politics* 32, no. 4 (2009): 792–809.

Masengu, Tabeth. "The Vulnerability of Judges in Contemporary Africa: Alarming Trends." *Africa Today* 63, no. 4 (2017): 3–19.

Masinde, Wanyama, and Christopher Otieno Omolo. "The Road to East African Integration." In *East African Community Law: Institutional, Substantive and Comparative EU Aspects*, edited by Emmanuel Ugirashebuja, John Eudes Ruhangisa, Tom Ottervanger, and Armin Cuyvers, 1–21. Leiden: Brill Nijhoff, 2017.

Mattern, Janice Bially, and Ayşe Zarakol. "Hierarchies in World Politics." *International Organization* 70, no. 3 (2016): 623–54.

Mattli, Walter, and Anne-Marie Slaughter. "Revisiting the European Court of Justice." *International Organization* 52, no. 1 (1998): 177–209.

Mawar, Deepak. "The Perils of Judicial Restraint: How Judicial Activism Can Help Evolve the International Court of Justice." *Goettingen Journal of International Law* 9, no. 3 (2018): 425–56.

Mawby, Spencer. *Ordering Independence: The End of Empire in the Anglophone Caribbean, 1947–69.* London: Palgrave Macmillan, 2012.

Mbori, Harrison. "Ingabire Victoire Umuhoza v. The Republic of Rwanda." *American Journal of International Law* 112, no. 4 (2018): 713–19.

McNamara, Kathleen. *The Currency of Ideas: Monetary Politics in the European Union.* Ithaca: Cornell University Press, 1998.

Melton, James, and Tom Ginsburg. "Does De Jure Judicial Independence Really Matter? A Reevaluation of Explanations for Judicial Independence." *Journal of Law and Courts* 2, no. 2 (2014): 187–217.

Meron, Theodor. "Judicial Independence and Impartiality in International Criminal Tribunals." *American Journal of International Law* 99, no. 2 (2005): 359–69.

Merry, Sally Engle. "What Is Legal Culture – An Anthropological Perspective Using Legal Culture." *Journal of Comparative Law* 5, no. 2 (2010): 40–58.

Milner, Helen. "The Assumption of Anarchy in International Relations Theory: A Critique." *Review of International Studies* 17, no. 1 (1991): 67–85.

Mitchell, Sara McLaughlin, and Emilia Justyna Powell. *Domestic Law Goes Global: Legal Traditions and International Courts.* Cambridge: Cambridge University Press, 2011.

Moravcsik, Andrew. "Taking Preferences Seriously: A Liberal Theory of International Politics." *International Organization* 51, no. 4 (1997): 513–53.

Morgan, Philip D. "Slavery in the British Caribbean." In *The Cambridge World History of Slavery: Volume 3*, edited by David Eltis and Stanley L. Engerman, 378–406. Cambridge: Cambridge University Press, 2011.

Morse, Julia C., and Robert O. Keohane. "Contested Multilateralism." *Review of International Organizations* 9, no. 4 (2014): 385–412.

Mpinganjira, Ernest. "Lawyers Protest Move to Weaken Regional Court." *The East African Standard*, December 19, 2006.

Mshomba, Richard E. *Economic Integration in Africa: The East African Community in Comparative Perspective*. Cambridge: Cambridge University Press, 2017.

Mugonyi, David. "Kenya Removes Judge from Arusha Court." *The Nation*, March 20, 2007.

Mujuzi, Jamil Ddamulira. "The African Court on Human and Peoples' Rights and Its Protection of the Right to a Fair Trial." *Law & Practice of International Courts and Tribunals* 16, no. 2 (2017): 187–223.

"The Islamic Law of Marriage and Inheritance in Kenya." *Journal of African Law* 65, no. 3 (2021): 377–401.

Murithi, Tim. "The African Union's Transition from Non-Intervention to Non-Indifference: An Ad Hoc Approach to the Responsibility to Protect?" *Internationale Politik und Gesellschaft* 1, no. 1 (2009): 90–106.

Mutinda, Jackson. "EACJ President Nestor Kayobera Says Court Needs More Autonomy." *The East African*, October 26, 2022.

Mutua, Makau. "Justice Under Siege: The Rule of Law and Judicial Subservience in Kenya." *Human Rights Quarterly* 23, no. 1 (2001): 96–118.

Mutyaba, Michael. "From Voting to Walking: The 2011 Walk-to-Work Protest Movement in Uganda." In *Popular Protest, Political Opportunities, and Change in Africa*, edited by Edalina Rodrigues Sanches, 163–80. Abingdon: Routledge, 2022.

Naldi, Gino J. "The African Union and the Regional Human Rights System." In *The African Charter on Human and Peoples' Rights: The System in Practice 1986–2006*, edited by Malcolm Evans and Rachel Murray, 20–48. Cambridge: Cambridge University Press, 2008.

Namunane, Bernard. "Leaders Petitioned Over Regional Court." *The Nation*, December 19, 2006.

Nathan, Laurie. "The Disbanding of the SADC Tribunal: A Cautionary Tale." *Human Rights Quarterly* 35, no. 4 (2013): 870–92.

Naurin, Daniel, and Øyvind Stiansen. "The Dilemma of Dissent: Split Judicial Decisions and Compliance with Judgments from the International Human Rights Judiciary." *Comparative Political Studies* 53, no. 6 (2020): 959–91.

Nielson, Daniel L., and Michael J. Tierney. "Delegation to International Organizations: Agency Theory and World Bank Environmental Reform." *International Organization* 57, no. 2 (2003): 241–76.

Niyungeko, Gérard. "National Sensitization Seminar." Speech at National Sensitization Seminar of the African Court on Human and Peoples' Rights. Accra, Ghana. December 12, 2011. Accessed August 25, 2024. www.african-court.org/wpafc/national-sensitization-seminar-on-the-african-court-on-human-and-peoples-rights-by-hon-justice-gerard-niyungeko/.

"The African Charter on Democracy, Elections and Governance as a Human Rights Instrument." *Journal of African Law* 63, no. S1 (2019): 63–80.

"The African Court on Human and Peoples' Rights and the Possible Role of the Pan-African Parliament in Promoting the Court." Speech at Fifth Ordinary Session of the Second Parliament of the Pan African Parliament. Midrand, South Africa. October 6, 2011. Accessed August 25, 2024. www.african-court.org/wpafc/the-african-court-on-human-and-peoples-rights-and-the-possible-role-of-the-pan-african-parliament-in-promoting-the-court-hon-justice-gerard-niyungeko/.

O'Brien, Derek. "CARICOM: Regional Integration in a Post-Colonial World." *European Law Journal* 17, no. 5 (2011): 630–48.

"The End of the Caribbean Court of Justice? On Failed Constitutional Referendums in Grenada, and Antigua and Barbuda," *ConstitutionNet*, November 26, 2018. https://constitutionnet.org/news/end-caribbean-court-justice-failed-constitutional-referendums-grenada-and-antigua-and-barbuda.

OAU. Decision AHG/Dec.115 (XVI), rev. 1, July 16–20, 1979. *Sixteenth Ordinary Session of the Assembly of Heads of State and Government*. Monrovia, Liberia: OAU, 1979.

Resolution AHG/Res.230 (XXX), June 13–15, 1994. *Thirtieth Ordinary Session of the Assembly of Heads of State and Government*. Tunis, Tunisia: OAU, 1994.

O'Brien, Derek, and S. Foadi. "CARICOM and Its Court of Justice." *Common Law World Review* 37, no. 4 (2008): 334–55.

"CARICOM: A New Legal Order?" *UK Constitutional Law Blog*, November 8, 2013. https://ukconstitutionallaw.org/2013/11/08/derek-obrien-caricom-a-new-legal-order/.

O'Donohue, Jonathan. "Financing the International Criminal Court." In *The Realities of International Criminal Justice*, edited by Dawn L. Rothe, James Meernik and Þórdís Ingadóttir, 269–96. Leiden: Brill, 2013.

Oba, Abdulmumini A. "The Future of Customary Law in Africa." In *The Future of African Customary Law*, edited by Jeanmarie Fenrich, Paolo Galizzi and Tracy E. Higgins, 58–80. Cambridge: Cambridge University Press, 2011.

Onoria, Henry. "Botched-Up Elections, Treaty Amendments and Judicial Independence in the East African Community." *Journal of African Law* 54, no. 1 (2010): 74–94.

Oré, Sylvain. "Presidential Speech." Speech at Opening Ceremony of the Third Continental Judicial Dialogue. Arusha, Tanzania. November 9, 2017. Accessed June 4, 2024. www.african-court.org/en/images/Speeches/Opening_Prez_3rd_JD_2017.pdf.

"Opening Statement by the President." Speech at 48th Ordinary Session of the ACtHPR. Arusha, Tanzania. February 26, 2018. Accessed February 26, 2024. www.african-court.org/en/images/Speeches/EG_48th_Opening_Statement_Prez_26_March_2018.pdf.

Orloff, Neil. "Economic Integration in East Africa: The Treaty for East-African Co-Operation." *Columbia Journal of Transnational Law* 7, no. 2 (1968): 302–32.

Oude Elferink, A. G. "The Russian Federation and the Arctic Sunrise Case: Hot Pursuit and Other Issues Under the LOSC." *International Law Studies* 92 (2016): 381–406.

Ouguergouz, Fatsah. "The Establishment of an African Court of Human and Peoples' Rights: A Judicial Premiere for the African Union." *African Yearbook of International Law* 11, no. 1 (2003): 79–141.

Palmtag, Tabea, Tobias Rommel, and Stefanie Walter. "International Trade and Public Protest: Evidence from Russian Regions." *International Studies Quarterly* 64, no. 4 (2020): 939–55.

Pasqualucci, Jo M. *The Practice and Procedure of the Inter-American Court of Human Rights.* 2nd ed. Cambridge: Cambridge University Press, 2013.

Pauwelyn, Joost, and Manfred Elsig. "The Politics of Treaty Interpretation: Variations and Explanations across International Tribunals." In *Interdisciplinary Perspectives on International Law and International Relations*, edited by Jeffrey Dunoff and Mark Pollack, 445–74. Cambridge: Cambridge University Press, 2014.

Pauwelyn, Joost, and Rebecca J. Hamilton. "Exit from International Tribunals." *Journal of International Dispute Settlement* 9, no. 4 (2018): 679–90.

Pauwelyn, Joost, and Krzysztof Pelc. "Who Guards the 'Guardians of the System'? The Role of the Secretariat in WTO Dispute Settlement." *American Journal of International Law* 116, no. 3 (2022): 534–66.

Pavone, Tommaso. "From Marx to Market: Lawyers, European Law, and the Contentious Transformation of the Port of Genoa." *Law & Society Review* 53, no. 3 (2019): 851–88.

The Ghostwriters: Lawyers and the Politics Behind the Judicial Construction of Europe. Cambridge: Cambridge University Press, 2022.

Payne, Anthony J. *The Political History of CARICOM.* Kingston, Jamaica: Ian Randle Publishers, 2008.

Pelc, Krzysztof J. "Googling the WTO: What Search-Engine Data Tell Us About the Political Economy of Institutions." *International Organization* 67, no. 3 (2013): 629–55.

Pevehouse, Jon C. W., Timothy Nordstrom, Roseanne W. McManus, and Anne Spencer Jamison. "Tracking Organizations in the World: The Correlates of War IGO Version 3.0 Datasets." *Journal of Peace Research* 57, no. 3 (2020): 492–503.

Phelan, William. "Enforcement and Escape in the Andean Community: Why the Andean Community of Nations Is Not a Replica of the European Union." *Journal of Common Market Studies* 53, no. 4 (2014): 840–56.

Pollack, Mark A. *The Engines of European Integration: Delegation, Agency, and Agenda Setting in the EU.* Oxford: Oxford University Press, 2003.

"International Court Curbing in Geneva: Lessons from the Paralysis of the WTO Appellate Body." *Governance* 36, no. 1 (2023): 23–39.

Pollard, Duke E. *The Caribbean Court of Justice: Closing the Circle of Independence.* Kingston, Jamaica: Caribbean Law Publishing Co., 2004.

Posner, Eric, and John Yoo. "Judicial Independence in International Tribunals." *California Law Review* 93, no. 1 (2005): 1–74.

Pratt, Tyler. "Deference and Hierarchy in International Regime Complexes." *International Organization* 72, no. 3 (2018): 561–90.

Prempeh, H. Kwasi. "Africa's 'Constitutionalism Revival': False Start or New Dawn?" *International Journal of Constitutional Law* 5, no. 3 (2007): 469–506.

"Marbury in Africa: Judicial Review and the Challenge of Constitutionalism in Contemporary Africa." *Tulane Law Review* 80, no. 4 (2006): 1239–1324.

Proctor, Jesse Harris. "The Framing of the West Indian Federal Constitution: An Adventure in National Self-Determination." *Revista de Historia de América* no. 57/58 (1964): 51–119.

Puig, Sergio, and Anton Strezhnev. "The David Effect and ISDS." *European Journal of International Law* 28, no. 3 (2017): 731–61.

Putnam, Robert D. "Diplomacy and Domestic Politics: The Logic of Two-Level Games." *International Organization* 42, no. 3 (1988): 427–60.

Rachovitsa, Adamantia. "On New 'Judicial Animals': The Curious Case of an African Court with Material Jurisdiction of a Global Scope." *Human Rights Law Review* 19, no. 2 (2019): 255–89.

Ramadhani, Augustino. "Statement to ACmHPR." Speech at Opening of the Fifty-Sixth Ordinary Session of the ACmHPR. Banjul, The Gambia. April 21, 2015.

"Statement." Speech at the Opening of the Validation of the African Court's Strategic Plan. Arusha, Tanzania. March 5, 2016.

Ratner, Steven R. "Persuading to Comply: On the Deployment and Avoidance of Legal Argumentation." In *Interdisciplinary Perspectives on International Law and International Relations: The State of the Art*, edited by Jeffrey Dunoff and Mark Pollack, 568–90. Cambridge: Cambridge University Press, 2010.

Ravenhill, John. "Regional Integration and Development in Africa: Lessons from the East African Community." *Journal of Commonwealth & Comparative Politics* 17, no. 3 (1979): 227–46.

Rawlins, Hugh. *The Caribbean Court of Justice: The History and Analysis of the Debate.* Georgetown, Guyana: CARICOM, 2000.

Reiss, Mariel. *Constructing the East African Community: Diffusion from African and European Regional Organizations.* Abingdon: Routledge, 2022.

Ríos-Figueroa, Julio, and Jeffrey K. Staton. "An Evaluation of Cross-National Measures of Judicial Independence." *Journal of Law, Economics, and Organization* 30, no. 1 (2014): 104–37.

Ríos Figueroa, Julio. "Fragmentation of Power and the Emergence of an Effective Judiciary in Mexico, 1994–2002." *Latin American Politics & Society* 49, no. 1 (2007): 31–57.

Risse, Thomas. "'Let's Argue!': Communicative Action in World Politics." *International Organization* 54, no. 1 (2000): 1–39.

Robinson, Tracy. "A Caribbean Common Law." *Race & Class* 49, no. 2 (2007): 118–24.

Rogowski, Ronald. *Commerce and Coalitions: How Trade Affects Domestic Political Alignments.* Princeton: Princeton University Press, 1989.

Romano, Cesare. "Trial and Error in International Judicialization." In *The Oxford Handbook of International Adjudication*, edited by Cesare Romano, Karen Alter and Yuval Shany, 111–34. Oxford: Oxford University Press, 2014.

Romano, Cesare, Karen Alter, and Yuval Shany. "Mapping International Adjudicative Bodies, the Issues, and Players." In *The Oxford Handbook of International Adjudication*, edited by Cesare Romano, Karen Alter and Yuval Shany, 3–26. Oxford: Oxford University Press, 2014.

"A Taxonomy of International Rule of Law Institutions." *Journal of International Dispute Settlement* 2, no. 1 (2011): 241–77.

Roopnarine, Lomarsh. "Indo-Caribbean Migration: From Periphery to Core." *Caribbean Quarterly* 49, no. 3 (2003): 30–60.

Ruhangisa, John Eudes. "The East African Court of Justice: Ten Years of Operation (Achievements and Challenges)." Sensitisation Workshop on the Role of the EACJ in the EAC Integration. Kampala, November 2, 2011. Accessed August 25, 2024. www.eacj.org/wp-content/uploads/2013/09/EACJ-Ten-Years-of-Operation.pdf.

Salmon, Hugh M. "The Caribbean Court of Justice: A March with Destiny." *Florida Coastal Law Journal* 2, no. 1 (2000): 231–40.

Sattler, Thomas, and Thomas Bernauer. "Gravitation or Discrimination? Determinants of Litigation in the World Trade Organisation." *European Journal of Political Research* 50, no. 2 (2011): 143–67.

Saunders, Adrian. "The Revised Treaty of Chaguaramas: Conflicts and Contradictions for the Island State." Speech at the Public Gathering, St Vincent and the Grenadines, May 16, 2017. Accessed August 25, 2024. www.ccj.org/wp-content/uploads/2021/02/Remarks-by-the-Honourable-Mr-Justice-Adrian-Saunder-on-the-Revised-Treaty-of-Chaguaramas-in-St-Vincent_20170516.pdf.

Saunders, Adrian D. "A Commentary on the Early Decisions of the Caribbean Court of Justice in Its Original Jurisdiction." *International and Comparative Law Quarterly* 59, no. 3 (2010): 761–78.

Scharpf, Fritz W. *Games Real Actors Play: Actor-Centered Institutionalism in Policy Research.* Boulder, CO: Westview Press, 1997.

"The Joint-Decision Trap: Lessons from German Federalism and European Integration." *Public Administration* 66, no. 3 (1988): 239–78.

Schimmelfennig, Frank. "The Community Trap: Liberal Norms, Rhetorical Action, and the Eastern Enlargement of the European Union." *International Organization* 55, no. 1 (2001): 47–80.

Segal, Jeffrey A., and Harold J. Spaeth. *The Supreme Court and the Attitudinal Model Revisited.* Cambridge: Cambridge University Press, 2002.

Shaffer, Gregory, Manfred Elsig, and Sergio Puig. "The Extensive (But Fragile) Authority of the WTO Appellate Body." *Law and Contemporary Problems* 79, no. 1 (2016): 237–73.

Shany, Yuval. *Assessing the Effectiveness of International Courts.* Oxford: Oxford University Press, 2014.

"No Longer a Weak Department of Power? Reflections on the Emergence of a New International Judiciary." *European Journal of International Law* 20, no. 1 (2009): 73–91.

Shelton, Dinah. *Remedies in International Human Rights Law.* Oxford: Oxford University Press, 2006.

Shirlow, Esmé. *Judging at the Interface: Deference to State Decision-Making Authority in International Adjudication.* Cambridge: Cambridge University Press, 2021.

Simmons, Beth A. *Mobilizing for Human Rights: International Law in Domestic Politics.* Cambridge: Cambridge University Press, 2009.

Simmons, David. "The Caribbean Court of Justice: A Unique Institution of Caribbean Creativity." *Commonwealth Law Bulletin* 31, no. 1 (2005): 69–90.

Smithey, Shannon Ishiyama, and John Ishiyama. "Judicial Activism in Post-Communist Politics." *Law & Society Review* 36, no. 4 (2002): 719–42.

Snyder, Jack. "The Broken Bargain: How Nationalism Came Back." *Foreign Affairs* 98, no. 2 (2019): 54–60.

Spackman, Ann. *Constitutional Development of the West Indies 1922–1968: A Selection from the Major Documents.* Barbados: Caribbean Universities Press, 1975.

Squatrito, Theresa. "A Comparative Analysis of Formal Independence." In *The Legitimacy of International Trade Courts and Tribunals*, edited by Robert Howse, Helene Ruiz-Fabri and Michelle G. Zang, 405–31. Cambridge: Cambridge University Press, 2018.

"The Democratizing Effects of Transnational Actors' Access to International Courts." *Global Governance* 24, no. 4 (2018): 595–613.

"Judicial Diplomacy: International Courts and Legitimation." *Review of International Studies* 47, no. 1 (2021): 64–84.

"Opening the Doors to the WTO Dispute Settlement: State Preferences on NGO Access as Amici." *Swiss Political Science Review* 18, no. 2 (2012): 175–98.

"Resourcing Global Justice: The Resource Management Design of International Courts." *Global Policy* 8, no. 5 (2017): 62–74.

Squatrito, Theresa, Oran Young, Andreas Follesdal, and Geir Ulfstein, eds. *The Performance of International Courts and Tribunals*. Cambridge: Cambridge University Press, 2018.

Squatrito, Theresa, Oran R. Young, Andreas Follesdal, and Geir Ulfstein. "A Framework for Evaluating the Performance of International Courts and Tribunals." In *The Performance of International Courts and Tribunals*, edited by Theresa Squatrito, Oran R. Young, Andreas Follesdal and Geir Ulfstein, 3–36. Cambridge: Cambridge University Press, 2018.

Staton, Jeffrey K., and Will H. Moore. "Judicial Power in Domestic and International Politics." *International Organization* 65, no. 3 (2011): 553–87.

Staton, Jeffrey K., and Alexia Romero. "Rational Remedies: The Role of Opinion Clarity in the Inter-American Human Rights System." *International Studies Quarterly* 63, no. 3 (2019): 477–91.

Steinberg, Richard H. "Judicial Lawmaking at the WTO: Discursive, Constitutional, and Political Constraints." *American Journal of International Law* 98, no. 2 (2004): 247–75.

Steinert, Christoph Valentin. "Elitist Remedies? Complaint Resources and Representation in International Human Rights Bodies." *International Studies Quarterly* 68, no. 2 (2024): 1–16.

Stiansen, Øyvind. "Directing Compliance? Remedial Approach and Compliance with European Court of Human Rights Judgments." *British Journal of Political Science* 51, no. 2 (2021): 899–907.

"(Non)Renewable Terms and Judicial Independence in the European Court of Human Rights." *Journal of Politics* 84, no. 2 (2022): 992–1006.

Stiansen, Øyvind, and Erik Voeten. "Backlash and Judicial Restraint: Evidence from the European Court of Human Rights." *International Studies Quarterly* 64, no. 4 (2020): 770–84.

"ECtHR Judgments." In *Georgetown/PluriCourts European Court of Human Rights Database*. Harvard Dataverse, 2019. https://doi.org/10.7910/DVN/OBYUO5.

Stirton, Lindsay, and Martin Lodge. "Constitutionalism and Colonial Legacies in the Caribbean." In *The Oxford Handbook of Caribbean Constitutions*, edited by Richard Albert, Derek O'Brien and Se-shauna Wheatle, 25–46. Oxford: Oxford University Press, 2020.

Stone Sweet, Alec, and Thomas L. Brunell. "Constructing a Supranational Constitution: Dispute Resolution and Governance in the European Community." *American Political Science Review* 92, no. 1 (1998): 63–81.

"The European Court of Justice, State Noncompliance, and the Politics of Override." *American Political Science Review* 106, no. 1 (2012): 204–13.

"Trustee Courts and the Judicialization of International Regimes: The Politics of Majoritarian Activism in the European Convention on Human Rights, the European Union, and the World Trade Organization." *Journal of Law and Courts* 1, no. 1 (2013): 61–88.

Tallberg, Jonas, and James McCall Smith. "Dispute Settlement in World Politics: States, Supranational Prosecutors, and Compliance." *European Journal of International Relations* 20, no. 1 (2014): 118–44.

Tallberg, Jonas, Thomas Sommerer, Theresa Squatrito, and Magnus Lundgren. "The Performance of International Organizations: A Policy Output Approach." *Journal of European Public Policy* 23, no. 7 (2016): 1077–96.

Tallberg, Jonas, and Michael Zürn. "The Legitimacy and Legitimation of International Organizations: Introduction and Framework." *Review of International Organizations* 14, no. 4 (2019): 581–606.

Tarrow, Sidney. "Bridging the Quantitative-Qualitative Divide." In *Rethinking Social Inquiry: Diverse Tools, Shared Standards*, 2nd ed, edited by Henry E. Brady and David Collier, 93–110. Lanham: Rowman & Littlefield Publishers, 2010.

Taye, Mihreteab Tsighe. "The Role of the East African Court of Justice in the Advancement of Human Rights: Reflections on the Creation and Practice of the Court." *African Journal of International and Comparative Law* 27, no. 3 (2019): 359–77.

Terris, Daniel, Cesare Romano, and Leigh Swigart. *The International Judge: An Introduction to the Men and Women Who Decide the World's Cases*. Oxford: Oxford University Press, 2007.

Toshkov, Dimiter. *Research Design in Political Science*. London: Bloomsbury Publishing, 2016.

Trochev, Alexei, and Rachel Ellett. "Judges and Their Allies: Rethinking Judicial Autonomy through the Prism of Off-Bench Resistance." *Journal of Law and Courts* 2, no. 1 (2014): 67–91.

Tsebelis, George, and Geoffrey Garrett. "The Institutional Foundations of Intergovernmentalism and Supranationalism in the European Union." *International Organization* 55, no. 2 (2001): 357–90.

Ubwani, Zephania. "Swearing-in of Kenyan MPs Blocked." *The Nation*, November 28, 2006.

"Why East African Court Wants More Financial Freedom." *The Citizen*, December 7, 2020.

"Why Financial Autonomy 'Is Good' for EACJ." *The Citizen*, July 5, 2021.

Udombana, Nsongurua J. "Toward the African Court on Human and Peoples' Rights: Better Late Than Never." *Yale Human Rights & Development Law Journal* 3, no. 45 (2000): 45–111.

UNDP. *Caribbean Justice: A Needs Assessment of the Judicial System in Nine Countries*. Panama City: UNDP, 2020. Accessed May 10, 2023. www.undp.org/sites/g/files/zskgke326/files/migration/bb/Caribbean-Justice_A-Needs-Assessment-of-the-Judicial-System-in-Nine-Countries.pdf.

Rule of Law and Access to Justice in Eastern and Southern Africa: Showcasing Innovations and Good Practices. Addis Ababa: UNDP, 2013. Accessed April 1, 2024. www.undp.org/sites/g/files/zskgke326/files/migration/africa/Rule-of-Law-and-Access-to-Justice-in-Eastern-and-Southern-Africa-2013_EN.PDF.

UN General Assembly. *Basic Principles on the Independence of the Judiciary*. Resolution A/RES/40/32 (November 29, 1985) and A/RES/40/146 (December 13, 1985). Adopted by the Seventh United Nations Congress on the Prevention of Crime and the Treatment of Offenders. 1985. Accessed August 25, 2024. www.ohchr.org/en/instruments-mechanisms/instruments/basic-principles-independence-judiciary.

UN International Law Commission. *Articles on the Responsibility of States for Internationally Wrongful Acts*. Report of the ILC on the Work of its Fifty-third Session, UNGA Official Record, 56th session, Supplement No. 10, A/56/10. 2001. Accessed August 25, 2024. https://legal.un.org/ilc/texts/instruments/english/draft_articles/9_6_2001.pdf.

US Trade Representative. *Report on the Appellate Body of the World Trade Organization*. 2020. https://ustr.gov/sites/default/files/enforcement/DS/USTR.Appellate.Body.Rpt.Feb2020.pdf.

Vanberg, Georg. *The Politics of Constitutional Review in Germany*. Cambridge: Cambridge University Press, 2005.

"Establishing and Maintaining Judicial Independence." In *The Oxford Handbook of Law and Politics*, edited by Gregory A. Caldeira, R. Daniel Kelemen and Keith E. Whittington, 99–118. Oxford: Oxford University Press, 2008.

Viljoen, Frans. "Forging a Credible African System of Human Rights Protection by Overcoming State Resistance and Institutional Weakness: Compliance at a Crossroads." In *Research Handbook on Compliance in International Human Rights Law*, edited by Rainer Grote, Mariela Morales Antoniazzi and Paris Davide, 362–90. Cheltenham: Edward Elgar Publishing, 2021.

International Human Rights Law in Africa. 2nd ed. Oxford: Oxford University Press, 2012.

"Understanding and Overcoming Challenges in Accessing the African Court on Human and Peoples' Rights." *International and Comparative Law Quarterly* 67, no. 1 (2018): 63–98.

Viljoen, Frans, and Lirette Louw. "The Status of the Findings of the African Commission: From Moral Persuasion to Legal Obligation." *Journal of African Law* 48, no. 1 (2004): 1–22.

Viola, Lora Anne. *The Closure of the International System: How Institutions Create Political Equalities and Hierarchies*. Cambridge: Cambridge University Press, 2020.

Voeten, Erik. "Borrowing and Nonborrowing Among International Courts." *Journal of Legal Studies* 39, no. 2 (2010): 547–76.

"The Impartiality of International Judges: Evidence from the European Court of Human Rights." *American Political Science Review* 102, no. 4 (2008): 417–33.

"The Politics of International Judicial Appointments." *Chicago Journal of International Law* 9, no. 2 (2009): 387–405.

"The Politics of International Judicial Appointments: Evidence from the European Court of Human Rights." *International Organization* 61, no. 4 (2007): 669–701.

"Populism and Backlashes Against International Courts." *Perspectives on Politics* 18, no. 2 (2020): 407–22.

"Public Opinion and the Legitimacy of International Courts." *Theoretical Inquiries in Law* 14, no. 2 (2013): 411–36.

Voigt, Stefan. "The Independence of International Courts – Making Reputation Work?" *Maastricht Journal of European and Comparative Law* 24, no. 4 (2017): 511–30.

von Borzyskowski, Inken, and Felicity Vabulas. "Hello, Goodbye: When Do States Withdraw from International Organizations?" *Review of International Organizations* 14, no. 2 (2019): 335–66.

VonDoepp, Peter, and Rachel Ellett. "Reworking Strategic Models of Executive-Judicial Relations: Insights from New African Democracies." *Comparative Politics* 43, no. 2 (2011): 147–65.

Waiswa, Abudu Sallam. "EACJ—Kenya's Move Shows Political Immaturity." *The East African*, January 2, 2007.

Walter, Stefanie. "Brexit Domino? The Political Contagion Effects of Voter-Endorsed Withdrawals from International Institutions." *Comparative Political Studies* 54, no. 13 (2021): 2382–2415.

Wasserfallen, Fabio. "The Judiciary as Legislator? How the European Court of Justice Shapes Policy-Making in the European Union." *Journal of European Public Policy* 17, no. 8 (2010): 1128–46.

Weiler, Joseph H. H. "The Transformation of Europe." *Yale Law Journal* 100, no. 8 (1991): 2403–84.

Wheatle, Se-shauna, and Yonique Campbell. "Constitutional Faith and Identity in the Caribbean: Tradition, Politics and the Creolisation of Caribbean Constitutional Law." *Commonwealth & Comparative Politics* 58, no. 3 (2020): 344–65.

WIC. *Time for Action: Report of the West Indian Commission.* Kingston: University of the West Indies Press, 1993.

Widner, Jennifer. *Building the Rule of Law: Francis Nyalali and the Road to Judicial Independence in Africa.* New York: W. W. Norton, 2001.

Windridge, Oliver. "Assessing Rwexit: The Impact and Implications of Rwanda's Withdrawal of Its Article 34(6) Declaration before the African Court on

Human and Peoples' Rights." *African Human Rights Yearbook* 2, no. 1 (2018): 243–58.

"A Watershed Moment for African Human Rights: Mtikila & Others v Tanzania at the African Court on Human and Peoples' Rights." *African Human Rights Law Journal* 15, no. 2 (2015): 299–328.

Zarbiyev, Fuad. "Judicial Activism." In *Max Planck Encyclopedia of International Procedural Law*, edited by Hélène Ruiz Fabri. Oxford: Oxford University Press, 2018.

"Judicial Activism in International Law: A Conceptual Framework for Analysis." *Journal of International Dispute Settlement* 3, no. 2 (2012): 247–78.

Zaum, Dominik, ed. *Legitimating International Organizations.* Oxford: Oxford University Press, 2013.

Zimmermann, Dominik. *The Independence of International Courts: The Adherence of the International Judiciary to a Fundamental Value of the Administration of Justice.* Baden-Baden: Nomos, 2014.

Zink, James R., James F. Spriggs, and John T. Scott. "Courting the Public: The Influence of Decision Attributes on Individuals' Views of Court Opinions." *Journal of Politics* 71, no. 3 (2009): 909–25.

Zips, Werner. "Laws in Competition: Traditional Maroon Authorities within Legal Pluralism in Jamaica." *Journal of Legal Pluralism & Unofficial Law* 28, no. 37–38 (1996): 279–305.

Zürn, Michael, Martin Binder, and Matthias Ecker-Ehrhardt. "International Authority and Its Politicization." *International Theory* 4, no. 1 (2012): 69–106.

INDEX

Suffix 'f' stands for figure, 't' for table and 'n' for footnote.

For EU product safety concerns, contact us at Calle de José Abascal, 56–1°, 28003 Madrid, Spain or eugpsr@cambridge.org.

www.ingramcontent.com/pod-product-compliance
Lightning Source LLC
LaVergne TN
LVHW011703200926
848484LV00004B/1049